AF528067

SHRUBS AND THEIR CULTIVATION

SHRUBS AND THEIR CULTIVATION

T.C. Mansfield

2002

BIOTECH BOOKS

Delhi - 110 035

First Indian Edition 2002
© Reserved

ISBN 81-7622-079-5

Published by : **BIOTECH BOOKS**
1123/74, Tri Nagar,
DELHI – 110 035
Phone: 7109765
e-mail: biotechbooks@yahoo.co.in

Showroom : 4762-63/23, Ansari Road, Darya Ganj,
NEW DELHI - 110 035
Phone: 3245578, 3244987

Printed at : **Chawla Offset Printers**
New Delhi – 110 052

PRINTED IN INDIA

CONTENTS

TO

MR. AND MRS. F. M. BURRIS

WITH GRATITUDE

FOR HAVING GRANTED ME THE PRIVILEGE

OF HELPING TO MAKE WHAT WAS BEAUTIFUL

MORE LOVELY STILL

PREFACE

IT IS NOW at least two years since the first book of the present series found its way to the public, and it would be ungracious if I did not express my great satisfaction with the generosity with which the gardening public have adopted the series.

One of the most gratifying features has been the large volume of correspondence, advice, and criticism, which I have received from readers, all of which I have read with considerable care, thought over, and endeavoured to put into effect.

The present book is the first one in which I have been fully able to take such criticism into account, and it is therefore more the work of the public than the author, who has found his part, though protracted, extremely congenial.

Once again the same method of photography has been employed, with the same excellent hand in control, and I again express my indebtedness to John Hinde, not only for his faithful reproductions, but for a measure of patience and kindness I have rarely found elsewhere.

It is quite unlikely that I shall ever again be able to devote as much time to the production of a book such as this, for I must confess that both the producers and the publishers have willingly given me such time as I have desired to make this book the work it deserves to be.

I must also convey my sincere thanks to the following: Col. F. R. Durham, of the Royal Horticultural Society; Mr. R. L. Harrow, of the R.H.S. Gardens, Wisley; Mr. F. J. Mitchell, of The Arboretum, Westonbirt; Messrs. John Waterer, Sons, and Crisp, of Twyford; and to my own staff at Baltonsborough for the ready way in which they have contrived to help and inspire me.

At a later stage a revision of the present book will undoubtedly be asked for, and I should like to include in it some indication of the comparative hardiness of various species in certain parts of the country.

For this reason I should welcome any correspondence dealing with this feature, as I should also in connection with some of the more unusual methods of propagation adopted throughout the country.

Of recent years a considerable advance has been made with the propagation and production of shrubs, work which has, in the main, been carried out by enthusiastic amateurs, and it is these experienced people to whom this suggestion is made.

We have found that it is usually the amateur who specialises in the production and perfect growth of certain individual varieties in which he exceeds in skill and in the beauty of his final productions the best efforts of his professional brothers.

It is to the advantage of all shrub lovers that they should pass on to their less fortunate neighbours such information as will help us all to make the cult of the Shrub Garden an even greater, wider and more universally pursued art, and it is only by the aid of such scientific knowledge, willingly passed on, that this much desired end can be brought into being.

To this end I invite correspondence, and express my desire to be of such assistance as I am able to all my amateur or professional friends in any part of the world. I must confess that such correspondence makes up a very large part of both my pleasure and my work, and I crave the indulgence of such of my friends as may write for any delay which may take place in replying, though my best endeavours will be given to replying as quickly as possible.

Chalice Hill Lane, Glastonbury

PREFACE TO THE SECOND EDITION

THE CHANGES which have been made in the second edition comprise only minor alterations to the captions of the plates to bring them into closer conformity with the text, and a corrected inversion. A Cross Index of Common Names has been added for the convenience of those readers who may be less familiar with the botanical nomenclature.

So little time has elapsed since the publication of the first edition that it has not been possible to compile sufficient information on the hardiness of different kinds of shrubs in varied localities, but the reader should not infer from this that any of the specimens photographed were not grown out of doors. Every plant mentioned or photographed can be successfully grown in the open, not necessarily in every part of the British Isles, but in selected positions in these islands.

The author will continue to welcome correspondence, and to reply as time will allow.

He also expresses his deep gratitude to Mr. S. F. Winter, of Messrs. Adprint Ltd., for his exceptionally able and conscientious assistance.

Chalice Hill Lane, Glastonbury

Abelia Schumanii

2

Abutilon megapotamicum

CHAPTER I

INTRODUCTION

IT has been said that any gardener who persists sufficiently long at his hobby eventually becomes a shrub addict. There is little doubt that this assertion is true.

Shrubs present collectively a galaxy so varied and replete with interest, that they must provide a suitable refuge for the more mature interests of questing minds.

They number among them evergreen and deciduous species, tall, medium, and dwarf varieties, upright, spreading, weeping, and even creeping forms; there are hardy, half-hardy, and tender kinds, and stolid and unimaginative sorts, together with others with all the grace and beauty of noble ancestry.

But in addition to the varied nature of the general picture they present they have an outstanding characteristic, offered by no other garden plants and one which is of great importance to the gardener; once established, they require little labour for their maintenance. They do however require, for their correct and efficient employment, a basic knowledge of their character, size, and requirements, greater than that necessary in any other form of gardening, since they are of a greater permanence, and though they can, even at a mature age, be moved with impunity, they can scarcely be so treated with ease.

It may be quite unfitting that a book about the beauties and glories of garden shrubs should begin with a criticism of what is normally called a "shrubbery." This is surely a detestable word which should rank with "rockery" in significance, for both words are those generally applied to examples which are the least outstanding in beauty, the most faulty in construction, and of mean design.

It is quite probable that literature concerning shrubs is in itself largely responsible for the dismal character of the so-called "mixed shrubbery," which generally develops into a place in which the strong and weak fight for existence with the inevitable result of the survival only of the fittest, and the loss of beauty and grace which this necessarily entails.

We take it for granted that the normal full-grown man is somewhere between 5 feet to 6 feet 6 inches in height, and that his weight may vary from, say, 100 to 250 lb., allowing considerable variation in the consideration of only one species! In the case of shrubs we have a multiplicity of species, any one of which may exhibit the same amount of variations, and which collectively vary so considerably that only an expert can say how big and how wide each may be expected to grow, and even then he may for his own peace of mind be forced to allow himself a considerable margin of speculation.

When one considers that the Shrub Garden must normally be planted while the component elements are immature, and a reasonable estimate of the eventual height and spread must be taken into account, the nature of the average shrubbery must be taken as an indication of ignorance rather than of knowledge!

Such a sweeping generalisation needs a measure of qualification. Of all attributes which the gardener should possess, patience is probably the most desirable. Too often have I found that even the expert, desiring quick effects, will plant three or even five shrubs in a spot which only one would eventually fill, intending obviously to remove two or four of them at some future date. How the practice should be deprecated! The proud possessor of the border, thrilled by immediate results, spurns all advice to be ruthless, and the slow process of deterioration sets in, to his eventual disappointment and disgust. On the whole, my considered advice is—plant with plenty of space to spare, to leave each individual component of your shrub garden to develop naturally and in perfect shape, and shun as you would the shadow of Lucifer, the temptation to plant for quick effect.

For this reason the "Glossary of Shrubs," with which this book concludes, gives an estimated height and spread for all the species described, and though there may be a measure of variation comparable with the example already given in the case of man, yet it will help the amateur to avoid the mistakes of crowding his species and not allowing living space.

Very few of us are sufficiently fortunate to possess gardens with natural scenic effects contributed by valleys and streams, hills, and declivities. We appreciate these as we travel through a beautiful countryside, but we find the maximum of beauty in that given by blending or contrasting colour—perhaps in the green of the grass, or of the trees—perhaps in the golden glory of fields of buttercups deepening in the shade cast by the trees, or in beauty of line of the trees which, with their variable heights and contours, add distinction to an otherwise insipid scene, and it is for this factor far beyond all others that the shrub is of paramount importance in the normal garden.

Indiscriminate planting merely for the purpose of screening

a distasteful view should be firmly eschewed; such a planting can be planned and all its factors well considered before the work is undertaken.

It is wise, therefore, to set out for ourselves a series of rules to which and by which we shall work. The first rule has already been stated, and is positive and all-embracing—leave ample room for the individual shrub to develop to its mature capacity. The natural corollary to this rule is quite obvious; since we are to allow full development it would be impractical to group slow-growing shrubs with the roistering kinds, and we must segregate our varieties so that within the confines of our shrub garden we can allow the weak to compete only with the weak, and the strong with the strong.

Among the weak, as a rule, all is well; the strong alone create the mischief. In the best-balanced and most perfectly designed shrub garden an occasional big fellow will aspire to giantism, and without attention would tend to spoil an otherwise beautiful plan. All can be well, however, if the primary aim of allowing sufficient space for the shrub to reach its average mature size has been followed, and the pruning knife must then be brought into operation to limit undue growth, which would encroach upon the development of contiguous species.

In planning the shrub garden we must allow a certain variation in the case of the large and the small gardens. It would be ridiculous to recommend that the small shrub border should consist of groups of varieties of the same kind, though in the case of very large gardens and public parks this is a practice strongly to be recommended, and as a practical proposition in design has much to commend it.

In the small shrub garden, symmetry of effect deserves little commendation. Nothing can be quite so dull as a border planted to slope from a straight line at the back, to a similar but less elevated line at the front. Thus it is wise to consider initially how far diversity of contour is desirable and to select with this end in view, using the taller-growing varieties either as backgrounds for contrasting species, as providers of broken sunlight for the shade-loving species, or for contrast in line with adjacent varieties.

The backbone trees or shrubs of any design should be indubitably hardy; nothing can be more annoying than to find that after the passage of ten or twelve years, and their welcome growth, an extra severe winter causes the passing of what has become an outstanding feature of one's garden. True, the consequent gap can be filled, but only by the expenditure of much labour, skill, and care can a really big tree or shrub be adequately replaced.

Planting to indicate the illusion of depth requires a measure of skill beyond the average ; but Figure 1 suggests a typical method in which every vista superimposes the outline of one tree upon another. Such a group set in carefully tended turf can exercise a screening effect, and also give a deceptive idea of depth, impossible to create by solid planting. Such a planting can also be used to conceal, until the last moment, features which it is intended to use as surprises, and which, upon the turning of a corner, leap to the eye, for no garden should reveal at a glance the sum total of its intrinsic beauty.

Going back over our recommendations, it would be well to summarise.

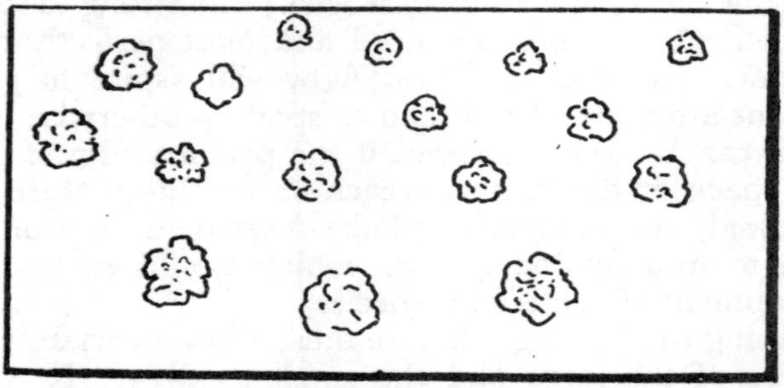

FIG. 1

For the small shrub garden one should:—

(*a*) Leave ample room for each individual plant to reach a mature (minimum) size.

(*b*) Segregate in mixed plantings shrubs of quick-growing characteristics from those with slower growth.

(*c*) Avoid formality.

(*d*) Keep the backbone of any design composed of shrubs of undoubted hardiness.

(*e*) Plant to create the illusion of depth.

(*f*) Utilise the larger features to provide broken sunlight for the shade-loving species, and for contrasts in silhouette.

A further consideration of the first rule suggests that seldom does the average gardener choose his material to fit the garden. I remember quite well a garden of excellent primary design, constructed by an eminent landscape artist, which I have always described as a pocket-handkerchief garden because of its tiny scope, which failed completely to maintain its early excellence because, though the designer was an artist, he was not a plantsman, and though his shrubs were selected for their excellent shape, colour, and size, he had completely forgotten that the passage of years would alter both shape and size alarmingly. Called in as a consultant, I must confess I could not improve his placing, but I could improve upon his selection of individual shrubs, since the obvious need was to employ those of extremely slow-growing characteristics. The owner of the garden was almost in tears when certain of the shrubs were removed, and we thought it advisable that she should take a holiday while the work was completed. On her return there was little doubt that she was duly appreciative, and though many years have since elapsed she still remains a faithful and grateful correspondent. The moral is an obvious one: select material which will be fitting to its sphere, with an eye to its mature size and shape.

One cannot end our introduction on this note. Though the small garden may preponderate, there is a still larger view. The people's personal gardens may be small, but their joint possessions are great and spacious, and it is in public gardens and parks that shrubs find their most ample locations, for it is here where one may plan not only for the present but for posterity. Given adequate facilities of space and time, trees and shrubs can so beautify our open spaces, and so transform mean views, that their employment is a necessity in order that the surroundings shall be fitting for the people.

It surely is not wise that the town dweller should be surrounded by privet, shaded by planes, dwarfed by poplars, with the occasional variation thrown in by limes. Let none descry these things ; in the well-ordered and designed city, there is yet place for other beauties, for in variety lies not only interest but the essential spur to understanding of things which are different, without which no true democracy of the spirit can live.

There are, of course, a multitude of uses for shrubs, which do not fall within the narrow view of the small garden, or of the grander and more spacious park, or of roadside plantings. The hedge, for instance, though utilitarian, may still be beautiful. It may be formal or it may exhibit as much variety of colour as Joseph's coat, and so much range of difference as the passes and peaks of the Himalayas. The formal hedge has its advantages as both a boundary and a screen and is always preferable to an iron railing ; but it is far from trouble-free. The mixed hedge is even less accommodating, and is the pastime of the expert rather than the hobby of the beginner.

The general test which should be applied is the one of fitness, that is, the ability to become an integral part of the surroundings, without offending the eye. Formality and informality must not be mixed and confused. If your mind and eye are satisfied by regular tidy hedges, neatly clipped and of orderly array, you may dislike the luscious profusion of the wild garden ; you will certainly dislike them in close proximity.

The reader will find as he peruses the Glossary that included among the varied shrubs there described are a number of climbing shrubs which must be regarded as part of the material for the shrub garden, as they form the most appropriate medium by which buildings and structures essential to the garden may be brought into harmony with it. It is no part of my purpose to enter into a discussion of the merits of pergolas and arches in the garden. They are essentially matters of personal taste. It will suffice to say that in small gardens certain outbuildings are a necessity—they may be screened, or suitably decorated with climbing plants where good taste directs this as necessary, and a personal preference of my own inclines to the view that it is better for a good climber to decorate a poor structure than a poor plant to decorate the work of a master architect.

" Nothing is so profusely given as advice," says Rochefoucauld, nor, he might add, so little taken, for the beginner is just as likely to confound the expert, if he has that intangible asset of all good gardeners, the ability to treat his plants with sympathy and understanding as he would living people, studying their whims and foibles, in addition to their primary needs. All the advice or instruction possible will not make a good gardener, nor, on the other hand, can one be produced cradled in ignorance. Gardening is essentially a living and growing art in which one gains proficiency by practice, and which grows in stature and spread like a tree, eventually reaching maturity. In some of us it grows quickly, in others but slowly, but the result is eventually the same—an incomplete but perfectly grown knowledge of the requirements of one's subjects.

So, while in the garden one's plants slowly reach to perfection, the gardener too acquires the knowledge of his art, knowing only too well that life itself is not sufficiently long for him to absorb one-half of all that is to be learned of the beauty which is our heritage, and which throughout his life induces a spirit of humility which grows with his understanding.

CHAPTER II

PROPAGATION

THERE is no phase of gardening of greater interest or of such fascination as the propagation of new stock, nor one which can be so profitable to the amateur.

This may be accomplished in the following ways :—

(*a*) By seeds
(*b*) By vegetative reproduction
 (i) from divisions of the root
 (ii) by layers
 (iii) by cuttings (α) of the stem
  (β) of the root
  (γ) of the leaves
 (iv) by budding or by grafting

Shrubs which have been derived from "sports" and have contorted, fastigiate, or weeping habits cannot be relied upon to reproduce themselves accurately from seed, and must be propagated by means of vegetative reproduction. They are seldom found in nature and rely for their continuance upon propagation by man for his own use and pleasure.

Trees and shrubs which do not produce seed in the country of their domicile must be also reproduced in this way, together with varietal hybrids of specific colour or shape.

Species which produce fertile seeds may, however, be best propagated from seed, and though they do not flower quite so quickly as those produced by budding or grafting, they provide, as a rule, healthy, clean stock destined for long life.

It is quite impossible to standardise a method for sowing seeds of trees or shrubs which will meet the individual requirements of all varieties.

Probably the most important item of all is that all the components of the soil should be sterilised ; this is vitally important in the case of very small seeds which give rise to tiny initial seedlings which would be crowded out by a heavy weed content in the soil and would be adversely affected by the presence of fungoid diseases. But it would also be idle to sow seeds in sterilised soil if the pots, pans, or boxes in which the soil is placed are contaminated, and these too should be well washed if previously used, and treated with a fungicide. Used pans should be soaked in a solution of Cheshunt Compound for a period of twenty minutes and then allowed to drain before using. Boxes should be treated with Cuprinol two days before use.

A standard seed compost, such as the John Innes Seed Compost, is a great boon to the amateur, and its components are given at the end of this chapter. Pans or boxes should be given a layer of sterile pot crocks to a depth of at least one inch, and then be filled to about one inch from the rim of the pot or edge of the box, when the soil should be well firmed with a smooth, flat board, or the base of another pan.

Large seeds should be sown upon the surface of the soil, and spread in such a way that their early growth is not crowded. It is particularly important that seeds should not be sown too thickly, since seeds distributed in this way become thin, weakly, and attenuated, and are particularly subject to attacks of "damping off."

Seeds should also not be sown too deeply; in fact, the depth at which they are sown should never be greater than their own diameter.

It is a mistake to assume that the soil which is in contact with the seed should necessarily be finely divided or sifted, and the best results are probably obtained by sowing the seed *thinly* over the surface of the compost, which should first of all have been perfectly firmed.

Excellent results are obtained if the seeds are then covered by a layer of approximately one-sixteenth of an inch in depth of sterile chipping, one-sixteenth of an inch in diameter. Washed grit is very suitable for this purpose.

In the case of very small seeds of species like the Rhododendron or Erica, excellent results are obtained by the use of sterilised moss, which has been thoroughly dried and rubbed through a very fine sieve, as a covering for the seed.

Pans containing shade-loving subjects should be kept sheltered either in cold frames with a north aspect, or under the shelter of a north wall. When watering is required it is an excellent plan to "soak up" a seed pan or box by placing it in a tray of water which does not cover the surface of the soil until the compost is uniformly moist. The pan is then taken out, allowed to drain, and replaced in its former position. A useful addition to the water is permanganate of potash in sufficient quantity to colour it a deep pink. This prevents to a large extent any trouble from damping off.

It is often advantageous to allow seed pans in which germination appears to have been delayed to be exposed to the full severity of a winter in the open, after which they may be returned

Acer palmatum aureum **ABDEFHKORS**

Veronica Hulkeana
BCGHLM

Acer palmatum septemlobum
atropurpureum **JNOPQTU**

4

Acer dasycarpum
ABEFJKN
Acer Ginnala **RSKPTU**

Acer rubrum **CDGHLMQ**

Agathaea coelestis

6

Anthyllís Hermanniae

Clematis macropetala
CDGHLM

Wistaria sinensis
EFJKNORS

Akebia quinata
GHPQ

Aster Pappei

to their former location, and germination will probably be accelerated.

As a rule microscopic seed germinates almost immediately or not at all. Certain seeds with hard bony coverings will often not germinate until they have spent a whole season in the soil, and not infrequently they are treated by being mixed with soil and left for a year before the actual sowing takes place. Soft or fleshy seeds require to be sown as soon as ripe, and should not under any circumstances be allowed to dry out in storage. A safe month in which to sow most of the seeds of shrubs is in February, but where it is desired to store seeds for subsequent sowing, they should be kept in cold but dry places.

The simplest method of propagation of certain shrubs is by division of the old plant into pieces, each with a separate root system. This is a process best put into operation in the spring when the rooted pieces may be disposed to their permanent homes. Where such divisions are insufficiently rooted for this purpose they may be encouraged to acquire the necessary root system by being potted in suitable soil, and be given the protection of a cold frame. The disadvantage inherent in most plants obtained by this method is the initial ugliness of contour of the divisions, which may be improved by the judicious use of the knife or secateurs, and in the case of the heaths by deep planting. In some cases artificial aid to separate the roots of the parent plant will be found necessary, and often the help of a saw may be employed with advantage to cut the hard, woody roots, and secateurs used to ensure that the rooted pieces each have sufficient roots to be able to support a separate existence.

Certain shrubs of low or pendent growth can be most appropriately increased by the process of layering, which in effect is to make a cutting of the plant and encourage it to produce a root system of its own, without detaching it completely from the parent plant. This operation is generally best performed in the spring and may take a full season or even, in the case of certain slow-rooting varieties, two seasons to complete. The process is dependent upon the interruption of the flow of the sap in the plant at the point at which it is buried in the soil. This may be brought about by notching or splitting the stem lengthwise, by ringing the bark with a cut which penetrates to the wood, or by twisting a piece of wire tightly round the stem. As an aid to efficient root production the point of constriction or of interruption of the flow of sap can be painted with Hortomone A. Figure 2 shows the methods used.

It is essential that, after the initial preparation of the layer, it should be firmly pegged into the ground by means of a layering pin or pins, or by means of a peg notched like a tent peg, or a cleft stick. It is of paramount importance that the soil into which the layer is pegged should be fertile and well drained, but also capable of retaining moisture so that it does not become readily dried out, and one recommends the incorporation of approximately one-third finely divided peat mould to all soils which dry out too quickly. Layering provides the answer for the amateur who has no facilities for the production of rooted cuttings in heat, for though it is slow in its results, it is probably the most certain method of all. Where soil and plant may be made to meet very few branches will prove so stubborn that they will not eventually provide a root system of their own.

Here the ingenuity of the gardener can exercise itself in a fashion seldom allowed elsewhere, for often he can improvise methods of making the mountain meet Mahomet, for where the branch will *not* bend the soil may be taken to the branch. A pot may be split longitudinally with a blunt wetted hacksaw

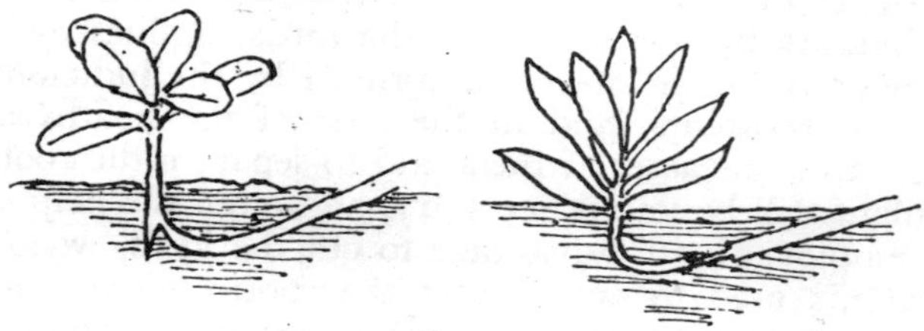

Fig. 2

blade, the stem of the tree ringed or split, the two halves of the pot bound firmly together around the treated tree, with the drainage hole in the base of the pot enlarged to take the stem if necessary, and then firmly filled with the appropriate soil. The problem which then presents itself is to keep the soil in the pot sufficiently moist. This may be provided by hanging a tin can of water above the level of the surface of the pot from which a thin lamp wick leads to the soil in the pot.

The same device may be used to keep moist a ball of moss bound around a ringed branchlet which will often lead to efficient rooting of the stem. Frequently in the case of Daphnes, Willows, and Currants it will be found sufficient to place a large stone across the branchlet, to bed it firmly into the ground, and rooting will take place with almost automatic certainty.

Cuttings provide the most important method of propagation in the case of shrubs, but though the method may be used with some success in the case of almost all trees, it cannot be claimed to do so with certainty, though a perusal of the Glossary will show that a surprising number of trees may be so produced.

The important difference between a cutting and a layer is self-evident. The fact that the cutting is completely detached from the parent plant renders it subject to the ability of the would-be propagator to keep it alive sufficiently long for it to obtain a root system of its own. It is essential, therefore, that this problem should be sufficiently studied at the outset. Dormant wooded cuttings with no leaves taken during the winter can be kept alive almost indefinitely since they have no leaf surfaces with which to transpire. Softwood or greenwood cuttings, generally taken from mid-July to the end of August, are usually generously provided with leaves which will perform their normal functions and must therefore be provided with a moist atmosphere, and sufficient encouragement in the matter of temperature, to promote rapid rooting.

It follows that dormant wood cuttings may generally be perfectly at home and happy, and will root quite readily in the open. They comprise side growths with from two to four buds planted firmly in the ground so that only the uppermost bud projects above the surface of the soil. Examples of suitable subjects are the Willow, Currant, Gooseberry, and Poplar.

In the case of cuttings of the green wood it is necessary to use a close atmosphere to prevent undue transpiration, and here one recommends a well-drained but fertile base of good sandy loam covered with a surface layer of two inches of sharp sand, covered with a well-shaded light, kept in a reasonably sunny position. Those who can afford the hourly attention required by the more intensive method in the hottest of sunlight, should cover with an unshaded light and water most copiously as often as necessary, never allowing flagging to take place ; this method undoubtedly gives the quickest results, but is not suitable to most shade-loving species.

The expert seems to know intuitively the type of green-wooded cuttings to take—so much so that he usually finds it extremely difficult to describe the exact appearance of the ideal cutting. He prefers as a rule to avoid the leading, soft or extra vigorous stems, and confines his attention to side branches, which are not too leafy, and may be anything from three to five inches in length. The ripeness of the wood is important, the time of its availability is variable in divergent summer conditions. In a hot, dry summer, suitable " wood " is available much earlier than in a cool or moist summer. Perhaps the best test which may be applied is to bend the current year's growth sharply—if the hard core cracks it is generally sufficiently ripe—if it bends and recovers it is not yet ripe enough. It should, however, be stressed that the correct time to take such cuttings is the earliest moment that the ripe wood can be found.

If the intensive method is used the importance of the ripeness of the wood is diminished, and it may be taken as an axiom that the harder the " wood " the longer the cutting will take to acquire roots of its own.

Generally speaking, cuttings are best made with a heel of the old wood. That is, the current year's growth is taken from the growth of the previous year by means of a sharp downward pull. If the heel is ragged it should be trimmed smooth with a sharp razor blade. In some cases it is better to detach the cutting by means of a cut both above and below the point at which it joins the old wood, thus making a shield-shaped heel. Where cuttings are taken without a heel they should be cut from the parent plant at a point just below a joint.

Some of the Clematis species and the Vines may be propagated in the spring by detaching " eyes "; that is, by taking short lengths, generally about an inch, with a central bud. They are then inserted into the soil or sand in such a way that the bud projects above the surface. Gentle bottom heat will ensure the quick formation of a good root system.

In the case of some of the Conifers it will be found upon examination that they will form the typical callous which is the necessary preliminary to the formation of roots quite quickly, but thereafter seem to hang fire. Often they may be persuaded to root quite readily if the resinous coat which covers the callous is removed by dipping momentarily into almost boiling water, or by rubbing the callous on a piece of fine sandpaper so that the coating is partially removed.

Frequently new plants may be readily obtained from cuttings of the thick, fleshy roots which some shrubs provide. Here the method of preparation is to cut the roots, which should be reasonably stout and never less in thickness than a matchstick, into pieces of about two inches in length. The pieces are then inserted in pans of soil which have been covered with a two-inch layer of sharp sand, with the end which was nearest to the stem of the plant towards the top. Examples of shrubs which may be thus obtained are Robinia, and Paulownia imperialis, and, in fact, any shrub or tree which in the course of its lifetime gives rise to " suckers."

Very few trees and shrubs can be propagated from cuttings of the leaves, though the species Camellia may be treated thus on occasion. Here the most appropriate method seems to be to take the whole leaf, with its bud and a short section of the stem, of about one inch in length, and insert in a pan of soil made up of one-third leaf mould, one-third loam, and one-third sand, so that the eye is just below the level of the surface of the soil. Gentle bottom heat will complete the work thus begun.

The practice of graftage is at best a necessary evil, justified only when it will produce a graft hybrid as in the case of Laburnum Adamii, or in such cases when it has been found impossible satisfactorily to grow the shrub upon its own roots; the process too may be properly employed when a tree or shrub of particular habit, such as a weeping beech, and which does not reproduce itself to type from seed, is grafted upon a stock of its own type. There is little justification for grafting, let us say, Daphne collina upon stocks of D. Mezereum, or D. pontica, since it roots most readily upon its own stems and keeps its character better thus.

It is, however, a great aid to the certain propagation of shrubs which do not root readily from cuttings, if graftage is done upon pieces of root of identical species. This method will be discussed later.

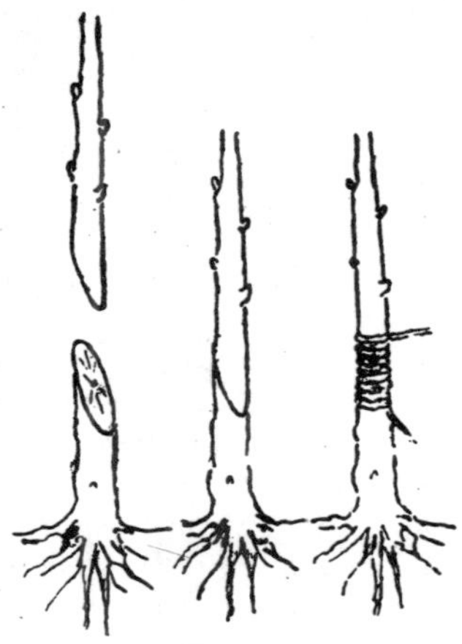

FIG. 3

Graftage, simply explained, may be said to be setting a cutting of one plant into a stock of another.

The processes of graftage, inarching, and budding, differ somewhat in method but have a common scientific principle. The stem of the normal plant consists of the central pith, encircled by the wood, which in its turn is surrounded by the cambium layer, which is covered by the bark. The only actively growing section of the stem is the cambium, and it is upon the expert matching of the cambium of the scion (that is, the cutting) with that of the stock (the other plant) that the success of the process depends. The more expert the carpentering the finer the results.

The simplest method of grafting, and that most applicable to the amateur, is known as whip-grafting. In order that this shall be as perfect as possible, the two-inch- to six-inch-long scion and the stock should be chosen of the same diameter. A long slanting cut is made both upon the stock and the scion, as in Figure 3, and the two surfaces are then placed together and tied firmly into place with wetted raffia so that the cambium layers are, so far as is possible, coincident. The joint should be sealed with grafting wax to exclude air.

Not infrequently heat is brought to the aid of the propagator, and the stocks are potted on early in the year and brought on, while the scions are cut and laid in the soil to keep them back. For the amateur who is desirous of adding graftage to his methods of propagation, a sharp budding knife is a necessary piece of equipment, and consistent practice in matching cuts will add much to his proficiency in graftage, since the art is one in which mechanical proficiency and dexterity are of paramount importance. Grafting should be done indoors at any time from January to March when suitable material is available, or in April out of doors.

The method of grafting a scion upon pieces of root of an identical plant has much to commend it, certainly to the amateur.

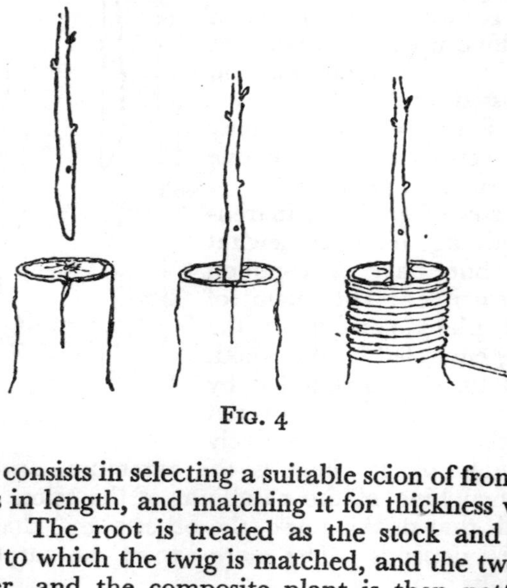

FIG. 4

The process consists in selecting a suitable scion of from two inches to six inches in length, and matching it for thickness with a piece of the root. The root is treated as the stock and cut with a slanting cut to which the twig is matched, and the two are firmly tied together, and the composite plant is then potted so that only the uncut portion of the scion is above the soil. Moderate bottom heat will then encourage the necessary growth. Many of the Daphne species readily respond to this process, and Wistarias are eminently suited by this kind of treatment.

A few words may be said of two other methods of graftage. Where it is impossible to find a stock and scion which match in diameter it is possible to use rind or wedge graftage.

In the case of rind grafting the stock is cut off two inches above the soil level and the bark is slit as in Figure 4, and is lifted to expose the cambium layer; the scion is prepared as before and slipped into the slit so that the cambium layers are in contact, and both components are tied firmly together.

Where wedge grafting is employed the scion should have about three eyes or buds, and be as short as is possible consistent with that fact. The scion is cut at its lower edge to a sharp wedge (Fig. 5). The stock is cut back to within two inches of the surface of the soil, and is then split down the middle with a sharp knife. The wedge is now inserted in the slit so that the cambium of the scion at one side is in contact with that of the stock. The joint is firmly bound with moistened raffia, and the air excluded from the cuts with the aid of clay or grafting wax.

Budding, a selective form of graftage, is much practised in the propagation of roses, and in the case of the flowering cherries,

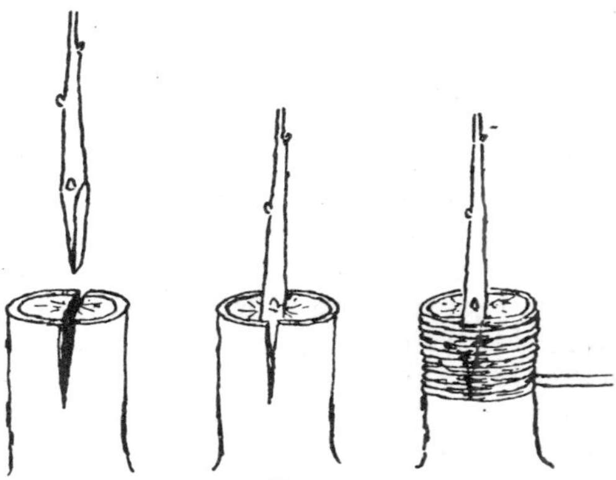

FIG. 5

and peaches. It differs little from graftage in its practice and advantage. Since it must be done while the cambium parts quite easily from the wood, it must generally be done during a dull day in July or August. The scion here consists only of one bud, selected as a rule from the more mature ones among the current year's growth. It is detached by means of a sharp knife with a shield of the bark, which should extend about half an inch above the bud, and about the same distance below, with about one-eighth of an inch on each side. A thin sliver of wood is always cut with the bud; this must be removed before the bud is inserted into the "T" cut, which is made in the bark of the stock. The bark may be lifted on each side of the down stroke with the handle of the budding knife to allow this to be done. The bark is then laid back over the shield and the junction should be firmly bound with raffia so that the bud only is left exposed. The bud will lie dormant until the following spring when, if the operation has been successful, growth will take place.

Seed Compost

Two parts by bulk medium loam (sterilised).
One part by bulk peat (or leaf mould).
One part coarse sand.
With the addition of superphosphate of lime 1½ oz., chalk ¾ oz. per bushel.

CHAPTER III

TRANSPLANTING

It must now be presumed that the gardener has gained such proficiency in his art that he now has at his disposal a large number of seedlings, rooted cuttings, layers, grafted or budded stocks, and their after-care becomes a matter for his immediate concern. In any case he will have a number of plants, varied in their methods of production, which will be too small to be placed in the shrub garden, and which will require to be "grown on" to suitable size before they may be built in to the garden plan. No matter how carefully seeds have been sown, little room exists in the original seed pan for the plants to develop in reasonable fashion, and sooner or later the time comes when it is imperative to "prick out" the little plants it is felt necessary to retain. From the point of view of the amateur, it is probable that he regards the many hundreds of seedlings of one variety which he may well obtain from a really good germination, with some dismay, and with much regret that he cannot hope either to cope with them all. I strongly recommend, however, that he should strictly limit his adventure into the field of mass production, unless he has unlimited means and illimitable plans for the disposal of his plants, to one pan, similar to that in which he raised his seedlings, to each variety, retaining in every case the remainder of the original pan of seedlings until the pricked-out plants are seen to be reasonably established, but trying again if they are observed to have failed. Such "pricking out" should be done in the case of seedlings as early in the year as is consistent with the progress of the seedlings. Care should be taken in transplanting the original seedlings that the roots are not

damaged. A small hardwood garden label sharpened to a long slender point, as in Figure 6, will be found of considerable assistance in lifting the seedlings from the pan, and may be used as a dibber for inserting them into their new quarters. After each pan has been completed it should be "soaked up" by being placed for a few minutes in a bowl of soft water, coloured rose-pink with the addition of a crystal or so of potassium permanganate. The pan should then be placed in a shaded frame which should be kept closed for a few days, and thereafter the air should be increased daily.

It is wise when selecting seedlings to "prick out" in this way to exclude those known to be of quick and hardy growth, reserving them for a more spartan treatment which will be later outlined.

These, together with vigorous rooted cuttings which have been produced by the intensive method, should be planted out in a nursery bed and shaded with slatted lights (constructed from

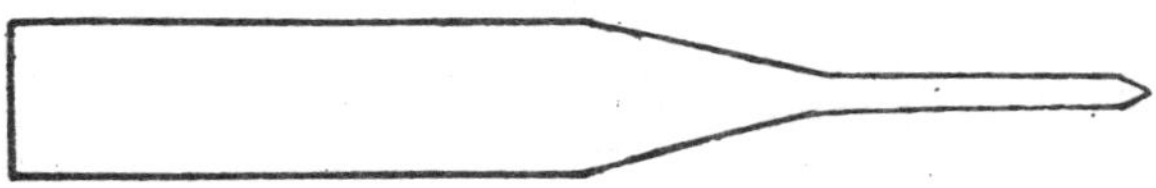

FIG. 6

laths) and well watered for the first week or two of their sojourn in their new home, which should be selected with some care, in a sheltered and preferably somewhat shaded site. Thereafter care of the plants will consist mainly in transplanting them as conditions require it, training where growth indicates it to be necessary, and pruning.

So far we have dealt only with those plants which will thrive in "any" soil, and which will be found in the Glossary which forms the main section of this book indicated by the letters "ANC," as an indication of their requirements in the matter of soil. There are those among the shrubs, however, which are only at home in a soil which consists mainly of peat, and others which only put on their best behaviour when thoroughly at home in a calcareous soil. For these it is wise to prepare, where it is desired to "line them out," a special bed consisting of peat with a little sand added to the ordinary soil of the garden, so that by bulk the peat consists of roughly one-third of the total soil to a depth of 1 foot. For the calcareous soil the addition of lime rubble at the rate of 7 lb. per square yard will suffice to keep the young plants both happy and in character.

For the choicer and more rare shrubs, raised with care and

nursed with patience to a stage when they call for individual quarters with a little more living room than the close company of their fellows in a seed-pan, one recommends the use of small pots; in the main those known to the trade as 60's are probably the best for the purpose. The soil to be used for all varieties should be similar at first, and the best basic soil from which to start is the John Innes potting compost—details of which will be found at the end of the chapter. In the case of the bulk of plants this will be found to keep them growing and healthy until such times that their size indicates that they are ready for planting out, when they should be transferred to the suitable section of the nursery bed. The pots, after potting has taken place, should be "soaked up" in the same way as the "pricked-out" seedlings in the pans earlier mentioned.

In the interim it is well for them to be located in cold frames, kept close for a few days after potting, and thereafter more air and light given. If the frame is situated in the fullest of sun, slatted lights should be used for shading on the hottest days.

It is an axiom that the older a tree or shrub the more difficult it is to transplant with success. Nevertheless a great deal depends upon the character of the root of the plant itself. Such plants as azaleas and rhododendrons, which form a tight mass of fine fibrous roots quite near to the surface of the ground, and which do not extend for long distances from the plant itself, transplant with the greatest ease, and, provided the soil into which they are transplanted is suitable to their growth, quickly become at home. In the case of many trees and shrubs, however, the root system under the ground is very similar to the branches above the ground. It consists of several branching, woody roots, radiating from which are more slender ones, which in turn give place to masses of active fibrous roots which spread farther and farther afield to extend the feeding ground of the tree.

Thus young trees and shrubs, which are not permanently sited, require occasional transplanting to render them fit to be moved when the time for their incorporation in the borders comes. In the case of the deciduous shrubs this should be done during the period of the year—generally commencing in November—when the shrub is dormant, and the root may be completely denuded of soil.

Deciduous shrubs protect themselves against undue winter transpiration by dropping their leaves, and consequently the functions of the roots during that period are considerably decreased. Root disturbance at that time is therefore less harmful than it would be at any other period, but if the transplanting is deferred until it is nearly time for the leaves to appear again, a great strain is thrown upon an attenuated root system, frequently with fatal results.

From this it may be seen that the longer a tree or shrub remains undisturbed the greater the ordeal it will have to undergo when the time comes for it to be removed, transported, and planted elsewhere.

Transplanting is an ordeal for any shrub ; but it would be idle to suggest that seedlings should be planted at first into their permanent homes, though this treatment would eventually give rise to plants with long clean leads, and an appearance of lusty strength. These characteristics are those of shrubs the roots of which have been undisturbed, and they are those to be avoided when selecting plants which it is desired to purchase and to have removed. The symptoms shown by shrubs which have been frequently transplanted are the somewhat stunted growth and short joints, and it is this type of shrub which the knowledgeable gardener selects as being likely to move well.

In the case of evergreens, and conifers, transplanting is a still greater hazard, and one recommends that they are taken with as large a " ball " of soil as possible ; where this is not practicable it is most important that the right time is chosen for the work. Here no falling of the leaves intervenes to compensate for the ruthless curtailment of the root systems, and the fall in supply of moisture from the roots is felt more considerably than in the case of a deciduous shrub. It is therefore essential that the root system should not be disturbed when it is at its slowest period of development, but when it is most likely to make immediate growth. For this reason, and with the proviso that reasonable precautions are taken to see that sufficient water is given during the ensuing summer, one recommends that it be done during the showery, warm, spring weather, usually experienced in May, that is, after all danger of excessive transpiration from the drying east winds is past.

The next best period is undoubtedly the similar period of weather experienced in the months of September and October, the earlier period for northern parts of the country and the later one in the south.

In certain cases a reduction of the surfaces which transpire (that is, the leaves) is to be strongly recommended, and one-third to one-half of the leaf surfaces of the hollies may be removed to advantage.

Where it is desired to move large shrubs known to have a widely spread root system, preparation is necessary generally at least a year in advance—and sometimes two years. The size of the " ball " is marked out, and a trench is dug just inside the measured space, to such a depth that all the roots are severed, for a distance of half-way (or less) round the shrub. The ball is then undermined to cut any tap roots, the soil replaced, the trench filled in and plentifully watered. In some cases the other half of the ball may then be similarly treated, but in the case of the larger and more valuable shrubs this should be undertaken the following year.

The ingenuity of the gardener comes fully into play when it is desired to remove a really large shrub. He will find planks useful as lifting boards, and accomplish much with the aid of rollers and planks which would at first seem impossible. He should, however, *not* attempt the impossible within the limits of his apparatus, which it is assumed is not of the most comprehensive type.

But with the removal of the tree or shrub only one-half of the process is complete, for replanting is still necessary for the fulfilment of the gardener's aim.

It is probably stating the obvious to say that in preparing the new site, the hole which it is required to dig should be sufficiently wide to accommodate the root system which has been lifted, *when it has been spread out to its fullest extent.* In other words, the hole should be dug to fit the roots, never should the roots be cramped into the hole.

The depth of the hole should be determined by the tree or shrub itself. In the case of trees deep planting should be avoided. Nature gives us plenty of examples of how trees grow, and invariably shows us the thickening of the trunk as it divides into its several main roots above the surface of the ground. In most cases, however, the shrub itself indicates to what depth it has been planted quite clearly upon its stems, and the object of the gardener should be to plant to a similar depth. He should remember that in the case of a prepared and dug hole, there is likely to be some subsidence of the freshly dug soil, and to allow for this in his planting.

The soil which is filled in about the fibrous roots should be fine, divided, and well worked in, and consolidated. In the case of very light soil, watering well will settle the shrub in probably better than a systematic ramming or firming. When the soil is very heavy *less* firming is required than in the case of a lighter loam.

John Innes Potting Compost

Seven parts medium loam.

Three parts peat.

Two parts sand.

With the addition of the John Innes base ¼ lb., and chalk ¾ oz. per bushel.

CHAPTER IV

MAINTENANCE

THE culminating pleasure which accrues to the gardener who propagates his plants from seed undoubtedly arises when, at long last, he produces a perfectly shaped shrub which will, in due season, gladden his eyes with an overwhelming display of bounteous colour, but there is betwixt promise and fulfilment a great deal of canny work flavoured with some hard labour.

Perhaps it may be said that the canny work includes one of the most important of all the gardener's arts, the art of pruning. Pruning may be said to be divided into two sections :—

(*a*) Shortening the growth of twigs or branches.
(*b*) Thinning out the growths, or eliminating the growth completely.

Pruning may be justified only on the following grounds :—

(1) It may serve to alter the line or beautify the appearance of the plant.
(2) It may be used as a type of surgery to improve the health of the plant.
(3) It may be used to improve the quality or size of the flowers of the plant.

It therefore follows that the purpose for which pruning is to be done should be kept in the forefront of the mind during its actual accomplishment ; but a great deal more than the reason for pruning must also be present. It is essential to know the normal outline of the shrub to be pruned, since pruning itself should aim at preserving the natural contours of the tree, or, if you wish, the most dignified outline, rather than to be an example of nightmarish topiary. Put in another way, pruning should be confined, when dealing with shape, to making its object as perfect a specimen of its kind as it is possible with the material at one's command.

Pruning for this purpose must also be based upon a knowledge of the flowering time of the plant, together with a knowledge of whether it flowers upon the growth of the previous season, or upon that of the current one.

Pruning for shape, therefore, should not be regarded as glorified clipping. As an example of pruning based upon insufficient knowledge one might instance the autumn pruning of Jasminum nudiflorum, or the autumn pruning of the Forsythias. As both these plants flower upon the wood produced in the previous year, they obviously should be pruned immediately after having flowered, for though it is possible by autumn pruning that they should acquire a good shape, it is also certain that such a method of pruning in these cases will give them the beauty of shape only, since flowers there will be none.

It is not often that one finds in amateur circles that the pruning of the larger trees is adequately practised, since these are normally allowed to attain whatever shape the vagaries of Nature allow them to take, and often their cribbed, cabined, and confined situation in the nursery garden leads them towards the fantastic rather than the beautiful.

It is essential in the case of the ornamental trees that systematic pruning for shape should begin quite early in the life of the tree. The primary aim is to lay a good framework of branches in such a way that the eventual tree will be graceful in shape and typical in character.

The gardener should not confuse his aims with those of the forester. The aim is not to provide a trunk which will give the maximum quantity of sound wood, but to produce in his garden a thing of beauty in which trunk, branches, leaves, and flowers each play their contributory parts.

In a spacious garden it is obvious that such trees should, where their natural habit dictates it, be covered with leafy branches almost to the ground. They should be evenly balanced and should have no aspect which needs concealment.

The first aim of pruning is to obtain a central trunk capable of bearing a suitable framework. This can best be done by keeping a watch upon the leading shoot while it is still young. A most important thing is to see that it is only a single shoot, and the formation of competitive leaders should be discouraged, or if they are produced they should be removed. If the original leader is broken, another side shoot near the top should be encouraged to take its place, trained into position by being tied to a stake, and kept in the lead by removing other shoots which might prove competitors of no mean order. Theoretically, trees so treated should continue to grow upwards if the side branches are constantly removed. In practice, however, they do so, but become very slender and unable to support their own top weight. It is better to shorten rather than remove the lower branches, so that they provide short branchlets with many leaves and build up sufficient fit material to give rise to a sturdy trunk which has its side branches removed by degrees as it gains strength.

Where the branches to be removed are large they should be cut off in at least two pieces, the last piece to be removed should be light and not exceed one foot in length—so that the final cut may be clean and unsplintered.

It is not wise to cut away all the branches from the lower part of the trunk at one time, particularly if it has been heavily shaded. The sudden exposure of a large area of trunk may lead to a considerable patch of the bark being killed. This may be obviated by the gradual reduction of the branches rather than their sudden expurgation. All the branches removed should be cut off as close to the bark as possible without the vestige of a stump remaining. The best time to do this is in November. The wound should be dressed with coal tar as a protection against the entry of spores and undue moisture.

It is stating the obvious to say that where branches are partly dead they should be cut back to about one foot behind the dead wood, and painted with tar as a similar protection. Broken branches should be treated in the same way. If allowed to stay, decay will set in and be ultimately transmitted to the trunk.

Where cavities are formed in trees by decay, all the decaying wood should be cleaned out and the cavity thus created sprayed with Cuprinol or a 20 per cent. solution of Phenol, after which it should be given a good thick coating of tar.

If the hole has a tendency to hold water, its lowest point should be found and a hole drilled through in such a way that any water which accumulates should be allowed to drain out. It will eventually be filled with Portland cement, or, in the case of very big holes, with concrete, or brickwork, which should be faced with a layer of cement, the surface of which should be coloured to match the bark as nearly as possible. It is important that all moisture should be rigorously excluded and a good surface provided for the bark to grow anew. If a suitable surface is not provided a continual tendency for the new bark to form thickened rolls at the edges of the hole is shown, and these will eventually fail to meet whatever the repair undertaken.

In the case of the smaller flowering trees less attention is required than is necessary with the large trees. It is rather a matter of educating the plant for the purpose of eradicating its faults and accentuating its most desirable characteristics.

The pruning in the early stages is therefore designed to encourage a short but sturdy trunk bearing shapely heads. Later it becomes necessary to prune the branches which have a tendency to bend their heads too near the ground and interfere with the passers-by. This does not consist in merely shearing away such awkward growths, but in treating the individual branches in such a way that they retain their grace of outline while they lose their apparent defects. This can generally be done by tracing back the longer pendent branchlets to their point of emission from the branch, and removing them entirely. This will enable the shorter ones which remain to display themselves to full advantage.

In the case of big, well-established, flowering trees such as the Cherries, Almonds, Laburnums, Peaches, Hawthorns, Birches, and Beeches, they should not have mature branches cut away since they produce these growths with difficulty, and quite often the final effect is worsened by so doing.

The genus Prunus is very prone to gumming after the removal of branches, and for this reason heavy pruning should be avoided. In the case of the Oaks and the Elms, response to pruning is exceptionally good, and can help considerably in the production of shapely trees.

When we come to shrubs one should not assume that every shrub needs pruning each year. It is not a case of "sparing the rod and spoiling the child." Many will grow well for several years without pruning, save for the shortening of extra and luscious growth. We might cite, as examples, most varieties of Azaleas, Rhododendrons, Daphnes, Camellias, Lilacs, Currants, Philadelphus, Honeysuckles, and Witch Hazels.

In the case of Forsythia, this should either be pruned immediately after flowering by cutting out the bulk of the old wood, or left completely unpruned to do its best under those circumstances.

In the case of practically all the evergreen shrubs little systematic pruning is necessary except to alter their shape where it is deemed necessary, or prevent them from spreading far and wide over less forward neighbours. This work is best performed as soon as the flowering season is over.

There is a tendency on the part of some shrubs to become over-tall and attenuated, and such an adventure into emaciated giantism should be discouraged just before spring growth is due to commence, since this will allow them as long a period as possible in which to become as fully clothed as the season will permit.

Most of the Heaths benefit by being cut back after flowering has finished to a point just above the commencement of the season's growth. This must be done with annual regularity if the plants are to be kept in character, and the looseness of growth to which they are so prone in the garden is to be obviated.

For the deciduous shrubs which need systematic pruning, one may set oneself a rule, which is that pruning is best done at that time of year which will allow the variety of shrub which one

proposes to prune the longest period of time before the shrub will again flower. Thus, the varieties which flower in the late summer and autumn should be pruned during the winter or early spring. Spring-flowering trees and shrubs should be similarly pruned as soon as the flowers are past. Thus it can be seen that it is necessary to study the peculiarities of the individual plant before attacking the problem of suitable pruning.

Pruning of such newly planted deciduous shrubs should merely consist of removing the tips of the shoots, but where the specimens are already sufficiently large in scope they may be pruned back hard, so that only a few buds are left at the base of the previous year's wood. This pruning should be done immediately after flowering in the case of those which flower in the spring, and in the winter or early spring in the case of those which flower later in the year upon the new wood.

But there is a class of shrubs which flower on the growth of the previous season, at the same time or later than they produce their maximum growth for the season. It must be obvious that these cannot be cut back early, since that would remove the flowering growth, neither can they be cut back immediately after flowering, since that would curtail the period in which the new shoots would make their best growth, and pruning must therefore consist of thinning the shoots rather than shortening them. Thus the gardener will confine his attention, after the shrub has flowered, to the process of eradicating thin, crowded, or unnecessary shoots, and generally opening up the plant so that it may produce better and finer flowers.

Thus for the shrub proper, we have variable treatment—plants which flower upon the new wood are cut back so that only a few buds of the previous year's growth are left, whereas in the case of plants which flower upon the previous year's wood, at the same time or later than the production of new growth, thinning only is the right procedure.

This treatment is of undoubted benefit to the Philadelphus (the Syringa of gardens), the Deutzias, and all those plants which have a tendency to make dense masses of twiggy growth.

As a rule shrubs require little care in the matter of staking unless they are of the type which for the first year or so after transplanting confine their growth to a single lengthening stem. The smaller flowering trees do, however, if transplanted into an exposed spot, require some form of support against the violence of the wind, especially if they have been transplanted bare of soil.

One fundamental function of the root system of the tree is to support it firmly in the ground, and the violent disturbance of this work brought about by transplanting calls for a while for the assistance of a stake to reinforce the reduced support of the shortened root system.

The stake to be used should be similar in diameter to the tree which it is to support, and pointed at the lower end. It should not, after it has been driven, extend to the full length of the trunk to the point where it first branches ; since its function in this case is merely to anchor the tree firmly to the soil. In the main it is better to drive in the stake before the tree is planted, and to arrange the roots of the tree about the stake, rather than to drive through them. If this method is adopted care must be taken to see that when the soil settles the ties do not prevent the tree from settling with it. The ties themselves should not be tied directly round the stem of the tree, but have a soft pliable material (once upon a time a piece of inner tyre was suitable) between the stem and the tie.

Often the practice of staking can be avoided if temporary help is given to the tree by first of all reducing the top branches so that less resistance is offered to the wind. This also has the effect of equalising the demands of the tree, and the ability of the reduced root system to supply.

In addition to this, three or more long wooden pegs, similar in shape and character to tent pegs, are driven into the ground on the circumference of a circle drawn about it, and joined to the top of the stem of the tree by ropes, cords, or wires bound round a protecting band of some resistant material.

As soon as the tree is self-supporting these artificial aids may be withdrawn with a consequent improvement of sightliness.

CHAPTER V

THE SOIL

THE ideal soil for the Shrub Garden is probably that which is possessed always by one's fortunate rivals but seldom lies in one's own garden. It is good loam, generally a light one, free of lime, and well drained. Such a soil would provide a perfect home for most shrubs, including all the ericaceous varieties, but since one is seldom likely to find such a soil dropped into the lap of one's garden, it is necessary to study how one can obtain the best results using the medium with which one is cursed or doubly blessed.

The subject of soil fertility is so great in its range that it would be idle to pretend that this slight chapter embodies a comprehensive study of the question, but it will help to clear up some of the difficulties which concern the average gardener.

The phrases " good fibrous loam," " coarse sand," " well rotted leafmould," are expressions conveying to the man of considerable experience definite, in fact almost rigid, descriptions of the appropriate materials, but are capable of a great variety of interpretations by the beginner and inexperienced. It is therefore essential that we should look at the study of the soil from an extremely elementary angle.

Soil may be said to be made up of four parts: the organic one, the inorganic one, together with air and water. The organic part consists of complicated chemical structures kept progressively in a state of decay by the action of bacteria which gradually reduce it to more simple compounds, finally to make them available to the plant as food. These bacteria are extremely numerous, an estimate of their number being roughly 3,000,000,000 in each gram of fertile soil. Thus roughly four parts per thousand of the actual weight of the top soil is made up of these tiny living things.

The bacteria may be likened to tiny plants growing within the soil. They, in their turn, are preyed upon by approximately three-quarters of a million protozoa in each gram of soil, and the relation between these two microscopic organisms is one of continual strife.

Bacteria also play an extremely important part in the production of nitrates which the plant can absorb readily, and any study of the soil must make it axiomatic that it is the vehicle in which they live, and where it is altered or treated such alteration and treatment must allow for the well-being of these tiny organisms. Since bacteria live primarily upon the organic part of the soil, the perfect soil must contain a set proportion of humus or organic matter.

The inorganic part of the soil has arisen from the constant and continued breaking-up of the surface rock into successively smaller particles, and ranges in size from stones to sand, to silt, and finally to clay. The division between each of these sections is arbitrary, so that at the finer end the smaller silt closely approximates to the coarser clay, and at the coarser end approximates to the finer sands.

In the normal soil clay is an extremely important constituent to the plant because it contains the only substance among the inorganic components of the soil in a state able to be assimilated by the plant. Finally, every soil should contain a small quantity of chalk, sufficient to neutralise any acidity caused by the presence of the decaying humus.

Loam is the name generally given to a natural mixture of sand, silt, clay, and humus, and a good loam is selected because of the benefit of its clay and humus content. A light loam is so called because it contains a rather higher percentage of sand than the medium loam, and a heavy loam contains much more clay and less sand than a light loam.

Marl is the name given to loams which contain chalk.

The ideal loam for the Shrub Garden is one which contains rather more sand than the heavy loam, and is, in fact, a light, decayed top-spit soil, and which will leave upon the hands the characteristic greasy stain of clay, but which will break apart with ease when handled.

The so-called good loam contains a mass of small root fibres. This is one form in which humus can be incorporated in the soil.

However, in the main one would not use loam merely to increase the quantity of humus in the soil, since there are many cheaper and better ways of obtaining the same results.

Peat is an almost purely organic soil in a state of suspended decay. It has been pointed out earlier that the bacteria in the soil bring about the successive reduction of the humus content into more simple chemical compounds. For their well-being they need also the presence of air within the soil. When the peat beds are flooded the air is excluded, and the bacteria can no longer thrive. Hence they no longer are able to perform their normal functions, and the decay of the peat is arrested ; in addition, certain organic acids are formed which help to continue the stoppage.

Peat is extremely useful in dry soils, since it can contain up to 95 per cent. of water, and as the average good loam can only contain 30 per cent. of water the ability of the soil to retain the moisture can obviously be considerably improved by the addition of peat.

Peat is normally deficient in phosphorus, potassium, and calcium, and not infrequently in magnesium, and where fertilisers are necessary these may be added when correctly balanced.

Sand is essential to the soil to aerate it, and to improve the drainage, since bacteria, which are so necessary to the well-being of the plant, require both air and moisture for their continued health.

The sand to be incorporated into any soil for the purpose of lightening it should be clean, should contain nothing in the way of shells, should be free of salt, and should not consist of particles of all one size, but should range from fine to coarse.

Little mention has been made of the functions of the protozoa in the soil. It has been said that they prey upon the bacteria, and it must be obvious that if they become too numerous the soil will suffer a reduction in its fertility, whereas if they are reduced the soil will temporarily improve. For this reason soils are often sterilised.

Sterilisation, whether chemical or mechanical, is used to kill protozoa and the bacteria at one and the same time. Fortunately the bacteria exist in an intermediate form as spores, and, relieved of the depredations of their natural enemies, proceed to thrive at an amazing rate after the sterilisation has been completed, and before the soil becomes repeopled by further protozoa. This gives rise to an immediate increase in fertility and a consequent improvement in the growth of the plant. Where bacteria are numerous and much organic material is present in the soil, the texture of the soil can be moist and somewhat sticky without being waterlogged, and at the same time crumble easily.

The presence of air in the soil is essential to the soil bacteria and to the growing plants themselves, and though there has recently been a great deal of controversy as to the merits and demerits of increasing the aeration of the surface soil by hoeing, no one can deny that complete exclusion of the air from the soil leads to the death of the plant and the soil bacteria. Water, too, is essential, since it provides the vehicle by which the plant foods are dissolved and made available to the root hairs.

The problem which arises from this elementary study of the soil is how to relate it to the needs of one's own garden. Perhaps the best way in which to render the information useful is to consider how to treat soils of various textures. Light, sandy soils most frequently suffer from a dearth of moisture owing to extraordinarily sharp drainage, and it is necessary to incorporate material which will retain moisture. For this purpose a well-shredded peat, leafmould, or farmyard manure, or even some form of cellulose, can well be used, and this should be added and well dug in.

In the case of the heavier soils composed mainly of sticky loams and clays, these are liable to suffer from the excessive retention of water at inappropriate periods. They can, of course, be improved by liming, which causes the soil to flocculate or gather together into larger particles with a consequent improvement in drainage. This, however, cannot be done where it is desired to preserve the neutrality of the soil, nor can it be put into effect when the ground has been freshly manured.

The texture of the soil in these cases can be considerably improved by adding any coarse organic or inorganic material such as coarse sand, burnt clay, boiler ash, leafmould, or peat.

In the case of soils consisting mainly of chalk, the soil presents a problem similar to that presented by a sandy soil, the problem being to create surface tillage and the incorporation of humus from the compost heap, turf, and, in fact, any available organic material will help to create the necessary surface layer of soil.

In the main, in such gardens deep-rooted trees should be avoided, since they will probably fail.

The gardener's aim should always be to produce from the existing soil one of balanced texture with no predominance given any one factor. Thus, in a sandy soil the object should be to increase the humus and clay content, in a clay soil to increase the sand and humus content, in a soil consisting mainly of peat to increase the sand and the loam content, and in one of chalk to incorporate if possible both clay and humus.

In the case of practically every soil considerable improvement may be brought about by dressing the surface with leaf soil or the product of the compost heap, and an early dressing of this kind will lead to considerable and progressive improvement in the surface soil and a consequent improvement in the growth of the shrubs.

It is a great mistake in the garden ever to burn green waste material; it should be stored until such times as it is reduced to a black, greasy humus, and used for this type of top dressing.

Having finally worked all the improvements to the soil which seem to be dictated by experience, one last factor must be borne in mind before planting one's Shrub Garden. Many species are found growing upon limy soils, but few of these species cannot be grown in neutral soils. If, however, the nature of one's soil is predominantly calcareous, it is idle to select plants which succeed best in neutral or acid soils, though if the soil is either neutral or slightly acid very little difficulty arises in the cultivation of plants said normally to appreciate lime, but in the case of certain species to which the presence of lime appears to be necessary, lime can be added if it is found that it does improve the cultivation of the shrub itself.

In the case of surface-rooted shrubs—the smaller type of Rhododendron is an example—provided aspect and rainfall are suitable, the acidity or alkalinity of the subsoil is not an important factor if the top six to nine inches of soil is correct in texture and humus content. Such plants may well be grown in a surface layer of sandy peat superimposed even upon chalk, provided always that the rainfall of the district is sufficient to support their growth without artificial aid, and if the suitable cool, sheltered aspect is available in a spot where surplus rainfall which has passed through the chalk cannot drain into the peat. Such a spot can usually be found halfway up a slightly sloping bank facing north or north-west. Continual top dressings of similar material to that in which they are growing are necessary to continue to feed them as the original layer of soil becomes impoverished.

NOTES ON USE OF GLOSSARY

NOMENCLATURE	In all cases where the plant has been named as a compliment to its producer, or discoverer, the information has been indicated by the abbreviation Comm.
DESCRIPTION	The heights given at the end of each description are the approximate heights in feet to which the varieties will grow under NORMAL conditions.
MONTH OF FLOWERING	The months indicated are the months in which the plant gives its most effective display. In foliage plants, this may be taken to be the period in which the foliage exhibits the greatest range of colour.
HABIT	A further note indicates whether the plant is deciduous (D) (leaf losing), evergreen (E), or semi-evergreen (DE).
SPREAD	The next note indicates the *scope* of the plant, that is, the approximate space to be allowed for its development. Thus 6-ft. indicates a space of six feet square (that is, 36 square feet).
PROPAGATION	Another note indicates the best method of propagation. Sd. (from seed), Cg. (by cuttings of the green wood), Ch. (cuttings with a heel of old wood), Cr. (root cuttings), D. (division of the old root), L. (layers), G. (graftage), Gr. (graftage upon root of the same plant), B. (budding). The figures which follow these indicate the best month in which to do this. Thus Ch.6 means that the plant is best propagated from cuttings with a heel of old wood during the month of June, and Cr.5 indicates root cuttings in May.
COLOUR	For some plants, a number indicates the colour of the flower as matched by the Horticultural Colour Chart (Parts I and II) published by

the Royal Horticultural Society in co-operation with the British Colour Council. In cases where the flowers have been definitely matched the sheet number is followed by a stroke and the shade number. It should be noted that colours are only true in daylight, preferably in a north light.

SOIL	Plants may be divided for the purpose into three classes : (*a*) those needing acid soils—the final note A indicates this ; (*b*) those needing calcareous soils—the final note C indicates this ; (*c*) those needing neutral soils—the final note N indicates this. Where the letters ANC are used the plant thrives in any soil; where the letters AN or NA are used neutral or acid soil will satisfy, but limy soil should be avoided; and where the letters CN or NC are used the plant will not tolerate an acid soil.
IDENTIFICATION	For the positive identification cf the plants illustrated in the plates the celluloid template provided will be found of great use ; thus in Plate 7 Clematis macropetala is identified by the letters CDGHLM, Wistaria sinensis by the letters EFJKNORS, and Akebia quinata by the letters GHPQ.

GLOSSARY

ABELIA (Caprifoliaceae) (named in honour of mr. abel, who discovered species a. chinensis in china in 1816).

A group of attractive deciduous and evergreen shrubs, which thrive mainly in well-drained, leafy soil, in a sunny and well-protected position. A few only of the species may be said to be hardy in all parts of the British Isles, except where they are given adequate wall protection.

A. chinensis (Chinese) China, forms a much-branched, rounded shrub, with reddish branches and light-green leaves, producing its flowers in groups in the leaf axils. The white flowers are sweetly scented and reminiscent of miniature foxgloves, and are surrounded by a calyx of rosy-red.

3-ft., July-August. D. 2-ft. Sq. Cg7. Ch10. N.

A. floribunda (Flowering abundantly) Mexico, is an evergreen species suitable for planting against sheltered walls, which will often reach a height exceeding ten feet, but grown as a shrub seldom

Berberidopsis corallina

Berberis Thunbergii atropurpurea ABCDEJ
Berberis Darwinii FGKLNOQU
Berberis Aquifolium PRST

exceeds six feet. The flowers, borne in clusters of twos or threes, in groups along the arching branches, are carmine-purple in colour and tubular in shape. The attractive rose-purple flowers in conjunction with the shiny evergreen leaves make it a most pleasing species. 6-*ft.*–10-*ft.*, *June*. *E*. 4-*ft. Sq*. *Cg*7. *Ch*10. *N*.

A. GRANDIFLORA (Large flowered), a hybrid of unknown origin, is a slender, gracefully disposed shrub, with dark-green leaves which persist in the mildest winters, and bears its white, pink-flushed, tubular, bell-shaped flowers in groups of from one to four in the leaf axils and terminals. It frequently masquerades as the A. chinensis of catalogues. 6-*ft*. *July-October*. *E*. 3-*ft. Sq*. *Cg*7. *Ch*10. *N*.

A. SCHUMANII (Comm.) China, is one of the most delightful of the species, the pale-green leaves become flushed with pale-red, and form a fitting setting for the bell-shaped flowers of rose-lilac.
3-*ft*., *July-September*. *D*. 2½-*ft. Sq*. *Cg*7. *Ch*10. *N*. *Pl*.1.

ABUTILON (MALVACEAE) (DERIVED FROM THE ARABIC NAME FOR AN INDIGENOUS PLANT WITH A FLOWER LIKE THAT OF A MALLOW).

These plants are tender and should strictly be regarded as half-hardy, but suitably placed against a south wall in full sun are so delightful, and generally satisfactory in the southern counties, that they cannot be omitted upon this score.

A. MEGAPOTAMICUM (From the great river) Brazil, is a pre-eminent beauty with eccentrically centred, simple leaves of deep green, with serrated margins, which seem to lie in a perpendicular plane with their apices down. The flowers, which are also pendent, are borne in the leaf axils, and have bright-red calices and lemon-yellow petals, and the exserted stamens of purple-brown form an attractive cluster of well-contrasted colour. Also known as A. vexillarium, the beauty of colour and of line of this plant make it greatly sought after.
3-*ft*., *June-October*. *D*. 3-*ft. Sq*. *Cg*7. *N*. *Pl*.2.

A. VITIFOLIUM (Vine-leaved) Chile, forms a tall shrub often exceeding eight feet in height, with low-forking tree-like growth, and bears large three- to seven-lobed, greyish, maple-like leaves, and has transparent " hollyhock " flowers of pale mauve.
12-*ft*., *June-July*. *D*. 8-*ft. Sq*. *Sd*3. *N*.

ACACIA (LEGUMINOSAE) (FROM THE GR. AKAZO—TO SHARPEN, FROM THE PRICKLY LEAVES OF SOME OF THE SPECIES).

Two only of these have been selected as being the hardiest of a tender family—both need careful siting in sheltered places and in favoured localities in the south and west.

A. JUNIPERINA (Resembling Juniper) Australia, is a prickly shrub with needle-like leaves, and long wand-like branches, bearing in the topmost leaf axils narrow, inch long, fluffy flowers, sweetly scented and bright yellow. 12-*ft*., *April-May*. *E*. 8-*ft. Sq*. *Cg*9. *N*.

A. VERTICILLATA (Whorled-leaved) Australia, is very similar in both appearance and characteristics in some of its forms, but is, if anything, less hardy. 12-*ft*., *April-May*. *E*. 8-*ft. Sq*. *Cg*9. *N*. *Pl*.17.

ACANTHOPANAX (ARALIACEAE) (FROM GR. AKANTHOS—A THORN; PAN—ALL ; AND AKOS—A REMEDY).

A group of attractive hardy shrubs, grown mainly for the benefit of their striking foliage and clusters of black berries which resemble those of the ivy.

A. HENRYI (Comm.) China, grows into a rounded bush about eight feet in height, with light brown stems armed with stout spines, and bearing leaves made up of five large leaflets, and inconspicuous flowers followed by groups of black berries which persist for a long time. *8-ft., June-July. D. 8-ft. Sq. Cr6. N.*

A. PENTAPHYLLUS (Five-leaved) China, is a most attractive shrub with upstanding stems of some eight feet, with arching branches, bearing three to five parted smaller leaflets and inconspicuous greenish-white flowers, followed by clusters of black berries.

8-ft., June-July. D. 8-ft. Sq. Cr6. N.

ACER (ACERACEAE) (FROM THE L. ACER—SHARP, FROM THE FACT THAT THE WOOD OF CERTAIN SPECIES WAS USED TO MAKE LANCES).

All the Maples are more correctly trees rather than shrubs, the Japanese Maples being trees of small size, frequently used in conjunction with shrubs. *Pls.* 3, 4, 16.

A. GINNALA (From the Amur River district) China, is a small tree with three-lobed, small, dark-green leaves, with reddish ribs, and sweetly scented, creamy-white flowers in May. The foliage assumes the most attractive colours in autumn upon a tree which is bushy and forked low. *15-ft., May-June. D. 15-ft. Sq. Sd2. ANC. Pl.4.*

A. GRISEUM (Grey) Central China, is another small tree with bark which peels, revealing the attractive coppery-orange new bark beneath. Foliage assumes attractive colours in autumn.

25-ft., May. D. 25-ft. Sq. Sd2. ANC.

A. JAPONICUM (Japanese) Japan, is still another small tree, with shapely leaves divided deeply into seven to eleven segments, sharply toothed. The flowers, produced before the leaves, are reddish purple, and borne in long-stalked hanging clusters. The variety A. japonicum aureum has golden leaves, and A. japonicum var. filicifolium has the segments of the leaves still farther dissected.

7-ft., May. D. 5-ft. Sq. G12. ANC.

A. PALMATUM (With palmate leaves) is extremely variable both in the shape and colour of the leaves, and has been divided into the following forms which cannot be regarded as anything but an attempt to bring them into practical divisions.

The DISSECTUM group : the green leaves are cut into seven to eleven segments which extend to the main leaf-stalk, and each segment is cut into fine sharply-toothed lobes. The sub-varieties are :—

A. PALMATUM VAR. DISSECTUM ORNATUM (Decorated) with leaves of blood red.

A. PALMATUM VAR. DISSECTUM MARGINATUM (Rose-margined) is similar in leaf structure, but has green leaves edged with rose.

A. PALMATUM VAR. DISSECTUM SESSILIFOLIUM (With stalkless leaves) is distinguished by its short-stalked green leaves and its short-stalked leaflets.

The PALMATUM group has its green leaves cut to about two-thirds of their depth into five lobes. The flowers are small, and of purple-red, and the winged seeds have their wings much incurved. The leaves assume the usual autumn tints. The sub-varieties are :—

A. PALMATUM VAR. ATROPURPUREUM (Dark-purple), has typical leaves of dark-purple.

A. PALMATUM VAR. AUREUM (Golden) is similar in leaf structure, but has its leaves of yellow colour turn to gold as the leaves age.

A. PALMATUM VAR. LINEARILOBUM (With parallel-sided lobes) has leaves deeply cleft into narrow green lobes.

A. PALMATUM VAR. RIBESIFOLIUM (With leaves like the currant) has green leaves cut into the base in wide lobes.

A. PALMATUM VAR. ROSEA-MARGINATUM (Rose-margined) has the typical green leaves of A. palmatum edged with rose.

A. PALMATUM VAR. VARIEGATUM (Variegated) differs only from the type in its variegated leaves.

The SEPTEMLOBUM group is generally distinguished by its young leaves being flashed with red, turning green with maturity, and blood-red in the autumn prior to falling. The leaves are larger than those of A. palmatum, and are cut into seven lobes.

A. PALMATUM VAR. SANGUINEUM (Blood red) has blood-red leaves.

A. PALMATUM VAR. SEPTEMLOBUM (Seven-lobed) is the type.

A. PALMATUM VAR. SEPTEMLOBUM ATROPURPUREUM (Deep purple) has similar leaves of deep purple.

ACTINIDIA (DILLENIACEAE) (FROM GR. AKTIS—A RAY, REFERRING TO STAR-LIKE STIGMAS OF THE FEMALE FLOWERS).

Plants of vigorous climbing growth which fare well in good soil in either sun or part shade.

A. ARGUTA (Serrated) Japan, is an exceptionally hardy, vigorous climber with broad, dark, shining green simple alternate leaves, suitable for rambling through a senile tree. The sweetly scented flowers have incurved rounded petals of white tinged with green, centred with purple anthers and star-like stigmata. The sweetly insipid fruits are edible with the added sauce of imagination.

15-ft. upwards, June. D. Variable. Sd2. Cg7. N.

A. CHINENSIS (From China) has large, broad, heart-shaped leaves, somewhat smaller upon the flowering shoots, green above and felted grey beneath, and bears from the previous year's wood white flowers about the size of a penny, turning buff-yellow with age, and

ACTINIDIA (continued)

centred by multiple stamens, followed by fruits covered with reddish-brown hair, about the size and flavour of a large gooseberry.
12-ft. upwards, June. D. Variable. Sd2. Cg7. N.

AEGLE (RUTACEAE) (IS NAMED AFTER ONE OF THE HESPERIDES).

The single species which follows is an extremely attractive plant, the sweetly scented flowers are followed by attractive fruits reminiscent in shape to a small downy orange. The fruits are too bitter and sharp to be eaten raw, but it is chronicled that they make a good conserve and a palatable beverage, and, if further excuse is needed, the pulp is reputed to have a medicinal value. Cultivation of this paragon consists of placing it in good deep loam in a sunny and sheltered position, when it will, at least in the south-west, fruit well when established.

A. SEPIARIA (Forming a hedge) China, is also known as CITRUS trifoliata, and makes a spring bush sparsely clad with green leaves made up of from three to five leaflets, borne upon angular green branches of irregular contour. The white, sweetly-scented flowers are produced in the axils of the spines before the leaves. It is recorded that the plant makes a good hedge and clips well.
9-ft., May. D. 9-ft. Sq. Sd2. Cg7. N.

AGATHAEA (COMPOSITAE) (FROM THE GR. AGATHOS—EXCELLENT; A REFERENCE TO THE BEAUTY OF THE FLOWERS).

A. COELESTIS (Heavenly) South Africa, is also Aster capensis, and is a hard-wooded, brown-leaved, evergreen shrub bearing long-stemmed daisy-flowers of pale sky-blue with central bosses of bright-yellow. A. coelestis is best placed in a sheltered spot where it may wax in strength from year to year, but it may also be propagated from greenwood cuttings and kept going as a bedding plant.
2-ft., June-Oct. E. 3-ft. Sq. Cg6. ANC. Pl.5.

AKEBIA (BERBERIDACEAE) (FROM THE JAPANESE NAME FOR THESE PLANTS).

Two climbers of very attractive appearance, to which distinction is given by the enlarged sepals of the freely produced flowers, and the elegance of the bright-green foliage. They roam at will through any suitable support, and require a sunny aspect and a good garden soil.

A. LOBATA (Lobed) China, has leaves composed of three leaflets, and bears female flowers with three incurved sepals of dark purple.
15-ft., April. D. Variable. Sd2. Cg8. N.

A. QUINATA (Five-leaved) Japan, is a quickly growing, twining climber with leaves made up of three, four or more, generally five, leaflets, and producing very sweetly scented flowers of chocolate-purple, forming a fitting and contrasting associate to Wistaria sinensis.
30-ft., May-June. D. or E. (according to location). Variable. Sd2. Cg8. L6. N. Pl.7.

ALYSSUM (Cruciferae) (from Gr. a—no; lyssa—madness; leaves from one of the species were once reputed to be the cure for the bite of a mad dog).

Many species are in cultivation which may be justly described as shrubby—notably the varieties of A. saxatile, which will be found dealt with in "Alpines in Colour and Cultivation."

AMELANCHIER (Rosaceae) (from the Fr. amelancier, the name given to the snowy mespilus—one of the species).

The foliage of all the varieties assumes most attractive colours in autumn, varying from bright yellow in some species to yellow in others.

AMELANCHIER ROTUNDIFOLIA

A. alnifolia (With leaves resembling Alder) Western N. America, is a small tree or shrub producing heavily-felted, immature leaves, eventually becoming smooth green with maturity, and which bears clusters of small, narrow-petalled, white flowers followed by attractively edible dark purple berries.

7-ft.–15-ft., May. D. 12-ft.–15-ft. Sq. Sd2. Cg7. D11. N.

A. florida (From Florida) Eastern N. America, is very near in appearance to A. alnifolia, the leaves being smooth when quite young and more heavily toothed.

7-ft.–10-ft., May. D. 8-ft.–10-ft. Sq. Sd2. Cg7. D11. N.

A. rotundifolia (Round-leaved) Europe, is the A. vulgaris of catalogues and the Snowy Mespilus, and is generally a small tree or shrub of about eight feet in height. The leaves when young are very white and felted, becoming smooth with age. The large, somewhat narrow-petalled flowers are followed by red fruits which

AMELANCHIER (continued)

turn black ; and which are edible if one can bring oneself to regard their consumption as a duty rather than a pleasure.

8-ft., May. D. 8-ft.–12-ft. Sq. Sd2. Cg7. D11. N.

AMORPHA (LEGUMINOSAE) (FROM THE GR. A—NO, AND MORPHE—FORM ; WITH REFERENCE TO THE IRREGULAR SHAPE OF THE LEAVES).

A group of attractive shrubs with pinnate leaves composed of from nine to forty-one leaflets, and bearing pea-flowers in which all but one petal have been atrophied, but since they are numerously and closely borne in spikes, this is more academically interesting than apparent. All the species thrive well in hot, dry positions.

A. CANESCENS (Grey) United States, is the "Lead Plant," so called because its presence was previously held to indicate the presence of lead in the soil. This is usually covered with dense white hair. The flower spikes are built up of closely-packed, dull, purple-blue, single petals, with grey hairy calyx. *4-ft., July. D. 4-ft. Sq. Cg7. N.*

A. FRUTICOSA (Shrubby) S. United States, is somewhat ungainly, requiring to be pruned back heavily in the spring, but which, with its attractively distributed dark-blue flower spikes, is worth a place in the rough shrubbery. *8-ft., July. D. 8-ft. Sq. Cg7. N.*

A. MICROPHYLLA (Small leaved) N. America, is a small, dainty shrub with sweetly-scented flowers in dainty, tight spikes of purple.

1½-ft., June. D. 2-ft.. Sq Cg7. D3. N.

ANDROMEDA (ERICACEAE) (NAMED AFTER THE GREEK PRINCESS RESCUED BY PERSEUS).

This delightful genus comprises three species, all of which closely resemble one another, and which thrive best in a moist, peaty soil. The common name of one of them, " The Bog Rosemary," gives a distinct clue to the type of soil and conditions of humidity conducive to the plant's well-being.

A. GLAUCOPHYLLA (With grey-blue leaves) N.W. America, with smooth, wiry stems and long, narrow, polished green leaves with heavy felting beneath, has clusters of small, pale pink, Lily-of-the-valley-like flowers. *1½-ft., April. E. 1½-ft. Sq. D10. A.*

A. POLIFOLIA (With leaves like Germander) Britain, has very narrow, almost spiny, leaves, and bears similar groups of attractive pink flowers in nodding terminal clusters.

1½-ft., April-May. E. 1½-ft. Sq. D10. A.

A. POLIFOLIA VAR. MAJOR (Larger) Britain, is similar in all its characteristics save in the width and length of its leaves, which adds a touch of the bizarre to a fairy who could well do without such a large size in boots. *1½-ft., April-May. E. 1½-ft. Sq. D10. A.*

ANTHYLLIS (LEGUMINOSAE) (FROM GR. ANTHOS—FLOWER, AND IOULOS—DOWN ; FROM THE PRESENCE OF A DOWNY CALYX IN SOME OF THE SPECIES).

Pre-eminently the species should be grown in a hot, dry spot.

A. HERMANNIAE (Hermann's) Europe, is a tightly growing, grey, spiny-leaved shrub which packs its branches tightly with masses of tiny, yellow pea flowers, each with a beauty patch of deeper orange. The attractive tight distribution of the wiry stems tend to make it appear an impenetrable thicket.

*1-ft.–2-ft., July-August. D. 2-ft. Sq. Cg*8. *N.* 2/1. *Pl.*6.

APLOPAPPUS (COMPOSITAE) (FROM THE GR. HAPLOOS—SINGLE, AND PAPPUS—DOWN).

A. ERICOIDES (Resembling Heather) California, is a pretty, heath-like shrub for a sheltered, sunny corner, which in late summer covers its grey cloud of foliage with masses of five-petalled, deep-yellow daisy flowers. *3-ft., August. E. 2-ft. Sq. Cg*7. *N.*

ARBUTUS (ERICACEAE) (DERIVED POSSIBLY FROM CELTIC ARBOISE—ROUGH-FRUITED, OR MORE PROBABLY FROM THE LATIN NAME FOR ONE OF THE SPECIES A. UNEDO).

A. UNEDO (Obscure) Ireland and S. Europe, is in reality a small tree which is seldom anything but a wide-topped shrub—the name of which is said to be derived from the Latin unus—one, and edo—to eat; which, coupled with the common name "The Strawberry Tree," gives a true picture of the palatability of the edible fruit. This beautiful, evergreen tree, which varies from fifteen to twenty feet in height, bears clusters of small, pinkish, pitcher-shaped flowers, followed by round hanging orange fruits which ripen at a time when the flowers of the following year are produced. In calcareous soils it seldom reaches its maximum height, rarely if ever exceeding ten feet. *15-ft., October-December. E. 15-ft. Sq. Sd*2. *NA.*

ARCTERICA (*see* "ALPINES IN COLOUR AND CULTIVATION").

ARCTOSTAPHYLOS (ERICACEAE) (FROM GR. ARKTOS—A BEAR, AND STAPHYLE—A BUNCH OF GRAPES; FROM THE FACT THAT THE BERRIES OF SOME OF THE SPECIES WERE EATEN BY BEARS).

A group of evergreen shrubs related to Erica. Soil and conditions should be as for Rhododendron—a reasonably deep layer of peat and sand, or lime-free soil rich in humus, and a location in which acute drying-out does not take place.

A. MANZANITA (The Spanish-American name for the genus) California, is really a small tree, seldom exceeding eight feet in height in this country, and generally less, with peeling bark with thick, oval, pale grey-green leaves, and bearing drooping panicles of white flowers, frequently tinged with pink, each reminiscent of a smaller and less rotund Lily-of-the-valley.

*4-ft.–8-ft., April-May. E. 6-ft.–8-ft. Sq. Sd*2. *AN.*

A. TOMENTOSA (Hairy) California, has foliage a little larger, felted beneath, and bluer in tinge, borne from hairy stems, and bearing

similar attractive white flowers which are followed by reddish-brown berries seldom produced in cultivation.
4-ft.–8-ft., April-May. E. 6-ft.–8-ft. Sq. Sd2. Cg8. AN.

A. UVA-URSI (Bear's grape) Europe, is a prostrate and creeping shrub with bright-green, polished leaves, bearing, in terminal clusters, pink, inverted, pitcher-shaped flowers, followed by shining red berries.
½-ft., April-May. E. 1½-ft. Sq. Sd2. Cg8. AN.

ARISTOLOCHIA (ARISTOLOCHIACEAE) (FROM GR. ARISTOS—BEST, AND LOCHEIA—CHILDBIRTH ; FROM THE ORIGINAL MEDICAL USAGE OF ONE OF THE SPECIES).

A group of vigorous climbing and twining shrubs, of exceptionally easy culture in a sunny site, and of curious rather than of beautiful appearance.

A. MOUPINENSIS (From Moupine) China, is a vigorous climber with large, heart-shaped, deep-green leaves, producing from the leaf axils solitary pipe-shaped, yellow flowers mottled with reddish-purple on the three lobes of the mouth.
12-ft.–20-ft., June-July. D. Variable. Cg8. ANC.

A. SIPHO (Tube-bearing) Eastern U.S.A., is also known as A. durior, and A. macrophylla, with the intriguing common name of "Dutchman's Pipe," and is an exceptionally vigorous climber with large, deep-green, heart-shaped leaves, and bearing upon short stems from the leaf axils, either solitary or in pairs, U-shaped flowers of yellowish-green, narrowing at the mouth, before spreading into three brown lobes. *20-ft., June. D. Variable. D3. ANC.*

A. TOMENTOSA (Covered with short hair) Southern U.S.A., is very similar to A. Sipho, but has somewhat smaller leaves, and has its young growth heavily felted, and the lobes of the calyx generally yellow.

ARTEMISIA (COMPOSITAE) (CALLED AFTER THE GODDESS ARTEMIS (DIANA)).

A group of aromatic shrubs which are evergreen in mild districts.

A. ABROTANUM (abrotonum, Latin name for Southernwood) S. Europe, is the Southernwood, Old Man, or Lad's Love, and has attractive, aromatic, deep-green, feathery foliage, and though the loose clusters of yellowish-green flowers have little appeal, A. Abrotanum provides an excellent colour contrast to grey-leaved shrubs, and must be deemed invaluable for its aromatic attractions.
3-ft., September-October. E or D. 3-ft. Sq. Cg7. ANC.

A. TRIDENTATA (Thrice-toothed) Western N. America, the Sage Brush, is another very pleasant aromatic shrub, at its best after a shower, with wedge-shaped, silvery-grey leaves tapering to the stalk, three- or six-toothed at the top. Unique both in colour and shape, the flowers, borne in long, slender clusters, more or less drooping, are

Berberis lologensis

Calluna vulgaris
var. Alportii ABCEFG

Daboecia cantabrica JFO

Calluna vulgaris
var. J. H. Hamilton NORS

Daboecia cantabrica
var. Watsonii KLHM

Erica vagans
St. Keverne LMOPQSTU

small and yellowish, but the whole plant has that touch of originality which, apart from its scent, would render it outstanding in any company. It should be planted in a dry, sunny site.

6-ft., October. E. 6-ft. Sq. Cg7. C.

ARUNDINARIA (GRAMINEAE) (FROM THE LATIN ARUNDO—A REED).

A group of large, shrubby grasses, differing from Bambusa in having three instead of six stamens, and the typical cylindrical stems and numerous side branches. They succeed best in rich, open, loamy soil or peat, in sheltered places where summer moisture may be had in plenty. The individual species are best propagated by division in May or September. Most of the species seldom flower, but a few have the curious habit of flowering simultaneously throughout the whole world and dying after flowering.

A. ANCEPS (Two-edged) Himalayas, is a Bamboo with brownish-green stems, purple branches, and bright-green leaves about four inches in length, grey-green below, spreading by underground runners.

12-ft. E. Indefinite. D9 or 5. ANC.

A. ANGUSTIFOLIA (With narrow leaves) Japan, is a variety with slender stems of variable height, clad with bright-green, narrow leaves, uniform in colour. *6-ft. E. Indefinite. D9 or 5. ANC.*

A. ARISTATA (Bearded like barley) Himalayas, has yellow canes bearing leaves of up to four inches in length, with smooth, green, rough-edged leaves, sharply pointed. *12-ft. E. Indefinite. D9 or 5. ANC.*

A. AURICOMA (Golden-tufted) Japan, has exceptionally thin, purple-green, tufted stems, and long, slender, dark-green leaves heavily striped with gold. It is also known as Bambusa Fortunei aurea.

4-ft. E. Indefinite. D9 or 5. ANC.

A. CHRYSANTHA (Golden-yellow) Japan, is another rapid runner with slender, dark-green stems, with green leaves sometimes striped with golden yellow, but more often not. Not such a striking plant as A. auricoma. *4-ft.–6-ft. E. Indefinite. D9 or 5. ANC.*

A. FALCATA (Sickle-shaped) Himalayas, has slender stems of greyish or yellowish-green, sheaths hairy at the apex and purple when young, but with pale-green leaves. *10-ft. E. Indefinite. D9 or 5. ANC.*

A. FASTUOSA (Stately) Japan, is probably the hardiest, tallest and most stately of all the species, with stout, dark-green canes, sometimes marked with purple and bearing long, dark, shining, green leaves up to seven inches in length. *20-ft. E. Indefinite. D9 or 5. ANC.*

A. FORTUNEI (Comm.) Japan, has very slender stems, bears silver leaves striped with green, and is withal the most attractive of the smaller varieties. *5-ft. E. Indefinite. D9 or 5. ANC.*

A. GRAMINEA (Grass-like) Japan, takes its name from the grass-like characteristics of its narrow leaves, very slender, long, crowded stems and tufted top growth. *10-ft. E. Indefinite. D9 or 5. ANC.*

A. HINDSII (Comm.) Japan, has the appearance of a stout-stemmed wider-leaved version of A. graminea, with olive-green stems.

10-ft. E. Indefinite. D9 or 5. ANC.

ARUNDINARIA (continued)

A. HUMILIS (Dwarf) Japan, is very similar to A. chrysantha, except in its tendency not to become anæmic either in colour or in growth, for what it lacks in inches it devours in space.

3-*ft.*–4-*ft.* *E.* *Indefinite.* *D*9 *or* 5. *ANC.*

A. JAPONICA (Japanese) is the Common Bamboo with stout canes and dark-green leaves 10-*ft.*–15-ft. *E.* *Indefinite.* *D*9 *or* 5. *ANC.*

A. MACROSPERMA (Bearing long seeds) has stout green stems, smooth green leaves to twelve inches long, finely toothed at the edge. A. VAR. TECTA is dwarf. 15-*ft.* *E.* *Indefinite.* *D*9 *or* 5. *ANC.*

A. MARMOREA (Marble-like) Japan, is a dwarf with purple-green stems, marbled or mottled sheaths and slender, bright-green leaves up to five inches in length. It spreads very rapidly, but is liable to be damaged in severe weather. 5-*ft.* *E.* *Indefinite.* *D*9 *or* 5. *ANC.*

A. MURIELAE (Comm.) China, is an attractive medium Bamboo with stems up to twelve feet, leafless at first, but eventually bending its yellow canes gracefully outwards, under the load of its slender, rich green leaves. 12-*ft.* *E.* *Indefinite.* *D*9 *or* 5. *ANC.*

A. NITIDA (Shining) China, is one of the best of bamboos for partial shade, the slender canes of purplish-black, bending similarly under their burden of small, deep-green leaves. Constant repetition of superlatives can be exceptionally annoying, and it is probably better to say that if medals were granted for good points, this would get them all save for the fact that it detests summer drought.

10-*ft.* *E.* *Indefinite.* *D*9 *or* 5. *ANC.*

A. PALMATA (Like a hand) Japan, has the doubtful merits of having the largest leaves of any of the species except A. Ragamowskii, fanning out finger-like, and an appetite for space which excludes it from the company of more sober relations, and sometimes leads it to a cataclysmic end. 4-*ft.*–6-*ft.* *E.* *Indefinite.* *D*9 *or* 5. *ANC.*

A. PUMILA (Small) Japan, can be distinguished from A. humilis if necessary and if one wanted to, but for garden purposes one is as good as the other, with the advantage in inches to A. humilis.

2-*ft.* *E.* *Indefinite.* *D*9 *or* 5. *ANC.*

A. RAGAMOWSKII (Comm.) is a dwarfer, larger-leaved variety than A. palmata, losing some of the grace of that variety.

3-*ft.* *E.* *Indefinite.* *D*9 *or* 5. *ANC.*

A. SIMONII (Comm.) China, resembles an even finer A. fastuosa.

20-*ft.* *E.* *Indefinite.* *D*9 *or* 5. *ANC.*

A. SIMONII VAR. CHINO is a dwarf sub-variety with dark-green leaves mottled with dull yellow. 4-*ft.* *E.* *Indefinite.* *D*9 *or* 5. *ANC.*

A. SPATHIFLORA (With sheath enclosing the flowers) Himalayas, closely resembles A. falcata. 12-*ft.*–20-*ft.* *E.* *Indefinite.* *D*9 *or* 5. *ANC.*

A. VAGANS (Scattered) Japan, is short and has bright-green, slender stems, bright-green leaves, and a demand for space which relegates it to the wild garden. 1-*ft.* *E.* *Everywhere.* *D*9 *or* 5. *ANC.*

A. Veitchii (Comm.) Japan, has round green stems and narrow leaves that yellow at the edge in autumn, and eventually wither.

2-ft. E. Indefinite. D9 or 5. ANC.

ASCYRUM (Hypericaceae) (from gr. a—not, and skyros—rough; that is, not rough to the touch).

A. hypericoides (Resembling Hypericum) resembles a Hypericum with four petals, generally distorted into the form of a crooked cross. It requires well-drained soil in a sunny site, and, though its life is of doubtful length, it may be kept going from the seed which it freely produces. *1-ft., July-September. D. 2-ft. Sq. Sd2. N.*

ASTER (Compositae) (from the gr. aster—a star).

A. Pappei (Comm.) South Africa, is a small shrub which produces many starry daisy-flowers of china-blue almost without end during the whole year. It flourishes in a hot, dry, sunny place and requires a measure of winter protection in any but seaboard districts.

1¼-ft., Jan.-Dec. E. 1½-ft. Sq. Cg6. N. Pl.8.

ASTRAGALUS (Leguminosae) (from the gr. astragalos—a knuckle bone; from the supposed resemblance of the seed).

A. Tragacantha (The Goat's Thorn) Asia Minor, is a low-growing, spiny shrub, with its attractive grey leaves, heavily felted, bearing small groups of three or four reddish-purple pea flowers, and is interesting as one of the sources of Gum Tragacantha.

1-ft., May-June. D. 3-ft. Sq. Sd2. ANC.

A. massiliensis (From the Red Sea Coast) differs but little except in the colour of its flowers, which are white.

1-ft., May-June. D. 3-ft. Sq. Sd2. ANC.

ATRAPHAXIS (Polygonaceae) (from gr. atraphaxus—the name given to the mountain spinach, to which the species bear some resemblance).

A group of deciduous, much branched, twiggy shrubs related to Polygonum which are perfectly hardy and thrive in any normal good garden soil.

A. Billardieri (Comm.) Greece, is a dwarf, somewhat spiny shrub, with long, lance-shaped leaves, bearing at the ends of the leafy twigs groups of small five-sepalled flowers of glowing pink, which persist in person and in colour long after the fruit has formed. A sunny site in well-drained, sunny soil is indicated.

2½-ft., June. D. 3-ft. Sq. Ch7. N.

A. buxifolia (Box-leaved) Caucasus, has wider, larger leaves of sombre green, and bears rather larger flowers of white flushed with pink,

ATRAPHAXIS (continued)

three sepals of which persist with enhanced colour after the fruit has formed, but lacks the loveliness of its predecessor.

2½-ft., June. D. 3-ft. Sq. Ch7. N.

ATRIPLEX (Chenopodiaceae) (possibly from Gr. a—no ; trophe—food ; relative to the fact that certain of the species grow in poor, sandy soils).

Both species grow well in dry, sandy soils, and are admirably fitted for exposed positions.

A. canescens (Hoary) Western N. America, is the Grey Sage Brush, and is outstanding, in spite of its small, unattractive flowers, and its shyness in producing berries, for its almost white, fleshy, narrow leaves. *5-ft., July. E. 6-ft. Sq. Cg7. N.*

A. Halimus (Old Name) S. Europe, is the Tree Purslane, an attractive shrub of loose, vigorous habit, with spreading, arching, silvery branches, clad with long, silvery leaves, suitable for seaside planting and for hedges, and providing an excellent contrast for other green-leaved shrubs. *6-ft., June. E. 8-ft. Sq. Cg7. N.*

AUCUBA (Cornaceae) (from the Japanese name for A. japonica).

Probably has one outstanding virtue—its ability to grow and to look bright and cheerful under the shade of trees. Generally unisexual, self-fertile varieties of at least one of the species are now available, but in most cases it is necessary to grow the male and female varieties, the latter only producing berries.

A. japonica (Japanese) Japan, has in the type large, glossy leaves resembling the laurel, followed by clusters of bright-red berries. Many variations of the species exist with variegated leaves, and one at least with white berries. *8-ft., April. E. 8-ft. Sq. Cg6. ANC.*

AZALEA (*see* **RHODODENDRON**).

BAMBUSA (*see* **ARUNDINARIA**).

BERBERIDOPSIS (Bixaceae) (from berberis, and opsis—resemblance).

Comprises at present only one species, B. Corallina, a magnificent, somewhat tender plant, suitable only to be grown upon sheltered walls. The plant figuring in Plate 9 was grown on a west wall at a height of 1,000 feet above sea-level.

B. corallina (Coral) Chile, is an evergreen, climbing plant with dark-green heart-shaped leaves, sharply toothed, bearing in the axils of the topmost leaves, clusters of pendent, nine- to fifteen-petalled flowers, of deep red, upon long, slender, deep-red stems. The flowering period is long and the plant deserves the protection it may well need for its successful growth.

10-ft., July-October. E. 10-ft.–20-ft. Sq. Cg7. AN. Pl.9.

BERBERIS (Berberidaceae) (from the arabic—berbery).

Of all shrubs the Barberries embrace some of the most satisfactory of all the species to grow. They are generally colourful in leaf, flower, and in berry, and have the added charm of easy culture. They comprise two sections, those which were earlier given the general name of Mahonia, which may be said to be those with pinnate leaves and generally evergreen, and Berberis (true) with simple leaves, spiny branches, and which may be either evergreen or deciduous. The whole genus has the following characteristics : the wood is yellow, the young roots are yellow, and the flowers are yellow. The flowers, divided into three parts, consist of six or nine sepals, six petals, and the six stamens move when touched from the petal recesses towards the centre of the flower. The berries are oval and contain one or two seeds. As a rule a sunny position suits the bulk of the species. Seeds are freely produced ; but where special forms are required cuttings of the half-ripened wood root readily.

B. aggregata (Clustered together) W. China, is an extremely attractive variety at its best in its sub-species, B. aggregata var. Prattii, with long, whip-like branches, bearing clusters of yellow flowers followed by masses of coral-pink fruits enhanced by the attractive coloration of the autumn leaves.

4-ft., July. D. 4-ft. Sq. Sd2. ANC.

B. amurensis (From Amur) N.E. Asia, is a tall-growing variety with three-parted spines, long, heavily-toothed leaves bearing drooping sprays of yellow flowers, followed by bright red berries. B. amurensis var. japonica is similar except that the leaf is wider, and the flower spray shorter. *10-ft., July. D. 6-ft.–8-ft. Sq. Sd2. ANC.*

B. angulosa (Having corners) Himalayas, is a deciduous shrub with dark, shining, green leaves of about one inch in length, borne from the axils of stiff spines, and is not one of the most outstanding, except that it has the largest flowers and berries of the species—and probably the most palatable dark-red ones.

4-ft., May-June. D. 6-ft. Sq. Sd2. ANC.

B. Aquifolium (Leaves resembling Holly) Western N. America, is one of the Mahonia group, and is known as the Oregon Grape ; is probably one of the most useful of the species for growing under trees, in sun or shade, or in game coverts. The evergreen, compound leaves are made up of from five to nine leaflets, each shaped like those of the holly, turning purple in winter. The flowers, which are produced in crowded sprays, are of bright yellow, and are followed by black berries heavily powdered with violet bloom. Of the sub-varieties, B. Aquifolium atropurpureum is a markedly purple-leaved form, and B. Aquifolium pinnata has smaller, dainty foliage. All the sub-varieties should be propagated by division of the root in the late autumn.

2-ft.–3-ft., February-May. E. 5-ft. Sq. Sd2. D10. ANC. Pl.10.

B. aristata (Bearded) Himalayas, is also known as B. floribunda var. B. petiolaris, and is a deciduous shrub rising upon occasion to ten feet in height, bearing its green, oval, pointed leaves in tufts of five to seven, with one to three spines, from which hang single racemes of bright yellow flowers, which are followed by largish, plum-shaped, red fruits with a bluish bloom. The variety B. aristata var. floribunda is more generous in flower and more sparing in inches. Each variety divides with some success.

10-ft., June-July. D. 8-ft. Sq. Sd2. D10. ANC.

B. ATROCARPA (Dark fruited) W. China, is a variety which resembles the better-known B. Sargentiana, but has smaller leaves and more arching habit of growth. The pale-yellow flowers are borne in stalkless clusters of from six to twelve, and are followed by jet-black fruits. *6-ft., April. E. 6-ft. Sq. Sd2. ANC.*

B. BEANIANA (Comm.) W. China, is a deciduous shrub which makes a neat, compact bush, turning an excellent colour in autumn before the leaves fall, and bears flowers of deep yellow in tight sprays, followed by slender, bright-purple fruits.

6-ft., May. D. 5-ft. Sq. Sd2. ANC.

B. BERGMANNIAE (Comm.) W. China, is an attractive variety in the way of the better-known B. Veitchii, with longish, coarsely-toothed leaves, and bears clusters of short-stalked yellow flowers, followed by black fruits heavily mealed with bluish bloom, upon red stems. The variety B. Bergmanniae var. acanthophylla has longer leaves.

6-ft., May. E. 6-ft. Sq. Sd2. ANC.

B. BRACHYPODA (With short foot-stalks) N.W. China, is distinctive in its downy young growth, slender, hanging clusters of pale-yellow flowers, and its bright red, oval berries.

6-ft., May. D. 8-ft. Sq. Sd2. ANC.

B. BUXIFOLIA (With Box-like leaves) Chile, is also known as B. dulcis, and is probably the first of the true Barberries to show its flowers in the spring, and though thus forward, redeems this immodesty by its otherwise decorous, not to say rigid, habit. The dark-green box-like foliage persists in most winters, and the beautiful orange-yellow flowers are produced, generally singly, from each tuft of leaves, followed by dark purple, globular fruits. Variety aureo-marginata has variegated foliage, but is otherwise similar. The variety B. buxifolia nana is neater and tighter in growth, forming a rounded bush of about two feet in height and scope.

6-ft., April. E. 6-ft. Sq. Sd2. Cg7. ANC.

B. CANADENSIS (Canadian) Eastern N. America, is also known as B. angulizans, and is an attractive, erect-growing shrub in the line of B. vulgaris, with rather large, narrow, oval leaves, and bearing groups of bright-yellow flowers, followed by nearly spherical, very persistent, red fruits. It assumes the most attractive colours in the autumn. *5-ft., May. D. 5-ft. Sq. Sd2. Cg7. ANC.*

B. CANDIDULA (Whitish) China, is a most attractive, slow-growing dwarf shrub of exceptionally charming disposition. The dark-green, sparingly spined, glossy foliage is white beneath. The flowers are large and of bright yellow, and are followed by dark, oval, purple, plum-like fruits. *2-ft., May. E. 3-ft. Sq. Sd2. Cg7. ANC.*

B. CHITRIA (From Chitral) Himalayas, for garden purposes is as good as B. aristata from which it differs only botanically.
10-ft., June-July. D. 8-ft. Sq. Sd2. D10. ANC.

B. CIRCUMSERRATA (Serrated all round) China, is an elegant, compact shrub resembling B. dictyophylla, with small pale-yellow flowers, generally one in each leaf cluster, and followed by pale-red fruits.
4-ft., May. D. 4-ft. Sq. Sd2. Cg8. ANC.

B. CONCINNA (Elegant) Himalayas, is a somewhat tender shrub of low growth with medium, deep-green leaves, solitary, deep-yellow flowers followed by large red berries.
2-ft., June. D. 3-ft. Sq. Sd2. ANC.

B. DARWINII (Comm.) Chile, is considerably variable in height, but seldom exceeds ten feet, and is always attractive with its small, holly-like, deep green, polished leaves, sometimes combined with its deep, orange-yellow flowers in hanging clusters, or with the small, bluish berries. B. Darwinii prostrata is a low-growing variety seldom reaching two feet in height. B. Darwinii nana is another dwarf. *10-ft., April-May. E. 8-ft. Sq. Cg7. ANC. Pl.10.*

B. DIAPHANA (Diaphanous) W. China, differs but slightly from B. dictyophylla, and is a little less tall with a brighter yellow flower, and magnificent autumn colouring.
5-ft., May. D. 5-ft. Sq. Sd2. D9. ANC.

B. DICTYOPHYLLA (With netted leaves) Yunnan, is an extremely graceful shrub with long wand-like strands, bearing tufts of small green leaves, grey-green beneath, each bearing a single pale-yellow flower, followed by a red, egg-shaped fruit. B. dictyophylla var. albicaulis has the underside of the leaves pure white.
6-ft., May. D. 8-ft. Sq. Sd2. ANC.

B. DIELSIANA (Comm.) W. China, is a tall-growing variety with multiple flower clusters of bright yellow, followed by bright-red berries. *10-ft., June. D. 10-ft. Sq. Sd2. ANC.*

B. EMPETRIFOLIA (Resembling the Crake berry) China, is a low-growing evergreen shrub well suited to the larger rock garden with thin, narrow leaves, golden-yellow, solitary flowers, and bluish-black fruits. *1-ft., May. E. 4-ft. Sq. Sd2. AN.*

B. FRANCISCI-FERDINANDII (Comm.) China, is a most attractive rounded shrub of some eight feet, with slender racemes of yellow flowers, followed by similarly shaped clusters of long, scarlet fruits.
8-ft., May. D. 6-ft. Sq. Sd2. ANC.

B. GAGNEPAINII (Comm.) W. China, is a neat evergreen species with elongated, dark-green, holly-like leaves, bearing in each leaf cluster groups of six or more bright-yellow flowers, yielding place to blue-black, plum-shaped berries.
4-ft., May-June. E. 4-ft. Sq. Sd2. ANC.

B. GILGIANA (Comm.) China, is a deciduous bush of some six feet, with largish, long leaves, well toothed and hairy beneath, bearing small clusters of bright-yellow flowers, followed by bright-red fruits.
6-ft., May-June. D. 6-ft. Sq. Sd2. ANC.

B. HAEMATOCARPA (Having blood-red fruit) Western N. America (MAHONIA haematocarpa) is an attractive evergreen shrub with compound leaves of from five to seven leaflets of grey-green colour, and armed with a few sharp teeth, with long sprays of pale-yellow flowers, followed by large clusters of bright red berries.
8-ft., May-June. E. 8-ft. Sq. Sd2. ANC. Shelter.

B. HAKEOIDES (Resembling the wooden cherry tree) Chile, is an outstanding, tall-growing species with almost round leaves, about the size of a halfpenny, strongly spined and sometimes long stalked, and bears tight round clusters of bright-yellow flowers, followed by blue-black fruits. To be seen at its best—which is indeed very good—it should be grown in a sheltered site.
10-ft., April-May. E. 8-ft. Sq. Sd2. L7. ANC. Shelter.

B. HETEROPODA (Unequally stalked) Turkestan, is a diffuse shrub with grey-green, oval leaves borne upon long stalks, bearing from each cluster of leaves up to three drooping clusters of bright, orange-yellow flowers, followed by slender, plum-shaped, blue-black fruits.
8-ft., May. D. 8-ft. Sq. Sd2. ANC.

B. HOOKERI (Comm.) Himalayas, has long, narrow, green leaves furnished with sharp teeth, and white beneath ; is of compact growth and bears rather large flowers of pale-yellow with reddish sepals in small clusters, followed by dark-purple berries which are very persistent. B. Hookeri var. latifolia is similar, with leaves green above and below, and reaches ten feet in height.
4-ft., April-May. E. 6-ft. Sq. Sd2. ANC.

B. INSIGNIS (Remarkable) Sikkim, is aptly named, for it carries the largest leaves of any of the true Barberries, sometimes up to seven inches in length, and of a dark, shining green with spiny margins, with the underside of pale green. The flowers, borne in the leaf axils, are in clusters of fifteen upwards and are large and orange-yellow in colour, with black fruits. The species carries no spines and deserves, indeed needs, a sheltered site.
6-ft., May. E. 6-ft. Sq. Sd2. Cg7. ANC. Shelter.

B. JAMESIANA (Comm.) Yunnan, is a fascinating Chinaman, the foliage starting life an attractive bluish-bronze, and ending in a blaze of red. The large clusters of yellow flowers are followed by clusters of transparent red berries of the size and characteristics of currants.
6-ft., May. D. 5-ft. Sq. Sd2. AN.

B. JAPONICA (From Japan) is one of the MAHONIA group with large, handsome, pinnate, compound leaves of bronzy-green, bearing clusters of sprays of sweetly scented lemon-yellow flowers in magnificent association with the outstanding foliage, followed by large

Camellia japonica

14

Caryopteris × clandonensis

purple-black berries. B. japonica var. Bealei is an even more aristocratic relation, its leaves being larger, a trifle glamorised, and the flowers, borne upon shorter stalks, have a wider distribution, and an air of breeding which, while detracting nothing from the charms of a less sophisticated sister, nevertheless invites comparison. Withal B. japonica var. Bealei is a little hardier, but resents transplanting at a mature age, and should therefore be caught young.

6-ft., March-April. E. 6-ft. Sq. L7. ANC. Shelter.

B. JULIANAE (Comm.) Central China, is a tight-growing evergreen with narrow, spiny, margined leaves, bearing many-flowered clusters of bright-yellow flowers, passing to blue-black fruits.

10-ft., May. E. 10-ft. Sq. Sd2. ANC.

B. KOREANA (Korean) Korea, resembles the better-known B. Sieboldii but has red, wax-like berries.

6-ft., May. D. 6-ft. Sq. Sd2. ANC.

B. LIECHTENSTEINII (Comm.) W. China, is also B. Potanini, a deciduous bush of some three feet with long, spiny, margined leaves and racemes of yellow flowers, replaced by berries of bright red.

3-ft., May. D. 4-ft. Sq. Sd2. ANC.

B. LEPTOCLADA (With thin twigs) China, is a low-growing shrub with grey-green foliage, typical yellow flowers borne from the leaf-clusters, and followed by red berries.

2-ft., May. D. 4-ft. Sq. Sd2. ANC.

B. LOLOGENSIS (From Lolol) Chile, is a natural hybrid of B. Darwinii ×B. linearifolia, and is an attractive, low-growing, evergreen shrub with small, holly-shaped leaves, bearing long sprays of golden-yellow flowers with reddish-orange sepals.

3-ft., April-May. E. 6-ft. Sq. L7. Cg7. ANC. Pl.11.

B. LOMARIAEFOLIA (With leaves like the Deer Fern) China, bears a close but transcendent resemblance to B. japonica var. Bealei, which causes one to exhaust one's superlatives in one explosive eruption brought into being by its refinement and grace.

6-ft., March-April. E. 6-ft. Sq. L7. ANC. Shelter.

B. LYCIUM (From the medical use) Himalayas, is a semi-evergreen shrub of lax habit, with pale-green, spine-tipped leaves, bearing clusters of largish yellow flowers, succeeded by purple-blue berries.

6-ft., May-June. D. 6-ft. Sq. C2. ANC.

B. MORRISONENSIS (From Mt. Morrison) Formosa, is a leaf-losing shrub with young red wood, reaching six feet in height, heavily armed with three-parted spines, and bearing clusters of small leaves, from which groups of pale-yellow flowers, up to five in number, appear on single stalks. The berries are bright-red and semi-transparent. It has the added advantage of being brilliantly coloured in the autumn. *6-ft., June. D. 6-ft. Sq. C2. ANC.*

B. NEPALENSIS (From Nepal) Kashmir, is also known as MAHONIA nepalensis, seldom exceeds eight feet in height, has composite, pinnate leaves, made up of about fifteen glossy green leaflets. The yellow flowers are carried on long, slender sprays up to twelve inches in length, giving place to blue-black berries which persist for a considerable time.

8-ft., October-April. E. 8-ft. Sq. C2. D10. ANC.

B. NERVOSA (Veined) Western N. America, is also known as MAHONIA nervosa, and is a very dwarf evergreen with luxurious, pinnately divided leaves, heavily veined beneath with spiny teeth on the margins. It has become extremely rare, and appears to be difficult to acclimatise. *1¼-ft., April. E. 3-ft. Sq. C2. D10. A.*

B. PALLENS (Palish) Yunnan, is unique because of the peculiar distribution of its angular branches, and the magnificence of its autumn colouring. The attractive yellow flowers are followed by narrowly oval, red berries. *5-ft., May-June. D. 6-ft. Sq. Sd2. ANC.*

B. PARVIFOLIA (Small flowered) is a dwarf with small green, sometimes evergreen, leaves, with golden-yellow flowers, followed by coral-red fruits, with exquisitely tinted autumn foliage.

2-ft., May-June. D. 4-ft. Sq. Sd2. ANC.

B. POIRETII (Comm.) Manchuria, produces slender, wand-like, arching branches clad with groups of green leaves, from each group of which hangs a two-inch spray of pale yellow flowers, succeeded by slender red berries. *5-ft., June. D. 6-ft. Sq. Sd2. ANC.*

B. POLYANTHA (Many-flowered) W. China, is one of the outstanding species, always delightful in autumn. The erect bush is decorated in the late spring with large, drooping sprays of bright yellow flowers, which give place to huge hanging clusters of bright-red fruits. *8-ft., May-June. D. 8-ft. Sq. Sd2. ANC.*

B. PRUINOSA (With frosted surface) is an evergreen shrub with smooth, leathery, bright-green leaves, lemon-yellow flowers produced either singly or in small clusters, succeeded by black fruits frosted with plum-like bloom. *8-ft., June. E. 8-ft. Sq. Sd2. ANC.*

B. REPENS (Creeping) Western N. America, is also MAHONIA repens, and a low-growing shrub, with pinnate, three to seven segmented leaves, producing crowded flower sprays of bright-yellow flowers at the tips of the growths. The berries are black, powdered with farina, and the autumn shade of the foliage is colourful but not startling.

1-ft., April-May. E. 4-ft. Sq. Sd2. ANC.

B. REPLICATA (Folded back) has attractively arching branches, smallish, narrow, green leaves, deep-yellow flowers, and red berries becoming black with age. *4-ft., March-May. E. 4-ft. Sq. Sd2. ANC.*

B. RUBROSTILLA (Red drops) is a garden hybrid, very similar to B. Wilsonae, the outstanding feature of its beauty being the large translucent, coral-red berries, which are borne in small hanging clusters of from two to four.

4-ft., May-June. D. 4-ft. Sq. Cg7. D10. ANC.

B. SANGUINEA (Blood-red) has rather long, narrow, evergreen leaves produced in groups of from two to five, which are packed with the golden-yellow flowers, enhanced in beauty by the red stalks and reddish sepals. The rather small berries are black.

8-ft., April. E. 6-ft. Sq. Sd2. D10. ANC.

B. SARGENTIANA (Comm.) China, is somewhat similar to B. Julianae with sharply pointed, rather long leaves of dark-green, pale beneath and with clusters of stemless, pale-yellow flowers. The ripe fruits, which are spheroidal, are black in colour.

6-ft., May. E. 6-ft. Sq. Sd2. D10. ANC.

B. SIEBOLDII (Comm.) Japan, is of compact habit, forming a neatly rounded bush with pale-yellow flowers in small clusters. The berries which follow are shining orange-red.

3-ft., May. D. 3-ft. Sq. Sd2. Cg8. ANC.

B. SOULIEANA (Comm.) China, has narrow, sharply spined, evergreen leaves, with yellow flowers followed by red fruits in small clusters.

6-ft., May. E. 6-ft. Sq. Sd2. Cg8. ANC.

B. STAPFIANA (Comm.) W. China, is a dwarf, almost evergreen shrub, allied to B. Wilsonae, with pale yellow flowers succeeded by bright-carmine, oval berries. *4-ft., June. D. 4-ft. Sq. Cg8. Sd2. ANC.*

BERBERIS STENOPHYLLA

B. STENOPHYLLA (Narrow leaved) is a garden hybrid of parentage B. Darwinii×B. empetrifolia and is one of the most beautiful and probably the most useful (a unique combination) of the Barberries. The slender branches are tightly interwoven and become wreathed in golden-yellow flowers, individually small but collectively stunning. The berries are black and heavily mealed. There are innumerable sub-varieties, all of which retain the usefulness of their progenitor, and add the meed of increased, amplified, or glamorised beauty. Some worthy of mention are B. stenophylla var. "Brilliant," coccinea, corallina, Irwinii and semperflorens, all of which are either more heavily rouged, or are so prolific as to be outstanding. B. stenophylla corallina var. compacta adds to its beauty the modesty of sedate and compact habit, and for such a retiring disposition earns especial praise, for what it lacks in inches it gains in charm. Give it only three feet in which to display it.

8-ft., April-May. E. 8-ft. Sq. Cg8. ANC.

B. SUBCAULIALATA (Somewhat short stemmed) is also known as B. Coryi, resembles B. Wilsonae, but is taller and has rather larger leaves, but otherwise has all its beauties somewhat enhanced.
6-ft., June. D. 8-ft. Sq. Cg8. Sd2. ANC.

B. SWASEYI (Comm.) Texas, is also MAHONIA Swaseyi, is another pinnate-leaved species with from five to eleven leaflets, resembling B. haematocarpa with the pale-yellow flower heads bearing broad bracts, and with attractive red fruits.
4-ft., May. E. 5-ft. Sq. Cg8. D10. ANC.

B. THUNBERGII (Comm.) Japan, is one of the most strikingly beautiful of the species, quite unsurpassed by any other in the refulgence of its autumn foliage, and prodigal in the production of its pale-yellow flowers with their orange-red sepals and ensuing red berries. It is outshone in summer brilliance by its variety B. Thunbergii var. atropurpurea, which has caught the colour of the red maples.
4-ft., April. D. 6-ft. Sq. Cg8. D10. ANC. Pl.10.

B. TISCHLERI (Comm.) W. China, is related to B. yunnanensis and is a tall variety with drooping clusters of yellow flowers followed by long, slender, bright-red berries.
8-ft., June. D. 6-ft. Sq. Cg8. D10. Sd2. ANC.

B. TRIFOLIOLATA (With three leaves) Mexico, is also MAHONIA trifoliolata, and a rigid bush with pinnate leaves made up of three glaucus leaflets, with short spires of bright-yellow. The large black berries which succeed the flowers are covered with bloom, and are preeminently the best for collection for preparing jelly, known to the Mexicans as Agrita. *8-ft., May. E. 8-ft. Sq. Sd2. AN.*

B. VEITCHII (Comm.) China, has elongated leathery leaves, yellow flowers with bronze sepals, succeeded by oblong black fruits.
6-ft., May. E. 6-ft. Sq. Sd2. ANC.

B. VERNAE (Comm.) W. China, is an exceptionally graceful shrub with spathulate green leaves in clusters of six or eight, with hanging clusters of small, bright-yellow flowers, giving place to rounded salmon-red berries. *8-ft., April. D. 12-ft. Sq. Sd2. ANC.*

B. VERRUCULOSA (Covered with small warts) China, is a dwarf evergreen shrub with its branches covered with tiny warts, with rosetted, dark-green leaves, golden-yellow flowers rather larger than ordinary, and blue-black berries. *3-ft., May. E. 5-ft. Sq. Sd2. ANC.*

B. VIRESCENS (Turning green) Himalayas, is tall growing, with orange-red stems, with shining pale green leaves, sulphur or greenish-yellow flowers, and dark-crimson, shining berries.
8-ft., April-May. D. 8-ft. Sq. Sd2. ANC.

B. VULGARIS (Common) Europe, is the Barberry, the host of wheat rust or mildew, and in spite of this a beautiful plant, unsurpassed in the late autumn in the luscious splendour of its scarlet berries. It has many sub-varieties, B. vulgaris foliis purpureis having leaves of

wine colour which provide a startling contrast to its hanging sprays of yellow flowers, and B. vulgaris purpurea macrophylla which has larger leaves and adds still further to its colour.
8-ft., May. D. 8-ft. Sq. Sd2. ANC.

B. WILSONAE (Comm.) W. China, is a magnificent dwarf shrub with reddish-brown branches, small grey-green leaves, and small golden-yellow flowers, but replaced with innumerable, almost transparent, coral-red berries, which are accompanied by foliage which colours attractively in autumn. *3-ft., May-June. D. 4-ft. Sq. Sd2. ANC.*

B. YUNNANENSIS (From Yunnan) China, is a tightly compacted shrub of spherical habit, rather small leaves, pale-yellow flowers produced in clusters, succeeded by bright-red berries up to eight in each cluster. *4-ft., May. D. 4-ft. Sq. Sd2. ANC.*

BERCHEMIA (RHAMNACEAE) (A GROUP OF CLIMBING SHRUBS NAMED AFTER THE FRENCH BOTANIST BERCHEM).

All thrive reasonably well in any soil.

B. GIRALDIANA (Comm.) China, is a pleasant climber with grey-green foliage and small white flowers, succeeded by red and black berries.
15-ft., August. D. 8-ft. Sq. Sd2. ANC.

B. RACEMOSA (Clustered) Japan, is a climber with small, oval, bright-green leaves, which turn lemon-yellow in autumn, and are followed by red berries which turn black as they age. Its variety B. racemosa var. variegata has pleasantly variegated leaves and is probably an outstanding climbing plant. *15-ft., August. D. 8-ft. Sq. Sd2. ANC.*

BETULA (BETULACEAE) (FROM THE LATIN NAME FOR THE BIRCH).

B. FRUTICOSA (Shrubby) N. Europe, is a small shrubby birch with pleasant dwarf characteristics. *8-ft., April. D. 8-ft. Sq. Sd2. ANC.*

B. NANA (Small) Europe, is another dwarf birch of shrubby habit, with dark-green leaves and erect catkins.
2-ft., April. D. 2-ft. Sq. D10. Sd2. ANC.

B. PUMILA (Small) Eastern N. America, has little garden value and may well be left undescribed.
9-ft., April. D. 8-ft. Sq. Sd2. ANC.

BIGELOWIA (COMPOSITAE) (NAMED AFTER JACOB BIGELOW—A NOTED BOTANIST).

B. GRAVEOLENS (Strong smelling) Western N. America, is a rather tender composite, suitable for a sheltered position against a south wall in a poor soil, producing large corymbs of five floretted yellow flowers in fascinating profusion.
6-ft., October. E. 6-ft. Sq. Sd2. ANC.

BIGNONIA (BIGNONIACEAE) (NAMED AFTER THE ABBÉ BIGNON, WHO WAS LIBRARIAN TO KING LOUIS XIV).

B. CAPREOLATA (Having tendrils) S.E. United States, is an attractive semi-evergreen climber with orange-red, funnel-shaped flowers with deep-green, heart-shaped leaves, which will do well upon a sheltered, sunny wall. B. capreolata var. atrosanguinea is deeper in colour.

20-ft., June. D. 20-ft. Sq. Sd3. ANC.

BILLARDIERA (PITTOSPORACEAE) (NAMED AFTER LA BILLARDIÈRE, A WELL-KNOWN FRENCH BOTANIST).

B. LONGIFLORA (Long flowered) Tasmania, is a rather attractive climbing plant with narrow, pointed, green leaves, five-petalled, tubular flowers of pale, yellowish-green, which eventually give place to luscious, dark-blue berries. *8-ft., June. E. 3-ft. Sq. Sd2. ANC.*

BRUCKENTHALIA (ERICACEAE) (THE NAME IS COMMEMORATIVE OF S. VON BRUCKENTHAL).

Only one species exists of the genus which is allied to ERICA, and requires the same kind of treatment.

B. SPICULIFOLIA (With foliage like small ears of corn) Europe, is a heather-like plant, with dark, needle-like, evergreen foliage, white beneath, loosely packed at the tips of the growth with small heather-like flowers of rose-pink.

1-ft., June. E. 2-ft. Sq. Cg7. D10. Sd2. AN.

BUDDLEIA (LOGANIACEAE) (NAMED IN HONOUR OF REV. ADAM BUDDLE).

A genus of attractive shrubs or small trees much loved by butterflies, and which thrive well in rich, deep loam in a sunny situation. The flowers are generally borne in terminal clusters, either as long tapering sprays or rounded clusters.

B. ALBIFLORA (With white flowers) China, is a strong-growing variety with scented, lilac-coloured flowers, each with an orange eye, borne in long sprays often exceeding a foot in length, and tapering from over two inches at the base. The long, green, pointed leaves are silvery-grey below, and though inferior to B. variabilis, B. albiflora is nevertheless an exceptionally good shrub.

10-ft., July-September. D. 8-ft. Sq. Cg7. Sd2. ANC.

B. ALTERNIFOLIA (With alternate leaves) China, is more decorous in its growth than B. variabilis, resembling a weeping willow in habit, and bearing sweet-smelling lilac flowers, inveigling the attention of errant bees, butterflies and moths, and spreading throughout and around its silver-green leaves the pervading scent of Heliotrope on a hot summer's day.

8-ft., July-September. D. 8-ft. Sq. Cg7. Sd2. ANC.

B. AURICULATA (Ear-shaped) S. Africa, is an almost evergreen shrub, best suited to growth upon a south wall, with sweetly scented, creamy-white, yellow-eyed flowers, borne in small sprays of about two inches in length.

10-ft., September-January. E. 10-ft. Sq. Cg7. Sd2. AN. Shelter.

B. CARYOPTERIDIFOLIA (With leaves resembling Caryopteris) W. China, forms a rounded bush, with its young leaves heavily felted with brown tomentum, and with the underside of the leaves and young stems covered with dense white wool. The lavender flower sprays are larger than those of B. auriculata. Blooming on the previous year's wood it requires protection in all but the most clement locations.

8-*ft.*, *June-July*. *D*. 10-*ft*. *Sq*. *Cg7*. *Sd2*. *ANC*. *Shelter*.

B. COLVILEI (Comm.) Himalayas, is in reality a tree attaining thirty to forty feet, and has the largest individual flowers of all the species, its pendulous sprays of rose-crimson flowers with white throats making it one of the most outstanding of all shrubs. Alas, pruning to keep it in bounds prevents it from flowering, as indeed do the frosts, but in a sheltered seaside location, on the west coast, one may at least hope that one day it will burst forth in full glory to convert still more souls to the gardener's art.

30-*ft.*, *June*. *D*. 30-*ft*. *Sq*. *Cg7*. *AN*.

B. DAVIDII (Comm.) W. China, is the better known B. variabilis, variable indeed, and available in many variations. Often fifteen feet high, its characteristics are almost too well known to need description. The long, slender, wedge-shaped leaves are often up to one foot in length, and the passably fragrant flowers are produced in crowded terminal sprays, sometimes more than two feet in length from tip to base. B. Davidii var. Veitchiana is more erect and has longer sprays of lilac flowers. B. Davidii var. magnifica has the habit of Veitchiana, but has flowers of violet-purple, var. amplissima is the best, deep mauve, var. serotina the latest to flower, and var. Pink Pearl the nearest to clear pink. All the varieties should be pruned back hard every spring, when they will often make strong, vigorous wood up to nine feet in length terminated by the finest sprays of flowers conceivable.

10-*ft.*, *July-October*. *D*. 10-*ft*. *Sq*. *Cg7*. *Sd2*. *ANC*. *Pl*.68.

B. FALLOWIANA (Comm.) China, is the most attractive of the dwarf varieties, and does remarkably well upon light soils. The foliage is probably more fascinating than the flowers, being so heavily felted with minute hairs as to appear white. Not quite as hardy as B. Davidii, it should be pruned very severely to encourage young vigorous growth. The flower sprays are typical and heavily scented, and in the type are lavender-blue, though B. Fallowiana var. alba has white flowers which, to my own mind, are far lovelier. As a rule the plant requires quite a large site, though its ultimate height may not exceed four feet.

4-*ft.*, *July-September*. *D*. 8-*ft*. *Sq*. *Sd2*. *Cg7*. *ANC*.

B. GLOBOSA (Ball-like) Chile, is an almost evergreen shrub with tall but sparse habit, with heavily netted green leaves, and rounded heads of many tiny flowers, looking at a distance like small oranges, and heavily scenting the surrounding air with the fragrance of honey. Indubitably hardy, it is well worth a place in every garden.

15-*ft.*, *May*. *ED*. 8-*ft*. *Sq*. *Cg7*. *ANC*.

B. PANICULATA (Flowering in tufts) Himalayas, has handsome, narrow, grey, downy foliage, and small but attractive, sweetly scented lilac-pink flowers. *8-ft., June-October. D. 12-ft. Sq. Sd2. Cg7. ANC.*

BUXUS (BUXACEAE) (PROBABLY DERIVED FROM THE GR. PUKNOS—SOLID OR DENSE, REFERRING TO THE QUALITY OF THE WOOD OF THESE SHRUBS).

A group of small evergreen trees or shrubs, growing well in almost any kind of soil, and of exceptional use in shady places or upon calcareous soils.

B. MICROPHYLLA (With small leaves) Japan, is a small, neat shrub rarely exceeding four feet in height, with square stems, small bright-green leaves, and excellent where a small, neat, slow-growing, green-leaved shrub is required.

B. SEMPERVIRENS (Evergreen) Europe, is the Common Box, which makes an excellent hedge which may be clipped to size.
10-ft., ——— E. Indeterminate. Ch6. ANC.

The following sub-varieties are noteworthy :—

B. VAR. AUREA MACULATA—leaves mottled with golden-yellow.

B. „ AUREA PENDULA—a weeping form of the preceding.

B. „ ELEGANTISSIMA—slow-growing with silvered margins to the leaves.

B. „ HANDSWORTHIENSIS—a very upright variety.

B. „ LATIFOLIA—a wide-leaved spreading variety.

B. „ MYOSOTIFOLIA—a very slow-growing variety with small, dark green leaves.

B. „ ROSMARINIFOLIA—a very slow-growing variety with leaves like Rosemary.

B. „ SUFFRUTICOSA—the Common Box edging.

B. „ SUFFRUTICOSA VARIEGATA—the variegated type.

CALCEOLARIA (SCROPHULARIACEAE) (DERIVED FROM THE LATIN CALCEOLUS—A SLIPPER, FROM THE SHAPE OF THE FLOWER, OR NAMED IN HONOUR OF F. CALCEOLARI, AN ITALIAN BOTANIST).

The two varieties which follow can only be safely grown out of doors in the south-western or western seaboard counties, elsewhere they are liable to extinction in an occasional winter of extra severity. They can, however, be kept going from cuttings of the half-ripened green wood, which root with ease and celerity. Both varieties are completely at home in well-drained soils in sheltered sites, C. integrifolia in particular providing a blaze of colour for a long period.

C. INTEGRIFOLIA (Having leaves with smooth edges) Chile, has upright growth, sage-like leaves of bright-green which are generally persistent, and throws its large, clear-yellow flowers in clusters, well

Ceratostigma Willmottianum

Acer saccharum ACDHKLQ

Cercidiphyllum japonicum
ABCEFGHLMPQTU

Euonymus alatus
FJKNORS

clear of the foliage on long, straight stalks. Thriving in well-drained good loam, it requires the protection of bracken or straw in the severest weather. *3-ft., June-October. E. 3-ft. Sq. Cg9. ANC.*

C. VIOLACEA (Violet-coloured) Chile, is another pretty but tender shrub, with small, irregularly toothed leaves, and open, diffuse sprays of helmet-shaped flowers, rather like truncated foxgloves, almost white, but with heavy flushes of pale violet, and spotted heavily within with orange, purple, and crimson. Propagation is easily accomplished from cuttings of the soft wood, and suckers which are freely produced. In nature the shrub will reach six feet in height, but in the average garden it seldom exceeds two feet in height. *2-ft., July. E. 2-ft. Sq. Cg7. ANC.*

CALLICARPA (VERBENACEAE) (FROM THE GR. KALOS—BEAUTIFUL; AND KARPON—FRUIT; ALLUDING TO THE CHARMINGLY COLOURED BERRIES OF SOME OF THE SPECIES).

The distinguishing features of the genus, from the point of view of the shrub garden, are the crowded clusters of small, pink flowers, which are later replaced by pale-violet fruits, and the attractive pink tones of foliage in late autumn. The flowers and fruits of most of the varieties which follow are almost identical in colour.

C. DICHOTOMA (With forked boughs) China, has narrow, oval, green leaves, serrated at the edges, and has pale-pink flowers, and lilac-violet berries the size of small peas.
4-ft., August. D. 4-ft. Sq. Sd2. AN.

C. GIRALDIANA (Comm.) W. China, is similar with larger leaves, pale lilac-pink flowers, and shiny bluish-lilac berries.
6-ft., Julv. D. 4-ft. Sq. Sd2. AN.

C. JAPONICA (Japanese) Japan, has larger leaves than C. dichotoma with pink flowers and violet berries.
4-ft., August. D. 4-ft. Sq. Sd2. AN.

C. KOREANA (From Korea) Korea, is a rather tighter, neater bush with small, much serrated leaves, pink flowers, and lilac-pink berries.
3-ft., August. D. 3-ft. Sq. Sd2. AN.

CALLISTEMON (MYRTACEAE) (FROM THE GR. KALLISTOS—MOST BEAUTIFUL; AND STEMON—A STAMEN; THE CHARACTERISTIC FEATURE OF THE INFLORESCENCES BEING THE DENSE FLOWER HEADS WITH LONG, EXSERTED STAMENS, WHICH GIVE THE PLANT ITS COMMON NAME, THE BOTTLEBRUSH).

All are indigenous to Australia and have small, simple, narrow, tough, sword-shaped leaves. In cultivation the following species are reasonably hardy in the south, west, and seaboard, but need sheltered positions in sunny aspects, and protection in the severest winters, and rarely reach more than a quarter of the height they attain in their native habitat.

C. LINEARIS (With linear foliage) Australia, has tough green leaves up

CALLISTEMON (continued)

to five inches long, borne upon stiff, woody stems, and bears dense spikes of bright scarlet, bottlebrush-like inflorescences.

5-ft., August. E. 4-ft. Sq. Sd2. ANC.

C. SALIGNUS (Resembling Willow) Australia, has rather shorter green leaves with a rather more yellow tinge, and similar flowers of deep yellow with pink-tipped stamens.

5-ft., August. E. 4-ft. Sq. Sd2. ANC.

C. SPECIOSUS (Showy) Australia, is similar but has very dense spikes of rich red stamens, surrounded with yellow anthers.

5-ft., August. E. 4-ft. Sq. Sd2. ANC.

CALLUNA (ERICACEAE) (FROM THE GR. KALLUNO—TO CLEANSE ; A REFERENCE TO THE USE OF THE TWIGS FOR MAKING BROOMS).

Calluna differs from ERICA in having a coloured calyx which is larger than the corolla. This shrub is the one which covers large areas of Northern England and Scotland, and is known as Ling. Only one species exists, but there are innumerable garden hybrids, all of which are attractive. Cultivation is simple in a light, peaty soil which serves to keep them from making the natural gaunt growth, which may also be remedied by cutting hard back in the spring before new growth begins. The following varieties are among the best :—

C. VULGARIS VAR. ALBA—white, normal habit.
C. „ „ ALBA PILOSA—white, normal habit, grey foliage.
C. „ „ „ PUMILA—white, dwarf habit.
C. „ „ „ TENELLA—white, tall habit.
C. „ „ ALPORTII—carmine, tall habit. *Pl.*12.
C. „ „ ARGENTEA—purple, dwarf habit, silvery foliage.
C. „ „ AUREA—purple, dwarf habit, golden foliage.
C. „ „ C. H. BEALE—double pink, normal habit.
C. „ „ COCCINEA—crimson, medium habit.
C. „ „ COUNTY WICKLOW—fully double pink, dwarf habit.
C. „ FL. PL.—double pale pink, normal habit.
C. „ VAR. FOXII—pink, very dwarf.
C. „ „ HAMMONDII—white, tall habit, pale green foliage.
C. „ „ HYPNOIDES—purple flowers, medium habit.
C. „ „ J. H. HAMILTON—fully double deep pink, dwarf habit. *Pl.*12.
C. „ „ MINIMA—purple, very dwarf, pale green foliage.
C. „ „ PYGMAEA—purple, very dwarf, dark green foliage.

2-ft., July-September. E. 2-ft. Sq. Cg5. AN.

The height given is for the normally habited varieties. Tall varieties are six inches taller, medium varieties are approximately six inches less in height, and the dwarf varieties are seldom more than one foot in height.

Chimonanthus fragrans **BCDGHM**

Acacia verticillata **AEFJKLNOPQ**

Clematis Viticella Ascotiensis
ABCDEFGHJK

Clematis Jackmanii
Comtesse de Bouchard
HMQU

Clematis lanuginosa
Nelly Moser LMPQSTU

Clematis Miriam Markham
JNOR

CALOPHACA (LEGUMINOSAE) (FROM GR. KALOS, BEAUTIFUL ; PHAKOS —LENS ; WITH REFERENCE TO THE SHAPE OF THE FLOWERS).

One delightful, low-growing shrub revelling in hot and dry exposures in any good soil.

C. WOLGARICA (From the Volga) Russia, has pinnate leaves made up of from seven to seventeen small leaflets, and carries groups of large yellow pea flowers on slender stems from the leaf axils.
3-ft., July-August. D. 6-ft. Sq. Sd2. ANC.

CALYCANTHUS (CALYCANTHACEAE) (FROM THE GR. KALYX—THE FLOWER CUP ; AND ANTHOS—A FLOWER ; HAVING ALLUSION TO THE COLOURED SEPALS).

A group of American plants with scented wood, producing flowers on short shoots of the current year's growth, or from the nodes of the previous season's wood. Best grown in moist, peaty, or loamy soil, they propagate most readily from layers, or from suckers which may be split off.

C. FERTILIS (Able to bear abundant fruit) Eastern N. America, is a rather busy shrub, usually about six feet in height, with large, oval, green leaves, and slightly scented flowers with petals and sepals of brown-purple. *6-ft., June-September. D. 6-ft. L7. D10. AN.*

C. FLORIDUS (Flowering freely) South-Eastern N. America, is of rather straggling habit, with rough, dark green elliptical leaves, with down undersurface, paler beneath, with red-brown, very fragrant flowers, made up of tongue-shaped petals, and sepals of brownish-red. Leaves, wood and roots have the pleasant camphor-like odour of the genus. *8-ft., June-July. D. 6-ft. Sq. L7. D10. AN.*

C. OCCIDENTALIS (Western) Western N. America, has larger, longer leaves than C. fertilis, and is of stronger and more ungainly growth, and has larger, paler flowers with a scent which is not so pleasant. To compensate, the scent of the leaves and wood are even more pleasantly aromatic than C. floridus.
12-ft., July-August. D. 8-ft. Sq. L7. D10. AN.

CAMELLIA (TERNSTROEMIACEAE) (SO NAMED AFTER A MORAVIAN JESUIT, CAMELLUS, WHO FOUND C. JAPONICA GROWING ON THE ISLAND OF LUZON IN THE PHILIPPINES IN THE LATE SEVENTEENTH CENTURY).

Live plants were introduced in 1739 and the genus became extensively cultivated as greenhouse plants. Important as a family, since they include also the Tea Plant, Camellias can be successfully grown out of doors, and no shrubs have a finer, greener, and more smooth foliage, no flower a smoother texture more fascinating to the touch, or so delicate a tint to soothe the eye. Nor indeed can any flower look quite so repulsive when bruised in passing. All the varieties do well upon a good lime-free soil, and are best suited by a western or north-western aspect. They are easily propagated from short cuttings of the firm wood cut to include a single leaf and bud, and given gentle heat.

CAMELLIA (continued)

C. CUSPIDATA (Tipped with a rigid point) W. China, make a comfortable bush of loose habit, with glossy, evergreen leaves, and produces single white flowers with yellow anthers in May.

4-ft., May. E. 3-ft. Sq. Cg6. L7. AN.

C. JAPONICA (Japanese) China, will reach thirty feet in height, but is generally considerably less, and is clad with dark green, glossy leaves like those of the laurel. In the type the flowers are single, red, five-petalled, and centred with yellow stamêns arranged in a circle, but many varieties have been produced with every shade of colour from white to red, and with considerable variation in the number of petals, ranging from single to fully double. The single varieties have a charm conferred upon them by the visual presence of the golden anthers, which makes their association with the deep green of the foliage of peculiar beauty, and should be grown much more considerably than they are. Among the best varieties are :—

C. JAPONICA VAR. ALBA SIMPLEX—single white flowers.

C. „ „ CAMPBELLII—single, semi-double rose flowers.

C. „ „ CHANDLERI ELEGANS—double, bright pink flowers.

C. „ „ DONCKELAARII—semi-double crimson flowers with white markings, and very hardy.

C. „ „ GLOIRE DE NANTES—soft pink, semi-double flowers, and is hardier than Lady Clare.

C. „ „ IMBRICATA RUBRA PL.—very double, deep carmine flowers.

C. „ „ IMBRICATA ALBA PL.—very double, white flowers.

C. „ „ LADY CLARE—is like Gloire de Nantes but more tender.

C. „ „ LATIFOLIA—has single, crimson flowers, and is very hardy.

C. „ MAGNOLIAEFLORA—has small, rather open, semi-double flowers of blush-pink.

C. „ VAR. MATHIOTIANA — double rose-red flowers, less crowded than C. imbricata.

C. „ „ ALBA—similar, with white flowers.

C. „ „ NOBILISSIMA—exceptionally beautiful double white flowers.

4-ft.–15-ft., April-May. E. 4-ft.–10-ft. Sq. Cg5. AN. Shelter. Pl.13.

C. RETICULATA (Netted) Yunnan, is an excellent shrub for a west wall, with large rose-crimson flowers, single to semi-double.

4-ft.–15-ft., March-April. E. 4-ft.–12-ft. Cg5. AN.

C. SASANQUA (Sasanquan) Japan, has rather smaller, shiny green leaves than C. japonica, and single white flowers produced in the middle of winter. It therefore deserves, and indeed needs, all the protection it can be given to encourage such robust liberalism.

4-ft.–15-ft., January. E. 4-ft.–12-ft. Cg5. Sd2. AN.

CAMPHOROSMA (CHENOPODIACEAE) (DERIVED FROM CAMPHOR, FROM THE AROMATIC SMELL OF THE PLANT).

C. MONSPELIACUM (Of Montpellier) S. Europe, is a low-growing shrub with tiny linear leaves and inconspicuous flowers of little merit, but its wood and foliage carry the heavy, aromatic odour of camphor.

2-ft., ——— *E. 2-ft. Sq. Cg5. ANC.*

CANTUA (POLEMONIACEAE) (THE NAME IS DERIVED FROM THE PERUVIAN NAME FOR THE GENUS).

The one species which follows is moderately hardy, but requires the shelter of a sunny wall in southern or south-western districts.

C. BUXIFOLIA (Box-leaved) Chilean Andes, is a shrub which, in the wild, will reach ten feet, but which, in the most favoured situation it can be offered, seldom exceeds four feet, and is clothed with small, unserrated, evergreen leaves, about one inch in length, and produces terminal clusters of long, funnel-shaped flowers of rose striped with yellow. A very handsome, but undoubtedly tender, shrub.

4-ft., May. E. 4-ft. Sq. Cg6. AN.

CARAGANA (LEGUMINOSAE) (DERIVED FROM CARAGAN, THE TATAR NAME FOR ONE OF THE SPECIES, CARAGANA ARBORESCENS OR PEA TREE).

The species are generally heavily spined, but this is not so evident in cultivation. The leaves are pinnate, but made up of an even number of leaflets, varying in the species from four to eighteen. Flowers are pea-shaped with the standard curled back at the sides. They also produce atrophied branches which are covered with scales, at the tip of which are produced tufts of leaves and flowers each year, but which fail from year to year to make further woody growth. The species grow best in poor soil, are easy to grow, are hardy, and can be propagated from the seeds which they produce, which should be soaked in warm water, or from root cuttings.

C. BOISII (Comm.) Tibet, is a small shrub with pinnate multiple leaflets, heavily spined, and with typical yellow pea flowers.

4-ft., May. D. 4-ft. Sq. Sd3. Cr3. AN.

C. CHAMLAGU (From Chamlagu) China, has dark-green leaves in two unequal pairs, the large flowers are reddish-yellow and borne singly, and makes a four-foot rounded bush with angular branches, with a smell of liquorice.

4-ft., May. D. 4-ft. Sq. Sd3. Cr3. AN.

CARMICHAELIA (LEGUMINOSAE) (THE GENUS IS NAMED IN HONOUR OF THE BOTANIST, CAPTAIN H. CARMICHAEL).

The characteristic of the genus is the replacement of the functions of the leaves by the flattened stems, each of which bears only a small, uneven number of tiny leaflets.

C. AUSTRALIS (Eastern) New Zealand, has curiously flattened stems and tiny leaves, but bears innumerable clusters of tiny, pale purple pea flowers with a fascinating scent.

6-ft., June-July. E. 6-ft. Sq. Sd2. AN.

C. Enysii (Comm.) New Zealand, is a tiny shrub making a mat of flattened twigs, which at the appropriate time becomes spangled with a number of tiny purple pea flowers.

⅓-ft., July. E. 1-ft. Sq. Sd2. AN.

C. Petriei (Comm.) New Zealand, differs from the other species in having rounded, rush-like twigs instead of flattened ones, producing many fragrant, small, purple pea flowers in small racemes, from an adult bush which is symmetrically rounded.

4-ft., July. E. 4-ft. Sq. Sd2. AN.

CARPENTERIA (Saxifragaceae) (named in honour of professor carpenter, a noted botanist of the state of louisiana).

An evergreen shrub with bright green leaves, whitely tomentose beneath, and which is allied to Philadelphus.

C. californica (Californian) Western N. America, bears sprays of from three to seven large, white, single, five-petalled flowers, centred with clustered yellow anthers, and with a sweet fragrance. Shelter is required in severe districts, and it is one of the worst of shrubs for growing in towns.

8-ft., June-July. E. 8-ft. Sq. Sd2. D3. ANC.

CARYOPTERIS (Verbenaceae) (the name is derived from gr. karuon—a nut ; and pteron—a wing ; a reference to the slightly winged seeds).

The so-called Blue Spiraea.

C. × clandonensis (From Clandon) Garden origin, is a hybrid between C. Mastacanthus and C. mongolica, and is probably one of the best of the species, making a bush up to six feet in height, with narrow grey-green serrated leaves, and bearing in August from the leaf axils semi-circular clusters of deep lavender-blue flowers, each individually small, but very impressive in the mass, and fascinating upon closer examination, when the fringed nature of the corolla lip can be really appreciated.

2-ft.–4-ft., August-October. D. 6-ft. Sq. Cg5. ANC. Pl.14.

C. Mastacanthus (An old name for the species) China, is also C. incana, is much more woody than the preceding, with more heavily felted and greyer, scented leaves ; the flowers, produced with less freedom, are pale violet-blue.

2-ft.–4-ft., August-October. D. 6-ft. Sq. Cg5. ANC.

C. mongolica (From Mongolia) N. China, is a tender dwarf with the uppermost parts of the current growth becoming fringed with flowers, with each flower made up of two shades of blue, very attractive, but it needs shelter except in the most favoured districts.

2-ft., August-October. D. 2-ft. Sq. Cg5. ANC.

C. tangutica (From Tangusa) East Siberia, has smaller leaves than C. Mastacanthus, but is harder, has deeper coloured flowers, which are less fringed. *3-ft., August-October. 2-ft. Sq. Cg5. ANC.*

Clematis Jackmanii Mme. Edouard André ABCDEGHJ
Clematis splendida FGKLM
Clematis Jackmanii Mrs. Chólmondeley NOPQRSTU

Clematis Jackmanii rubra ABCDEFJ
Clematis purpurea elegans plena FGJKLNO

Clematis Jackmanii
Comtesse de Bouchard
LMPQ

CASSANDRA (ERICACEAE) (FROM A MYTHICAL NAME).

This shrub can only be well grown in a moist, lime-free soil.

C. CALYCULATA (Small-calyxed) Eastern N. America, is also known as ANDROMEDA calyculata and CHAMAEDAPHNE calyculata, and is a somewhat sparse shrub, with oblong, leathery, green leaves, rusty underneath, and producing singly in the uppermost leaf axils, small, white, Lily-of-the-valley flowers.
3-*ft.*, *March-April.* *E.* 11-*ft. Sq.* *Cg5.* *AN.*

CASSIA (LEGUMINOSAE) (DERIVED FROM KASIA, THE GREEK NAME OF A PLANT MENTIONED IN THE BIBLE).

C. MARYLANDICA (From Maryland) is a pleasant plant with annual growths of about three feet long, which die back each year and have pinnate leaves made up of even pairs of leaflets up to eighteen in number, ending in a bristle, and produces from the leaf axils sprays of yellow pea flowers with purple anthers.
3-*ft.*, *July-October.* *D.* *Sd2.* *D3.* *ANC.*

CASSINIA (COMPOSITAE) (NAMED IN HONOUR OF A FRENCH BOTANIST, M. CASSINI).

A group of heath-like plants with inconspicuous flowers, liable to be browned off during the winter with an extra severe frost, and to perform the same service for many a gardener by failing to provide anything worthy of his idea of a flower. Nevertheless the foliage is pleasant.

C. FULVIDA (Tawny) New Zealand, leads a double life with the catalogue alias of DIPPLOPAPPUS chrysophyllus, has deep green, heathery foliage, brown below, and has very small and very numerous, tiny aster-(Michaelmas-Daisy)-like flowers. A plant for those who value neatness, and a gem for those who like miniatures which flower at an early age.
3-*ft.*–6-*ft.*, *July.* *E.* 3-*ft. Sq.* *Cg4–8.* *ANC.*

C. VAUVILLIERSII (Comm.) New Zealand, has wide leaves of a pleasant, bluish-green tinge, is smaller, and is otherwise similar, and, according to point of view, charms or fails to do so, by being more shy in flowering. 2-*ft.*–5-*ft.*, *July.* *E.* 4-*ft. Sq.* *Cg4–8.* *ANC.*

CASSIOPE (ERICACEAE) (NAMED AFTER THE MOTHER OF ANDROMEDA).

This group comprises a number of evergreen plants with dense, overlapping, needle-like leaves like those of the heathers, which thrive in moist, cold, peaty soil, and are best grown on a site with a north aspect.

C. FASTIGIATA (Pointed and erect) Himalayas, is a small, upright bush with tightly pressed, square branches of lapping green, needle-like foliage, producing at the topmost leaf axils large, white, Lily-of-the-valley flowers. ½-*ft.*, *May-June.* *E.* ½-*ft. Sq.* *Cg7.* *AN.*

C. HYPNOIDES (Resembling feather moss) Arctic Regions, forms a flat tuft of tangled, deep green, the white, bell-like flowers hanging on thread-like stems produced from the ends of the branches.

¼-ft., May-June. E. ½-ft. Sq. Cg7. Sd10. AN.

C. MERTENSIANA (Comm.) Western N. America, is an upright growing plant with wider leaves and the four-angled appearance of C. fastigiata, with hanging, bell-shaped flowers, with red sepals.

1-ft., April-May. E. 1-ft. Sq. Cg7. Sd10. AN.

C. SELAGINOIDES (Resembling Selago) Himalayas, has tiny green foliage like club-moss, and bears the flowers typical of the group upon short, hair-like stems.

¼-ft., April-May. E. ½-ft. Sq. Cg7. Sd10. AN.

C. TETRAGONA (Four-angled) Arctic Regions, is larger than C. fastigiata, is taller, and has smaller flowers, but redeems these faults, if faults they be, by being more tractable and easier to grow.

1-ft., May-June. E. 1-ft. Sq. Cg7. Sd10. AN.

CEANOTHUS (RHAMNACEAE) (FROM THE GR. KEANOTHOS—A NAME USED BY THEOPHRASTUS TO DENOTE A NOW UNIDENTIFIED SPINY PLANT).

This group of attractive plants requires, as a rule, a sheltered position, generally against a wall, all but C. rigidus are reasonably hardy, but they are liable to be cut by frosts, and should be pruned heavily immediately after flowering. Propagation from cuttings is not difficult. The hybrids are, as a general rule, the most satisfactory garden varieties.

C. ARNOULDII (Comm.) is also C. Delilianus, is a popular hybrid with large deciduous leaves, and has large panicles of powder-blue flowers. Requires heavy pruning.

8-ft., July-October. D. 12-ft. Sq. Cg7. ANC.

C. BURKWOODII (Comm.) is a hybrid of C. floribundus with C. hybridus indigo, with small evergreen leaves, and dense sprays of bright blue flowers borne from the leaf axils on the current year's wood.

9-ft., July-October. E. 15-ft. Sq. Cg5. ANC.

C. CYANEUS (Cornflower-blue) S. California, comes from a reasonably high altitude, and is probably among the hardiest of the evergreen species, which, added to the fact that its panicles are without doubt the largest of the evergreen group, generally in excess of five inches in length, and of clear blue. Against a sheltered wall it will reach twenty feet, but is normally less than half that height.

8-ft., May-July. E. 10-ft. Sq. Cg7. ANC.

C. DENTATUS (Toothed) California, is regarded by some authorities as a variety of C. papillosus, and has small, notched, evergreen leaves, small clusters of deep blue flowers, rather rounder in contour, and is a magnificent wall plant, or in the open in mild districts. C. dentatus var. Russellianus is the best blue.

10-ft., May. E. 10-ft. Sq. Cg7. ANC.

Clematis tangutica

Coriaria terminalis xanthocarpa **FKOS**

Coriaria terminalis **BGLQ**

C. Fendleri (Comm.) N.W. America, is a dwarf, deciduous species with narrow, small leaves, and white or very pale-blue flowers, and is not particularly beautiful.

4-ft., May. D. 4-ft. Sq. Cg7. ANC.

C. hybridus (Hybrid) Garden origin. For convenience it has seemed necessary to group the deciduous garden hybrids under this title which has already been used for a hybrid between C. arboreus and C. spinosus, and American practice indicates many of the varieties given below under C. Delilianus and C. pallidus.

C. Albert Pittet has large leaves, bright pink flowers, and is the pink counterpart of Gloire de Versailles.

C. hybridus Ceres has mauve-pink panicles, not so large.

C. hybridus Charles Detriche is a rich, dark blue.

C. „ Gloire de Versailles has probably the largest sprays of deep powder-blue flowers.

C. „ Marie Simon is one of the best of the pink varieties with small leaves, and needing less vigorous pruning than most. Six feet is a good maximum height.

C. „ Perle Rose is bright carmine.

C. „ Topaz is slightly smaller in inflorescence to C. Gloire de Versailles, but darker in colour.

8-ft.–20-ft., July-October. D. 5-ft.–15-ft. Sq., Cg7. ANC.

C. rigidus (Stiff) California, has small evergreen leaves, short joints, and tightly packed, deep-blue flowers in very small heads, but dispersed in graceful fashion along the whole branch.

8-ft., April-May E. 6-ft. Sq. or more. Cg7. ANC. Shelter.

C. thyrsiflorus (Flowering in bunches) is the hardiest and tallest of the evergreen species, with pale-blue flowers. C. thyrsiflorus var. griseus has grey flowers but is otherwise similar. Very good on a north wall. *25-ft., June-August. E. 10-ft. Sq., or more. Cg7. ANC.*

C. Veitchianus (Comm.) is a hybrid between C. rigidus and C. thyrsiflorus, and somewhat similar to C. dentatus, but has larger leaves, deep blue flowers, and is a little less hardy.

10-ft.–15-ft., May-June. E. 12-ft. Sq. Cg7. ANC.

CELASTRUS (Celastraceae) (from Gr. kelastros—a particular evergreen tree; probably a reference to the fact that these vine-like shrubs retain their fruits throughout the winter).

The group comprises a collection of deciduous twining shrubs, with alternate simple green leaves, clusters of greenish-white flowers, and fruits which split open to display brilliantly coloured seeds. All are useful for covering trellis, walls, and the like, will grow well in ordinary soil, and propagate easily from seed, suckers, or cuttings of the half-ripened wood.

CELASTRUS (continued)

C. ANGULATUS (Angled) China, has large, green, wide, oval leaves and orange-red fruits with red seeds.

20-ft., June. D. Indeterminate. Sd10. D3. Cg7. ANC.

C. ARTICULATUS (Jointed) China, has young, spiny branches, becoming smooth with age, and smaller leaves than the foregoing. The white flowers are followed by orange-red fruits, which open to show golden-yellow interiors and scarlet seeds. C. articulatus var. punctatus has smaller leaves and is generally less vigorous. The leaves of both varieties turn clear yellow in autumn.

40-ft., June. D. Indeterminate. Sd2. ANC.

C. LOESENERI (Comm.) China, has dull green leaves, glaucous upon the underside, greenish-white flowers, yellow fruits and red seeds.

20-ft., June. D. Variable. Sd2. ANC.

C. ROSTHORNIANA (Comm.) W. China, has still smaller, shiny green leaves, and is generous in the display of its orange fruits with red seeds. *15-ft., June. D. Variable. Sd. ANC.*

C. SCANDENS (Climbing) N. America, is probably best known, but the least satisfying of the species. A unisexual plant, one of each sex are required to be planted in close proximity before the orange fruits with scarlet seeds can be freely produced. They are best planted in an old tree, through which they may ramble at will.

20-ft., June. D. Variable. Sd2. ANC.

CEPHALANTHUS (RUBIACEAE) (FROM GR. KEPHALE—A HEAD ; AND ANTHOS—A FLOWER ; THE FLOWERS ARE DISPOSED IN HEADS).

The one species which follows is interesting rather than beautiful, and grows well in a moist spot in sandy peat.

C. OCCIDENTALIS (Western) N. America, has oval, lanceolate, shiny, green-surfaced leaves, with small, creamy-white flowers arranged in heads of about one inch in diameter, either singly upon the ends of the shoots, or in groups of four.

5-ft.–8-ft., August. D. 6-ft. Sq. Cg8. AN.

CERATOSTIGMA (PLUMBAGINACEAE) (FROM GR. KERAS—A HORN ; AND STIGMA—REFERRING TO THE BRANCHED APPEARANCE OF THE STIGMA).

A small group of deciduous shrubs, with deep-blue flowers succeeding in, and deserving, good garden soil.

C. GRIFFITHII (Comm.) Himalayas, is a low-growing shrub, reputed to be evergreen, but never deserving this reputation, with dull-green leaves with red margins, and bearing loose heads of deep-blue flowers. It is best grown in a hot, dry position sheltered by a backing wall.

1-ft., July-September. D. 2-ft. Sq., or more. Ch7. AN.

C. WILLMOTTIANUM (Comm.) China, makes a shrub of two feet or slightly more, with angular growth, and small rhombic leaves, and produces loose heads of deep but bright blue flowers. It needs some slight protection from keen winds, such as can be provided by nearby shrubs.

2-ft., August-September. D. 2-ft. Sq. Ch7. AN. Pl.15.

CERCIDIPHYLLUM (CERCIDIPHYLLACEAE) (FROM GR. KERKIS—A SHUTTLECOCK ; AND PHYLLON—A LEAF ; THE LEAVES HAVING A RESEMBLANCE TO CERCIS, THUS NAMED BY THEOPHRASTUS).

In reality a small tree, C. japonicum is more often represented in gardens by a multiple-stemmed shrub, but small or large as it may be, the delightful distribution of its rounded leaves, and their delightful colour in autumn, render it indispensable to every garden which will allow it to grow.

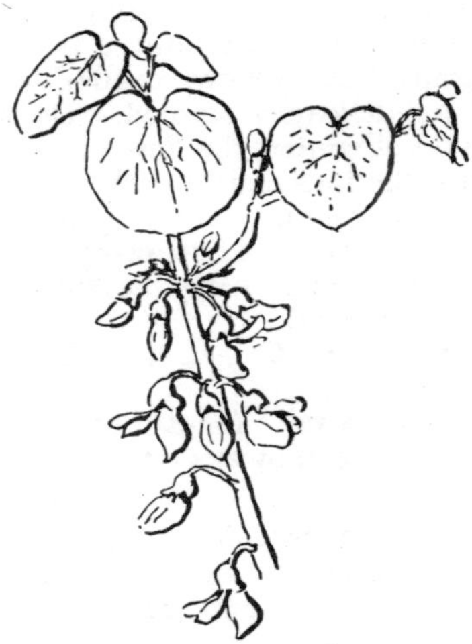

CERCIS SILIQUASTRUM

C. JAPONICUM (Japanese) Japan, is tender and suited only to the south, south-west and western seaboard, or sheltered gardens inland. The predominant feature of this grand tree is the attractive way in which its rounded, glaucous leaves turn apricot-yellow, flushed with rose, as the year progresses to its close. Good but moist soil suits it best. *8-ft.–20-ft. D. 5-ft.–10-ft. Sq. Sd2. AN. Pl.16.*

CERCIS (LEGUMINOSAE) (*see derivation under* CERCIDIPHYLLUM).

Again in reality a tree, but under cultivation generally represented by a low-spreading shrub, seldom exceeding fifteen feet in height, and succeeding best in a sheltered position in sun, and in a good soil.

C. SILIQUASTRUM (From Siliqua), a generic name given to a species with partitions between the seeds in the pod ; is an attractive small tree or shrub with glaucous, round leaves, slightly flattened or pointed at the tips. The very attractive, bright rosy-lilac pea flowers are produced in clusters, before the leaves appear, at the joints of the old wood, often upon the mature branches or the trunk itself. *10-ft.–15-ft., May. D. 10-ft.–15-ft. Sq. Sd2. ANC.*

CHIMONANTHUS (CALYCANTHACEAE) (FROM GR. CHEIMA—WINTER; AND ANTHOS—A FLOWER; FROM THE FACT THAT C. FRAGRANS FLOWERS IN THE WINTER).

The two varieties are easily grown in good garden soil, in a reasonably sunny site where the wood will fully ripen.

C. FRAGRANS (Fragrant) China, is also MERATIA praecox, is a deciduous shrub with elliptical, ovate, rough, green leaves, produced after flowering. The nodding flowers, produced between November and February, are a translucent yellow, centred with smaller purple inner petals, and are delicately scented. Designed by nature to withstand the ravages of winter, the flowers are impervious to rain, snow, or frost, and if the inclement weather causes the gardener to default, the plant is not unduly damaged by having some at least of its flowering branches removed to bring its ineffable fragrance with it to the sick-room! The variety GRANDIFLORUS has larger and just as sweetly scented flowers.
6-ft.–10-ft., November-February. D. 5-ft.–9-ft. Sq. Sd2. L5. ANC. Pl.17.

CHIONANTHUS (OLEACEAE) (FROM GR. CHION—SNOW; AND ANTHOS—A FLOWER; THE FLOWERS OF SOME VARIETIES PRESENTING THE APPEARANCE OF SNOW).

Both varieties appreciate moist, deep loam and a position with a sunny aspect, and produce compound clusters of white flowers with four or five long petals, giving the appearance of snow.

C. RETUSA (Blunt leaves) China, is a very handsome shrub under cultivation, usually met with about ten to twelve feet in height, but which, in its native habitat, is a small tree of some thirty feet high.
15-ft.–30-ft., June-July. D. 8-ft.–24-ft. Sq. Gr5. ANC.

C. VIRGINICA (Virginian) N. America, is a shrub (under cultivation) with long, slender, green leaves with loose sprays of slightly fragrant, five-petalled flowers.
10-ft.–12-ft., June. D. 8-ft.–10-ft. Sq. Sd2. ANC.

CHOISYA (RUTACEAE) (NAMED AFTER J. D. CHOISY, A SWISS BOTANIST).

C. TERNATA (With three leaflets) Mexico, is known as the Mexican Orange Flower, and makes a rounded bush of from six to ten feet in height, more against a wall, clad in three-parted, bright, glossy green leaves, and with large clusters of five-petalled, white flowers about the size of a halfpenny, scenting the air with the fragrance of hawthorn. Easily cultivated in good, light loam, in a position where the wood will fully ripen to resist spring frosts. Sometimes flowers twice a year. *6-ft.–10-ft., April-May. E. 6-ft. Sq. Cg6. ANC.*

CISTUS (CISTACEAE) (FROM GR. KISTOS—A ROCK-ROSE; ITSELF DERIVED FROM KISTE—A BOX; FROM THE FORMATION OF THE SEED CAPSULE).

This is a large group of shrubs which are allied to Helianthemum, differing in having the seed capsules divided into multiples of five instead of three in Helianthemum. Very few of the varieties can be said to be indubitably hardy, they can withstand all but severe winters, but as an insurance should be kept going from cuttings, which root with ease, and should be given a measure of winter protection, or should be protected with bracken or straw. All the species are best grown in light loam in a sunny and well-drained, sheltered site.

C. ALBIDUS (Nearly white) S.W. Europe, takes its name from the appearance of the leaves which are covered with whitish down. Often surviving to reach its ultimate height of five feet, it has large flowers, exceeding two inches in diameter, of pale lilac-pink with a patch of yellow at the base of each petal. C. var. albiflorus is similar in growth with white flowers.

5-ft., May-June. E. 4-ft. Sq. Cg6. ANC.

C. CORBARIENSIS (From Corbière) S. France, is an attractive, dwarf, round shrub, with dark green, netted leaves, and red buds opening to white, yellow-centred flowers, about the size of a penny.

2-ft.–3-ft., May-June. E. 4-ft. Sq. Cg7. ANC.

C. CRISPUS (Curly) S. Europe, is so named because of its wavy-edged leaves, which are coated with down and accompanied by larger, deep-rose flowers in May and June.

2-ft., May-June. E. 3-ft. Sq. Cg7. ANC.

C. CYPRIUS (From Cyprus) S. Europe, has dull green leaves, sticky to the touch, and has larger flowers than any species so far mentioned, with several in a cluster and of clear white with a blood-red patch at the base of each petal. The variety C. cyprius var. albus is white and rare, and has nothing more than this to commend it above the species. *6-ft., May-June. E. 6-ft. Sq. Cg7. ANC.*

C. FLORENTINUS (Florentine) Italy, has rough, netted, green leaves, producing its flowers several upon a stalk, and each of clear white splashed with a patch of yellow at the base.

2-ft.–3-ft., May-June. E. 4-ft. Sq. Cg7. ANC.

C. LADANIFERUS (Yielding ladanum, a gum) S.W. Europe, is notable for its extremely large, crinkled white flowers, touched with five chocolate patches at the bases of the petals, produced in solitary glory at the ends of the side shoots, and its gummy stems and leaves. C. ladaniferus var. albiflorus lacks the "beauty patches" of the species, and for those of you who prefer unspotted beauty, is an alternative choice. *5-ft., May-June. E. 7-ft. Sq. Cg7. ANC.*

C. LAURIFOLIUS (With leaves resembling laurel) S.W. Europe, is a very hardy and strong-growing shrub, with a peeling bark, and with dark-green, smooth, leathery leaves, and large white flowers with basal patches of yellow.

8-ft., May-June. E. 8-ft. Sq. Cg7. ANC.

C. Loretii (Comm.) Natural hybrid, is a low-growing bush with large white flowers stained with crimson splashes at the bases of the petals. *2-ft., May-June. E. 2-ft. Sq. Cg7. ANC.*

C. lusitanicus (Of Portuguese origin) Natural hybrid, is similar to C. Loretii but is taller and wider growing.
4-ft., May-June. E. 4-ft. Sq. Cg7. ANC.

C. obtusifolius (With blunt leaves) Portugal, is a prostrate, low-growing variety with smallish white flowers.
1-ft., May-June. E. 2-ft. Sq. Cg7. ANC.

C. populifolius (Poplar leaves) S.W. Europe, has the largest leaves of any of the species, and bears its white, yellow-stained flowers in clusters of four or five. *5-ft., May-June. E. 5-ft. Sq. Cg7. ANC.*

C. purpureus (Purple) Garden origin, makes a well-rounded bush with long, narrow leaves of grey-green, and produces one at a time from clusters of three or four buds, large purplish-red flowers, with a maroon patch at the base of each petal. It requires, and will certainly suffer without, a sheltered position.
3-ft., May-June. E. 4-ft. Sq. Cg7. ANC.

C. salvifolius (Sage-leaved) S. Europe, has green leaves like those of the Salvia, and bears yellow-stained, white flowers, produced from groups of buds, or singly.
2-ft., May-June. E. 3-ft. Sq. Sg7. ANC.

C. Skanbergii (Comm.) Lampedusa, is one of the most attractive of all, forming a neat and shapely bush of under three feet in height, with narrow, grey-green leaves and long clusters of small, clear pink flowers, shaped like buttercups. Somewhat variable in colour, it welcomes, and shows its approval of, a sunny and dry exposure.
2½-ft., June-August. 2½-ft. Sq. Cg8. ANC.

C. Silver Pink (Descript.) Garden origin, is a wonderful hybrid raised by Messrs. Hilliers—the name of which is fully descriptive of its colour, and whose beauty is combined with a constitution which belies the idea that beauty and frailty are a necessary combination. *3-ft., June-July. 3-ft. Sq. Cg7. ANC.*

C. villosus (Hairy) S. Europe, has rounded leaves, usually covered with down, and grey beneath, and produces from groups of three to five buds its large, rose-purple flowers, flushed at the base of the petals with yellow. C. villosus var. creticus is similar in all its characteristics except the colour of the petals, which are pale-mauve.
3-ft., June-July. E. 3-ft. Sq. Cg7. ANC.

C. Wintoniensis (Of Winton) Garden origin, provides a fitting close to the series. C. Wintoniensis, also known as Halimocistus Wintoniensis (a bigeneric cross) is, whichever name it is to be known by, one of the best of all. Low growing, seldom if ever exceeding two feet in height, the greyish-green, rather wide foliage is a fitting foil for the pearly-white flowers with the crimson-maroon patches fading to a central yellow zone. Even the winters of '40 and '41 failed at altitudes in excess of 1,000 feet to harm it in this district, and I doubt if elsewhere. *2-ft., May-June. E. 2-ft. Sq. Cg7. ANC.*

CLADOTHAMNUS (ERICACEAE) (FROM GR. KLADOS—A BRANCH; AND THAMNOS—A BUSH).

A deciduous shrub related to the heathers, and needing a peaty soil and a cool situation.

C. PYROLIFLORUS (With flowers resembling the Winter Green), is a neat and attractive small shrub with narrow leaves and white flowers, shell pink at the centre and yellowish at the margins, borne singly at the ends of the shoots and in the leaf axils.
2-ft., June. D. 3-ft. Sq. Sd2. AN.

CLEMATIS (RANUNCULACEAE) (FROM GR. KLEMA—A VINE; A REFERENCE TO THE CLIMBING HABIT OF SOME OF THE SPECIES).

These relatives of the buttercups number among them some of the most beautiful of climbing plants, but though the hybrids of CC. lanuginosa, patens, florida, and Viticella are probably the best known in gardens, they do not contain among them all the most beautiful climbers. The flowers of the Clematis are interesting, among other reasons, because the flowers have no petals, the highly coloured and large sepals numbering from four to eight having replaced them. Considerable variation exists in the shape and size of the flowers of the various species which are dealt with in the descriptions. Cultivation consists in giving them in the main cool, moist, but well-drained soil, and pruning, except where otherwise especially stated, to confine to their allotted space, and remove dead or superfluous wood.

C. ALPINA (Alpine) S.E. Europe, is an early flowering climbing or trailing plant, well suited to ramble through a low bush, or trail down a steep bank. This graceful plant will enchant with the artistry of its blend of deep lavender and cream, and the queer symmetry of its twisted sepals. *5-ft., April-May. E. 3-ft. Sq. Sd4. N.* 063/2.

C. ARMANDII (Comm.) China, is a very delightful evergreen species with large, glossy, deep green, three-parted leaves with twisted stalks, and compound clusters of large white flowers borne in threes, fading to pink with age. *20-ft., April. E. Indefinite. Sd3. N.*

C. BALEARICA (From the Balearic Islands) Minorca, etc., is also C. calycina, and has dark green, finely divided foliage which gives it its common name "the Fern Leaved Clematis," and which turns bronze in winter when the greenish-yellow flowers, spotted and flushed with irregular, reddish-purple stains are produced.
10-ft., September-March. E. 8-ft. Sq. Sd6. ANC. Shelter.

C. CHRYSOCOMA (With tufts of golden hair) Yunnan, is a deciduous, shrubby species with trifoliate leaves, and bears at the joints of the previous year's wood its solitary, four-sepalled flowers of white flushed with pink.
6-ft., August. D. 6-ft. Sq. Sd2. ANC. Shelter.

C. CIRRHOSA (With curled tendrils) S. Europe, is an evergreen climber in the style of C. balearica, with a similar involucre in the flower stem, and with simple leaves and yellowish-white flowers produced from the leaf axils in winter.
8-*ft.*, *January-March.* *E.* 8-*ft. Sq.* *Sd*6. *ANC.* *Shelter.*

C. DURANDII (Comm.) Garden origin, is a fascinating climber of parentage C. integrifolia × C. Jackmanii, with oval, pointed, undivided leaves of glossy green, with very large, dark violet-blue flowers with golden stamens, freely produced in June and from then onwards to September. 9-*ft.*, *June-September.* *D.* 6-*ft. Sq.* *Ch*5. *ANC.*

C. FLAMMULA (Little flame) Europe, is an evergreen climber with a large tangled head and bare legs, with bright green leaves made up of three or five leaflets, and which bears foot-long sprays of exquisitely scented, small, clear-white flowers. The hawthorn-scented flowers provide one of the greatest attractions of the garden in the autumn. 10-*ft.*, *August-October.* *D.* 8-*ft. Sq.* *Sd*2. *ANC.*

C. FLORIDA (Flowering abundantly) Japan, is interesting mainly because it is one of the parents of the so-called Florida hybrids, and is a semi-evergreen with three-parted leaflets, and which bears solitary flowers of creamy-white up to three inches in diameter, with a clear green band at the back of each sepal, which number four to six ; closely related to C. patens, it can be distinguished by the presence of a pair of bracts upon the flower stem. The Florida hybrids bear their flowers from the old wood and, if pruned, this should consist of the removal of the old flowering wood immediately after flowering. The best are :—

Belle of Woking—has pale mauve double flowers.
Countess of Lovelace—is bluish-lilac with double flowers.
Duchess of Edinburgh—is double white, heavily scented.
Lucie Lemoine—is a very hardy, double white variety.
sanguinea plena—has double, deep-claret flowers.

10-*ft.*, *June-July.* *D.* *Variable.* *Ch*7. *ANC.*

C. GLAUCA VAR. AKEBIOIDES (Sea-green, resembling Akebia) Yunnan, is a fascinating variety in the style of C. tangutica with bronze-yellow flowers, and the same honey fragrance.
15-*ft.*, *June-October.* *D.* 8-*ft. Sq.* *G*5. *ANC.*

C. INDIVISA (Undivided) New Zealand, is an evergreen with exceedingly variable foliage, and very large, white flowers with rose anthers, which is suitable only for the mildest districts.
10-*ft.*, *July.* *E.* ——— *Sd*2. *ANC.*

C. JACKMANII (Comm.) Garden origin, is the name given to the most popular group of hybrid Clematis, originally raised by Messrs. Jackman of Woking, in 1860, from seeds resulting from a cross of C. Hendersonii with C. lanuginosa. They have given rise to the magnificent group of garden varieties known as the Jackmanii group, which are vigorous growers, flower on the new growth from

Colquhounia coccinea

Pieris japonica
ABCFGKO

Corylopsis pauciflora
DGHLMPQ

July to October, and which benefit by being pruned back hard each spring. Some of the best varieties are :—

Alexandra—has pale, reddish-violet flowers.
Comtesse de Bouchard—is mauvish-pink. *Pls.*18, 20.
Duke of Edinburgh—has large violet-purple flowers.
Gipsy Queen—is dark purple.
Jackmanii—is the original dark purple.
" alba—has fine white flowers.
" rubra—is as good, but has red flowers. *Pl.*20.
" superba—has wide petals of violet-purple.
Madame Edouard André—has reddish-purple flowers of velvety texture. *Pl.*19.
Mrs. Cholmondeley—is light blue, and flowers early. *Pl.*19.
Perle d'Azure—is bright blue with flowers of medium size.
Proteus—has mauve-pink flowers with yellow centre.
Rubella—is deep claret-purple.
Snow-White Jackmanii—is the freest flowering white.
Star of India—is plum-red with deeper bands in the middle of the sepals.
Velutina purpurea—has sepals the colour of ripe mulberries.
Victoria—has transparent, purple-mauve sepals.

10-*ft.*, *July-October.* *D.* *Variable.* *Ch*7. *ANC.*

C. JOUINIANA (Comm.) Garden origin, is a vigorous climber with parentage C. Vitalba × C. Davidiana, with leaves made up of from three to five leaflets, and which produces from the uppermost leaf axils large sprays of small white flowers tinted with lilac, giving the effect of one large inflorescence over a foot in length, and is a splendid climber to ramble through an old tree.

10-*ft.*, *August-October.* *D.* *Variable.* *Sd*2. *ANC.*

C. KOREANA (From Korea) Korea, is a prostrate-growing species with leaves made up of three notched leaflets, and which produces solitary, nodding, violet flowers. C. koreana var. lutea has yellow flowers.

1-*ft.*, *June-September.* *D.* *Variable.* *Sd*2. *ANC.*

C. LANUGINOSA (With woolly down) China, is a deciduous climber, interesting as the parent of the Lanuginosa hybrids, and can be distinguished by its very large flowers, and woolly young growth, and woolly underside to the leaves. In the original varieties the flowers were white or pale lilac, but by cross breeding purple-reds and pinks have been produced. C. lanuginosa flowers upon short lateral shoots successionally throughout the summer, and succeeds with but moderate pruning. The varieties considered worthy of individual mention are :—

Beauty of Worcester—has bluish-violet flowers with yellow stamens, single and double flowers on the same plant.
Belle Nantaise—is pale lavender.
Blue Gem—has sky-blue flowers.
Crimson King—is rosy-red with paler bands down each sepal

Duke of Portland—is flushed cream with a crimson bar down each sepal.
Elsa Spath—has bright blue flowers with darker centre.
Empress of India—has well-proportioned flowers of light-purple, deeper bars and brown stamens.
Fairy Queen—is pale flesh colour with pink bars.
Gloire de St. Julien—has very large, pale-mauve flowers with yellow stamens.
Grand Duchess—has very large, bluish-white flowers.
Henri—has perfectly proportioned, large, creamy-white flowers.
King Edward VII—is magenta-violet with the main rib of the sepal shaded violet-purple.
Lady Caroline Neville—is pale grey with pink shading down the sepals.
Lady Northcliffe—has deep lavender sepals shaded purple at the base, and with white stamens.
La France—is violet-purple with brown anthers.
lanuginosa candida—has white flowers, tinted grey.
Lawsoniana—has flowers of clear lavender.
Lord Neville—is dark plum colour.
Marie Boisselot—is pure white.
Mrs. Bush—has very large flowers of deep-lavender.
Mrs. Hope—has shiny sepals of mauve shaded with darker colour.
Nellie Moser—has lilac-pink sepals with crimson bars. *Pl.*18.
Otto Frobel—has very large flowers of white shaded with grey.
Princess of Wales—has satiny sepals of bluish-mauve.
Queen Alexandra—is pale-lavender with a lilac-purple base with white bars.
Sensation—has shiny mauve flowers.
Sieboldii—has sepals of pale mauve, prettily reflexed.
W. E. Gladstone—has very large flowers of lilac with lighter bars.
William Kennett—is very large with deep-lavender flowers.

9-ft., July-October. D. Variable. Ch7. ANC.

C. MACROPETALA (With long petals) China, is similar to C. alpina in habit, but is also a grand climber for a south wall, where its many sepals of powder-blue, giving way to cream in the centre, form a fitting decoration during the early summer, and are followed by the silky tasselled seed heads in the autumn. Among the seedlings deeper violet forms, and even pink forms, are found. A very good pink form is C. macropetala var. Markhamii.

5-ft., April-May. D. 3-ft. Sd4. N. Pl.7.

C. MONTANA (Of the mountains) Himalayas, is a most attractive deciduous climber with three parted leaves, producing in May masses of clear white flowers reminiscent both in size and shape of the Wood Anemone. C. montana is most useful for covering arbours and similar structures. C. montana rubens is another attractive variety with rose-pink flowers and bronze-green foliage. C. montana undulata has flesh-pink flowers, and C. montana Wilsonii has larger white flowers which are very pleasantly scented and flowering in the autumn.

To 20-ft., May. D. Variable. Sd2. ANC.

C. ORIENTALIS (Eastern) China, is a variety now badly confused with C. tangutica, and is a vigorous grower with slightly scented, golden-yellow, four-petalled flowers, reminiscent in the unopened buds of Chinese lanterns. C. tangutica—held by some to be a variety of C. orientalis—is similar, but very fragrant.

15-*ft., August-September. D. Variable. Sd2. ANC.*

C. PANICULATA (Flowering in clusters) Japan, is an even more vigorous edition of C. Flammula, and becomes covered in autumn with a mass of small, fragrant, white flowers.

30-*ft., September-October. D. Sd2. ANC.*

C. PATENS (Opening out) Japan, is probably not now in cultivation in its original white form, but is of importance as the progenitor of the Patens hybrids, of which the following are probably among the best. Pruning consists of removing the dead wood, and any weak, straggling, or overcrowded branches.

Edouard Desfosse—has large, violet-mauve flowers with darker bars.

Etoile de Paris—has violet flowers, paling towards the centre.

Fair Rosamond—is very pale-pink with crimson-purple bars.

King of the Belgians—has pale-lavender flowers deepening at the centre of the sepals.

Lady Londesborough—is silvery-grey, paling towards the centre.

Lasurstern—has deep purple-blue flowers.

Miss Bateman—is white with chocolate anthers.

Mrs. George Jackman—is satiny white with cream bars.

Sir Garnet Wolseley—is blue with plum-red bars and touched with bronze.

The Bride—is late flowering, large white flowers, yellow stamens.

The President—is dark violet and late flowering.

The Queen—is pale lavender.

9-*ft.* (*Early varieties, May-July. Late varieties, June-October.*) *D. Variable. Ch6. ANC.*

C. REHDERIANA (Comm.) W. China, is also known as C. nutans, and is a very vigorous climber, which, if cut to the ground, will still reach twenty feet in a year, and is a magnificent plant to ramble through an old tree; the large flower clusters, produced from the leaf axils, are composed of small, nodding, bell-shaped flowers of primrose-yellow, bearing the characteristic fragrance of the primrose.

20-*ft., July-October. D. Variable. Sd2. Ch8. ANC.*

C. SERRATIFOLIA (With serrated leaves) Korea, is as beautiful as C. tangutica, which it closely resembles, but differs in its doubly divided, three-parted leaves, and its smaller flowers.

10-*ft., August-September. D. Variable. Sd2. ANC.*

C. TANGUTICA (From E. Siberia) W. Mongolia, is, in spite of its many competitors, the finest of the yellow-flowered Clematis, for from

June to late autumn it is spangled with deep-yellow, sweetly scented Chinese lanterns, converted by age to silvery-grey, hoary heads of fluffy seeds which continually add charm to the whole.

10-ft., June-October. D. Variable. Sd2. ANC. Pl.21

C. TEXENSIS (From Texas) U.S.A., loses its climbing top growth in cultivation each winter, but is unique in the colour of its small, nodding, pitcher-shaped flowers, smaller than a halfpenny but of variable colour from scarlet to purple-grey. As a species it needs the shelter of a south wall, but it has given rise to a number of interesting hybrids, of which the following are suitable examples, and are sometimes known as the Wokingensis type :—

Admiration—is salmon, edged with violet, and white on the reverse.

Countess of Onslow—is bright-violet with a scarlet band down the centre of each sepal.

Duchess of Albany—has flowers of bright-pink with a deeper bar.

Duchess of York—is pale blush-pink, darkening down the ribs of the sepals.

Grace Darling—has star-shaped blooms of bright-carmine.

Sir Trevor Lawrence—is crimson with deeper throat.

6-ft., July-October. D. 3-ft. Ch6. ANC.

C. VEDRARIENSIS ROSEA (Vedrare, rose) Garden origin, is also C. Spooneri rosea, and is very similar to C. montana rubra, but with flowers a little larger—about three inches in diameter.

10-ft., May-June. D. Variable. Sd2. ANC.

C. VITALBA (The Traveller's Joy) Great Britain, is the Old Man's Beard of our native hedgerows.

C. VITICELLA (Vine bower) S. Europe, is a deciduous woody climber with pinnate or bipinnate leaves, with blue, purple, or rose-purple flowers, two inches across, with yellow stamens, flowering from June to August. C. Viticella var. rubra grandiflora has double, reddish-purple flowers.

The following hybrids are interesting, and among the best :—

Ascotiensis—has large, azure-blue flowers. *Pl.18.*

Daniel Durondo—has purple-blue flowers with yellow eye.

Duchess of Sutherland—has bright-red flowers with paler ribs to the sepals.

Kermesina—has bright-red flowers.

King George V—is light flesh colour with bright-pink bars.

Lady Betty Balfour—is a strong-growing climber with glossy purple flowers.

Madame Grange—has large crimson-purple flowers.

Mrs. Spencer Castle—has pinkish-heliotrope flowers.

rubra grandiflora—has double crimson-claret flowers.

Ville de Lyon—is bright carmine with deeper edges.

viticella alba luxurians—has large white flowers.

8-ft., July-October. D. Variable. Ch6. ANC.

CLERODENDRON (VERBENACEAE) (IS SAID TO BE DERIVED FROM GR. KLEROS—CHANCE; AND DENDRON—A TREE; FROM ITS DISPUTED MEDICINAL PROPERTIES).

A group of small trees and shrubs which may be said to be hardy in the south and in sheltered districts, and thrive in an open loamy soil, preferably backed by a sheltering wall to the north.

C. BUNGEI (Comm.) China, is also C. foetidum, has large heart-shaped leaves clothed with violet hair, and bears late in the year rounded heads of tightly packed, rosy-red flowers. Behaving in most districts as a herbaceous plant, but throwing strong new wood each year, it requires a hot, dry summer and a sheltered spot in which to give of its best. The flowers are sweetly scented and belie the old name which refers to the odour of the crushed leaves.
4-ft.–6-ft., August-September. D. 6-ft. Sq. Suckers. Cr4. D3. ANC.

C. FARGESII (Comm.) China, is also C. trichotomum Fargesii, and is a vigorous shrub reaching to about ten feet in height, with ovate leaves up to five inches in length, reddish-purple when young, but turning glossy-green, and produces clusters of white, fragrant, star-shaped flowers which are followed by small pale-blue berries set in pink calyces. *10-ft., July-September. D. 8-ft. Sq. Cr4. ANC.*

C. TRICHOTOMUM (With three points) China, derives its name from the fact that some of its leaves, notably the lower ones, are three-lobed, and has leaves which are generally larger and have the underside covered with down. The white flowers, set in maroon calyces, are followed by bright-blue berries which ultimately turn black.
10-ft., July-September. D. 10-ft. Sq. Cr4. ANC.

CLETHRA (ERICACEAE) (FROM THE GR. KLETHRA—THE NAME FOR ALDER, TO WHICH SOME OF THE SPECIES BEAR A RESEMBLANCE).

All the Clethras are best planted in lime-free soils, and bear white flowers in sprays or clusters, differing from the related Ericas in having the corolla divided into five separate petals.

C. ALNIFOLIA (Alder-leaved) Eastern N. America, is the Sweet Pepper Bush, a very handsome shrub with upright branching habit, and with leaves thrice as long as wide, tapering sharply at the points, and which bears compound, erect sprays of small, sweetly scented, white flowers. C. alnifolia is best grown in a moist soil, and is a fine plant for both its scent and late flowering character. C. alnifolia var. paniculata is notable in having ampler panicles of larger flowers.
8-ft., August. D. 5-ft. Sq. Suckers. Cg6. Sd2. AN. Pl.43.

C. ARBOREA (Tree-like) Madeira, is the gem of the genus, and is popularly called the Lily-of-the-valley Tree, and is only hardy in very mild south-western districts, elsewhere it must grace the cold greenhouse. Its narrow, dark, shining, green leaves are accompanied in autumn by clustered sprays of open-mouthed Lily-of-the-valley flowers. *20-ft., August. E. ——— Cg6. Sd2. AN.*

CLETHRA (continued)

C. BARBINERVIS (With bearded fibre) Japan, is not so tall as C. alnifolia, but is more diffuse ; is not so hardy, but has larger leaves ; has more compact flower clusters, but has slightly smaller flowers.
6-ft., August. D. 6-ft. Sq. Suckers. Cg6. Sd2. AN.

C. DELAVAYI (Comm.) China, is a deciduous shrub—more probably a tree—which should be in every garden in which it proves hardy, perhaps in the south-west and west, for it has attractive, dark green, deeply veined, serrated leaves, and bears horizontal sprays of sweetly scented Lily-of-the-valley flowers, open at the mouth.
—— August. D. ———— Sd2. Cg5. AN.

C. TOMENTOSA (Covered with short, dense hair) Eastern N. America, is more grey in its young growth than C. alnifolia, but is otherwise very similar. *8-ft., August. E. 5-ft. Sq. Suckers. Cg6. Sd2.*

COLLETIA (RHAMNACEAE) (COMPRISES TWO CULTIVATED SHRUBS NAMED IN HONOUR OF M. P. COLLET, A FRENCH BOTANIST).

They are peculiar in that they are made up of grey-green branches, fleshy and round or triangular in sections, and needle-like or triangular in shape. The leaves, of which very few are generally produced, are almost insignificant. Both plants need sunny, warm sites.

C. ARMATA (Armed with thorns) Chile, makes a ferociously spined shrub which bears hawthorn scented flowers a little smaller in size than those of the Lily of the valley, but similar in shape and colour.
8-ft., October. D. 8-ft. Sq. Cg5. ANC.

C. CRUCIATA (Cross-shaped) Uruguay, has an even more frightening appearance, the spiny branches here are composed of triangular, sharply pointed protuberances with the occasional appearance of rounded spines in addition. The flowers, which are creamy-white in colour, are similar in shape.
8-ft., September-October. D. 8-ft. Sq. Cg5. ANC.

COLQUHOUNIA (LABIATAE) (NAMED IN HONOUR OF SIR ROBERT COLQUHOUN, A ONE-TIME PATRON OF THE BOTANIC GARDEN, CALCUTTA).

A shrub of loose growth, fitted by this circumstance for, and needing for its protection, the shelter of a south wall.

C. COCCINEA (Scarlet) Nepal, has squarish stems, rather woolly in texture, leaves of variable size, but generally heart-shaped, large and woolly, green above and white felted beneath, with a pleasant odour when crushed. The long sprays of flowers, which are typically those of a Labiate, are heavily felted, and the individual flowers of bright orange-scarlet are yellow within.
6-ft., August-October. D. 8-ft.–10-ft. Cg5. AN. Pl.23.

COLUTEA (LEGUMINOSAE) (THE DERIVATION IS OBSCURE BUT IS BELIEVED TO BE FROM THE GREEK NAME FOR A PLANT NOT NOW KNOWN).

A group of shrubs with pinnate leaves, and pea-shaped flowers, generally yellow, which are suitable for any poor soil, and producing flowered racemes followed by bladder-like pods, which, when sharply pressed, give rise to a good report pleasing to children of all ages, and deserved by the plant.

C. ARBORESCENS (Like a tree) S. Europe, is said to populate the slopes of Vesuvius, and is a vigorous, bushy shrub which produces its clusters of yellow pea-flowers in the leaf axils from June until the end of the year, and is an easily grown but quite attractive large shrub. *12-ft., June-October. D. 9-ft. Sq. Sd2. ANC.*

C. ARBORESCENS VAR. BULLATA (Puckered) is a dense, dwarf form with crinkled leaves, adding daintiness to other virtues.
4-ft., June-October. D. 6-ft. Sq. Ch8. ANC.

C. ISTRIA (Istrian) Asia Minor, is another attractive dwarf with coppery-yellow flowers and small, neat leaves.
3-ft., May-September. D. 4-ft. Sq. Sd10. ANC.

C. MEDIA (Medium). Hybrid origin, is a hybrid between C. arborescens and C. orientalis, often known as C. purpurea, and similar to C. arborescens but with bronzy-yellow flowers.
12-ft., June-October. D. 9-ft. Sq. Ch8. ANC.

C. ORIENTALIS (Eastern) E. Europe, has foliage of grey-green and has small copper-coloured flowers in small groups of from two to five flowers. *6-ft., June-September. D. 6-ft. Sq. Sd2. ANC.*

COMPTONIA (MYRICACEAE) (THE NAME IS COMMEMORATIVE OF HENRY COMPTON, A SEVENTEENTH-CENTURY BISHOP OF LONDON, AND BOTANIST).

The one species is sometimes regarded as part of the genus MYRICA, but differs by being seldom unisexual.

C. ASPLENIFOLIA (With leaves like Asplenium) has dark green leaves, resembling those of Asplenium trichomanes, and bears cylindroid male catkins and spherical female ones. The attractively cut leaves and pleasant bay scent make it a very pleasing shrub to grow in a peaty soil. *3-ft., April-May. D. 4-ft. Sd2. AN.*

CONVOLVULUS (CONVOLVULACEAE) (FROM LATIN CONVOLVO—TO ENTWINE; DECIDEDLY MISAPPLIED IN THE CASE OF THE FOLLOWING SHRUB).

C. CNEORUM (Meaning obscure) S. Europe, is a shining silvery-leaved bush with narrow, elliptical leaves, which bears clusters of pink buds which open to typical, white, trumpet-shaped flowers about the diameter of a penny, and requires a sheltered aspect.
1½-ft.–3-ft., June-September. E. 2½-ft.–4-ft. Sq. Cg6. N.

COPROSMA (RUBIACEAE) (FROM THE GR. KOPROS—DUNG; AND OSME—SMELL; FROM THE FACT THAT SOME OF THE SPECIES GIVE OFF A BAD SMELL).

COPROSMA (continued)

C. ACEROSA (Sharp) Australasia, is a dwarf-growing, evergreen shrub forming a mat of interknitting stems, and bearing unisexual, inconspicuous flowers, generally upon separate plants, the female flowers being followed by small, round, translucent, pale-blue berries, very attractive when grown in mild districts.

1-ft., ——— *E. 2-ft. Sq. Sd2. AN.*

C. PROPINQUA (Related) New Zealand, is similar to C. acerosa, but has shorter leaves, is taller in growth, and has dark blue-black berries. *1-ft.,* ——— *E. 2-ft. Sq. Sd2. AN.*

C. PETRIEI (Comm.) New Zealand, is a very small shrub forming a flat mat of dense stems, and small linear leaves edged and covered with short hair, the female flowers being followed by larger bluish-purple berries. *¼-ft.,* ——— *E. 1-ft. Sq. Sd2. AN.*

CORIARIA (CORIARIACEAE) (FROM THE LATIN CORIUM—LEATHER; PROBABLY FROM THE USE OF THE LEAVES OF C. MYRTIFOLIA FOR TANNING LEATHER).

Comprises a group of deciduous shrubs with handsome, deeply veined, green foliage, borne upon arching, annual stems, and with inconspicuous, green, five-petalled flowers, the female flowers in fruit being distinguished by the curiously inflated petals which swell and change colour, and appear as brightly coloured five-fold berries of exceptionally attractive appearance, but there is no definite confirmation of the fact that these berries are poisonous to human beings though a measure of care should be exercised in their consumption.

C. JAPONICA (Japanese) Japan, is a low-growing shrub with almost herbaceous stems with unisexual sprays of green flowers, produced two or three together from the axils of the year-old wood. The petals of the female flowers swell when the fruits are formed, and turn cherry-red and then black.

2-ft., May. D. 3-ft. Sq. Sd2. ANC.

C. TERMINALIS (Terminal flowering) China, differs from C. japonica in its nine-nerved leaves, and in the colour of its thickened fruits which may be black, red, or yellow. Treated as an herbaceous plant, and planted in a warm spot, it almost always fruits reasonably well in a hot, dry season. The yellow-petalled form is known as C. terminalis var. xanthocarpa.

2-ft., May. D. 4-ft. Sq. Sd2. Suckers. 3. ANC. Pl.22.

CORNUS (CORNACEAE) (FROM THE LATIN CORNU—A HORN; FROM THE HORNY OR HARD WOOD).

The Cornels may be grown for a variety of reasons, among which may be given the following: the colour of the stems as in C. alba, for beauty of habit as in C. Hessei, for the beauty of the flower as in C. Mas, or for the colour of the leaf as in C. alba sibirica var. variegata.

C. ALBA (White) N. Asia, is a deciduous, rampant shrub, making a thicket of stems which turn a brilliant red in autumn and winter,

Cydonia japonica
BCDEFJKNOR

Cydonia Lagenaria fl. pl.
GHLMPQ

Cydonia Lagenaria Knaphill Scarlet
PSTU

Cytisus Battandieri

and is fitted for massing in isolation where, in a moist position, the red colour of its stems may be duly appreciated. To encourage the growth of the attractively coloured young wood C. alba and its varieties, except the first, should be cut back in the spring.

8-ft., June. D. 12-ft. Sq. C11. ANC.

The following varieties have all attractive variations from the species :—

C. ALBA VAR. ATROSANGUINEA—is much more dwarf, is less rampant, and has deeper red stems.

C. „ VAR. GOUCHAULTII—is variegated with gold and rose.

C. „ SIBIRICA—is a crimson-barked variety.

C. „ SIBIRICA VAR. VARIEGATA—has leaves irregularly mottled and edged with silver.

C. „ VAR. SPAETHII—has golden variegated leaves and red bark in winter.

C. „ VARIEGATA—has leaves of greyish-green with a narrow white margin.

C. AMOMUM (Resembling Cardamon) Eastern N. America, is deciduous, compact, and has purplish stems, small yellowish-white flowers, and small, pea-like, pale-blue fruits.

8-ft., June. D. 8-ft. Sq. Cg11. ANC.

C. CANDIDISSIMA (Very white) N. America, is another deciduous shrub, generally much branched, with dull, grey-green, long, slender leaves and with large clusters of short-stemmed white flowers in great profusion. *10-ft., June-July. D. 10-ft. Sq. Cg11. ANC.*

C. HESSEI (Comm.) Origin unknown, is a very dwarf, slow-growing variety with dark-green, narrow leaves, much crowded with small clusters of pinkish-white flowers, and is so restrained a representative of an otherwise exuberant family as to be especially noteworthy.

2-ft., June. D. 3-ft. Sq. Cg11. ANC.

C. KOUSA (A Japanese name) Japan. This small tree of bushy habit owes its excellence to the fact that the insignificant flower clusters are surrounded by four large, creamy-white bracts, and to the beautiful colour the leaves assume before they fall in the autumn.

12-ft.–20-ft., May. D. 12-ft.–20-ft. Sq. Sd2. AN.

C. MAS (Probably contraction of Mascula) S.W. Europe, a small, or more generally a multiple-stemmed shrub up to fifteen feet in height, known as the Cornelian Cherry, which bears upon its bare branches, in February, short-stemmed clusters of small yellow flowers, the petals of which turn back to resemble a yellow-flowered Ceanothus. The flowers are followed by large, red, cherry-like fruits which flatter only to deceive, since only birds appreciate their flavour. The other varieties are :—

C. MAS VAR. AUREA—with foliage flushed with gold.

C. „ „ AUREA ELEGANTISSIMA—has similar foliage tinted with pink.

C. „ „ VARIEGATA—is variegated with silver.

20-ft., February. D. 10-ft.–15-ft. Sq. Sd10. ANC.

12

CORNUS (continued)

C. Nuttallii (Comm.) N. America, is a tree-like Dogwood, in nature reaching seventy-five feet, but seldom represented in this country by anything in excess of fifteen feet, and owing its not inconsiderable beauty to the bracts, numbering from four to eight, which surround the small flower clusters, and the excellence of its autumn colour. The bracts, which develop during May, are at first creamy-white but persist and turn pink with age. Young plants are best transplanted from pots. ——— *May.* ——— *D. Sd10. ANC.*

C. paucinervis (Few veined) China, is a dwarf, rather slow-growing shrub with pointed, narrow, elliptical leaves and small, clustered, white flowers produced in July and August and followed by small, rounded, black berries.
6-ft., July-August. D. 8-ft. Sq. Sd10. ANC.

C. stolonifera flaviramea (Bearing suckers; yellow branched) is effective as a contrast to the red-stemmed varieties, having smooth, shiny bark of bright-yellow. Should be cut back as for C. alba.
8-ft., July. D. 8-ft. Sq. Cg11. ANC.

COROKIA (Cornaceae) (derives its name from the Maori name korokia).

A group of rather angular shrubs, usually with a quaint appearance, small, evergreen leaves, and yellow flowers followed by berries.

C. Cotoneaster (Resembling Cotoneaster) New Zealand, is a very slow-growing, small tree, reaching six feet after many years, with angular branches, small dark green leaves, spathulate at the tips, and dotted in May with five-petalled, starry flowers of bright yellow, which are succeeded by bright red berries.
6-ft., May. E. 3-ft. Sq. Ch7. A.

C. virgata (Composed of willowy twigs) New Zealand, has larger leaves of grey-green, silvery upon the underside, and bears yellow, starry flowers a little larger, which are succeeded by orange-yellow berries. *6-ft., May. E. 3-ft. Sq. Ch7. A.*

CORONILLA (Leguminosae) (from Latin corona—a crown; hence a little crown, a reference to the crown-like appearance of the flower clusters).

C. Emerus (Old generic name; cultivated) Central and Southern Europe, is very hardy and tractable, growing well in almost any soil. The bright green, seven-parted, pinnate leaves are a fine setting for the yellow pea-flowers which are marked with a brown stripe, and are produced from the leaf axils in groups of three or less. Against a wall the shrub will reach a height of nine feet, but in the open is more generally less than five feet in height. As if to add full measure it flowers twice a year, from April to May and again in September to October.
9-ft., April-May. September-October. D. 6-ft. Sq. Ch7. ANC.

C. GLAUCA (Sea-blue) S. Europe, has pinnate, grey-green leaves, and makes a dense bush which bears small heads of butter-yellow pea flowers from June throughout the winter if given the sheltered, warm position it requires, and is not too ambitiously placed for slaughter by winter frosts and early morning thaws.

3-ft., June-December. E. 3-ft. Sq. Ch7. ANC. Shelter.

CORREA (RUTACEAE) (FROM CORREA, THE NAME OF A PORTUGUESE BOTANIST).

A group of shrubs only possible for those in southern and western districts, and liable even then to suffer from "the slings and arrows of outrageous fortune," but well worth experimenting with against a sheltered wall.

C. ALBA (White) Australia, has scurfy, wide, elliptical, green leaves, white beneath, and produces attractive, tubular, white flowers, half an inch long, in April continuing until June.

4-ft., April-June. E. 4-ft. Sq. Cg7. AN. Shelter.

C. HARRISII (Comm.) Hybrid origin, is even less robust, but has flowers of dark crimson.

3-ft., April-June. E. 3-ft. Sq. Cg7. AN. Shelter.

C. MAGNIFICA (Magnificent) Australia, is also C. speciosa and C. virens, and the strongest and most virile of the species, with green, ovate to lanceolate leaves, and hanging, tubular flowers about an inch or more in length, primrose-yellow within and green without, produced for over six months each year.

8-ft., March-September. E. ——— Cg7. AN. Shelter.

CORYLOPSIS (HAMAMELIDACEAE) (FROM LATIN CORYLUS, *q.v.*; AND OPSIS—A RESEMBLANCE; FROM THE RESEMBLANCE OF THE LEAVES TO THE HAZEL).

All the varieties are hardy, and welcome good, rich soil, though they are not difficult to grow. All have scented flowers of various shades of yellow offset by flower bracts of pale green, produced before the leaves. Layering should be done in early spring, and cuttings should consist of short side shoots. The general picture presented is that of paler, smaller-flowered and more gracefully disposed Forsythias.

C. GLABRESCENS (Becoming nearly hairless) Japan, is also C. Gotoana, is a comparatively rare species said to reach twenty feet in height, but less in cultivation, with almost round, strongly veined leaves about three inches in diameter, with drooping one-inch sprays of yellow, cowslip-like flowers.

12-ft., March-April. D. 10-ft. Sq. Ch7. L3. ANC.

C. PAUCIFLORA (Few-flowered) Japan, is a small shrub, rounded and dense, with many twig-like branches with drooping sprays of two to three sweetly scented, primrose-yellow flowers breaking in great profusion from creamy-green bracts.

4-ft., March. D. 3-ft. Sq. Ch7. L3. ANC. Pl.24.

CORYLOPSIS (continued)

C. PLATYPETALA (Wide-petalled) China, has wider-tipped, five-petalled, scented, yellow flowers than most species, borne in larger clusters, and its rounded green leaves turn bright-yellow in autumn. Its habit is more open than the preceding.

6-*ft.*, *March.* *D.* 6-*ft. Sq.* *Ch*7. *L*3. *ANC.*

C. SINENSIS (Chinese) W. China, is a small tree, often over ten feet in height, with large, somewhat oblong, green leaves, grey-green beneath, bearing before their full development larger sprays of small, sweetly scented, primrose-yellow flowers.

12-*ft.*, *March-April.* *D.* 10-*ft. Sq.* *Ch*7. *L*3. *ANC.*

C. SPICATA (Spiked) Japan, is a spreading shrub with heart-shaped, hazel-like leaves about four inches in length, producing its one-and-

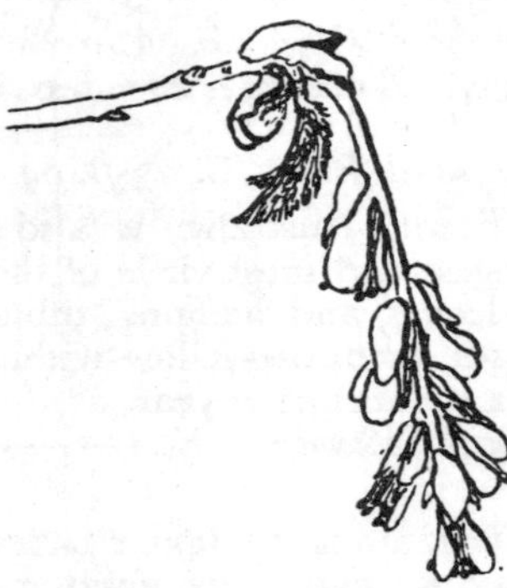

CORYLOPSIS SINENSIS

a-half-inch sprays of pale-yellow, cowslip-scented flowers in February and March, and assuming a bold yellow colour in autumn.

6-*ft.*, *February-March.* *D.* 7-*ft. Sq.* *Ch*7. *L*3. *ANC.*

C. VEITCHIANA (Comm.) China, has large, rounded, coppery-green leaves, grey-green upon the underside; strong, bold branches and two-inch long racemes of scented, primrose-yellow flowers with red-brown anthers, and is of bushy growth.

6-*ft.*, *March-April.* *D.* 7-*ft. Sq.* *Ch*7. *L*3. *ANC.*

C. WILLMOTTIAE (Comm.) China, is one of the quicker growing of the species, with the added joy of having still longer hanging sprays of yellowish-green flowers.

9-*ft.*, *March-April.* *D.* 8-*ft. Sq.* *Ch*7. *L*3. *ANC.*

C. WILSONII (Comm.) China, is an erect-growing, tree-like shrub with widely oval leaves, with very long racemes of primrose-yellow flowers produced before the leaves.

10-*ft.*, *March-April.* *D.* 8-*ft. Sq.* *Ch*7. *ANC.*

CORYLUS (BETULACEAE) (FROM THE GR. KARYON—A NUT).

The following species has a decidedly ornamental value, and is easily grown in any good garden soil.

C. MAXIMA PURPUREA (Large; purple) Europe, W. Asia, rivals the Copper Beech in the intensity of its coppery-purple leaves, and excels it in its vigour.
15-ft.–20-ft., —— *D.* *16-ft.–25-ft. Sq.* *Suckers.* *ANC.*

COTONEASTER (ROSACEAE) (POSSIBLY DERIVED FROM THE GR. KOTONEON—QUINCE; AND ISTES—ASSOCIATED WITH; FROM THE RESEMBLANCE OF THE SPECIES).

Cotoneasters are accommodating shrubs which will do well in any soil in sun or shade, and are particularly useful for planting under trees, upon north walls, or dry or wet banks. The small, five-petalled flowers are either white or tinted with pink, and are followed by attractive red, yellow, or black berries which persist for a long period into the winter. Related to CRATAEGUS and PYRACANTHA, the Cotoneaster differs in being spineless, but provides many a garden with the backbone of its winter colour. There are both evergreen and deciduous species. Species may be reproduced from cuttings of the current year's wood about four to six inches in length. Seeds should be sown as soon as gathered, and wintered in the open.

C. ACUMINATA (Long pointed) Himalayas, has large, oval to lanceolate leaves two-and-a-half inches long, is upright in its habit, bears large, bright-red berries in groups of from two to five, and becomes attractively coloured in autumn before it drops its leaves.
10-ft., June. *D.* *8-ft. Sq.* *Sd12.* *Cg8.* *ANC.*

C. ADPRESSA (Pressed against) China, has small, bright-green leaves with wavy edges, is very close growing, and has pinkish-white flowers followed by bright red berries in ones or twos. The foliage colours brightly in autumn before falling.
1-ft., June. *D.* *3-ft. Sq.* *Sd12.* *Ch6.* *ANC.*

C. AFFINIS (Related to) Himalayas, is related to C. acuminata and C. bacillaris, is very vigorous and has long green leaves, grey beneath, and bears large clusters of small white flowers, followed by brownish-black berries.
15-ft., June. *D.* *10-ft.–15-ft. Sq.* *Sd12.* *Cg8.* *ANC.*

C. AMBIGUA (Doubtful) W. China, is a small shrub seldom exceeding four feet in height, with diamond-shaped leaves up to two inches in length, with clusters of from five to ten pinkish flowers followed by black fruits. *4-ft., June.* *D.* *4-ft. Sq.* *Sd12.* *Cg8.* *ANC.*

C. AMOENA (Lovely) Yunnan, is a neat and tidy small shrub with half-inch-long greyish leaves, with clusters of pinkish-white flowers of from six to ten, followed by bright orange-red berries.
3-ft., June. *E.* *4-ft. Sq.* *Sd12.* *Cg8.* *ANC.*

C. APICULATA (With pointed ends) W. China, has six-foot arching branches, small rounded leaves, generally sharply pointed at the apex, and bears small white flowers followed by bright red berries in great profusion, and is one of the most pleasing of the smaller varieties. *6-ft., June. D. 8-ft. Sq. Sd12. Cg8. ANC.*

C. BACILLARIS (In small rods) Himalayas, is sometimes known as C. affinis var. bacillaris, and is a vigorous shrub with large oval leaves, and small white flowers produced in many flowered clusters, which are followed by large clusters of blackish-brown berries. *15-ft., June. D. 10-ft.–15-ft. Sq. Sd12. Cg8. ANC.*

C. BULLATA (Puckered or wrinkled) W. China, is one of the outstanding varieties of the genus, its long rugged leaves vying in colour with the bright-red, cherry-like fruits, which are borne in clusters of from three to seven following the fall of the pinkish-white petals, and it is regrettable that one must chronicle that C. bullata var. floribunda has more flowers in each cluster and consequently more crimson berries to intermingle with its scarlet leaves in autumn. *6-ft., June. D. 8-ft.–10-ft. Sq. Sd12. Cg8. ANC.*

C. BUXIFOLIA (Box-leaved) Himalayas, has the pleasing habit of producing the largest fruits of any variety in the genus, and has small, round, shining green leaves with dense, hairy covering beneath, and groups of two to six white flowers. Its habit is somewhat rambling, but the intense scarlet berries are a measure of compensation. C. buxifolia var. vellaea is smaller in all its details. *8-ft., June. E. 12-ft. Sq. Sd12. Cg8. ANC.*

C. CONGESTA (Crowded) Himalayas, is also known as C. microphylla var. glacialis, and is a creeping shrub of crowded habit with small shining leaves and small pink flowers, followed by berries of sealing-wax-red. C. congesta var. procumbens is more dwarf and slower growing. *1½-ft., June. E. 3-ft. Sq. Sd12. Ch8. ANC.*

C. CONSPICUA (Remarkable) Tibet, is a more recently introduced species with branches clad with small, deep green, rounded leaves, and tight growth, threaded in winter with bright orange-red berries along the branches. *4-ft., June. E. 5-ft. Sq. Sd12. Cg8. ANC.*

C. DAMMERI (Comm.) Central China, is also C. humifusa, and gives rise to long, slender strands, closely interknit, clothed with small, oval, dark shining green leaves, with white flowers singly borne, followed by bright-red, bead-like fruits, and will sit so tightly upon a rock as to become a part of it. C. Dammeri var. radicans has smaller leaves and adds variety by producing some of its flowers in pairs. *½-ft., June. E. 5-ft. Sq. Sd12. Ch6. ANC.*

C. DIELSIANA (Comm.) China, is also called C. applanata, and has long, arching sprays with green leaves, felted below, small pinkish flowers in clusters of from three to seven, followed by clusters of bright-scarlet berries placed along the branches with mathematical precision. C. Dielsiana var. elegans has smaller leaves, almost evergreen, on thinner stems and is quite distinct, though no better. *10-ft., June. D. 10-ft. Sq. Sd12. Ch6. ANC.*

C. DIVARICATA (Spreading widely apart) W. China, is aptly named, for its graceful, diffuse habit is one of its greatest charms, which, when added to the glorious scarlet hues which autumn brings to its small, green, polished leaves, interspersed with its trios of bright red fruits, may well be said to put it among the best.

6-*ft.*, *June*. *D*. 8-*ft. Sq*. *Sd*.12. *Cg*8. *ANC*.

C. FOVEOLATA (Having small depressions) China, has long, dull-green leaves with distinct deep veins, clusters of from three to six flowers followed by red fruits turning black, with the leaves brightening to scarlet in late autumn.

12-*ft.*, *June*. *D*. 12-*ft. Sq*. *Sd*2. *Cg*6. *ANC*.

C. FRANCHETII (Comm.) Yunnan, makes a rounded bush with silvery-grey leaves on gracefully arching branches, has small, pinkish-white flowers in groups of seven to eleven followed by pear-shaped, orange-scarlet fruits, and is among the best.

10-*ft.*, *June*. *E*. 12-*ft. Sq*. *Sd*2. *Cg*6. *ANC*.

C. FRIGIDA (Frosty) Himalayas, is an attractive, quick-growing semi-evergreen, grand for screening and with masses of large, bright crimson fruits, persisting in spite of the birds through much of the winter. C. frigida var. fructu-luteo varies the monotony by having yellow fruits, and C. frigida var. Vicarii has larger leaves and red berries which are more attractive to human eyes than to those of the birds.

15-*ft.*–24-*ft.*, *June*. *D*. 15-*ft.*–20-*ft. Sq*. *Sd*2. *Cg*6. *ANC*.

C. GLABRATA (Hairless) W. China, has large glaucous leaves like those of C. frigida, but almost hairless beneath, and makes an outstanding and quickly established tree, bearing dense clusters of small white flowers, developing into orange-scarlet fruits accompanied by brilliantly coloured foliage.

15-*ft.*, *June*. *E*. 15-*ft. Sq*. *Sd*2. *Cg*6. *ANC*.

C. GLAUCOPHYLLA (With grey-blue leaves) China, has leaves which are blue-grey on the underside, has scented flowers, is late to flower and to produce its berries of bright orange-red, and if berried beauty is the standard by which one should judge, this ranks among the very best and has other attractions similarly unhidden.

9-*ft.*, *July*. *E*. 9-*ft. Sq*. *Sd*2. *Cg*6. *ANC*.

C. HARROVIANA (Comm.) China, is outstanding in flower, the symmetrically disposed, tightly packed clusters of white flowers are followed by bright red berries on pyramidal bushes of gracefully arching, red stems with persistent, long, evergreen leaves.

10-*ft.*, *June*. *E*. 9-*ft. Sq*. *Sd*2. *Cg*6. *ANC*.

C. HEBEPHYLLA (With leaves resembling Hebe) China, is a most gracefully disposed shrub with arching branches, small, grey-green, oval leaves, with white flowers from six to sixteen in a group, followed by dull-red, hawthorn-like fruits.

10-*ft.*, *June*. *D*. 10-*ft. Sq*. *Sd*2. *Cg*6. *ANC*.

C. HENRYANA (Comm.) China, has long, narrow, oval, dark-green leaves, very grey beneath, on open, horizontally produced branches, pendent at the tips, and loose sprays of small white flowers followed by crimson-brown fruits. The large leaves turn bronze-red in mid-winter. *12-ft., June. E. 15-ft. Sq. Sd2. Cg6. ANC.*

C. HORIZONTALIS (Horizontal) Himalayas to China, is also C. Davidiana, spreading with fan-like branches on an horizontal plane, and is the complete maid-of-all-work, for covering up unsightly banks and siting in positions where little else will grow. The attractive autumn colours of the small leaves, the cheerfulness of the bright red, openly spaced berries all add to its attractions. Common maybe, but certainly not vulgar! C. horizontalis var. perpusilla is decidedly more aristocratic, has smaller leaves, spineless, is much slower in growth, and is much too good to use to hide a bank, even if it would! C. horizontalis var. variegata hovers between the two in its speed of growth, and its prettily silvered leaves are pleasantly enlivened with touches of pale-green and pink, but it usually drops its berries quite quickly as if to assert that beauty should not be expected to carry so heavy a burden.
Type: 1½-ft., June. D. 8-ft. Sq. Ch6. ANC.

C. HUPEHENSIS (From Hupeh) has arching branches, pendent at the tips, green leaves, grey beneath, white flowers in clusters of from six to twelve, followed in due season by large, shining, red berries.
7-ft., June. D. 8-ft. Sq. Ch6. ANC.

C. LACTEA (Milky) China, is in the style of C. Harroviana, with tightly packed, two-inch clusters of white flowers, long, evergreen leaves, milky-white beneath, and magnificent clusters of brilliant red fruits three times as wide as the flower clusters.
15-ft., June. D. 10-ft. Sq. Ch8. ANC.

C. LUCIDA (Shining) Siberia, is dwarf and compact, has dark, shining green leaves which assume beautiful colours in autumn, and pale-pink flowers in groups of from three to eight, which turn to shining black berries. C. lucida is also C. sinensis and C. acutifolia.
6-ft., June. D. 6-ft. Sq. Ch8. ANC.

C. MELANOCARPA (Bearing black fruits) Siberia, has dark green leaves, white beneath, pink flowers in the normal groups followed by black berries. C. melanocarpa var. laxiflora has larger leaves and larger groups of flowers. *6-ft., June. D. 8-ft. Sq. Ch8. ANC.*

C. MICROPHYLLA (Small-leaved) Himalayas, is very well known as a wall shrub, and has small, shiny, green leaves, is of upright growth and bears solitary coral-red berries with a distinct bloom. It can be made to run and root if its branches are pegged down, and thus treated is a magnificent shrub for covering banks.
3-ft., June. E. 8-ft. Sq. Sd12. Ch6. ANC.

C. MICROPHYLLA VAR. COCHLEATA (Snail-shaped) Hybrid of garden origin, raised at the Cambridge Botanic Gardens, is an excellent variety, hugging the ground closely, and a magnificent picture in the autumn when the large carmine berries are set in the dark-green, shining carpet. *½-ft., June. E. 8-ft. Sq. Cg8. ANC.*

Cytisus Cornish Cream
ABCDEFJKNO

Cytisus albus
DGHLMPQ

Daphne Somerset
ABEFJLO

Daphne collina var. neapolitana
CDGHMQ

C. MICROPHYLLA VAR. THYMIFOLIA (Thyme-leaved) is a dwarf, very compact variety with tiny, glossy green leaves, and at the correct season these are accompanied by cerise-red berries with a bluish bloom. *1½-ft., June. E. 3-ft. Sq. Ch6. ANC.*

C. MOUPINENSIS (Of Moupine) China, is an erect-growing species with large leaves less than half as wide, bears clusters of many small, almost inconspicuous flowers followed by black berries, and for garden purposes may be dismissed as just another variety.
12-ft., June. D. 15-ft. Sq. Sd12. Ch6. ANC.

C. MULTIFLORA (Many-flowered) W. China, is also C. reflexa, a delightful shrub with whip-like reflexed branches with distinctive charm of outline, and oval leaves wreathed with open clusters of white flowers reminiscent of the Hawthorn, followed by round red fruits. C. multiflora var. calocarpa has larger leaves and berries.
12-ft., June. D. 15-ft. Sq. Sd12. Ch6. ANC.

C. NITENS (Shining) W. China, grows to a small bush of pleasing outline, wearing small, dark-green, shining leaves, the perfect foil for the clusters of three small, pink flowers, which are superseded by purplish-black fruits. The leaves assume bright scarlet tones before they eventually fall. *6-ft., June. D. 8-ft. Sq. Sd12. Ch6. ANC.*

C. OBSCURA (Dull) China, is a diffuse variety with large, diamond-shaped, green leaves, heavily felted beneath, and short-stemmed clusters of from three to seven pinky-white flowers, replaced in time by small, pear-shaped, dull-red fruits. The attractive orange and red tints of the autumn foliage make it a worth-while species.
10-ft., June. D. 15-ft. Sq. Sd12. Cg6. ANC.

C. PANNOSA (Woolly) S.W. China, is a charming species with its arching red branches and small, oval, green leaves, woolly white below, and clustered white flowers in groups of from six to twenty, which are followed by dark red berries.
10-ft., June-July. E. 12-ft. Sq. Sd12. Cg6. ANC.

C. RACEMIFLORA VAR. MICROCARPA (Flowering in clusters; small-fruited) Himalayas, is of semi-weeping habit similar to C. multiflora, and has small leaves up to one inch in length or a little larger, white flowers in clusters of from three to twelve, followed by long, narrow, red berries. C. racemiflora var. songarica has leaves which are less grey. *8-ft., June. D. 10-ft. Sq. Sd12. Cg8. ANC.*

C. RHYTIDOPHYLLA (With wrinkled leaves) grows upright, and has large, wrinkled, green leaves, yellowish-white beneath, some of which become coloured in autumn, and tight heads of small white flowers yielding place to small, pale-salmon berries.
8-ft., June. E. 8-ft. Sq. Sd12. Cg8. ANC.

C. ROTUNDIFOLIA (Round-leaved) Himalayas, is sometimes known as C. disticha, and C. Hookeri, is a grand semi-evergreen shrub with stiff, erect, branching habit, small leaves reminiscent of Box, and brilliant, shiny red fruits threaded singly upon the plant like beads in great profusion. The foliage colours well in autumn and its persistence throughout the winter is dependent upon weather conditions. *5-ft., June. D. 6-ft. Sq. Sd12. Cg8. ANC.*

COTONEASTER (continued)

C. SALICIFOLIA (Willow-leaved) China, has somewhat willow-like, long leaves of light green, rough and wrinkled above, woolly beneath, and its white flowers, borne in tight clusters, are followed by small orange-red berries. *12-ft., June. E. 15-ft. Sq. Sd12. Cg8. ANC.*

C. SALICIFOLIA VAR. FLOCCOSA (Fleecy) China, is not so tall but has narrower, shiny leaves, very woolly below, and is of very graceful habit. The branches become wreathed with clusters of small, round, red berries. C. salicifolia var. rugosa has wrinkled, coarser leaves, shiny above, and bears innumerable coral-red berries.
8-ft., June. E. 12-ft. Sq. Sd12. Cg8. ANC.

C. SEROTINA (Late in the year) W. China, is a very handsome shrub with long, evergreen leaves, wide trusses of small white flowers, and many orange-red berries in winter.
10-ft., July-August. E. 12-ft. Sq. Sd12. Cg8. ANC.

C. SIMONSII (Comm.) Himalayas, is a grand shrub for a hedge, with smallish, glossy green leaves, white beneath, and persistent in mild winters, when the brilliantly tinted leaves are accompanied by small groups of one to four orange-scarlet berries.
10-ft., June. D. 8-ft. Sq. Sd12. Cg8. ANC.

C. TOMENTOSA (Covered with short hair) Alps, has large, roundish leaves, heavily felted beneath with grey down, which become enlivened and brightened in autumn with gold, orange, and crimson, with bright red fruits.
6-ft., June. D. 6-ft. Sq. Sd10. Cg7. ANC.

C. TURBINATA (Inverted-cone-shaped) C. China, has medium size, green leaves, silkily grey-white upon the underside, and bears many-flowered clusters of white flowers, followed by pear-shaped, dark red fruits, and is a very pleasant shrub of conical habit.
6-ft., July. E. 6-ft. Sq. Sd12. Cg8. ANC.

C. WARDII (Comm.) Tibet, has handsome grey-green leaves, silvery below, turning orange-red in autumn, when the matching and contrasting colour of the berries make it an outstanding sight.
8-ft., June. E. 8-ft. Sq. Sd10. Cg8. ANC.

C. WATERERI (Comm.) Garden origin, is a hybrid between C. frigida and C. Henryana; is a quick-growing variety with many bright red berries in autumn. *20-ft., June. E. 18-ft. Sq. Cg8. ANC.*

C. ZABELII (Comm.) China, is a six-foot shrub with graceful weeping habit, pale grey-green leaves, creamy-grey beneath, with pale pinky-white flowers in clusters of from eight to nine. The ensuing berries are pear-shaped and reddish-purple.
6-ft., June. D. 8-ft. Sq. Cg8. Sd12. ANC.

CRINODENDRON (*see* TRICUSPIDARIA).

CYATHODES (EPACRIDACEAE) (FROM GR. KYATHOS—A CUP).

One shrub, suited to a sandy, peaty soil, and of dwarf habit and handsome appearance.

C. COLENSOI (Comm.) New Zealand, is an upright shrub whose chief beauty consists of its small, linear, silver or blue-grey leaves, pink at the tips of the branches, which are produced in compact array. The small, creamy-white flowers, produced in clusters of about half a dozen, are sweetly scented and are succeeded by rose-red berries.
1-ft., August. E. 1-ft. Sq. Ch7. A.

CYDONIA (ROSACEAE) (THE NAME IS DERIVED FROM THE OLD NAME FOR THE QUINCE WHICH GREW AT CYDON IN CRETE).

It is reputed to have been the forbidden fruit of the Bible, and to have been used in pagan wedding rites. The genus is an outstanding one for three reasons. Firstly because of the complete hardiness of the species, secondly for their ability to thrive in almost any soil, and finally for their own intrinsic beauty. Most varieties are suitable to grow against walls, either shaded or sunny, or in the open. The best method of propagation is from cuttings of the stem, which should be taken from side shoots, with a heel (with no exposed pith) and placed under a sunny light. The genus is not an isolated instance in the matter of its names, for it is also known as CHAENOMELES, and certain of its varieties as PYRUS japonica, or, more simply to the gardener, as the JAPONICA; but, to add still further to the confusion, CYDONIA japonica of gardens is now CYDONIA Lagenaria, and what was once CYDONIA Maulei is now named CYDONIA japonica. Under these circumstances it seems best to note that, while the generic name of CYDONIA has been retained, the name of the species given below is that at present correct, with the older and more generally known names quoted in the text for reference.

C. JAPONICA (Japanese) Japan, is the shrub known to most gardeners as C. Maulei, and makes a thick bush of rather thin branches with smaller and rounder green leaves than those of C. Lagenaria, and seldom exceeds three feet in height, and is of symmetrical growth. The five-petalled flowers are orange-red or orange-scarlet, about the size of a penny, produced in short-stemmed clusters of three or four, and are succeeded by rather larger yellow fruits with the characteristic scent of the Quince. The alpine variety, C. japonica var. Sargentii, shows no difference in cultivation.
3-ft., April-May. D. 8-ft. Sq. Ch7. ANC. Pls.25, 36, 76.

C. JAPONICA ALBA (White) varies only in its white flowers.

C. JAPONICA INCENDIE has orange flowers.

C. JAPONICA SIMONII is slower growing, not quite so tall, and has larger flowers of deep geranium-scarlet, and requires about half the space of the other species.

C. LAGENARIA (Like the Bottle Gourd) Japan, is the Japonica of gardens, is also Pyrus japonica, and was once called C. japonica; is a magnificent shrub for covering walls, and is decorated in early spring with larger flowers than those of the true C. japonica of bright red. Fruits greenish-yellow.
6-ft.–9-ft., March-April. D. Indefinite. Ch7. ANC.

CYDONIA (continued)

The following varieties are all excellent, varying in colour only, except where stated :—

APRICOT—Semi-double flowers of orange-red with dwarfer habit.

ATROPURPUREA—Single dark-crimson flowers are the feature of this slow-growing species.

AURORA—has rose flowers blended with orange, and is extra dwarf.

CARDINALIS—has cup-shaped flowers of salmon-red.

FLORE PLENO—has double rose-pink flowers. *Pl.*25.

KNAPHILL SCARLET—is dwarf and has brilliant orange-scarlet flowers of globular form. *Pl.*25.

MOERLOESII—has appleblossom-pink flowers.

NIVALIS—has pure white flowers.

RUBRA GRANDIFLORA—has large crimson flowers.

UMBILICATA—has flowers of bright-pink.

CYRILLA (CYRILLACEAE) (THE NAME IS DERIVED FROM THAT OF D. CIRILLO, AN ITALIAN BOTANIST).

The beauty of the one species which follows, and is the only one suitable for outdoor cultivation in the most favoured localities, is the autumn colour of the oblong, shiny green leaves.

C. RACEMIFLORA (Flowering in racemes) Southern U.S.A., is a handsome bush for the woodland, with racemes of white flowers resembling ITEA, and long, polished green leaves which turn crimson in autumn. *6-ft., September. D. 6-ft. Sq. Cg6. A.*

CYTISUS (LEGUMINOSAE) (FROM GR. KYTISOS—TREFOIL ; A REFERENCE TO THE TRIFOLIATE LEAVES OF SOME OF THE SPECIES).

The Brooms are essentially lovers of the sun and should be situated so that they obtain what they require. As a rule varieties which grow upon their own roots are the best for soils which are acid or neutral, but grafted plants on Laburnum stocks are probably better for calcareous soils. Pruning should be done with discretion immediately after flowering in order that they shall not become " leggy." Apart from grafting the most successful method of propagation is by stem cuttings. These should be made from the short side shoots with a heel of the old wood, inserted in sandy peat in July or August, placed in a close frame with a sunny exposure.

C. ALBUS (White) Spain, is the common White Spanish Broom, and is a delightful shrub with grey-green foliage, with wand-like sprays of small white flowers extending five or six feet in length. *8-ft., May. D. 12-ft. Sq. Ch7–8. AN. Pl.27.*

C. ALBUS VAR. DURUS (Hard) is more compact in habit and flowers later.

C. ALBUS VAR. INCARNATUS (Flesh-coloured) is similar to the type, but pleasantly flushed with pink.

C. Ardoinii (Comm.) S.E. France, is an exceptionally dwarf-growing Broom with a multiplicity of short upright branches, which become densely clad with small butter-yellow pea flowers.

½-ft., April-May. D. 1-ft. Sq. Ch6. N. 2.

C. austriacus (Austrian) S.E. Europe, is an upright shrub with inch-long leaflets and terminal clusters of bright-yellow flowers.

C. austriacus var. Heuffelii (Comm.) Hungary, is a low-growing shrub with trifoliate leaves, and terminal clusters of bright-yellow flowers, and seldom exceeds one foot in height or spreads over more than a square yard. *3-ft., July-August. D. 4-ft. Sq. Ch6. N.*

C. Battandieri (Comm.) Morocco, is an exceptionally beautiful, tall-growing variety with large, three-parted, silvery-grey leaves and white woolly stems, which terminate with tightly packed spires of golden-yellow, sweetly-scented flowers. It is magnificent as a small tree or planted against a wall.

15-ft., June-September. D. 15-ft. Sq. Ch6. Sd2. N. Pl.26.

C. Beanii (Comm.) Garden origin, is a hybrid of C. Ardoinii with C. purgans, and makes a pretty, symmetrical bush about a foot in height, with arching stems which bear many small golden-yellow flowers. *1-ft., April-May. D. 1½-ft. Sq. Ch6. N.* 3/1.

C. ciliatus (Fringed) E. Europe, resembles C. hirsutus, has hairy, trifoliate leaves, and bears its flowers of golden-yellow in the uppermost leaf axils. *2-ft., May. D. 3-ft. Sq. Ch7. N.* 3/1.

C. Dallimorei (Comm.) Garden origin, is a hybrid of C. albus with C. scoparius var. Andreanus, and is outstanding with its short heads of twiggy growths, which in May are congested with deep rose flowers flushed with claret.

C. Dorothy Walpole (Comm.) Garden hybrid, resembles C. Dallimorei, but is probably a better grower and has flowers of deep pink and shining crimson-maroon, and is of stiff habit. C. Burkwoodii is similar with an even deeper shade of colour, and is very hardy.

C. Enchantress (Garden hybrid) has flowers of two shades of rose-pink, and is bushy and of spreading habit.

C. Geoffrey Skipwith (Garden hybrid) has rose-purple wings and cerise-red keels, and is bushy with arching branches.

C. glabrescens (Becoming hairless) C. Europe, is a very low-growing shrub with sweetly scented, golden-yellow pea flowers produced upon short, stiff stems. *1-ft., May-June. D. 2-ft. Sq. Ch7. N.*

C. hirsutus (Hairy) S. Europe, is another dwarfish variety with three-parted, hairy leaves, and large, butter-yellow flowers produced from the uppermost leaf axils.

2-ft., May-June. D. 2-ft. Sq. Ch7. N.

C. hirsutus var. demissus (Hanging down) Greece, is a delightful prostrate-growing variety with trifoliate, grey, hairy leaves, and its almost stemless yellow flowers, which deepen to bronze, sit tightly upon the tuft. ½-*ft.*, *May-July*. *D*. *Indefinite*. *Ch7*. *Sd2*. *ANC*.

C. KEWENSIS (Of Kew) Garden origin, is a hybrid of C. Ardoinii with C. albus, and is a delightful trailing shrub with pale green, small leaves and long strands of sulphur-yellow flowers.
½-*ft.*, *May*. *D*. 3-*ft. Sq*. *Ch7*. *AN*. 64/3.

C. LADY MOORE (Garden hybrid) has yellow wings flushed with pink, with an orange keel, of loose and branching habit.

C. LEUCANTHUS (Bearing whitish flowers) S.E. Europe, is a dwarf spreading shrub with terminal clusters of pale cream flowers.
1-*ft.*, *June*. *D*. 4-*ft. Sq*. *Ch7*. *N*.

C. LORD LAMBOURNE (Garden hybrid) has sulphur-yellow wings flushed pink with maroon keel, and is of spreading and branching habit. 5-*ft.*, *May*. *D*. 6-*ft. Sq*. *Ch7*. *N*.

C. MONSPESSULANUS (From Montpellier) S. Europe, is a somewhat tender Broom of attractive habit with almost evergreen, three-parted leaves, and produces masses of bright yellow flowers in the spring and again in the autumn.
8-*ft.*, *May-September*. *D*. 10-*ft. Sq*. *Ch8*. *N*.

C. NIGRICANS (Becoming black) C. Europe, is also C. Carlieri, is a fine shrub for autumn colour, for it produces foot-long racemes in great quantities upon neat, bushy and compact bushes, and is a grand addition to the small garden.
4-*ft.*, *July-September*. *D*. 4-*ft. Sq*. *Ch8*. *N*. *Pl.40*.

C. OSBORNII (Comm.) Garden origin, resembles the better-known C. praecox with its bushy, arching habit, and bears its long sprays of canary-yellow flowers later.
6-*ft.*, *May-June*. *D*. 8-*ft. Sq*. *Ch8*. *N*.

C. PRAECOX (Appearing early) Garden origin, is a hybrid of C. purgans and C. albus, and is the well-known Warminster Broom, a gracefully habited, grey-green-leaved shrub, with arching sprays of sulphur-yellow flowers.

C. PRAECOX VAR. ALBUS (White) is stiffer in habit, a trifle dwarfer, and has clear white flowers. 6-*ft.*, *May*. *D*. 8-*ft. Sq*. *Ch8*. *N*.

C. PROCUMBENS (Trailing) S.E. Europe, makes a mat of interknitting branches, gradually adding height until about one foot is reached, and covered with clustered heads of bright-yellow flowers in May.
1-*ft.*, *May-June*. *D*. 3-*ft. Sq*. *Ch6*. *N2*.

C. PURGANS (Purgative) S.W. Europe, is one of the best known, but one of the most attractive of the species, with half-inch, narrow leaves, and masses of deep golden-yellow flowers borne in the leaf axils of the sturdy upright sprays. It sometimes produces other flowers in autumn. 3-*ft.*, *May-June*. *D*. 4-*ft. Sq*. *Ch8*. *N*.

C. PURPUREUS (Purple) E. Europe, has low, arching strands of green, woody stems clothed with three-parted green leaves, and becomes covered with very pretty pale-purple pea flowers. C. purpureus var. albus is similar in characteristics but has white flowers, and C. purpureus var. albo-carneus is more dwarf but even prettier with its long strands of bright-rose flowers.

2-ft., May-July. D. 3-ft. Sq. Ch8. N. 630/3.

C. SCOPARIUS (Brush-like) Europe, is the Common Yellow Broom and is a magnificent plant which would find a place in every garden if it were twice as rare.

C. SCOPARIUS ANDREANUS—is a sport found in Normandy with yellow and mahogany-red flowers.

C. „ DAISY HILL—is a combination of sulphur-yellow.

C. „ DRAGONFLY—has brownish-red flowers flushed with yellow.

C. „ FIREFLY—has fiery-red flowers flushed with gold.

C. „ FULGENS—has flowers of orange-yellow and crimson fading to crimson and dark-red.

C. „ MAYFLY—has flowers of yellow and buff.

C. „ SULPHUREUS—is pale sulphur-yellow.

C. „ SUNLIGHT—has large flowers of golden-yellow turning sulphur-yellow.

6-ft., May. D. 7-ft. Sq. Ch8. N.

C. SESSILIFOLIUS (With stalkless flowers) S. Europe, is a particularly graceful shrub with long, slender stems, bearing short sprays of bright yellow flowers at the tips of the laterals.

5-ft., June. D. 6-ft. Sq. Ch8. N.

C. VERSICOLOR (Changing colour) Garden origin, a hybrid of C. purpureus and C. hirsutus, is an attractive dwarf with flowers of pale buff-yellow shaded with pale-pink and mauve, and is pretty but not striking. *2-ft., May-June. D. 3-ft. Sq. Ch8. N.*

DABOECIA (ERICACEAE) (CALLED AFTER AN IRISH SAINT, ST. DABEOC).

A genus consisting only of two species which will only thrive in a peaty or lime-free soil. Propagation may be made of the species from seed, or of the varieties by cuttings of the tips of the side shoots placed in sandy peat, and kept close under a handlight. The species have wider foliage and larger bells than the Ericas to which they are related.

D. AZORICA (From the Azores) Azores, has small, rather wide, hairy, bronze-green leaves, and has ample oval bells of barbaric crimson held aloft upon long, reddish stems, often in excess of three inches in length. *⅔-ft., May-July. E. 1-ft. Sq. Cg6–8. AN.*

D. CANTABRICA (Cantabrian) S.W. Europe, is the D. polifolia (D. Don) of catalogues, and in the type has short, pointed, but wider leaves than Erica vagans, and has rounded, oval flowers of rose-purple held well above the foliage. D. cantabrica alba has similar white flowers. D. cantabrica bicolor has white flowers with red markings at the mouths. D. cantabrica globosa has wider habit and more round, pale purple flowers. D. cantabrica purpurea has dark-green foliage with crimson-purple flowers.

1½-ft., June-October. E. 1½-ft. Sq. Cg68. AN. Pl.12.

DALIBARDA (Rubiaceae) (from Dalibard, a French botanist).

D. repens (Creeping) N. America, is a prostrate, creeping bramble with quaintly shaped, scalloped and very rugose leaves, and which bears large, white, bramble flowers. The foliage assumes the most delightful tones of red and orange in autumn, and is splendid for covering shady banks. *¼-ft., May. D. 2-ft. Sq. Cg6. A.*

DAPHNE (Thymelaeaceae) (named after Daphne who, pursued by Apollo, was rescued by being turned into a spurge laurel —which was given the same name).

The Daphnes number among them the hardiest, the most beautiful, and the most perfectly perfumed inhabitants of the shrub borders, and at least one representative of the genus should be found in every garden. There is considerable variation among the species in height, habit, colour, and cultural needs. Propagation can be made of certain of the varieties in various ways, from seed, from cuttings of the stems, by graftage, by layering. It is essential that in the case of graftage suitable stocks are chosen, and, though in all cases Daphnes are more in character " on their own roots," one can thoroughly recommend seedling plants of D. acutiloba as a suitable stock for many of the more rare varieties, which grow but slowly if produced from cuttings. The Daphnes of European origin, in my own opinion and experience, thrive best in a mixture of peatmould (not peat) liberally laced with limestone chippings when grown upon their own roots, but, when grown upon stocks of C. acutiloba, flourish best upon a straightforward neutral soil.

D. acutiloba (With pointed lobes) W. China, has shiny, pointed, narrow leaves, and bears terminal clusters of from five to seven scentless, white, sharply pointed petalled flowers, followed by large, shiny, scarlet berries, each containing one seed.

4-ft.–5-ft., June-August. E. 6-ft. Sq. Sd2. AN.

D. alpina (Alpine) S. Europe, is deciduous, with spathulate, lanceolate, grey-green leaves, and seldom exceeding a foot in height, bears clusters of up to ten sweetly scented, white flowers, succeeded by orange-red fruits. *1-ft., May-June. D. 1-ft. Sq. Sd2. C.*

D. arbuscula (A small tree) Hungary, is a dwarf, woody shrub of rounded habit, generally upon more than a single stem, with polished, green, grooved leaves and clusters of attractive, sweetly scented, rose-pink flowers.

½-ft., May-June. E. 1-ft. Sq. Ch6. D3. C. See above.

Daphne Mezereum **ABCDEFGHJKMNOQ**

Daphne Mezereum var alba
LP

30

Desfontainea spinosa

D. **Blagayana** (Comm.) S.E. Europe, may be said to fan out bare, woody stems in all directions, clothed at the tips with rosettes of polished, oval, bright-green leaves, in which are borne the clusters of creamy-white flowers which diffuse the most fascinating fragrance characteristic of the genus. Propagation consists of holding the stems down with a piece of rock, and covering with light leafy soil containing limestone, when at a later stage the rooted runners may be detached. *¾-ft., March-April. E. 3-ft. Sq. D8. A or C.* *See p.* 96.

D. **Burkwoodii** (Comm.) Garden hybrid, is of the parentage D. Cneorum × D. caucasica, is a free-growing species with narrowly oval, pointed, bright-green leaves, and forms a symmetrical bush which becomes covered in May with sweetly scented, flesh-pink flowers produced in tight clusters, and fading to white with age. There is little difference between this and D. Somerset.

3-ft., May-June. E. 4-ft. Sq. Ch7. N. 627/3.

D. **caucasica** (Caucasian) Caucasus, has sophisticated beauty rather than commonplace prettiness. The woody stems are heavily clothed for the top three-quarters of their length with long, narrow, pale-green leaves, and the white, scented flowers are produced at the ends of the previous year's growth.

3-ft.–4-ft., May-June. D. 3-ft. Sq. Ch7. N.

D. **Cneorum** (Origin obscure) C. and S. Europe, makes a mat of neat stems, well clothed with long, narrow, bright-green leaves of symmetrical distribution round the stems, and covers itself in May, at the tips of the shoots, with bright-red buds which open into starry-mouthed, tubular, rose-pink flowers of waxy texture. The rules for its successful culture seem to be to plant it in a mixture of loam, leafmould, and limestone in equal quantities, with its roots in the shade and its head in the sun, and to cover the total growth to a half of its height each year with the same mixture. D. Cneorum var. alba is a little more diffuse and of less height, and bears clear white flowers which are just as attractive. D. Cneorum var. eximia (Of great size—beauty) has large foliage of more glaucous green, has stronger stems, is redder in the bud, larger in the flower and deeper in colour, and, for all who prefer these perfections, is a shrub much to be desired. D. Cneorum var. Verlotii is a variety narrower in leaf and deeper in colour, and considerably more rare.

1-ft., May-June. E. 2-ft. Sq. Cg6. C. 24/2.

D. **collina** (Of the hills) S. Italy, is one of the outstanding Daphnes, has narrowly oval, deep-green leaves, overlaid with short, light brown hair, and bears exquisitely scented lilac, rose-pink flowers in groups of about a dozen, and is the D. sericea of some catalogues.

1-ft., May-June. E. 1½-ft. Sq. Cg6. C. *See p.* 96. 2.

D. **collina var. neapolitana** (Neapolitan) Italy, is sometimes the D. sericea of catalogues and generally D. Fioniana. It is later than D. collina, has deep-green leaves, grey or light-brown beneath, and bears clusters of lilac-pink flowers, somewhat smaller than those of D. collina. *2-ft., May-June. E. 2-ft. Sq. Cg6. C.* *See p.* 96. *Pl.*28.

D. HYBRIDA (Hybrid) Garden origin, is also D. Dauphinii, and a hybrid of D. sericea with D. odora, and is a stout, wooded, open shrub with wide, shiny, green, pointed leaves and clusters of large, reddish-purple, deliciously scented flowers.

3-ft., May-June. E. 4-ft. Sq. Cg6. C. See p. 96.

D. INDICA (*see* D. ODORA).

D. LAUREOLA (The Spurge Laurel) Europe, is a strong shrub with wide, pointed, oval leaves of deep, shining green, and bears yellowish-green, sweetly scented, spidery-petalled flowers from the top leaf axils of the previous year's growth in groups of from four to eight, followed by black, poisonous berries. It thrives upon heavy soils.

3-ft., February-March. E. 4-ft. Sq. Sd2. Cg7. C. See p. 96.

D. MEZEREUM (Possibly deadly—the berries of this variety are poisonous) Europe, is extremely variable, growing into an upright twiggy bush of two feet and over. The flowers, which vary considerably in colour in seedlings, are borne tightly upon the stem before the leaves appear, are very sweetly scented, and are purplish-red at their deepest and lilac-pink at their palest. The flowers are succeeded by red berries from which, when ripe, the plant may be freely propagated, but their acrid taste should warn the would-be experimenter that they are poisonous. A number of varieties have been selected. D. Mezereum var. grandiflora has larger flowers, D. Mezereum var. autumnalis flowers at the end of the year instead of the beginning, but pride of place undoubtedly goes to D. Mezereum var. alba, which has so far lost its claim to purple as to be a clear, pure white, and improves upon this by following its flower with clear yellow (poisonous) berries.

2-ft. upwards, February-March. D. 2-ft. Sq. Ch7. Sd2. ANC.
Type 031/1. *Pl.*29.

D. ODORA (Sweet-smelling) China, Japan, is the Daphne indica rubra of catalogues, and, except in the south-west, should be grown in the shelter of the cold house. A delightful shrub with polished, deep-green, pointed leaves, of rhomboidal shape, it bears heavily scented, large, reddish-purple flowers from late winter to late spring. D. odora alba has white flowers but is otherwise similar, and D. odora variegata (the D. japonica of catalogues) has leaves margined with yellow and bears pink flowers and a reputation for hardiness in excess of that of D. odora.

3-ft., February-April. E. 4-ft. Sq. Cg6. ANC.

D. OLEOIDES (Resembling the Olive Tree) Mediterranean Region, is a small, woody shrub with shiny green leaves variously reported as pale pink, purple, or creamy-white. There is little doubt, however, that the species, in its natural habitat, has white flowers, as do those in cultivation, which can justly lay claim to the name.

1½-ft., April-May. E. 2-ft. Sq. Sd2. C.

D. PETRAEA (Growing on stony ground) Tyrol, is the D. rupestris of catalogues, and in it the genus Daphne reaches its high-water mark.

It is a tiny, woody shrub with small, neat, dark-green, shiny foliage, bearing in the shelter of rosettes of leaves, clusters of three or four rose-pink, tubular flowers with wide petals, spread starwise. Very fragrant, it is generally found grafted upon stocks of D. Mezereum, which may be the cause of its occasional and incomprehensible demise. Grafted upon stocks of D. acutiloba, or D. oleoides, this seems less probable, but it *can* be made to grow upon its own roots, when it is slow in growth but of a character which is breath-taking. D. petraea var. grandiflora has larger flowers.

$\frac{1}{3}$-ft., May-June. E. $\frac{2}{3}$-ft. Sq. Ch8. 627/1.

D. PONTICA (From the shores of the Black Sea) S.E. Europe, is a shade-loving species in the style of D. Laureola, but with more spreading habit, and sweetly scented, greenish-yellow flowers freely produced.

3-ft., April. E. 4-ft. Sq. Ch7. ANC.

DAPHNE ODORA

D. RETUSA (Blunted) W. China, is another of the gems of the genus, and looks like a stout miniature tree with dark-green, thick leaves, from the terminal rosettes of which are borne large clusters of deep-purple buds which open to four-petalled, tubular flowers of clear white with a waxy texture, and are exceptionally fragrant. D. retusa appears to be best grown in a peaty soil.

1$\frac{1}{4}$-ft., May-June. E. 1$\frac{1}{4}$-ft. Sq. Ch7. Sd2. A.

D. STRIATA (With longitudinal grooves) European Alps, appears stiffer and more turgid than any other variety, with more congested growth. The deeply grooved, short, deep-green leaves are decorated in July with clusters of rose-pink flowers.

$\frac{1}{2}$-ft., July. E. 1-ft. Sq. G3. Sd2. C. *See p.* 96.

D. SOMERSET (Comm.) Garden origin, resembles D. Burkwoodii but is not identical. A hybrid of similar parentage, it has plentiful pale-green leaves, makes a rounded bush, and bears innumerable clusters of pale-pink, sweetly scented flowers. It has one great advantage over all the other species, it grows so easily anywhere.
2½-ft., May-June. E. 3-ft. Sq., or more. Ch7. ANC. 627/3. *Pl.*28.

D. TANGUTICA (Tangusian) E. Siberia, is a strongly growing species reaching three feet in height, with dark-green, diamond-shaped leaves, strong, woody branches and white flowers touched here and there with purple within, and pale-purple without. The flowers are produced in rather large clusters at the tips of the branches.
3-ft., March-May. E. 3-ft. Sq. Ch7. AN.

DAPHNIPHYLLUM (EUPHORBIACEAE) (THE NAME IS DERIVED FROM DAPHNE AND PHYLLON—A LEAF; THE LEAVES RESEMBLING THOSE OF THE DAPHNES).

D. MACROPODUM (With long footstalk) Japan, is a tall, spreading shrub which is interesting rather than beautiful. The stems, which are red, are clad with alternate pale-green leaves like those of a Rhododendron, the flowers are inconspicuous and green, and the berries, produced only upon the female plants, are small and black. The foliage is attractive and may turn red in autumn.
8-ft., May-June. E. 12-ft. Sq. Sd2. Cg8. ANC.

DECAISNEA (LARDIZABALACEAE) (NAMED AFTER THE FRENCH BOTANIST, J. DECAISNE).

D. FARGESII (Comm.) W. China, is a most attractive shrub with large, long, pinnate leaves made up of six to twelve pairs of leaflets, and grey beneath. The long racemes of yellowish-green flowers are followed by large, metallic purple-blue pods about four inches in length and reminiscent of broad beans. Seed germinates slowly.
10-ft., June. D. 12-ft. Sq. Sd2. ANC.

DECUMARIA (SAXIFRAGACEAE) (FROM THE LATIN DECEM—TEN; WHICH IS THE PREVAILING NUMBER IN THE DISTRIBUTION OF THE PARTS OF THE FLOWER).

D. BARBARA (Foreign) South-E. U.S.A., is a semi-evergreen climber, climbing by means of aerial roots, which will, in sheltered districts, reach twenty feet in height, and is clothed with shining, green, ovate leaves, and bears small white flowers in terminal clusters.
20-ft., June. D. Indefinite. Cg6. ANC.

DESFONTAINEA (LOGANIACEAE) (NAMED AFTER R. L. DESFONTAINES, A FRENCH BOTANIST).

D. SPINOSA (Spiny) Chile, is a magnificent plant which will reach eight feet in height in a sheltered, shady and somewhat moist site, but is seldom more than three feet elsewhere, and in foliage resembles a light-green holly, but bears tubular flowers of scarlet, tipped with gold. Propagation may be from seed if obtained, but the seedlings should be kept growing in shady, moist conditions. Cuttings of the side shoots, about three inches, rooted in a frame, should be similarly treated.

8-*ft.*, *July-October*. *E*. 6-*ft. Sq*. *Sd3*. *Cg7*. *ANC*. *Pl.30*.

DEUTZIA (SAXIFRAGACEAE) (NAMED IN HONOUR OF J. D. VAN DE DEUTZ, ONCE A SHERIFF OF AMSTERDAM).

A group of very floriferous shrubs with opposite serrated leaves, which bear five-petalled flowers produced in clusters. Double-flowered varieties are plentiful, and are often forced for indoor decoration. Deutzias flourish in well-drained but moist soils, and are best suited by a good loam. Propagation is made from either hardwood or greenwood cuttings, by division or from seeds. Cuttings should be about four inches in length and of the current year's wood.

D. CORYMBOSA (Flowering in wide corymbs) Himalayas, is a small shrub with three-inch-wide clusters of five-petalled, snowy-white flowers beautified by golden-yellow anthers, and spreading the scent of Hawthorn around and about.

4-*ft.*, *June-July*. *D*. 4-*ft. Sq*. *Cg7*. *D11–3*. *ANC*.

D. DISCOLOR GRANDIFLORA (Varied colours, large-flowered) C. and W. China, is the larger flowered of the species with flat, wide-petalled flowers of white flushed with pink.

4-*ft.*, *June*. *D*. 6-*ft. Sq*. *Cg7*. *D11–3*. *ANC*.

D. DISCOLOR MAJOR (Large) C. and W. China, is similar, with clear white flowers in large, wide clusters.

4-*ft.*, *June*. *D*. 6-*ft. Sq*. *Cg7*. *D11–3*. *ANC*.

D. GRACILIS (Slender) Japan, is a variety with large, flat, milky-white flowers which, except in certain favoured districts, is fit only for forcing. 3-*ft.*, *May-June*. *D*. 4-*ft. Sq*. *Cg7*. *D11–3*. *ANC*.

D. KALMIIFLORA (Kalmia-flowered) Garden origin, is a hybrid between D. purpurascens and D. parviflora, has branches pendent at the tips, and bears large pink flowers in clusters, each resembling an inverted umbrella. 3-*ft.*, *May*. *D*. 4-*ft. Sq*. *Cg7*. *D11–3*. *ANC*.

D. LONGIFOLIA (With long leaves) China, is a magnificent species with upright growth and bears rose-pink flowers about the size of a halfpenny, and is best grown in a shaded site. D. longifolia var. Veitchii has rougher, larger leaves, and even larger flowers of rose-pink. 8-*ft.*, *June*. *D*. 6-*ft. Sq*. *Cg7*. *D11–3*. *ANC*.

D. MACROCEPHALA (Large-headed) Garden origin, is a bold, free-growing shrub of erect habit, with large, pure-white flowers borne in great profusion.

8-*ft.*, *June*. *D*. 8-*ft. Sq*. *Cg7*. *D11–3*. *ANC*.

D. MAGNIFICA (Magnificent) Garden origin, is a hybrid of D. scabra and D. Vilmorinae, and has large clusters of double white flowers held erect, and is reminiscent of sprays of white (double) lilac.

8-*ft.*, *June*. *D*. 8-*ft. Sq*. *Cg7*. *D11–3*. *ANC*.

D. MAGNIFICA VAR. LATIFOLIA has large flowers about the size of a halfpenny, and D. magnifica var. longipetala has flowers with the edges of the petals fringed.

8-ft., June. D. 8-ft. Sq. Cg7. D11–3. ANC.

D. MONBEIGII (Comm.) China, has small green leaves with grey undersides, borne upon slender branches with pendent tips, and bears star-shaped, clear white flowers in large clusters.

6-ft., June. D. 6-ft. Sq. Cg7. D11–3. ANC.

D. PARVIFLORA (With small flowers) N. China, is a plant of upright habit, bearing clusters of small white flowers with very graceful distribution. *5-ft., June. D. 5-ft. Sq. Cg7. D11–3. ANC.*

D. PULCHRA (Beautiful) Formosa, is also D. taiwanensis, has pointed, leathery, bright-green leaves borne upon gracefully arching branches, which bear innumerable clear white flowers in June and July. *8-ft., June-July. D. 8-ft. Sq. Cg7. D11–3. ANC.*

D. PURPURASCENS (Purplish) China, has wand-like branches, and bears clusters of rounded-petalled, white flowers tinted with purple-crimson, and is only suitable for a sheltered site.

6-ft., June-July. D. 6-ft. Sq. Cg7. D11–3. *ANC.*

D. ROSEA (Rose) Garden origin, is also known as D. gracilis carminea, and is a hybrid of D. gracilis with D. purpurascens, is of graceful habit, and has large, frilled, carmine-pink flowers shading to pale pink. D. rosea var. venusta has large white flowers, D. rosea var. grandiflora has large clusters of smaller pink flowers.

3-ft., May. D. 4-ft. Sq. Cg7. D11–3. ANC.

D. SCABRA (Rough) Japan, has large rough leaves and bears large clusters of clear white flowers upon very strong-growing, erect branches. D. scabra var. candidissima is also Pride of Rochester, and has clear-white, double flowers, D. scabra flore pleno has double white flowers tinged with rose-purple, D. scabra var. latiflora has large clusters of many large, single white flowers (6-ft.), D. scabra var. longipetala is dwarf and has white flowers with fringed petals (3-ft.), D. scabra var. staphyleoides has long, pointed leaves, neat habit, windswept clusters of fringed, white flowers (5-ft.), and D. scabra var. Watereri has single white flowers purple on the outside. *10-ft., June-July. 8-ft. Sq. Cg7. D11–3. ANC.*

D. SETCHUENENSIS (From Setchuen) China, is a slender branched species with long, pointed leaves, green above and very woolly beneath, which bears loose clusters of clean white flowers with the petals rounded at the tips. D. setchuenensis var. corymbiflora differs only in its larger leaves, and both varieties are best grown in a semi-shady site.

6-ft., May-June. D. 6-ft. Sq. Cg7. D11–3. ANC.

D. SIEBOLDIANA (Comm.) Japan, is a dwarf with heart-shaped leaves, and bears small white flowers in loose, compound clusters.

4-ft., June. D. 4-ft. Sq. Cg7. D11–3. ANC.

D. VILMOREANAE (Comm.) China, has large, long leaves and bears open clusters of very large, pure-white flowers with golden anthers, and deserves and requires a sheltered spot.

8-ft., June. D. 8-ft. Sq. Cg7. D11–3. ANC.

D. WILSONII (Comm.) China, also bears compound clusters of large white flowers. *7-ft., June. D. 7-ft. Sq. Cg7. D11–3. ANC.*

DIAPENSIA (DIAPENSIACEAE) (FROM GR. DI—DOUBLE ; AND PENTE—FIVE ; A REFERENCE TO THE FACT THAT THE FLOWERS HAVE FIVE PETALS AND FIVE STAMENS).

D. LAPPONICA VAR. OBOVATA (From Lapland ; egg-shaped) is a prostrate shrub making a mat of small, shining, evergreen leaves, from which arise short-stemmed, numerous, small, clear white flowers. It flourishes in a soil which is both moist and peaty, and is best grown in shade.

$\frac{1}{6}$-ft., June-July. E. 1-ft. Sq. D8. A. White.

DIERVILLA (CAPRIFOLIACEAE) (THE NAME IS GIVEN IN HONOUR OF N. DIERVILLE, A FRENCH SURGEON).

The genus is probably better known to most gardeners under the name of WEIGELA. The Diervillas are an extremely useful and ornamental group of shrubs, the flowers resembling most closely the flowers of Digitalis (the Foxglove) but produced in clusters in the topmost leaf axils. They flower upon the wood of the previous year, and flourish in rich, moist soils. The average height of the species is about six feet. Propagation is from cuttings of the current year's wood, about four inches in length.

D. FLORIDA (Floriferous) Korea, is an attractively disposed shrub with arching branches wreathed with clusters of deep-rose flowers, shading to pink.

D. FLORIDA CANDIDA—is similar with white flowers.

D. „ FOLIIS PURPUREIS—has purple foliage and pink flowers (4-ft.).

D. „ VARIEGATA—has silver variegations in its leaves.

6-ft., May-June. D. 6-ft. Sq. Cg7–8. ANC.

D. HORTENSIS (Of the garden) Garden origin, is also known as D. japonica var. hortensis, and includes :—

D. HORTENSIS VAR. LOOYMANSII AUREA—a pleasant shrub with bright-yellow leaves and pink flowers.

D. „ NIVEA—with green foliage and large white flowers.

8-ft., May-June. D. 8-ft. Sq. Cg7. D11–3. ANC.

D. HYBRIDA (Hybrid) Garden origin, comprises the following :—

D. ABEL CARRIÈRE—with soft rose flowers.
D. AVANTGARDE—has bright-pink flowers.
D. BOUQUET ROSE—has large flowers of silver-pink.
D. CONQUÊTE—has large flowers of deep rose-pink.

DIERVILLA (continued)

D. DESCARTES—is very dark-crimson.

D. EVA RATHKE—has flowers of deep-crimson, and is of slow growth. *Pl.*31.

D. FLEUR DE MAI—is the earliest to flower, and is carmine fading to pink.

D. HÉROINE—has flowers of pale-pink.

D. LA PERLE—has creamy-white flowers.

D. LAVALLEI—has crimson flowers.

D. LE PRINTEMPS—has large pink flowers.

D. MONT BLANC—has large white flowers.

D. OTHELLO—is very robust, and has clear-pink flowers in profusion.

D. SATURNE—is carmine, turning to pink.

D. STELZNERI—is bright-pink.

D. STYRIACA—has rose and crimson flowers.

D. JAPONICA (Japanese) Japan, has elliptical leaves, is of very vigorous growth, and freely bears clusters of deep-pink flowers.

8-ft., May-June. D. 8-ft. Sq. Cg7. D11-3. ANC.

D. LONICERA (Resembling Honeysuckle) Eastern N. America, has green, smooth, oval, long, pointed leaves, and bears in the leaf axils clusters of small, pale-yellow flowers flushed with brown.

4-ft., June. D. 5-ft. Sq. D11-3. ANC.

D. MIDDENDORFIANA (Comm.) Japan, has whip-like branches, green, wrinkled, long, pointed, oval leaves, and bears clusters of small, sulphur-yellow flowers, marked with orange on the lips, in the topmost leaf axils, looking in the aggregate like a terminal cluster. D. Middendorfiana requires a sheltered position.

3-ft., April-May. D. 3-ft. Sq. D11-3. ANC.

DIOSTEA (VERBENACEAE) (FROM GR. DI—TWO; AND OSTEA—BONES).

The hard fruits contain two nuts or seeds. DIOSTEA is also known as BAILLONIA.

D. JUNCEA (Rush-like) S. America, is a tall, graceful shrub with green, rush-like branches similar in growth to, but taller than, SPARTIUM junceum, and bears sweetly scented, small, pale-lavender, verbena-like flowers with yellow throats.

15-ft., June-August. D. 8-ft. Sq. Sd2. Cg7. ANC.

DIPELTA (CAPRIFOLIACEAE) (FROM THE GR. DI—TWO; AND PELTE—A SHIELD; A REFERENCE TO THE WINGED FRUITS OF THE SPECIES, WHICH APPEAR TO BE COMPOSED OF TWO SHIELDS).

This genus is related to DIERVILLA, and has similar bell-shaped flowers, with five spreading lobes, borne in small axillary clusters. The best method of propagation is from greenwood cuttings of quickly grown wood of the current year's growth. These shrubs flourish in a good, rich loam, preferably in a shaded or semi-shaded site.

Diervilla hybrida Eva Rathke

Rhododendron Falsia
×campylocarpum ABEF

Rhododendron discolor
×campylocarpum CDGHM

Enkianthus campanulatus
JKLNOP

D. FLORIBUNDA (Floriferous) China, is very lovely, the fragrant pink flowers with yellow throats are borne upon upright bushes with slender branchtips in great abundance, and are followed by large, brown fruit bracts of quaint appearance.

9-ft., May. D. 8-ft. Sq. Cg7. D11–3. ANC.

D. VENTRICOSA (Inflated) W. China, has longer, more pointed, hairy leaves, rose flowers with an orange throat, with wider calyces, but is similar in other respects.

9-ft., May. D. 8-ft. Sq. Cg7. D11–3. ANC.

D. YUNNANENSIS (From Yunnan) China, is more dwarf and bears flowers resembling those of D. floribunda in shape, white in colour, but more or less flushed with rose, and with the throats marked with orange. *6-ft., May. D. 6-ft. Sq. Cg7. D11–3. ANC.*

DIRCA (THYMELAEACEAE) (FROM THE NAME OF A GRECIAN SPRING).

The one species is a neat shrub related to the Daphnes, needing a moist, peaty soil in a shaded site.

D. PALUSTRIS (Swamp-loving) N. America, has elliptical, green leaves, flexible, tough branches, and bears its yellow, pendent, tubular flowers in groups of three upon the bare stems before the leaves appear. *5-ft., March. D. 5-ft. Sq. Cg7. ANC.*

DISANTHUS (HAMAMELIDACEAE) (FROM GR. DI—TWO ; AND ANTHOS—A FLOWER ; A REFERENCE TO THE TWIN-FLOWERED CLUSTERS).

The one species which follows requires good fertile loam in which to grow, and is grown for the beauty of its autumn foliage.

D. CERCIDIFOLIUS (Leaves resembling Cercis) Japan, resembles Hamamelis and has heart-shaped leaves, dark red-purple, star-shaped flowers borne in twos back to back upon short stalks, produced from the leaf axils and, grown in a moist atmosphere, the leaves assume the most startling shades of claret and orange before they fall. *8-ft., September-October. D. 10-ft. Sq. Ch6. ANC.*

DISTYLIUM (HAMAMELIDACEAE) (FROM GR. DI—TWO ; AND STYLOS—A STYLE ; THE TWO-STYLE DIVISION OF THE FLOWERS PERSISTING ON THE FRUITS AS TWO HORNS).

D. RACEMOSUM (Clustered) Japan, is eighty feet high in nature, but shrubby in cultivation, five feet high in the open and up to twenty feet on a sheltered north wall, and has elliptical, dark-green, shiny leaves with irregular margins, and has small, reddish flowers made up of sepals only with a group of purple anthers. It is best grown in a shaded site. *5-ft., March-April. E. 5-ft. Sq. Sd10. ANC.*

DOCYNIA (ROSACEAE) (AN ANAGRAM OF CYDONIA, TO WHICH THE GENUS IS RELATED AND BEARS SOME RESEMBLANCE).

D. DELAVAYI (Comm.) is also PYRUS Delavayi, and has long, pointed, oval, green leaves and bears small, white, quince-like flowers in clusters, and green, shiny leaves upon wood which is armed with two-inch spines.

8-ft., April-May. E. Indefinite. Cg7. ANC. Shelter.

D. DOCYNIOIDES (Docynia-like) S.W. China, has green, elliptical leaves with sharp points, and serrated near the tips, and bears clusters of clear-white Cydonia flowers, flushed with pink.

8-ft., April-May. E. 10-ft. Sq. Cg7. ANC. Shelter.

DORYCNIUM (LEGUMINOSAE) (DERIVED FROM THE GREEK NAME FOR ANOTHER PLANT, THE CONVOLVULUS, DORO—A SPEAR; KNAO—RUB).

One species, D. hirsutum, is sometimes known as CYTISUS Lotus.

D. HIRSUTUM (Hairy) S.W. Europe, is a low shrub with leaves which are clover-like, covered with a grey sheen, and with white pea flowers flushed with pink, borne in small heads.

2-ft., July-September. D. 3-ft. Sq. Sd2. ANC.

DRIMYS (MAGNOLIACEAE) (FROM GR. DRIMUS—BITTER; FROM THE ACRID TASTE).

A group of evergreen shrubs with scattered, simple, narrow leaves with oil glands, and which are aromatic when crushed. One species, D. Winteri, is the source of Winter's Bark, a cinnamon substitute, and the dried seedpods as a pepper substitute. All species flourish on good loam, even if calcareous. The species enumerated below are extremely variable in height, some reaching twenty-five feet in mild localities, but in more severe districts rarely a third of that height.

D. AROMATICA (Aromatic) Australia, has pleasantly scented leaves, young red wood, narrow green leaves and loose panicles of small white flowers made up of many petals.

6-ft.–10-ft., April-May. E. 8-ft.–12-ft. Sq. Cg6–7. L6. ANC. Shelter.

D. WINTERI (Comm.) S. America, is a magnificent evergreen with the appearance of a giant Rhododendron, with terminal panicles of many-petalled, creamy-white flowers. D. Winteri var. latifolia has larger leaves and larger flowers.

8-ft.–25-ft., May. E. 8-ft.–25-ft. Sq. Cg6–7. L6. ANC.

DRYAS (ROSACEAE) (FROM GR. DRUAS—A DRYAD, GODDESS OF THE WOODS; OR POSSIBLY FROM GR. DRUS—OAK, THE LEAVES OF THE PLANT RESEMBLING OAK LEAVES).

Close-growing or creeping sub-shrubs with oak-like, evergreen leaves which grow well in any well-drained, good soil. Propagation is from cuttings of the ripened wood.

D. OCTOPETALA (Eight-petalled) Europe, make a low-growing mat of shining green oak leaves, grey below, over which are borne large, eight-petalled flowers of snow-white, followed by fluffy seed heads. D. octopetala var. minor is a smaller edition.

$\frac{1}{2}$-ft., May-July. E. 2-ft. Sq. Ch6. ANC.

Escallonia hybrida var. Ingramii ABCEFG

Escallonia alba CDH

Escallonia sanguinea JNO

Escallonia hybrida var. Donard Seedling GHKLM

Escallonia hybrida var. edinensis LPQ

Clethra alnifolia **ABCDFG**

Eucryphia glutinosa
JKNOPSU

Oxydendrum arboreum
CDHLMQ

ECCREMOCARPUS (Bignoniaceae) (from Gr. ekkremes—hanging; and karpos—pods).

Is represented by one species, E. scaber, which is a tender climber with opposite, pinnate, tendrilled leaves, and which is tender inland but may be safely relied upon to grow to a good old age in seaboard and sheltered districts if placed to advantage upon a south wall.

E. scaber (Rough) Chile, is a most attractive climber, the numerous tubular, bright-orange flowers borne in long, open clusters are produced in great profusion.

10-*ft.*–20-*ft.*, *June-October*. *D*. *Indefinite*. *Sd*2. *ANC*.

EDGEWORTHIA (Thymelaceae) (named in honour of M. Edgeworth).

E. chrysantha (Golden-yellow) Himalayas, is also known as E. papyrifera and Daphne chrysantha, and is a beautiful and interesting plant needing a sheltered position in all but the south and west. The stems are very pliable, more so than Willow, and the plant has for years been used in Japan as the raw material for the production of high-quality paper. In spite of its utility it is very beautiful with its dark-green, narrow leaves and hanging, spice-scented, small, clear, bright-yellow flowers, borne in crowded clusters.

3-*ft.*, *February-March*. *D*. 5-*ft. Sq*. *Cg*6. *ANC*.

ELAEAGNUS (Elaeagnaceae) (the name is an old Greek one for the willow, but possibly derived from elaios—an olive, from the berry; and agnos, from the resemblance of the leaf to that of the chaste tree—Vitex agnus castus).

This is a group of both deciduous and evergreen shrubs, the young growth of which is covered with silvery or brown scales. The flowers, which are small and fragrant, resemble very tiny Fuchsias and are produced in clusters in the leaf axils, and are followed by attractive berries. The common name is Oleaster.

E. angustifolia (With narrow leaves) Europe, is a very tall, handsome species with long, narrow, silvery, willow-like leaves, flowers small and fragrant in groups of two or three in the leaf axils.

20-*ft.*, *May*. *D*. 20-*ft. Sq*. *Sd*2. *ANC*.

E. argentea (Silver) N. America, is the Silverberry, with thin stems, narrow leaves, silver upon both sides, with small, sweet-scented, silvery-yellow flowers borne in groups of one to three in the leaf axils, and replaced by silver berries on very short stalks.

6-*ft.*–8-*ft.*, *May*. *D*. 8-*ft. Sq*. *Sd*2. *ANC*.

E. glabra (Smooth) China, is a vigorous, spreading, evergreen variety with large, green, oval leaves, silvery beneath, with small, fragrant flowers followed by grey or brown berries.

20-*ft.*, *October-November*. *E*. *Indefinite*. *Cg*6. *ANC*.

E. macrophylla (Having long leaves) is a pretty shrub with rounded habit with broad, elliptical, shining, grey-green leaves, silvery upon the underside, and bearing in groups of from four to six small silvery fuchsia flowers, followed by red fruits.

8-ft.–10-ft., October-November. E. 8-ft.–10-ft. Sq. Cg6. ANC.

E. MULTIFLORA (Many-flowered) China, has green leaves, silvery beneath, small, scented, creamy-white flowers, followed by deep-orange, oblong, edible fruits borne in great quantities, and making a most attractive display in July when ripe.

6-ft., April-May. D. 6-ft. Sq. Sd2. ANC.

E. ORIENTALIS (Eastern) Orient, bears some resemblance to E. angustifolia but has broader leaves which are green upon the upper side and silver below, and amber fruits overlaid with silver.

20-ft., June. D. 20-ft. Sq. Sd2. ANC.

E. PUNGENS (Sharp) Japan, has wavy margined, spiny, green leaves, rather like Holly, silvery beneath, and speckled with brown scales. The flowers are small, silvery-white and borne in the leaf axils, and followed (but rarely in this country) by red, silvery, and brown fruits. The varieties are :—

E. PUNGENS VAR. AUREO-VARIEGATA—has bright-golden leaves.
E. „ „ DICKSONII—has golden leaves.
E. „ „ VARIEGATA—has green leaves variegated with cream.

10-ft.–15-ft., October-November. E. 10-ft.–15-ft. Sq. Cg6. ANC.

E. UMBELLATA (Umbelled) Japan, has branches covered with brown scales, bright-green, narrow, elliptical leaves, silvery beneath, with small silvery flowers, white within, borne in clusters up to three and followed by small silvery fruits turning red.

15-ft.–18-ft., May-June. D. 20-ft.–25-ft. Sq. Sd2. ANC.

ELSHOLTZIA (LABIATAE) (IS NAMED AFTER J. S. ELSHOLTZ, A GERMAN BOTANIST).

E. STAUNTONII (Comm.) China, is a lax shrub of rather untidy habit, with leaves which, when crushed, smell strongly of mint, and which is quite useful for late flowering. The leaves are oval to oblong, green above and paler beneath, and the flower spikes are woolly, dense, and one-sided, and bear lilac-purple flowers in congested heads at the ends of the branches.

6-ft., September-October. D. 6-ft. Sq. Cg6. ANC.

EMPETRUM (EMPETRACEAE) (FROM GR. EN—IN ; PETROS—A ROCK ; A REFERENCE TO THE NATURAL HABITAT OF THE PLANT).

E. NIGRUM (Black) Europe, makes a close-growing mat of dark-green, evergreen foliage, with small, pinkish flowers followed by black berries. It should be grown in a sandy, peaty soil in a sunny exposure. *½-ft., May. E. 2-ft. Sq. Ch6. A.*

E. RUBRUM (Red) Falkland Islands, is a low-growing shrub with small, grey, narrow leaves and small, crimson flowers, followed by red fruits. *1-ft., April. E. 2-ft. Sq. Ch6. Sd2. A.*

ENKIANTHUS (ERICACEAE) (FROM THE GR. ENKUOS—PREGNANT ; AND ANTHOS—A FLOWER ; A REFERENCE TO ONE FLOWER OPENING IMMEDIATELY AFTER ANOTHER).

A group of deciduous shrubs with leaves and branches arranged in tiers with white or pink bell flowers in pendent clusters at the tips of the branches. Among the attractions of the species must be counted the exquisite colour of the autumn foliage before it is shed with fierce tones of orange and red. All the species are best grown in lime-free soils, and are happier if grown in semi-shade. Propagation is from short cuttings of the young wood, but layering the more mature small branches will produce quicker results.

E. CAMPANULATUS (Bell-like) Japan, has numerous dull-green, fine-toothed, simple leaves, and bears many racemes of pendent, cream, Lily-of-the-valley flowers, exquisitely veined and edged with crimson.
6-ft.–8-ft., May. D. 6-ft.–8-ft. Sq. Cg6–7. L6–7. AN. Pl.32.

ENKIANTHUS SINENSIS

E. CERNUUS (Nodding) Japan, is a rare shrub with marked tiers of branches and small, obovate, dark-green leaves. The closely packed racemes have pretty, creamy-white, quaintly fringed flowers. E. cernuus var. rubens is similar with flowers of deep-red.
3-ft.–5-ft., May-June. D. 3-ft.–5-ft. Sq. Cg6–7. L6–7. AN.

E. PALIBINII (Comm.) Japan, is a very attractive shrub, very compact, and resembling E. campanulatus except in its rich, red, bell-shaped flowers.
6-ft.–8-ft., May-June. D. 6-ft.–8-ft. Sq. C6–7. L6–7. AN.

E. PALLIDIFLORUS (With pale flowers) Japan, is also E. campanulatus var. albiflorus, and bears clusters of creamy-yellow flowers passing to white, on a very close-growing plant of neat habit, with the added attraction of a clear golden colour before the leaves fall.
6-ft.–8-ft., May. D. 6-ft.–8-ft. Sq. Cg6–7. L6–7. AN.

ENKIANTHUS (continued)

E. PERULATUS (Very broad) Japan, is also E. japonicus, and has its branches divided and arranged in tiers, and produces its hanging white bell flowers with constricted mouths, in clusters of four or five at the tip of every small shoot. The leaves assume the most startling colours in the late autumn when it appears to be a compound of brilliant red and fiery orange.

6-ft.–8-ft., May. D. 6-ft.–8-ft Sq. Cg6–7. L6–7. AN.

E. RECURVUS (Bent down) Japan, is a taller and more slender variety with its growth arranged in the typical tiers of the genus, and with many clusters of hanging, bell-shaped flowers, this time of pearl-white tinted and edged with pink.

6-ft.–10-ft., May. D. 5-ft.–8-ft. Sq. Cg6–7. L6–7. AN.

EPIGAEA (ERICACEAE) (FROM THE GR. EPI—UPON ; GE—THE EARTH ; A REFERENCE TO THE HABIT OF GROWTH OF THE PLANT).

The common name MAYFLOWER is said to have been given to it by the Pilgrim Fathers after their ship. The various species are all best suited by a moist, peaty soil in some shade, generally among the Rhododendrons.

E. ASIATICA (Asiatic) Japan, makes a mat of rough, hairy, leathery, pointed, oval, bronze-green leaves, and bears clusters of starry, tubular, sweetly-scented flowers which are bright-red in the bud, white to rose when opened, and surrounded by bracts. This plant is eminently suited for growing upon a north slope, in a lime-free soil such as will adequately support the Rhododendrons.

½-ft., April-May. E. 2-ft. Sq. D9. Sd10. A.

E. REPENS (Creeping) N. America, is the Mayflower of North America, has pointed oval leaves of bright green, and bears starry, white, sweetly-scented flowers on hairy stems, from pink buds.

½-ft., April-May. E. 2-ft. Sq. D9. Sd10. A.

ERICA (ERICACEAE) (FROM THE GR. EREIKE—HEATH ; TO BE CORRECT THE NAME SHOULD BE PRONOUNCED ERÍCA).

The genus comprises the Bell Heathers and Heaths, and numbers over five hundred species, many of them not hardy in this country. In the main all the species and their varieties grow best in light, sandy loam with some peat, but many of the English species will persist even in limy soils. E. carnea seems completely indifferent to the presence of lime. Propagation of the true species is comparatively easy if the seed is sown in February upon a sandy, peaty soil, and left uncovered and exposed to the weather, though "damping off" should be guarded against. For the varieties, cuttings one inch long inserted in sandy peat under a bell glass or handlight, in a cold frame in June, July, and August, is the easiest method, and more easy the earlier within these months that the work is undertaken. The cuttings should be selected from side growths, and care must be taken when the bottom leaves are removed not to damage the bark. Erica cuttings

Euonymus yedoensis

Forsythia suspensa ABCDHNORS
Salix lanata JNOR

Cydonia japonica FGKLMPQSTU

appear to root more readily in peat in which Ericas have already been grown, probably due to the production of beneficial root fungi.

E. ARBOREA (Like a tree) Mediterranean region, is the Tree Heath which will reach ten feet in height and has stout, hairy stems, smooth, greyish leaves arranged in threes, and bears sweetly fragrant, white flowers in large compound clusters in March and April.

6-ft.–10-ft., March-April. E. 7-ft.–10-ft. Sq. Sd2. AN.

E. ARBOREA VAR. ALPINA (Alpine) Spain, is a dwarfer growing variative with bright-green leaves and more conical habit, and the benefit of greater hardihood.

5-ft.–8-ft., March-April. E. 6-ft.–9-ft. Sq. Cg6. AN.

E. AUSTRALIS (Southern) Spain, is the Spanish Heath, a strong shrub with open and somewhat straggling habit with its small, smooth, dark-green leaves arranged in fours, and smothered with purplish-rose flowers produced on the young shoots in April.

4-ft.–5-ft., April-May. E. 4-ft.–5-ft. Sq. Sd2. AN.

E. AUSTRALIS MR. ROBERT (Comm.) S. Spain, is a delightful variety with freely produced, waxy, clear-white flowers.

4-ft.–5-ft., April-May. E. 4-ft.–5-ft. Sq. Cg6. AN.

E. CARNEA (Flesh-coloured) C. and S. Europe, has normally prostrate branches, the smooth green leaves arranged in fours, and has rose-pink flowers produced in one-sided clusters about two inches in length. E. carnea will grow in any loamy soil in an open position, despite the presence or absence of lime, and flowers from December to March. The following varieties are good :—

E. CARNEA ALBA—has greeny-white flowers.
E. ,, ATRORUBRA—is late in flowering and has dark, almost crimson flowers on dark-green foliage.
E. ,, CECILIA N. BEALE—has very white flowers, and is erect.
E. ,, C. J. BACKHOUSE—has creamy-white flowers.
E. ,, KING GEORGE—is deep-pink and is very dwarf.
E. ,, MRS. DONCASTER—has clear-pink flowers, is earlier and has larger trusses than the type.
E. ,, PINK PEARL—has flowers of pearly pink.
E. ,, PRAECOX RUBRA—is a very deep-pink variety.
E. ,, QUEEN MARY—has deep-pink flowers.
E. ,, QUEEN OF SPAIN—is light-pink.
E. ,, RUBY GLOW—is a late flowering variety with carmine flowers paling to pink.
E. ,, SPRINGWOOD WHITE—has white flowers, brown anthers and prostrate habit.
E. ,, SPRINGWOOD PINK—has clear-pink flowers, brown anthers, and the same habit.
E. ,, THOMAS KINGSCOTE—pale-pink, late flowering.
E. ,, VIVELLI—has crimson-carmine flowers with bronze-green foliage in winter.
E. ,, WINTER BEAUTY—has deep-pink flowers.

¾-ft.–1-ft., December-March. E. 1½-ft. Sq. Cg6. ANC.

E. CILIARIS (Fringed with hairs) W. Europe, is the Fringed or Dorset Heath, and has inverted, bell-shaped flowers of bright rose-red, very freely produced, in sprays up to five inches in length, upon grey-green, low bushes with hairy-edged leaves arranged in threes. E. ciliaris needs a lime-free soil, and is not particularly easy to grow in inland gardens. The varieties are :—

E. CILIARIS VAR. ALBA—with white flowers.
E. „ „ GLOBOSA—has pale rose-pink flowers.
E. „ „ MAWEANA—has rose-crimson flowers.

2-ft., July-October. E. ½-ft. Sq. Cg6. A.

E. CINEREA (Grey) N.W. Europe, is the Grey, or Scotch, or Twisted Heath, with its small, deep-green leaves arranged in whorls of threes, grey beneath, while still juvenile, and reaching eighteen inches in height, clad with large, purple, bell-shaped flowers, restricted and toothed at the mouth, in sprays of from four to eight. It is found in wide distribution upon the English moors. A considerable number of varieties, all more or less distinctive, exist, of which the following are representative :—

E. CINEREA VAR. ALBA—adds the purity of its clear-white flowers to the other distinctions of the species, and rises to still greater heights in E. cinerea var. alba minor which, by reason of its dwarf and compact habit, is a coveted and precious plant, never exceeding six inches in height.

E. „ „ APPLE BLOSSOM—has light-green foliage and white flowers flushed with pink, and is of normal habit.

E. „ „ ATRORUBENS—is one of the outstanding heathers bearing long sprays of ruby-red flowers, which are produced in prodigality and received with wide-open eyes.

E. „ „ ATROSANGUINEA—is later flowering than the type, and has a dwarfer, more compact habit, and freely produced, dark-red flowers.

E. „ „ CARNEA—is semi-prostrate in its growth and ornaments the garden from early summer to late autumn with its large, pale-pink flowers.

E. „ „ C. D. EASON—is neat in habit and has bright-red flowers.

E. „ „ COCCINEA—has very dark foliage, is more dwarf than the type, and has flowers of very bright red.

E. „ „ FRANCES—has bronzy foliage and bright-cerise flowers.

E. „ „ KNAP HILL—green leaves, rose-red flowers.

E. „ „ LILACINA—has lilac flowers.

E. „ „ MR. DILL—is very dwarf and spreading, and has flowers of very bright, shining pink.

Salix lanata BCFGJNORST
Fothergilla major ABHMPQU

Fuchsia magellanica alba

E. CINEREA VAR. PALLIDA—is dwarf with dark-green foliage and attractive white flowers modestly tinted with pink.

E. „ „ PURPUREA—has deep-green foliage and dark-red flowers.

E. „ „ ROSEA—is one of the easiest varieties to grow, and has flowers of bright, clear-rose.

E. „ „ ROSE QUEEN—is of matted habit and bears masses of rose-pink flowers for a long period.

E. „ „ SCHIZOPETALA—is distinctive because of its split petals, and bears curious pale-purple flowers on plants with green leaves with an overlay of bronze.

½-ft.–1½-ft., May-October. E. 1½-ft. Sq. Cg6. AN.

E. DARLEYENSIS (Comm.) Garden origin, is a natural hybrid of E. carnea × E. mediterranea, and forms a rounded and compact bush tightly packed with small green leaves, distinctive for its propensity to flower in the heart of winter; and if its flowers are more pallid than those of the best of the carnea hybrids, they may be excused on the grounds of their generous production.

2-ft., November-April. E. 2-ft. Sq. Cg7. ANC.

E. HYBRIDA (Hybrid) comprises a number of natural hybrids of diverse characteristics :—

E. HYBRIDA VAR. DAWN—is a hybrid of E. Tetralix with E. ciliaris and has nicely rounded bell flowers of deep rose, borne well above the foliage.

E. „ „ GWEN—is a natural hybrid of doubtful parentage, distinctive because of its young coppery growth, dwarf habit, and pink flowers.

E. „ „ H. MAXWELL—is a hybrid of E. Tetralix with E. ciliaris, and is of easy growth and has large rose-red flowers borne in long sprays well above the foliage.

1¼-ft., July-October. E. 1½-ft. Sq. Cg6. AN.

E. LUSITANICA (Portuguese) Spain, Portugal, is also E. codonoides, and a tree heath which, in open weather, is wreathed with sprays of white flowers surmounted by pink buds.

10-ft., March-June. E. 8-ft. Sq. Cg7. AN. Shelter.

E. MACKAYI (Comm.) N.W. Spain, is also known as E. Tetralix var. Mackayi, and is a very effective dwarf with pale grey-green, rather hairy foliage, and clusters of bright-pink, globular flowers freely produced in July and August. E. Mackayi var. plena is also known as E. Crawfurdii, and is equally attractive with its double flowers of flushed pearly-pink.

1-ft., July-August. E. 1½-ft. Sq. Cg7. AN.

E. MEDITERRANEA (Mediterranean) S.W. France, makes a dense, upright bush of from six to eight feet in height, with dark-green leaves in whorls of four, which becomes covered with small rosy-red

globular flowers. E. mediterranea is best suited by a sheltered site.
6-ft.–8-ft., March-May. E. 5-ft.–6-ft. Sq. Cg7. AN. Shelter.

E. MEDITERRANEA VAR. ALBA (White) is much more dwarf and compact, and bears its clear-white flowers in great prodigality when it is situated in a place which does not become sun-parched in summer.
2½-ft.–3-ft., February-May. E. 2-ft.–3-ft. Sq. Cg7. AN. Shelter.

E. MEDITERRANEA BRIGHTNESS—garden origin, is a useful dwarf hybrid with deep rose-red flowers, and a strong constitution.
1½-ft., January-April. E. 2-ft. Sq. Cg7. AN.

E. MEDITERRANEA VAR. HIBERNICA (W. Ireland) has grey-green foliage, pale-grey flowers tinged with red, and makes a neatly rounded bush up to four feet in height.
2-ft.–4-ft., March-May. E. 2-ft.–4-ft. Sq. Cg7. AN.

E. MEDITERRANEA VAR. SUPERBA—garden origin, is a fine variation with compact and tidy, rounded growth, and a predilection to produce its pretty pink flowers with the most complete freedom.
3-ft.–4-ft., February-April. E. 3-ft.–4-ft. Sq. Cg7. AN.

E. PAGEANA (Comm.) S. Africa, is a very attractive, though tender, shrub with large, tubular, waxy, deep-yellow flowers.
2-ft.–6-ft. April-June. E. 2-ft.–4-ft. Sq. Cg7. Sd2. AN. Shelter.

E. STUARTII (Comm.) Ireland, is a natural hybrid between E. Mackayi and E. mediterranea, with long, narrow, pink flowers marked with deep-rose. *2-ft., July-August. E. 2-ft. Sq. Cg7. AN.*

E. TERMINALIS (With terminal flowers) S. Europe, is also E. stricta, a really beautiful shrub with many heads of soft rose-coloured flowers, produced with freedom in mild and seaboard districts, but shy to flower elsewhere.
2-ft.–5-ft., July-November. E. 3-ft.–5-ft. Sq. Cg7. AN.

E. TETRALIX (Four leaves arranged in a cross) N. and W. Europe, is the Cross-leaved Heath, and that most commonly found growing wild throughout Britain ; a low spreading shrub with small, dark-green leaves, densely white beneath, arranged cross-like in whorls of four. The flowers are borne in groups of upwards of four and are rose in colour. The varieties outstanding are :—

E. TETRALIX VAR. LAWSONIANA—a dwarf form with pale-pink flowers.

E. „ „ MOLLIS—has its leaves and young shoots densely hoary, and bears large, globular, snow-white flowers.

E. „ „ PINK GLOW—has greyish foliage and shining pink flowers.

E. „ „ RUBRA—is dwarf, has ash-grey foliage and bears clusters of dark-red flowers.

½-ft.–1½-ft., June-October. E. 1-ft.–2-ft. Sq. Cg7. AN.

E. UMBELLATA (Umbelled) W. Mediterranean regions, is a shrub of few inches in height, never above a foot, with very small grey-green leaves, and small pink flowers throughout spring and early summer. Its beauty is only fitted to the most clement parts of the British Isles.

1-ft., April-October. E. 3-ft. Sq. Cg7. AN.

E. VAGANS (Widespread) S.W. Europe, is the Cornish Heath, a spreading shrub with woody stems with dark green, channelled leaves arranged in whorls of four or five, and bearing upon the season's growth six- to eight-inch sprays of pinkish-rose flowers from July to October. The outstanding varieties are :—

E. VAGANS VAR. ALBA—with white flowers, is rather more dwarf and compact.

E. „ „ CARNEA—is more compact than the type, and has flesh-pink flowers.

E. „ „ GRANDIFLORA—has longer sprays of flowers than the type.

E. „ „ LYONESSE—has clear-white flowers with brown anthers.

E. „ „ MRS. D. F. MAXWELL—is the outstanding variety with sprays of clear-cerise flowers.

E. „ „ ST. KEVERNE—is very similar but with flowers of bright rose-pink. *Pl.12.*

1½-ft., July-October. E. 1½-ft. Sq. Cg6. AN.

E. VEITCHII (Comm.) Garden origin, is a hybrid of E. ciliaris with E. Tetralix and has rose-coloured flowers freely produced.

1-ft., July-September. E. 2-ft. Sq. Cg7. AN.

ERINACEA (LEGUMINOSAE) (DERIVED FROM GR. ERINEOS—WOOLLY ; THE CALYX OF THE FLOWER HAVING A WOOLLY APPEARANCE ; OR POSSIBLY FROM LATIN ERINACEUS—A HEDGEHOG ; FROM THE SPINY NATURE OF THE GROWTH).

E. PUNGENS (Spiny) S.E. Europe, is a low-growing, spiny, shrub, reminiscent of a very dwarf broom, with grey-green, round, spiny stems and almost inconspicuous leaves, and which bears, if and when it flowers, blue-grey pea flowers of more than ordinary charm. Opinion seems to be divided as to the appropriate culture for the plant, most authorities regarding a sun-parched site paramount to the production of its flowers, but conceding a difficulty in encouraging it to flower. The only plants I have grown which have flowered freely have had open positions upon a north-west slope, open to the sun but with the roots deep among rocks.

1-ft., April-May. E. 2-ft. Sq. Ch10. Sd2. ANC.

ESCALLONIA (SAXIFRAGACEAE) (THE NAME IS GIVEN IN HONOUR OF A SEÑOR ESCALLON, A SPANISH TRAVELLER AND BOTANIST).

The Escallonias comprise a group of plants of great range, adapted to hedging in the milder districts, as specimen shrubs in the open borders, or in the less clement parts of the country for growing against walls. Easily adapted to almost any soil they may be readily propagated from the seed which they freely produce, or from cuttings of the half-ripened wood about three inches in length, inserted in a cold frame in July or August.

E. HYBRIDA (Hybrid) Garden origin, comprises a large number of varieties of mixed parentage and of variable characteristics, and all of great charm, often outshining the species.

E. HYBRIDA VAR. ALICE—has slender, arching stems, bright-green, polished leaves, and long spikes of rose-red flowers.
3-ft.–4-ft., April-August. E. 4-ft.–6-ft. Sq. Cg7. ANC.

E. HYBRIDA VAR. C. F. BALL is a hybrid between E. macrantha and E. Ingrami, and eventually makes a large bush of open, branching habit bearing carmine-crimson flowers from May till autumn.
6-ft., May-August. E. 6-ft.–8-ft. Sq. Cg7. ANC.

E. HYBRIDA VAR. DONARD BEAUTY has the slender habit of Alice and bears bright, rose-red flowers.
4-ft., April-August. E. 4-ft.–8-ft. Sq. Cg7. ANC.

E. HYBRIDA VAR. DONARD BRILLIANCE is a strong-growing variety with open branching habit and crimson flowers.
6-ft., May-July. E. 8-ft. Sq. Cg7. ANC.

E. HYBRIDA VAR. DONARD GEM has the advantage of neatness and compactness of growth, and sweetly-scented, pale-pink flowers larger than those of the type.
3-ft.–4-ft., May-June. September-October. 4-ft. Sq. Cg7. ANC.

E. HYBRIDA VAR. DONARD SEEDLING is of parentage E. langleyensis × E. virgata, is an extremely vigorous variety with strong, arching stems and pale-pink flowers, paling with age to white.
8-ft.–9-ft., June-July. E. 8-ft.–9-ft. Sq. Cg7. ANC. Pl.33.

E. HYBRIDA VAR. EDINENSIS is a hybrid of E. rubra and E. virgata, and is of strong growth with slender, arching branches bearing many clusters of rose-pink flowers accompanied by bright-green leaves.
6-ft., June-July. E. 7-ft. Sq. Cg7. ANC. Pl.33.

E. HYBRIDA VAR. EXONIENSIS has as its parents E. pterocladon and E. rubra, and is a strong, erect-growing variety with bright-green, glossy leaves and pink buds opening to white flowers, and is excellent for forming screens in mild districts.
12-ft., June-October. E. 12-ft. Sq. Cg7. ANC.

E. HYBRIDA VAR. INGRAMII was derived from E. macrantha and E. punctata and is one of the best of the hedge-forming Escallonias, its dark-green, polished leaves forming an adequate foil for the sprays of deep-red flowers which it produces with generosity.
12-ft., June-September. E. 12-ft. Sq. Cg7. ANC. Pl.33.

E. HYBRIDA VAR. IVEYANA (E. montevidensis × E. exoniensis) has dark green, glossy leaves and bears large clusters of sweetly-scented white flowers flushed with pink.
6-ft., June-October. E. 8-ft. Sq. Cg7. ANC.

E. HYBRIDA VAR. LANGLEYENSIS is of parentage E. punctata × E. virgata, and has small, bright-green leaves borne upon arching branches carrying clusters of carmine flowers, sometimes losing part or all of its foliage in winter.

6-ft.–8-ft., June-July. S.E. 8-ft. Sq. Cg7. ANC.

E. HYBRIDA VAR. SLIEVE DONARD has open semi-pendulous branches, and bears, often twice during the same year, pleasantly placed and scented flowers of flesh-pink, deepening in colour as they mature.

6-ft., June-July. September-October. E. 6-ft. Sq. Cg7. ANC.

E. ILLINITA (Varnished) Chile, is one of the most hardy species, being distinctive in its rounded clusters of white flowers, and occasionally evil smell. *10-ft., June-July. E. 10-ft. Sq. Sd2. Cg7. ANC.*

E. MACRANTHA (Long-flowered) Chile, is a grand hedging shrub for coastal districts where its large, shining, deep-green leaves are enlivened by clusters of bright-red flowers from midsummer to autumn. It is also a very good wall shrub.

6-ft.–9-ft., July-October. E. 8-ft.–10-ft. Sq. Sd2. Cg7. ANC.

E. MONTANA (Of the mountains) is a miniature with small leaves and attractive deep-red flowers, freely produced for a long period, and is suitable to the rock garden or for the front of the shrub border.

1½-ft., June-October. E. 3-ft. Sq. Sd2. Cg7. ANC.

E. MONTEVIDENSIS (From Montevideo) S. America, is a tender but very beautiful species with long sprays of clear-white flowers late in the year, and is best suited to a south wall.

12-ft., September. E. 12-ft. Sq. Sd2. Cg7. ANC.

E. ORGANENSIS (From the Organ Mountains) Brazil, is a tender shrub needing the shelter of a wall, but with the protection of it will produce its dense clusters of waxy, rose-pink flowers.

6-ft., August. E. 6-ft. Sq. Sd2. Cg7. AN.

E. PTEROCLADON (With winged branches) Patagonia, is well suited to be grown against a south wall, which will ensure the production of its sweetly-scented, clear-white flowers.

4-ft.–8-ft., June-August. E. 8-ft. Sq. Cg7. ANC.

E. PUNCTATA (The underside of the leaves speckled) is a most vigorous variety with its juvenile growth of sticky, rather large, glossy green leaves, and rich crimson flowers.

12-ft., June-August. E. 12-ft. Sq. Sd2. Cg7. ANC.

E. REVOLUTA (Rolled back) is also E. coquimbensis and E. mollis, and another shrub well suited to be grown upon a wall, with grey-green leaves, and attractive pink flowers which are freely produced in the latter part of the year.

10-ft., September. E. 12-ft. Sq. Sd2. Cg7. ANC.

E. RUBRA (Reddish) Chile, is also E. microphylla, a very dense shrub with small leaves, and bears with great freedom, and for a long period, clusters of tubular, red flowers. E. rubra pygmaea, which originated as a witches' broom upon a plant of the type, is smaller, seldom exceeding one and a half feet, and even neater, well suited to the front of the shrub garden, or to the rock garden, though its tendency to revert to the type must be rigorously discouraged by pruning the more robust growths.

3-ft.–4-ft., June-September. E. 3-ft.–4-ft. Sq. Sd2. Cg7. ANC.

E. VIRGATA (Made of willowy twigs) Valdivia, is also E. Phillippiana and, though sub-evergreen, is of extreme grace, its small green leaves providing the most fitting background for its sweetly-scented, starry, white flowers.

4-ft., June-September. DE. 4-ft. Sq. Sd2. Cg7. AN.

E. VISCOSA (Sticky) Chile, is also E. glutinosa ; differs but slightly from E. illinita in its hairy undercoating and stickier foliage, and its more pronounced evil odour. As compensation it adds an even stronger constitution.

10-ft., June-August. E. 10-ft. Sq. Sd2. Cg7. ANC.

EUCRYPHIA (EUCRYPHIACEAE) (FROM THE GR. EU—GOOD ; AND KRYPHIOS—CONCEALED ; A REFERENCE TO THE CAP-LIKE COVERING OF THE CALYX).

The species and their hybrids are best suited by woodland conditions, in soils which are either acid or neutral, and are best raised from seeds sown in light, sandy, peaty soil in February or March, when they germinate freely. Young seedlings require suitable care and are best grown on in pots until well established. Some of the species grow into appreciable trees and, in spite of their reputation for tenderness, persist permanently if nursed through their earlier years, even in the severest weather. Cuttings of the half-ripened wood root, but not readily, in sandy peat in June.

E. CORDIFOLIA (Leaves heart-shaped) Chile, is probably the most beautiful of all the species, and is also the most tender, but is worth all the protection and care the gardener can bestow. The dull green, heart-shaped leaves are produced upon downy branches, and the four- or five-petalled flowers of clear-white with terracotta anthers are reminiscent of the Rose of Sharon.

10-ft., September-October. E. 10-ft. Sq. Sd2. AN.

E. GLUTINOSA (Sticky) Chile, is also E. pinnatifolia, and makes an erect-growing but well-branched shrub, with three or five parted pinnate leaves which assume bright autumn tints before falling, and with large, open, white, Hypericum-like flowers with golden stamens. E. glutinosa plena has an extra petal or so, which is its only claim to mention.

12-ft.–18-ft., August. D. 12-ft. Sq. Sd2. AN. Pl.34.

E. INTERMEDIA (Intermediate) Garden origin, is a hybrid of E. lucida and E. glutinosa, and is also known as E. Rodgersii, and has evergreen, polished leaves of bright green, either simple or trifoliate, and bears large, white, typical flowers with a central cluster of thread-like stamens with pink anthers.

12-ft.–15-ft., August-September. E. 12-ft. Sq. Ch8. AN.

E. LUCIDA (Shining) Tasmania, is also E. Billardieri, and is a quick-growing, somewhat tender species with slender stems, and dark-green, shining leaves, with distinctly cup-shaped, white flowers holding thread-like stamens tipped with pink anthers, and pervading the surrounding air with its exquisite hawthorn scent.

10-*ft.*, *August.* *E.* 8-*ft. Sq.* *Sd*2. *AN.*

E. LUCIDA VAR. MILLIGANII (Comm.) Tasmania, differs only in its slow and more compact growth, and is a shrub to covet, to cajole, and to cosset. 6-*ft.*, *August.* *E.* 4-*ft. Sq.* *Sd*2. *AN.*

E. MOOREI (Comm.) Tasmania, is another to place in a warm and sheltered spot, and to watch and tend with care. Its distinctive features are its pinnate, eleven- to thirteen-parted leaves, green above and grey beneath, and its tabulate form, and smaller, but just as beautiful, clear-white flowers.

8-*ft.*, *August.* *E.* 8-*ft. Sq.* *Sd*2. *AN.*

E. NYMANSAY (Comm.) Garden origin, is a child of the parentage E. glutinosa and E. cordifolia, with a lusty vigour and incomparable beauty, which develops into a most attractive small tree. The leaves, which are similar to those of E. glutinosa, but are evergreen, and the flowers have the beauty of those of both parents.

30-*ft.*, *August.* *E.* 30-*ft. Sq.* *Cg*6. *AN.*

EUONYMUS (CELASTRACEAE) (FROM THE GR. EU—GOOD, ONOMA—A NAME, THAT IS, LUCKY; FROM THE PURPORTED ABILITY TO ENSURE GOOD FORTUNE).

The Spindle Trees number among them some of the most attractive of all garden shrubs, some deciduous, some evergreen. For autumn colour many of the varieties cannot be excelled, and though the flowers of most of the species are inconspicuous, and even if examined closely can be said only to be dingy in colour, they are generally followed by seed pods which have all the beauty of the most exotic of flowers. The deciduous varieties are best propagated from seed, which generally germinates freely, but if it fails to germinate during its first month or so should be weathered outside during the winter and brought into a warm house in March. Layers are an alternative where seed is not produced. The evergreen species are best propagated from cuttings three to four inches long, taken when the shrub is not in active growth, and placed in a frame with gentle bottom heat.

E. ALATUS (Winged) Japan, is a stiffly symmetrical, slow-growing, small shrub with winged stems of cross-like sections, the chief beauty of which is the habit of its leaves to turn to deep pink and crimson in colour as if to persuade the onlooker that the shrub has turned to one huge flower.

6-*ft.*, ——— *D.* 6-*ft. Sq.* *Sd*2. *ANC.* *Pl.*16.

E. ALATUS VAR. APTERUS (Wingless) China, is also E. subtriflorus, and lacks the winged stems of E. alatus, has narrower leaves, is more lax, and a trifle more free in growth, but assumes just as brilliant colours in the autumn. 8-*ft.*, ——— *D.* 8-*ft. Sq.* *Sd*2. *ANC.*

EUONYMUS (continued)

E. ALATUS VAR. COLORATUS (Coloured) Garden origin, is a seedling of E. alatus which is even brighter in its autumn colours, if such a thing is really possible. 6-*ft.*, ——— *E.* 6-*ft. Sq.* *Cg*6. *ANC.*

E. BUNGEANUS (Comm.) Manchuria, would indeed be a beauty if it could be compelled, cajoled, coaxed, or constrained to produce with freedom and regularity its fascinating, pale-yellow fruits, so tantalisingly tinted with pink.
10-*ft.*, ——— *D.* 10-*ft. Sq.* *Cg*6. *Sd*2. *ANC.*

E. EUROPAEUS (European) Europe and W. Asia, is the native Spindle Tree, so attractive because of its fascinating pink fruits which open to emit, for the pleasure of all who have eyes to see, its orange-red seeds. E. europaeus var. aldenhamensis is even better because it produces its fruits with greater freedom. E. europaeus var. atropurpureus has deep-purple foliage, turning scarlet in autumn, and E. europaeus var. fructu albo has white fruits which persist for a long period, and E. europaeus var. intermedius has large fruits of bright-rose. 5-*ft.*–7-*ft.*, ——— *D.* 7-*ft. Sq.* *Cg*6. *Sd*2. *ANC.*

E. FARRERI (Comm.) China, is a most attractive species with bright red fruits, narrow, almost insignificant, green leaves, which provides the most fascinating picture of all when its brilliant fruits are silhouetted upon the winter snow.
1-*ft.*, ——— *D.* 2-*ft. Sq.* *Sd*2. *ANC.*

E. GRANDIFLORUS (Large-flowered) W. China, is a very beautiful evergreen shrub with long, narrow, deep-green leaves, and large, primrose-yellow flowers which are followed by red and black fruits.
6-*ft. May-June.* *E.* 6-*ft. Sq.* *Sd*2. *ANC.*

E. LANCIFOLIUS (With lancet-like leaves) has leaves like those of the laurel, sometimes persistent, turning bright gold and red in autumn when the rose-coloured fruits are also in evidence.
6-*ft.*, *May-June.* *D.* 6-*ft. Sq.* *Sd*2. *ANC.*

E. LATIFOLIUS (With broad leaves) W. Asia, is a wide shrub with large, wide leaves turning dark-red in autumn at the same time as the large red fruits upon long, thread-like stems are also present.
12-*ft.*, *May-June.* *D.* 12-*ft. Sq.* *Sd*2. *ANC.*

E. NANUS (Small) Caucasus, is a rather larger shrub than E. Farreri, to which it bears a general resemblance.
2-*ft.*, *May-June.* *E.* 2-*ft. Sq.* *Sd*2. *ANC.*

E. OXYPHYLLUS (With pointed leaves) Japan, is a quickly growing shrub with long, pointed leaves which in autumn become crimson to match the masses of crimson fruits which it so freely bears.
10-*ft.*, *May-June.* *D.* 8-*ft. Sq.* *Sd*2. *ANC.*

E. PAUCIFLORUS (With few flowers) Korea, has pointed, oval leaves which colour brilliantly in autumn, young red wood gradually turning brown, and rose-coloured fruits.
6-*ft.*, ——— *D.* 6-*ft. Sq.* *Sd*2. *ANC.*

Fuchsia magellanica gracilis

Cytisus nigricans

E. PENDULUS (Pendulous) Himalayas, has red juvenile foliage, gradually paling through salmon to pink.

15-*ft.*, ——— *E.* 12-*ft. Sq.* *Sd2.* *ANC.*

E. PHELLOMANUS (With corky hands) resembles E. alatus, but has larger leaves and is more free in its growth, and bears rose-red fruits.

6-*ft.*, *May-June.* *D.* 8-*ft. Sq.* *Sd2.* *ANC.*

E. PLANIPES (With a flat foot) Japan, has some resemblance to E. latifolius but is less tall, though even more magnificent in its autumn colour. 6-*ft.*–8-*ft.*, *May-June.* *D.* 8-*ft. Sq.* *Sd2.* *ANC.*

E. RADICANS (Rooting) Japan, is a useful evergreen which will run over the surface of a bed, bank, or wall, and if its flowers and fruits seldom bother the eye, it will not often allow anything else to do so.

$\frac{1}{4}$-*ft.*, ——— *E.* *Variable.* *Cg5.* *ANC.*

E. RADICANS COLORATUS (Coloured) is a glamorised version with the underside of the leaves dark-red, the veins pale-yellow or pink, or even red, and if you like this sort of plant you just won't be able to be without it. $\frac{1}{4}$-*ft.*, ——— *E.* *Variable.* *Cg5.* *ANC.*

E. RADICANS MINIMUS (Tiny) is also E. kewensis, and adds the decorum of tiny leaves to the virtues or deficiencies of its larger brethren.

$\frac{1}{12}$-*ft.*, ——— *E.* *Variable.* *Cg5.* *ANC.*

E. SANGUINEUS (Blood-red) is one of the most beautiful of the species in the prodigality of its autumn colour, which combines crimson with intense scarlet. The loose, open branches are dull-red, the deep-green leaves are red upon the underside, and the fruits, which are not quite lost in the gallimaufry of colour, are deep crimson with yellow seeds. 8-*ft.*, ——— *D.* 10-*ft. Sq.* *Cg5.* *ANC.*

E. SIEBOLDIANUS (Comm.) China, has modestly winged branches, long, large, serrated leaves of deep-green assuming autumn colours, with its crimson fruits carried for a long period from late summer until the severe frosts. 8-*ft.*, ——— *D.* 10-*ft. Sq.* *Cg5.* *Sd2.* *ANC.*

E. WILSONII (Comm.) China, is remarkable among the genus Euonymus for its peculiar spiny fruits—rather like those of the Chestnut, enclosing yellow seeds. The small flowers are yellowish.

12-*ft.*, *June.* *E.* 10-*ft. Sq.* *Sd2.* *ANC.*

E. YEDOENSIS (From the Yedo or Tokio district) Japan, is one of the finest of all the varieties, the strong, branching stems being clad with large, minutely toothed leaves, which assume the most attractive colours in autumn when the bright rose-pink fruits are also present, and which persist after the leaves have fallen, and open to display the orange seeds.

5-*ft.*–8-*ft.*, *June.* *D.* 8-*ft. Sq.* *Sd2.* *ANC.* *Pl.*35.

E. YEDOENSIS VAR. KOEHNEANUS (Comm.) C. China, is another fine variety with deeper rose-coloured fruits.

5-*ft.*–8-*ft.*, *June.* *D.* 8-*ft. Sq.* *Sd2.* *ANC.*

EUPATORIUM (Compositae) (named after Mithridates "Eupator," King of Pontus, said by Pliny to have discovered among its species an antidote for poison).

E. micranthum (Bearing minute flowers) Chile, is also E. ligustrinum and E. Weinmannianum, and a quick-growing shrub with oblong, few-toothed leaves up to three inches in length, and flat heads of small, sweetly-scented, white flowers.

5-ft.–7-ft., August-November. E. 7-ft. Sq. Sd2. ANC.

EUPHORBIA (Euphorbiaceae) (of doubtful origin, said by some to be derived from Euphorbus, a physician to the King of Mauritania, by others from an old Latin name for the biting juice of a North-African cactus).

E. Wulfenii (Comm.) Dalmatia, gains place as a shrub in spite of its lack of woody growth, mainly because of its evergreen nature, and its long, narrow, bluish-green leaves are fittingly overtopped by sprays of small, pale-yellow flowers in any place.

3-ft., January-April. E. 3-ft. Sq. Sd2. ANC.

EXOCHORDA (Rosaceae) (from the Gr. exo—outside; and chorde—a cord; from the threads left when the seeds break out of the seed vessel).

The species are of easy growth in good soil in a sunny site, and can be propagated from seed where it is obtained, sown in February. Sucker growths can also be carefully detached with roots, or cuttings two or three inches long with a slight heel may be inserted in a cutting frame with gentle bottom heat in June.

E. Giraldii (Comm.) China, is a bush of rather erect habit with its young foliage of delicate pink tones developing to oval, green, elliptical leaves with pink main ribs, and small clusters of five-petalled, clear-white flowers, larger than a penny, centred by a cluster of twenty or more stamens. *6-ft.–8-ft., May. D. 8-ft. Sq. Sd2. Ch6. ANC.*

E. Giraldii var. Wilsonii (Comm.) C. China, has larger flowers in larger clusters, and bears the characteristic scent of the Hawthorn.

8-ft.–12-ft., May. D. 12-ft. Sq. Sd2. Cg6. ANC.

E. Korolkowii (Comm.) Turkestan, is also E. Albertii, and an upright growing species with clusters of clear-white flowers about the size of a halfpenny, produced from groups of buds which resemble pearls, and have given it the common name of the Pearl Bush.

8-ft.–12-ft., April. D. 12-ft. Sq. Sd2. Ch6. ANC.

E. macrantha (With long flowers) Garden origin, is a hybrid of E. Korolkowii with E. racemosa, and bears clusters of upwards of six large, pure-white, five-petalled flowers, produced with the greatest freedom in such a way as to make this one of the most beautiful of all spring flowering shrubs.

9-ft.–12-ft., May-June. D. 12-ft. Sq. Ch6. ANC.

E. RACEMOSA (Flowering in racemes) C. China, is also E. grandiflora, has flowers rather larger than those of E. Korolkowii, produced with the utmost freedom.

10-ft., April-May. D. 12-ft. Sq. Sd2. Ch6. ANC.

FABIANA (SOLANACEAE) (NAMED IN HONOUR OF A SPANISH ARCHBISHOP, E. FABIANO, A KEEN STUDENT OF BOTANY).

These members of the Nightshade family, near relatives of the Potato, are pleasing, heath-like shrubs with tiny, stiff, evergreen leaves crowded along the stems, and with erect, tubular flowers, widening at the mouth. They are propagated with ease if cuttings of the ripened wood, three to four inches long, are taken in July and placed in sandy soil (or sand) with gentle bottom heat.

F. IMBRICATA (With broad scales like tiles) Chile, is an attractive tender shrub reputed to reach ten feet in height in sheltered coastal districts, but more often met not exceeding four feet in height, wreathed from May to August with its small trumpet-like flowers of waxy white. *4-ft.–10-ft., May-August. E. 6-ft. Sq. Ch7. AN.*

F. IMBRICATA VAR. VIOLACEA (Violet) Garden origin, is variable, but generally more prostrate in its habit than E. imbricata, and either clad with flowers of dirty grey, euphemistically described as blue, or with pale-blue flowers which miss the purity of the type but gain somewhat in glamour, which at least is mitigated to some extent by the desire of the connoisseur to at last see a real blue Fabiana.

4-ft., May-August. E. 6-ft. Sq. Ch7. AN.

FATSIA (ARALIACEAE) (FROM THE JAPANESE NAME).

F. JAPONICA (Japanese) Japan, is also Aralia japonica and A. Sieboldii, is a most attractive bush with very large, smooth, evergreen leaves, cut into very wide, deep lobes, generally met as a greenhouse shrub but quite successful out of doors, and which bears whitish flowers in large panicles. It is best grown in a shady spot.

8-ft., October. E. 8-ft. Sq. Ch8. ANC.

FEIJOA (MYRTACEAE) (NAMED IN HONOUR OF J. DA FEIJO, A BOTANIST OF SAN SEBASTIAN).

The one species in general cultivation, F. Sellowiana, has a predilection for a chalky soil in which it is very hardy, but is generally best suited by a flanking wall with a southerly or westerly aspect. It is best propagated from cuttings of the half-ripened wood, taken in July and given gentle bottom heat.

F. SELLOWIANA (Comm.) Brazil, has deep green, opposite leaves, very white beneath, and is exceptionally pretty when the large, four-petalled, white flowers, centred with very numerous red stamens, are produced. *8-ft., August-September. E. 8-ft. Sq. Cg7. ANC.*

FENDLERA (SAXIFRAGACEAE) (NAMED IN HONOUR OF A. FENDLER, ONE OF THE EARLIEST BOTANICAL EXPLORERS OF NEW MEXICO).

The one species is a slow-growing shrub which required much sun and plenty of shelter, and can be propagated from cuttings of the half-ripened wood, about three inches in length, taken in July and placed in sandy soil with gentle bottom heat.

F. RUPICOLA (Growing in stony places) S.W. United States, is a low-growing, much-branched shrub with white, four-petalled flowers, tinted at the base with rose, about the size of a halfpenny.

4-ft., May-June. D. 4-ft. Sq. Cg7. AN. Shelter.

FORSYTHIA (OLEACEAE) (NAMED IN HONOUR OF WM. FORSYTH, AN ENGLISH BOTANIST, SOMETIME SUPERINTENDENT OF THE ROYAL GARDENS).

The species are fortunately of easy growth, succeeding always beyond one's expectations, in spite of the fact that the early flowers provide suitable food for innumerable sparrows in numberless towns, and that its branches are cut while still in bud to brighten many a room with their borrowed sunshine, never so bright as when silhouetted against a brilliant spring sky. Propagation may be made from cuttings four to six inches long from the young shoots in late June, placed in a warm sand frame, or alternatively cuttings twelve inches long of the hardened wood placed in sheltered places out of doors from October to December. Pruning should take place immediately after flowering as the flowers are borne upon the wood of the previous year.

F. GIRALDIANA (Comm.) Yunnan, is a slender-branched, spreading shrub with delicate, hanging, pale-yellow, scented, bell-flowers produced as early in the year as any of the flowers of the other varieties, but with a more graceful disposition. The broad leaves, produced after the flowers, are bronzy-green in colour.

6-ft.–8-ft., February-March. D. 8-ft. Sq. Cg7. Ch12. ANC.

F. INTERMEDIA (Intermediate) Garden origin, is a hybrid of F. suspensa with F. viridissima, and combines the pliant gracefulness of the former with the robust growth of the latter and, though it reaches ten feet when left unpruned, it may be trimmed to any desired height, when it will still be ornamented by its small clusters of golden-yellow flowers in March.

10-ft., March. D. 8-ft. Sq. Cg7. Ch12. ANC.

F. INTERMEDIA VAR. PRIMULINA (Primrose-like) Garden origin, is a very beautiful shrub with strong annual growths which become wreathed with primrose-yellow flowers with turned-back lobes.

7-ft., March-April. D. 7-ft. Sq. Cg7. Ch12. ANC.

F. INTERMEDIA VAR. SPECTABILIS (Showy) Garden origin, is probably the most floriferous variety of all, its robust stems being wreathed with dense clusters of flowers, larger than those of any other variety, of intense golden-yellow.

7-ft.–10-ft., March-April. D. 7-ft.–10-ft. Sq. Cg7. Ch12. ANC.

F. INTERMEDIA VAR. VITELLINA (The colour of the yolk of an egg) is a strong-growing variety with many clusters of deep yellow flowers, borne somewhat later than those of the other varieties.

6-ft.–10-ft., April-May. D. 6-ft.–10-ft. Sq. Cg7. Ch12. ANC.

F. JAPONICA (Japanese) Japan, is a rare shrub of rather slower growth than the other varieties, and of more compact habit, but with the typical flowers of the species.

4-ft.–6-ft., March-April. D. 4-ft.–6-ft. Sq. Cg7. Ch12. ANC.

F. OVATA (Elliptic, with wider base) Korea, is slow growing and much more compact than any other variety, and the exceptionally pretty, scented, golden-yellow bell flowers are freely produced in February.

4-ft.–5-ft., February-March. D. 4-ft.–6-ft. Sq. Cg7. Ch12. ANC.

F. SUSPENSA (Hanging downwards) Japan, is the most widely grown of the species, and is of spreading habit, so easy to grow that it will propagate itself, and will ramble anywhere and produce its golden-yellow flowers with complete disregard for place but not time.

10-ft., March-April. D. 12-ft. Sq. Cg7. Ch12. ANC. Pl.36.

F. SUSPENSA VAR. SIEBOLDII (Comm.) Japan, is rather more bushy in habit, and pendulous, clothing its own base much more adequately.

7-ft., March-April. D. 8-ft. Sq. Cg7. Ch12. ANC.

F. VIRIDISSIMA (Of deep green) China, is more robust, has larger flowers than F. suspensa, and if you prefer your charmers this way, must be your favourite, though its flowers have a tint of green which most of the others miss, but provide an effective contrast to its brilliant green stems.

12-ft., March-April. D. 12-ft. Sq. Cg7. Ch12. ANC.

FOTHERGILLA (HAMAMELIDACEAE) (IS NAMED IN HONOUR OF A DR. FOTHERGILL, A DISTINGUISHED GARDENER).

The genus consists of a group of deciduous shrubs with broadly oval leaves, with white flowers borne in round clusters, fragrant, and produced generally just before the leaves are in evidence. The best method of propagation is from cuttings three to four inches long, made with a slight heel and placed in a sand frame with a gentle bottom heat, and potted on singly when rooted and given the protection of a cold frame during the first winter. Fothergillas delight in a sandy peat and in a semi-shady site.

F. GARDENII (Comm.) Eastern U.S.A., is also F. alnifolia, and a shrub of somewhat tardy but certain growth, with witch-hazel-like leaves which assume the most attractive colours in autumn, and are preceded by sweet-scented, bottle-brush flowers, illuminated by bright-yellow anthers, in March and April.

5-ft., March-April. D. 5-ft. Sq. Sd2. Ch7. AN.

F. GARDENII VAR. GLAUCOPHYLLA (With glaucous leaves) Eastern U.S.A., is smaller in all its characteristics, with blue-green surfaces to its leaves, which are blue-grey beneath. In other particulars it closely resembles its type.

4-ft., March-April. D. 4-ft. Sq. Sd2. Ch7. AN.

F. MAJOR (Larger than the type) is a most fascinating shrub with cordate, much-netted leaves, and rounded spikes of sweetly-scented, white flowers, which deserves, but seldom obtains, a place in any garden.

6-ft., March-April. D. 4-ft. Sq. Sd2. Ch7. AN. Pl.37.

FOTHERGILLA (continued)

F. MONTICOLA (Growing on hills) N. Carolina, has hazel-like leaves and creamy-white flowers, and every shade of an autumn sunset in its autumn foliage.

3-ft., March-April. D. 3-ft. Sq. Sd2. Ch7. AN.

FRANKENIA (FRANKENIACEAE) (NAMED AFTER J. FRANKENIUS, A PROFESSOR OF BOTANY AT UPSALA IN 1660).

F. LAEVIS (Not rough) Europe, is the Sea Heath, a creeping shrub which forms a mat of heather-like foliage which turns crimson and orange in autumn, and bears small, five-petalled, stemless, pink flowers. *1/12-ft., July-August. E. Variable. Cg4. ANC.*

F. THYMIFOLIA (With thyme-like leaves) Europe, varies only in its ability to produce large flowers with greater freedom.

1/12-ft., July-August. E. Variable. Cg4. ANC.

FREMONTIA (STERCULIACEAE) (NAMED IN HONOUR OF THE AMERICAN COL. J. FREMONT, WHO DISCOVERED F. CALIFORNICA).

One shrub which reaches ten feet in height and is best grown in an impoverished soil, which will induce the production of a greater number of flowers. Unfortunately, this beautiful shrub is only hardy in sheltered sites in the more clement parts of Great Britain. The best methods of propagation are from seed, which should preferably be soaked for a few days before sowing singly in pots, and then potted on as may become necessary, or from greenwood cuttings taken in July and coaxed along with gentle bottom heat.

F. CALIFORNICA (Californian) Western U.S.A., is a partially evergreen tree with long-lobed, dull-green leaves, and which bears for a long period large, bright-yellow flowers made up of five sepals, and provides one of the most beautiful of all garden shrubs.

10-ft., May-October. DE. 10-ft. Sq. Sd2. Cg7. AN.

FUCHSIA (ONAGRACEAE) (NAMED AFTER LEONARD FUCHS, A SIXTEENTH-CENTURY GERMAN BOTANIST).

In spite of the tender reputation of the Fuchsias, all of which may or may not be cut to the ground in severe winters, many are delightfully beautiful, and when grown in protected surroundings can and do survive, and may be so freely produced with such ease from cuttings of the young, unhardened wood at any period of the year, that they should never be absent from the garden of a single enthusiast.

F. FULGENS (Glowing) Mexico, is one of the most tender, but one of the most exotic of the species, fitted only for the shelter of a south wall, which it will bedeck and bedizen sufficiently to attract the curious and the sophisticated with its large, lush green leaves, and its clusters of long, slender flowers made up mostly of a long, cerise-scarlet tube, but with its sepals tipped with pale green. It is so easily produced from cuttings that, even if an extra severe winter whisks it away, a little forethought will ensure that it can be easily replaced. 3-*ft.*–6-*ft.*, *May-October*. *D*. *Variable*. *Cg*6–12. *ANC*.

F. MAGELLANICA (From Magellan) S. America, is still known most often as F. macrostemma, and is the parent of all the garden Fuchsias. It has long, pendulous flowers made up of a scarlet calyx divided into four sepals, with a bright purple corolla composed of four petals, and will reach six feet or more in sheltered gardens. 6-*ft.*, *June-October*. *D*. 6-*ft. Sq*. *Cg*6–12. *ANC*.

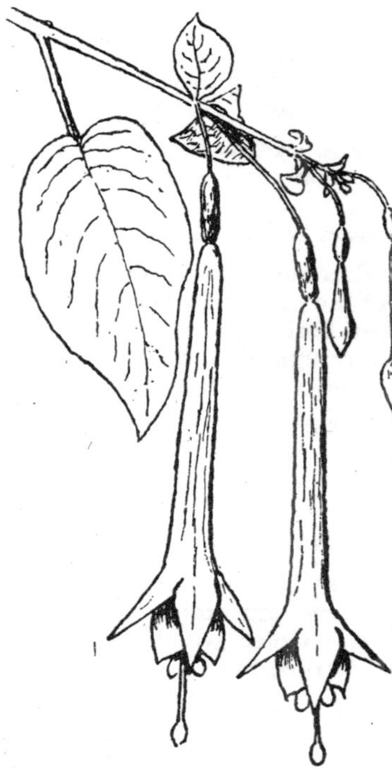

FUCHSIA FULGENS

F. MAGELLANICA VAR. ALBA (White) S. America, is undoubtedly misnamed, and is one of the hardiest of the species, a hedge here having survived—no, flourished—for the past ten years despite the most severe winters. The leaves are a paler green than those of the type, and the flowers, which have an elegant grace, are composed of very pale pink sepals and very pale lavender petals. 6-*ft.*, *June-October*. *D*. 6-*ft. Sq*. *Cg*6–12. *ANC*. *Pl*.38.

F. MAGELLANICA VAR. CORALLINA (Coral-red) Garden origin, is either more prostrate or more climbing in its habit according to its situation, and few plants exist which are better for either purpose, the bright green leaves providing the ideal background for the entrancingly beautiful flowers of coral-red and purple.

¼-ft., June-October. D. 6-ft. Sq. Cg6–12. ANC.

F. MAGELLANICA VAR. GRACILIS (Slender) Garden origin, has small red and purple flowers with very round buds.

5-ft., June-September. D. 5-ft. Sq. Cg6–12. Ch6. ANC. Pl.39.

F. MAGELLANICA VAR. PRUNELLA (Comm.) Garden origin, is another variety rescued from a cottage garden, with larger leaves and flowers than the foregoing, but which covers itself with its flowers for such long periods as to be indispensable.

1-ft., June-September. D. 1-ft. Sq. Cg6–12. Ch6. ANC.

F. MAGELLANICA VAR. PUMILA (Dwarf) Garden origin, is a tiny plant very seldom exceeding one foot, with very slender, hanging flowers with scarlet sepals and a purple corolla.

1-ft., June-September. D. ⅔-ft. Sq. Cg6–12. Ch6. ANC.

F. MAGELLANICA VAR. RICCARTONII (Grown at the Riccarton Gardens), Edinburgh, is one of the most magnificent of all hedging plants, but also one of the most floriferous of shrubs, its slender, purple and scarlet flowers being produced in the utmost profusion.

5-ft., June-September. D. 5-ft. Sq. Cg6–12. Ch6. ANC.

F. MICROPHYLLA (Small-leaved) Mexico, is a very low-growing bush of less than three feet in height, with very small leaves but profuse, tiny, quaintly shaped, pink flowers borne all along the willowy branches.

2½-ft., July-October. D. 3-ft. Sq. Cg6–12. Ch6. ANC.

F. PROCUMBENS (Prostrate) New Zealand, is prostrate in its habit, and has circular green leaves and amber and green flowers with bent-back sepals tipped with violet, which are outshone by the large red fruits which ultimately turn black.

¼-ft., June-October. D. 1½-ft. Sq. Cg4. AN.

F. THYMIFOLIA (With thyme-like leaves) Mexico, is somewhat similar to F. microphylla but has larger leaves, and larger flowers of coral-pink and of delicate and quaint shape, borne upon willow branches clad with small, bright-green leaves.

2½-ft.–4-ft., July-October. D. 2½-ft. Sq. Ch6. Cg6–12. ANC.

GALAX (DIAPENSIACEAE) (FROM GR. GALA—MILK ; AN ALLUSION TO THE WHITE FLOWERS OF THE SPECIES).

A shade-loving shrub suited best to a soil composed of sandy peat.

G. APHYLLA (No leaves, that is, upon the flower stalks) N. America, has round, green, shiny, serrated leaves edged with scarlet, of exceptional charm, which excuse and compensate for the fact that the flowers which the plant bears are indifferently displayed upon foot-high spikes. *1-ft., June. E. 1-ft. Sq. D8. AN.*

Hibiscus syriacus

Hibiscus syriacus fl. pl.

GARRYA (Garryaceae) (named by douglas in honour of a w. garry of the hudson bay company, who rendered him considerable assistance in his expeditions in n.w. america).

The genus is given the general name Silk Tassel Bush from the appearance of the unisexual flowers without petals, borne in catkin-like racemes. Indifferent as to soil, the species are best propagated from cuttings four to six inches long, taken in August and placed in sand, and given gentle bottom heat. Seeds will produce plants of both sexes, but however raised the young plants are best grown on singly in pots until they may be finally planted out in permanent quarters.

G. elliptica (With elliptical leaves) California, is unfortunately tender, but the male form is a grand shrub for coastal gardens, and just as good inland where it is given the protection of a backing wall. The leaves call to mind those of the evergreen oak, and are ornamented by the long, drooping, catkin-like inflorescences of silvery-grey, produced in January and February.
6-ft.–12-ft., January-February. E. 6-ft.–12-ft. Sq. Cg8. Sd2. ANC.

G. macrophylla (With long leaves) Mexico, displays but little beauty in flower, but is undeniably an extremely attractive evergreen shrub. *10-ft., February. E. 8-ft. Sq. Cg8. Sd2. ANC.*

G. Thuretii (Comm.) Garden origin, is a tender, evergreen shrub of attractive appearance, which seldom, in spite of its vigour, troubles to flower and, if it did, would add little to its otherwise attractive appearance. *10-ft., —— E. 8-ft. Sq. Cg8. Sd2. ANC.*

GAULNETTYA (Gaulnettyaceae) (gaultheria × pernettya).

A bigeneric cross between a Gaultheria and a Pernettya, which can only be propagated from division or cuttings, and needs a sandy peat soil in which to succeed. The one species is a result of artificial hybridisation successfully accomplished at the Royal Horticultural Society's Gardens at Wisley.

G. Wisleyana (Of Wisley) Garden origin, is an attractive bush which bears sprays of pearly-white, Lily-of-the-valley flowers, which are followed by large purple, or almost black, berries.
2-ft.–2½-ft., May-June. E. 2½-ft. Sq. Cg7. D10. AN.

GAULTHERIA (Ericaceae) (the species is named in honour of dr. gaulthier, a physician who lived in quebec).

This group of evergreen sub-shrubs generally produces bell-shaped flowers reminiscent of those of the Lily of the valley, followed by fruits consisting of the swollen calyx which is generally brightly coloured. All are best suited to lime-free or acid soils, and sites from which the maximum of summer sunlight is naturally excluded. Propagation of the small-leaved varieties should consist of two-inch cuttings, taken in August and brought to manhood in a cold frame. The varieties with larger leaves should have similar treatment but deserve the added insurance of an extra three inches in the length of the cutting. All the species may also be propagated from seed which should, of course, be sown in a lime-free soil.

G. ADENOTHRIX (With glandular hair) Japan, has, as its enviable distinction, the largest flowers of the species, white flushed with pink, and succeeded by red berries very like those of the Holly.
1-ft., June. E. 1½-ft. Sq. Cg4–8. Sd2. AN.

G. ANTIPODA (From the Antipodes) Tasmania, New Zealand, is an exceptionally hardy, compact and erect shrub with small, round, brown-green leaves, and sprays of pearly-white flowers followed by fruits of a similar colour.
2-ft., June. E. 2-ft. Sq. Cg4–8. Sd2. AN.

G. CAUDATA (With a tail) W. China, is a much larger shrub, with olive-green, heavily netted leaves, grey-green beneath, and short sprays of small, round, greeny-white flowers.
5-ft., May-June. E. 5-ft. Sq. Cg4–8. Sd2. AN.

G. CUMINGIANA (Comm.) Formosa, is a small shrub with irregularly jointed red stems of angular pattern, clothed with oval, acutely pointed, serrated, shining green leaves, and short sprays of globular, greeny-white flowers flushed with crimson and followed by red-brown fruits.
1½-ft., June-October. E. 2-ft. Sq. Sd2. Cg8. AN. Tender.

G. CUNEATA (Wedge-shaped) W. China, is a very attractive dwarf with reddish-brown stems, long sprays of white Lily-of-the-valley flowers which are succeeded by large snow-white fruits.
1-ft., June-September. E. 1-ft. Sq. Sd2. Cg8. AN.

G. DEPRESSA (Lying down flat) New Zealand, makes a mat of upright, wiry stems clad with round, green leaves, red underneath, and bears very small white flowers, which are followed by handsome, large, red fruits. G. depressa var. fructu albo is similar but has white fruits. *6-in., June-September. E. 1-ft. Sq. Sd2. Cg8. AN.*

G. FAGIFOLIA (With beech leaves) New Zealand, is a natural hybrid of G. oppositifolia and G. antipoda, and has round, deckle-edged, shiny leaves, with small white flowers followed by either white or red fruits. *1½-ft., June-September. E. 1½-ft. Sq. Sd2. Cg8. AN.*

G. FRAGRANTISSIMA (Most fragrant) India, has the red stems so often found in the species, and oblong, blunt-toothed, dark-green leaves with turned-back edges, and small sprays of white bell flowers appearing at the leaf axils are followed by fruits which may be white or pale blue. *2-ft., June-September. 2-ft. Sq. Sd2. Cg8. AN.*

G. GRIFFITHII (Comm.) Himalayas, has bright-green, oblong, sharp-pointed, serrated leaves, and is of weeping habit, and bears axillary sprays of small, white, Lily-of-the-valley flowers which, as a rule, prove abortive.
2-ft.–4-ft., June-September. E. 4-ft. Sq. Cg8. AN.

G. HISPIDA (Somewhat rough) Australia, makes a medium-sized bush with lance-shaped, deep-green leaves, much mottled, which turn bright red in autumn. The attractive white flower sprays are succeeded in autumn by large white fruits.

2-ft., June-July. E. 2-ft. Sq. Cg4. Cg8. Sd2. AN.

G. HOOKERI (Comm.) Himalayas, is a tender species with large, deep-green, netted leaves, and the typical white bell flowers are seldom followed in this country by fruits.

2-ft., June. E. 4-ft. Sq. Cg8. Sd2. AN.

G. HUMIFUSA (Creeping along the surface of the ground) N.W. America, is also known as G. myrsinites, and has small, round, shiny, wavy-edged leaves, white bell flowers sometimes tinged with pink, and fruits of bright holly-red.

1/6-ft., June. E. 1-ft. Sq. Cg8. Sd2. AN.

G. MERILLIANA (Comm.) Formosa, is another tender species with small, oval, green leaves enlivened with reddish veins, white typical flowers, and white fruits sometimes becoming pinkish.

1/2-ft., June. E. 2-ft. Sq. Cg8. Sd2. AN.

G. MIQUELIANA (Comm.) Japan, has heavily netted, apple-green foliage, very pretty sprays of clear white flowers followed by large, ridged, white fruits. *3/4-ft., June. E. 2-ft. Sq. Cg8. Sd2. AN.*

G. NUMMULARIOIDES (Resembling Moneywort) Himalayas, makes a flattish mat of long strands of heart-shaped leaves edged with hairs, and becoming increasingly smaller towards the tips, and bears, generally in complete privacy beneath the branches, pendent, dull pink, bell flowers, which may, or may not, be followed by black berries. *1/2-ft., June. E. 3-ft. Sq. Cg4. Cg8. Sd2, AN.*

G. NUMMULARIOIDES VAR. NUMMULARIFOLIA (With leaves like Moneywort) W. China, is also G. minor, and is an exceptionally pretty carpeter with small leaves, more diffuse growth, and is generally sufficiently shy not to produce either flowers or fruit.

1/6-ft., June: E. 3-ft. Sq. Cg8. AN.

G. NUMMULARIOIDES VAR. MINUTA (Tiny) W. China, is smaller still, just creeping along the surface of the ground, but can provide the enthusiast with many a thrill when spangled with its brown, and red solitary flowers in the leaf axils.

1/12-ft., June. E. 2-ft. Sq. Sd2. Cg8. AN.

G. OVATIFOLIA (With ovate leaves) British Columbia, is a most attractive variety with semi-weeping, hairy stems and small, pale-green leaves, white flowers flushed with pink, succeeded by bright-red flattened fruits. *1-ft., May-June. E. 1-ft. Sq. Sd2. Cg8. AN.*

G. PROCUMBENS (Prostrate) N. America, is the Wintergreen, Checkerberry, or Teaberry, has foliage of polished green, reddening in autumn, each white Lily-of-the-valley flower tinged with pink, maturing to a large, holly-red berry curiously cut at the apex.

1/2-ft., May-June. E. 3-ft. Sq. Dg. Cg8. Sd2. AN.

GAULTHERIA (continued)

G. PYROLIFOLIA (With leaves like Wintergreen—Pyrola) Himalayas, mats the surface of the ground with small, bluntly round, netted, bright-green leaves, and bears small sprays of tiny, pale-pink flowers.
¼-ft., May-July. E. 2-ft. Sq. Dg. Cg8. AN.

G. SHALLON (An American native name) N.W. America, is the Salal, and makes an impenetrable bush clad with broad, oval, dark green leaves, with sprays of white flowers more or less deeply flushed with pink, and purple to black fruits good to eat. This plant will succeed completely under and in the shelter of trees.
2-ft., May-June. E. 6-ft. Sq. D9. Cg8. Sd2. AN.

G. TETRAMERA (In whorls of four) S.W. China, is a pleasing bush with dark-green, netted leaves, and many small white flowers, and light-blue to dark-violet, pear-shaped fruits.
2-ft., May-June. E. 4-ft. Sq. D9. Cg8. Sd2. AN.

G. TRICHOPHYLLA (With hairy foliage) Himalayas, is one of the most fascinating of all the species, making a dwarf mat of wiry stems, neatly clothed with small, shining, green, hairy leaves, and followed by berries which are at first dirty brown, then, as they increase in size, pale pink, and finally become bright pale-blue.
¼-ft., May-June. E. 1-ft. Sq. Sd9. D9. Cg8. AN.

G. VEITCHIANA (Comm.) C. China, is one of the most beautiful of the larger-growing species, with larger elliptical to oblong, sage-green, netted leaves, sprays of white Lily-of-the-valley flowers, and copious, large, bright-blue fruits which persist well into the winter.
3-ft., May-June. E. 3-ft. Sq. Sd9. Cg8. AN.

G. WARDII (Comm.) Tibet, is a tender variety with sharply pointed leaves, white flowers upon the old wood, and blue berries powdered with white farina. *4-ft., May-June. E. 4-ft. Sq. Sd9. Cg8. AN.*

GAYLUSSACIA (VACCINIACEAE) (NAMED IN HONOUR OF L. J. GAY-LUSSAC, THE FRENCH SCIENTIST).

These shrubs, commonly called HUCKLEBERRIES, are all best suited by woodland conditions in peaty soil, and are grown mainly for the exquisite beauty of the autumn colours assumed by their pretty leaves. They are best propagated from cuttings made of the tips of the current growth, taken during August and inserted in sandy peat in a cold frame.

G. BACCATA (Berried) N. America, is also G. resinosa, which name it has acquired from the dots of gum which it bears upon the underside of its oval green leaves. The sprays of flowers, which resemble those of Gaultheria, are pale-red and are followed by blue berries.
5-ft., June. D. 5-ft. Sq. Cg8. AN.

G. BRACHYCERA (Short-horned) Eastern N. America, is the Box Huckleberry, a dwarf, small-leaved shrub, the leaves of which are initially red, ultimately becoming dark glossy green. The white bell flowers, like those of the Pyrola, are streaked with pink and are followed by blue fruits. $1\frac{1}{2}$-*ft.*, *May-June.* *E.* 2-*ft. Sq.* *Cg*8. *AN.*

G. FRONDOSA (Covered with leaves) Eastern U.S.A., is also G. glauca and the Dangleberry, a thinly branched shrub with young, grey-green leaves which age to markedly blue-green, and short sprays of pale greenish-purple flowers, followed by blue berries with a white "bloom." 4-*ft.*, *June.* *D.* 4-*ft. Sq.* *Cg*8. *AN.*

G. URSINA (Liked by bears) Carolina, is the Bear Huckleberry or Buckberry, and a very attractive shrub with long, oval, green leaves and bell-shaped flowers of creamy-white tinged with red, followed by shining black berries.
6-*ft.*, *May-June.* *E.* 6-*ft. Sq.* *Cg.* *AN.*

GENISTA (LEGUMINOSAE) (FROM THE CELTIC GEN—A SMALL BUSH; OR FROM THE OLD LATIN NAME GENISTA, FROM GENU—JOINT).

A genus allied to Cytisus, in general suited to reasonably light soil and a fully sunny exposure. The true species are best increased from seeds which should be sown in February. Cuttings are best made of the thin side shoots, taken with a heel so that no pith is exposed, and inserted in sandy soil, in April or August, in a frame freely exposed to sun and light. They should be left undisturbed until the following spring, when they should be potted on.

G. AETNENSIS (From Etna) Sicily, is a very fast-growing, rush-like shrub with inconspicuous leaves, with the tops of the slender stems covered with masses of golden-yellow pea flowers.
10-*ft.*–15-*ft.*, *July-August.* *D.* 10-*ft.*–12-*ft.* *Sd*2. *ANC.*

G. CINEREA (Ash-grey) S.W. Europe, has long, slender, silky, whip-like branches tipped with sprays of butter-yellow pea flowers which persist for long periods.
3-*ft.*–8-*ft.*, *July-September.* *D.* 3-*ft.*–6-*ft. Sq.* *Sd*2. *ANC.*

G. DALMATICA (Dalmatian) is G. sylvestris var. pungens.

G. DELPHINENSIS (From the Dauphiné) W. Europe, is a very small shrub with winged stems, like a tiny edition of G. sagittalis, sometimes classified as G. sagittalis var. minor. It makes a tight tuft of flattened, knitted stems, from the ends of which rise many clusters of golden-yellow flowers.
$\frac{1}{4}$-*ft.*, *June-July.* *D.* 1-*ft. Sq.* Cg4–8. *A.*

G. GERMANICA (Of German origin) Europe, is a dwarf, spiny shrub with small, dark-green, narrow leaves, and short sprays of bright-yellow pea flowers with turned-back standards.
2-*ft.*, *June.* *D.* 2-*ft. Sq.* *Sd*2. *ANC.*

G. HISPANICA (Spanish) S.W. Europe, is the Spanish Gorse, makes a dwarf, neatly rounded, spiny shrub, seldom more than two feet in height, which becomes obscured by the innumerable sprays of small, golden-yellow flowers in May and June.
2-*ft.*, *May-June.* *D.* 2-*ft. Sq.* *Sd*2. *Cg*8. *ANC.*

G. HORRIDA (Horrid, spiny) France, Spain, makes a small, rounded shrub of spiny, silver stems, like ERINACEA pungens, and covers itself with clusters of the brightest golden pea flowers of the genus.

½-ft., June-July. D. 1-ft. Sq. Cg4–8. ANC.

G. JANUENSIS (Looking both ways) S. Europe, is G. triquetra of catalogues, and makes a mat of triangular stems with lance-shaped, shiny, green leaves, and large cylindrical heads of rather small, bright-yellow flowers.

½-ft., May-June. D. 2-ft. Sq. Sd2. Cg8. N.

G. LYDIA (From Lydia) Asia Minor, is a most graceful shrub with rising, pale-green stems which become pendent at the tips, and distributes its fascinating clusters of butter-yellow pea flowers with artistry linked with symmetry.

1½-ft., May-June. D. 2-ft. Sq. Cg4. N.

G. PILOSA (Covered with soft hair) S. Europe, is a delightful prostrate shrub, gradually increasing in height but seldom exceeding half a foot. The thin, neat growths are clothed with small, deep-green leaves richly patterned with small clusters of deep-yellow flowers.

½-ft., June. D. 2-ft. Sq. Cg4. ANC.

G. PULCHELLA (Little and beautiful) Dalmatia, is G. Villarsii of catalogues, and has thin, grey, microscopic leaves and bright-yellow flowers. Two forms appear to exist in commerce, one of which is perfectly prostrate and the other with its thin stems pointed heavenwards, but both deserve equal praise.

⅙-ft.–¼-ft., June-July. D. ⅛-ft. Sq. Cg4–8. N.

G. RADIATA (Rayed) S.E. Europe, forms a bush of silvery-grey, spidery stems, well rounded and shapely, and symmetrically ornamented by neat, terminal heads of deep golden-yellow flowers.

1½-ft., June-July. D. 1½-ft. Sq. Cg4. Sd2. N.

G. SAGITTALIS (Like an arrow) S. Europe, is the Austrian Arrow Broom, and forms itself into a tangled mat of green leaves which rise from flat, angular stems and become tipped with long sprays of bright golden-yellow flowers.

¾-ft., June-July. D. 1½-ft. Sq. Cg4. Sd2. N.

G. SYLVESTRIS VAR. PROCUMBENS (Wild ; prostrate) Balkans, is a rock-clinging, prostrate mass of twiggy stems, ornamented with small, deep-green leaves, and becomes covered with small golden clusters of pea flowers. *¼-ft., June-July. D. 1½-ft. Sq. Cg4. Sd2. N.*

G. SYLVESTRIS VAR. PUNGENS (Wild ; piercing) Balkans, is also known as G. dalmatica (Bartl) and is a dwarf, running bush of very sharp, spiny stems of neatly symmetrical habit, with small clusters of minute golden flowers.

¾-ft., June-July. E. 1-ft. Sq. Cg4. Sd2. N.

G. TINCTORIA (Used for dyeing) Europe, is the Dyer's Greenwood, and covers a number of plants differing in certain characteristics, but all bearing marked resemblance to each other. The type may be said to be a low shrub with dark-green, spear-shaped leaves, and branching heads of large, deep-yellow pea flowers.

1-ft., June-September. D. 3-ft. Sq. Cg4. Sd2. N.

G. TINCTORIA VAR. ANXANTICA (Making yellow) Italy, is a delightful prostrate variety with slender stems, and flowers larger than those of the type. *¼-ft., June-August. D. 2-ft. Sq. Cg4–8. Sd2. N.*

G. TINCTORIA VAR. HUMIFUSA (Creeping on the surface) is a charming prostrate shrub with small, oval, pointed, green leaves and many small clusters of small bright-yellow flowers.

¼-ft., June-July. D. 2-ft. Sq. Cg4–8. N.

G. TINCTORIA VAR. MANTICA (From Mantua) Italy, is an upright-growing, slender-branched shrub with long spires of brilliant yellow flowers. *3-ft., June-August. D. 3-ft. Sq. Cg4–8. N.*

G. TINCTORIA VAR. PLENA (With double flowers) Europe, is prostrate in growth but sends its double flowers in long sprays upwards, becoming at such times a brilliant display of golden-yellow heads.

1-ft., June-July. D. 3-ft. Sq. Cg4–8. N.

G. VIRGATA (Made up of willowy twigs) Madeira, is a tall shrub of very compact, upright habit, with grey-green leaves and short, terminal sprays of rather large, golden-yellow pea flowers with a neatly rounded standard.

12-ft., June-July. D. 8-ft. Sq. Cg4–8. Sd2. N.

GORDONIA (TERNSTROEMIACEAE) (NAMED IN HONOUR OF ALEXANDER GORDON, AN EAST-END NURSERYMAN).

Both species are tender and suited only to the more clement districts of Great Britain, and are best grown in semi-shaded sites. They may be propagated from cuttings of the half-ripened wood three to four inches in length, taken in late July or August and placed in sandy peat with gentle bottom heat.

G. ALATAMAHA (From the banks of the Alatamaha River) is generally spelt Altamaha, but was not originally so, and is a deciduous shrub or small tree with large, long, green leaves, delightfully tinted in autumn, with large, white, cup-shaped flowers singly produced on short, stout stalks.

8-ft.–20-ft., August. D. 8-ft.–20-ft. Sq. Cg7–8. N.

G. AXILLARIS (Growing in the axils) China, is a large evergreen shrub with long, dark-green leaves and almost stemless, single white Camellia flowers, produced at the tops of the shoots at any time from November to May according to climatic conditions. G. axillaris is only fitted to be grown in the most sheltered and favourable sites and is not a shrub for everyone.

8-ft.–12-ft., November-May. E. 12-ft. Sq. Cg7. AN.

GREVILLEA (PROTEACEAE) (THE NAME IS COMMEMORATIVE OF CHARLES E. GREVILLE, A PRESIDENT OF THE ROYAL SOCIETY).

The Grevilleas succeed in sheltered sites in lime-free soils, and are best propagated from cuttings of the fully hardened wood, taken in July and placed in sandy peat in a cold frame.

G. ALPINA (Alpine) S. Australia, is a most attractive shrub with grey-green, narrow leaves, rounded habit, and curious snail-like buds of bright cerise-red, uncurling into queer-shaped flowers of pink and bright-red with a long protruding yellow style.

1-ft., January-December. E. 1-ft. Sq. Ch7. A.

G. ROSMARINIFOLIA (Rosemary-leaved) New South Wales, has longer and deeper-green leaves, and rather larger flowers of the same shape but of brighter rose-red, and is a very graceful shrub for seaside districts.

5-ft.–6-ft., January-August. E. 8-ft. Sq. Ch7. A. Pl.65.

G. SULPHUREA (Sulphur-yellow) New South Wales, is more hardy, has shorter leaves, is more upright and has similarly shaped flowers of bright pale-yellow. *8-ft., May-June. E. 6-ft. Sq. Ch7. A.*

G. THYRSOIDES (With compact clusters of flowers) New South Wales, is more upright than G. rosmarinifolia, has narrower leaves and even brighter flowers.

5-ft.–6-ft., January-August. E. 6-ft. Sq. Ch7. A.

HALESIA (STYRACACEAE) (NAMED IN HONOUR OF DR. STEPHEN HALES, AN EIGHTEENTH-CENTURY ENGLISH BOTANIST).

The Halesias or Snowdrop Trees flourish in soils which are free from lime, and are best produced from layers made in early spring, or from root cuttings taken at the same time.

H. CAROLINA (From Carolina) N. America, is also H. tetraptera and an exceedingly beautiful small tree or shrub of spreading habit, with alternate, toothed, oval leaves and drooping sprays of white, four-petalled, snowdrop-like flowers which are followed by four winged seeds.

15-ft.–20-ft., May-June. D. 15-ft.–20-ft. Sq. Cr4. L4. A.

HALIMIOCISTUS (CISTACEAE) (FROM GR. HALIMOS—SEA COAST; AND KISTOS, THE OLD GREEK NAME FOR THE ROCK ROSE).

The species grows well in good garden soils, in positions which are sunny. Propagation is from three-inch cuttings of the tips of the branches, taken in August, placed in sandy soil and left until the following spring in the frame into which they are put.

H. SAHUCII (Comm.) France, is more commonly known as Cistus Sahucii, and is a low-growing shrub with rounded, grey-green leaves and white, buttercup-like flowers produced in profusion. A bi-generic natural cross, H. Sahucii is very beautiful.

1-ft., July-September. E. 2-ft. Sq. Cg8. ANC.

Hibiscus syriacus coelestis

Hydrangea hortensis, florists' varieties

HALIMIUM (*see* **HELIANTHEMUM**).

HALIMODENDRON (LEGUMINOSAE) (FROM GR. HALIMOS—SEA COAST; AND DENDRON—A TREE; A REFERENCE TO THE NATIVE HABITAT OF THE PLANT).

The one species is best grown on lime-free soils and propagated from seeds sown in February.

H. HALODENDRON (Salt-tree) Siberia, is also known as H. argenteum, and is a very handsome shrub with grey foliage, with leaves divided into two or four leaflets enlivened with small, pinkish pea flowers in June and July. A splendid shrub for light or poor soils, it is also resistant to sea spray, as its common name, the Siberian Salt Tree, indicates. *6-ft., June-July. D. 6-ft. Sq. Sd2. ANC.*

HAMAMELIS (HAMAMELIDACEAE) (FROM GR. HAMA—TOGETHER; AND MELA—FRUIT; THE FRUIT AND FLOWERS OF THE SHRUB OFTEN BEING PRESENT TOGETHER).

As a rule the best method of propagation is from seeds, but these generally take two years in which to germinate, and scions of the better flowering kinds are grafted upon stocks of H. virginiana. All varieties require a deep, rich soil, and cannot be regarded as a success upon chalky soils.

H. JAPONICA (Japanese) Japan, is extremely variable, both in habit and in the colour of its flowers, but in the type is a large, spreading shrub with many branching shoots, with large, simple, toothed, rough, green-surfaced leaves up to four inches in length, but which bears its curious flowers, made up of undulating, strap-like petals of pale yellow, before the leaves appear, beginning in January with a touch of sunshine, but shining with a blaze of colour in February. In addition, it diffuses a fascinating scent.
10-ft., January-February. D. 10-ft. Sq. Sd2. Gr3. AN.

H. JAPONICA VAR. ARBOREA (Like a tree) Japan, is a grand shrub of open or almost tree-like habit and fine fan-shaped branches, which, from December to March, are thickly set with scented, tawny-yellow flowers, claret at the base, composed of golden tinsel, and is admirably placed against a wall which faces north or east.
10-ft.–25-ft., December-March. D. 10-ft.–25-ft. Sq. G3. AN.

H. JAPONICA VAR. FLAVO-PURPURASCENS (Yellowish-purple) Japan, is also H. rubra, and is variable, but in its best forms has petals of old gold with reddish-purple calyx.
10-ft.–25-ft., December-March. D. 10-ft.–25-ft. Sq. G3. AN.

H. JAPONICA VAR. ZUCCARINIANA (Comm.) Japan, is of less robust growth, is later-flowering, and has lemon-yellow flowers based upon a green calyx. *10-ft., March. D. 10-ft. Sq. G3. AN.*

H. MOLLIS (Downy) China, is the Chinese Witch Hazel, has dark-green, large leaves, often six inches in length, dark-green above and downy below, turning golden-yellow with age, and ineffably scented, golden-yellow flowers made up of strap-like petals under which appears the claret calyx.

7-ft.–9-ft., December-February. D. 9-ft. Sq. Sd2. G3. AN.

H. VERNALIS (Flowering in spring) Southern U.S.A., is a gracefully branched shrub, reproducing from suckers, with grey-green leaves almost smooth beneath and turning bright-yellow in autumn, which are followed by sweetly-scented, small red flowers with a dark-red calyx.

6-ft., January-February. D. 6-ft. Sq. Sd2. G3. Suckers. AN.

H. VIRGINIANA (Virginian) N. America, is the Witch Hazel, source of the precious unguent beloved by our forefathers, which loses much of its glamour because it produces its many pleasant, sweetly-scented, small, golden-yellow flowers while its leaves still remain to hide and subdue them.

8-ft.–15-ft., September-November. D. 8-ft.–15-ft. Sq. Sd2. AN.

HARRIMANELLA (ERICACEAE) (A COMMEMORATIVE NAME).

One species, allied to CASSIOPE, requiring a shady site and sandy, peaty soil in which to grow, and which may be propagated from seed.

H. STELLARIANA (Starry) Japan, is a pretty, prostrate shrub with thin, wiry stems closely clothed with small brown-green leaves, and throws up, on two-inch stems, small white bell flowers, each with a crimson calyx. *¼-ft., April-June. E. 1-ft. Sq. Sd2. AN.*

HEDYSARUM (LEGUMINOSAE) (FROM THE GR. HEDYS—SWEET; AND SARON—BROOM).

One shrubby species which grows well in any good garden soil, and reproduces most readily from seed.

H. MULTIJUGUM (Having many pairs of leaves) S. Mongolia, is a curious shrub with zig-zag stems, pinnately divided leaves made up of ten to twenty pairs of leaflets, and sprays of magenta pea flowers produced in late summer. Generally an untidy shrub, it requires careful pruning. *5-ft., July-August. D. 6-ft. Sq. Sd2. AN.*

HELIANTHEMUM (CISTACEAE) (FROM GR. HELIOS—SUN; AND ANTHEMON—A FLOWER).

These are the Sun Roses, which may be regarded as the dwarf section of the Cistus family, and are eminently suited for sunny positions at the front of the shrub garden. The best method of propagation is from cuttings of the half-ripened wood, about eight inches in length, taken in June and placed in a sand frame or in sandy loam. Included in the varieties specified below are some now more correctly to be known as HALIMIUM, the old name being retained because it is more widely used.

H. ALPESTRE (Of the Lower Alps) S. Europe, forms a low mat of small shining green leaves which is obscured with sprays of small yellow flowers. *⅙-ft., June-July. E. 1-ft. Sq. Cg6. ANC.*

H. ALPESTRE VAR. SERPYLLIFOLIUM (With leaves resembling Thyme) S. Europe, is smaller in all its parts, has grey-green foliage, but rises a little higher from the ground.

¼-ft., June-July. E. 1-ft. Sq. Cg6. ANC.

H. ALYSSOIDES (Like Alyssum) S.W. Europe, is an attractive shrub with grey leaves, blunt at the tips, and which bears large, golden, open, flattened, buttercup-like flowers, completely unmarked. Is more correctly Halimium alyssoides.

1-ft., June-July. E. 1½-ft. Sq. Cg6. ANC.

H. APENNINUM (From the Apeninnes) Europe, is a low spreading bush with grey leaves and large white flowers.

1½-ft., June-July. E. 1½-ft. Sq. Cg6. ANC.

H. FORMOSUM (Beautiful) Portugal, has very grey, pointed leaves, grey-green stems and golden-yellow flowers about the size of a penny, stained at the base of each petal with a purple-brown patch, and is more correctly known as H. lasianthum or Halimium lasianthum.

3-ft., June-July. E. 3-ft. Sq. Cg6. ANC.

H. HALIMIFOLIUM (With leaves like Halimus) Mediterranean Region, is also known as Halimium halimifolium, and bears a close resemblance to H. formosum, from which it may be said to differ only botanically. *3-ft., June-July. E. 3-ft. Sq. Cg6. ANC.*

H. LIBANOTIS (From Mount Libanus) Spain, is also known as H. rosmarinifolium and Halimium Libanotis, and has narrow green leaves closely resembling Rosemary, but has a more open habit and produces sprays of lemon-yellow flowers.

1½-ft., June-July. E. 1-ft. Sq. Cg6. ANC.

H. LUNULATUM (Crescent-moon-shaped) Mediterranean Region, is a dwarf, grey-green leaved shrub which decorates itself with sprays of small, clear yellow flowers later in the year than those of most other varieties. *½-ft., July-September. E. ⅔-ft. Sq. Cg6. ANC.*

H. OCYMOIDES (Like Basil) Spain, Portugal, is also Cistus algarvensis, but more correctly Halimium ocymoides, is a very charming and hardy shrub with very grey, pointed leaves, and out-thrown clusters of bright-yellow flowers, heavily stained at the base of each petal with a purple-brown patch.

2½-ft., June-July. E. 2-ft. Sq. Cg6. ANC.

H. UMBELLATUM (Umbelled) Mediterranean zone, is also Halimium umbellatum, is very similar in leaf and habit to H. libanotis, and bears similar flowers of clear white.

1½-ft., June-July. E. 1-ft. Sq. Cg6. ANC.

H. VULGARE (Common) S.E. Europe, is also H. nummularium and H. Chamaecistus, and is made up of the well-known Sun Roses of the garden, than which no dwarf shrub could be more prodigal in its display of colour. All the varieties below-mentioned should be ruthlessly pruned back to the base each year after flowering, and should be replaced by new stock from cuttings each fourth year. For convenience the single-flowering varieties have been separated from the double-flowering varieties.

HELIANTHEMUM (continued)

Low-growing varieties with single flowers :—

H. VULGARE AMY BARING—has single flowers of glowing orange.
H. „ APRICOT—has apricot flowers with a deeper eye. 09/3.
H. „ BEN HECKLA—has brick-red flowers. 5/1.
H. „ SULPHUREUM—has sulphur-yellow flowers.

⅓-ft.–½-ft., June-August. E. 1½-ft. Sq. Cg6. ANC.

Upright-growing varieties with single flowers :—

H. VULGARE BEN AFFLICK—has orange flowers with terra-cotta centres. 6/1.
H. „ BEN ALDER—is terra-cotta red.
H. „ BEN ATTAW—is cream with a primrose eye.
H. „ BEN DEARG—is bright-red in colour.
H. „ BEN FHADA—is yellow with a small orange eye.
H. „ BEN HECKLA—has flowers of soft brick-red.
H. „ BEN HOPE—is soft carmine. 025/1.
H. „ BEN LAWERS—has flowers of pale orange-yellow.
H. „ BEN LEDI—has flowers of deep-crimson.
H. „ BEN LOMOND—is pink with a white eye.
H. „ BEN LUI—is deep crimson-magenta. 822.
H. „ BEN MARE—has flowers of even flame colour.
H. „ BEN VANE—is bright terra-cotta in colour.
H. „ BEN VENUE—has flowers of signal-red.
H. „ BEN VORLICK—has flowers of coppery-orange, shaded with pink.
H. „ CHAMAECISTUS—is crimson-carmine.
H. „ CROFTIANUM—is pink with an orange eye.
H. „ FIREBALL—has orange-scarlet flowers.
H. „ FIREFLY—has flowers of fierce red.
H. „ GOLDEN QUEEN—is of even gold.
H. „ JOCK SCOTT—has rather small flowers of soft rose.
H. „ MAGNIFICUM—is terra-cotta red.
H. „ MISS MOULD—has fringed flowers of salmon. 19/1.
H. „ MRS. J. SMITH—is coppery-orange.
H. „ PEGGY—has flowers of pink, deepening in colour in the centre.
H. „ PRAECOX—has grey-green leaves and bright-yellow flowers.
H. „ RED DRAGON—is another red variety.
H. „ RHODANTHE CARNEUM—earns the right to an extra line by having silvery-grey leaves and soft silvery-pink flowers.
H. „ SUDBURY GEM—is crimson-pink, nearing magenta.
H. „ ST. JOHN'S COLLEGE YELLOW—is real gold.
H. „ TAYLOR'S SEEDLING—has flowers of orange-scarlet.
H. „ THE BRIDE—has grey leaves and white flowers.
H. „ VENUSTUM—is red in colour.
H. „ WISLEY PRIMROSE—has grey-green leaves with deep primrose flowers.

The double-flowered varieties :—

H. VULGARE ALBUM PLENUM—with double white flowers.
H. „ BRONZE JUBILEE—has bronze-yellow flowers.
H. „ COCCINEUM—is deep-red in colour.
H. „ JUBILEE—has small, pale-yellow flowers. 2/2.
H. „ LUTEUM—is bigger and deeper. 3/1.
H. „ MRS. EARLE—is red with a glimpse of yellow at the base.
H. „ ROSE OF LEEWOOD—is pink.
H. „ RUBENS—is orange.
H. „ VENUSTUM PLENUM—has bright-scarlet double flowers.
H. „ WATLAND'S RED—has double flowers of deep-red.

HELICHRYSUM (COMPOSITAE) (FROM GR. HELIOS—THE SUN ; AND CHRYSOS—GOLD).

The following shrubs have quaint everlasting flowers, are excellent in light, well-drained soil, and can be freely produced from cuttings which, in the case of H. selaginoides, should be pulled from the plant and not cut.

H. ROSMARINIFOLIUM (With leaves like Rosemary) Tasmania, resembles the Rosemary in growth and bears sprays of small, white, daisy flowers, exquisitely scented.
5-ft.–7-ft., June-August. E. 7-ft. Sq. Cg7. ANC.

H. SELAGINOIDES (Resembling Club-moss) Austialia, resembles the Whipcord Veronicas, and looks a little tree with its leaves pressed tightly against the stems and separated only by threads of white wool. The flowers, borne at the tips of the stems, are small, cream, and yellow-centred. *½-ft., July-August. E. 6-ft. Sq. Cg4. ANC.*

HIBISCUS (MALVACEAE) (AN OLD GREEK NAME APPLIED BY VIRGIL TO A MALLOW-LIKE PLANT, AND SAID TO BE DERIVED FROM IBIS, THE EGYPTIAN GOD, AND ISKO—LIKE).

A deciduous shrub, rising sometimes to nine or ten feet, but generally about half that height, and which displays a disregard for the knife by continuing to flower even though vigorously pruned, and can be produced from cuttings of the stem with a heel of the old wood, placed in sandy peat in a closed frame in July and left until rooted in the following spring. The shrub is commonly called the "Tree Hollyhock," and bears flowers which, fully opened, closely resemble the flowers of the hollyhock, and more than deserve a place in the sun.

H. SYRIACUS (Syrian) China, is represented by the following varieties, which are varieties known to be in cultivation but must not be considered to be exhaustive. *Pls.*41 *and* 42.

H. SYRIACUS ADMIRAL DEWEY—has double white flowers.
H. „ AMPLISSIMUS—has double rose-purple flowers.
H. „ COELESTIS—is single and the flowers blue. *Pl.*43.
H. „ COELESTIS PLENUS—has double flowers of matching blue.

HIBISCUS (continued)

H. SYRIACUS DUC DE BRABANT—has deep-rose double flowers.
H. „ ELEGANTISSIMA—has white double flowers, maroon in the centre.
H. „ JEANNE D'ARC—has double white flowers flushed with rose outside.
H. „ MONSTROSUS—has large, single white flowers with a dark centre.
H. „ PUNICEUS PLENUS—is double purple-rose.
H. „ ROSEUS PLENUS—is double pink.
H. „ RUBIS—is a fine variety with large single red flowers.
H. „ SPECIOSUS—has double flowers of peach blossom pink.
H. „ TOTUS ALBUS—has single flowers of pure white.

8-*ft.*, *August-November*. *D*. 6-*ft*. *Sq*. *Ch*7. *ANC*.

HIPPOPHAE (ELEAGNACEAE) (FROM THE GR. HIPPOS—HORSE; AND PHAOS—AN EYE; AS AN EXTRACT FROM THE PLANT WAS USED TO CURE EYE AFFLICTIONS IN HORSES, BUT POSSIBLY FROM HYPO—UNDER; AND PHAINO—TO SHOW LIGHT; A REFERENCE TO THE FACT THAT THE UNDERSIDE OF THE LEAVES IS WHITE).

The Sea Buckthorn is an exceptionally attractive shrub in autumn which succeeds in almost any good soil, but requires to be planted with plants of both sexes in close association if the orange-coloured fruits are to be produced. Layering is the best way to increase female plants.

H. RHAMNOIDES (Like Buckthorn) Europe, Asia, has silvery-grey leaves, and in autumn becomes covered with bright-orange, shiny, round fruits which emit a foul odour in closed places and are therefore unsuitable for indoor decoration, but which, perhaps for this reason, are distasteful to birds in the open.

4-*ft*., *June-July*. *D*. 6-*ft*. *Sq*. *L*5. *ANC*. *Pl*.67.

HOHERIA (MALVACEAE) (THE NAME IS DERIVED FROM A NATIVE NAME).

Comprises a beautiful genus of tender shrubs generally best suited to sheltered positions near south walls. Propagation is from cuttings of the half-ripened wood. It seems indifferent to soil.

H. LYALLII (Comm.) New Zealand, is the hardiest of the species with glaucous green leaves, and becomes covered with white flowers resembling cherry blossom, but with almost transparent petals and bright-yellow stamens.

10-*ft*.–15-*ft*., *July*. *D*. 8-*ft*.–12-*ft*. *Sq*. *Cg*6. *ANC*.

H. LYALLII VAR. GLABRATA (Hairless) New Zealand, is even better, but a little more tender.

10-*ft*.–15-*ft*., *July*. *D*. 8-*ft*.–12-*ft*. *Sq*. *Cg*6. *ANC*. *Shelter*.

H. LYALLII VAR. RIBIFOLIA (With leaves like the Currant) New Zealand, has downy, blue-grey leaves, and is just as beautiful but just as tender. 8-*ft*.–15-*ft*., *July*. *D*. 8-*ft*.–10-*ft*. *Sq*. *Cg*6. *ANC*. *Shelter*.

H. POPULNEA (Like Poplar) New Zealand, has wide, pointed, oval leaves, with clusters of clear white flowers borne in profusion. Unfortunately it is tender and requires a fully sheltered position.

8-ft.–15-ft., September-October. DE. 8-ft.–12-ft. Sq. Cg6. ANC. Shelter.

H. SEXSTYLOSA (Six-styled) New Zealand, has lance-shaped, serrated leaves of bright green, and flowers similar to those of the other varieties.

8-ft.–15-ft., July-August. DE. 8-ft.–12-ft. Sq. Cg6. ANC. Shelter.

HYDRANGEA (SAXIFRAGACEAE) (FROM THE GR. HYDOR—WATER; AND ANGEION—A VESSEL; A REFERENCE TO THE SHAPE OF THE SEED VESSEL).

The Hydrangeas are among the most beautiful and easily cultivated of all garden shrubs, and are equal in hardiness to almost any other genus of flowering shrubs. Among the varieties from China may be said to be some of the hardiest and most handsome. All varieties do well in soils which do not dry out too easily in summer, and are best propagated from cuttings of the half-ripened wood of the current year's growth, placed in a heated sand frame during August, or from suckers detached with root.

H. ARBORESCENS VAR. GRANDIFLORA (Tree-like; large-flowered) is a very hardy variety with large leaves, tree-like growth, and covering itself with terminal clusters of large, clear-white, sterile flowers surrounding a "powder-puff" of small, fertile flowers.

4-ft., July-September. D. 6-ft. Sq. Cg8. ANC.

H. ASPERA (Rough) Himalayas, is a very hardy variety with very large, rough leaves and terminal clusters of porcelain-blue, fertile flowers surrounded by pale-pink, sterile florets.

12-ft., August-October. D. 12-ft. Sq. Cg8. ANC. Pl.45.

H. BRETSCHNEIDERI (Comm.) China, has large, oblong, green leaves and large clusters of sterile, white florets, closely resembling Viburnum Mariesii. *8-ft., August-October. D. 8-ft. Sq. Cg8. ANC.*

H. HORTENSIS (Said to be commemorative as the genus was originally named HORTENSIA) China and garden origin, is also known as H. opuloides, and is the well-known florists' Hydrangea, not particularly suited for growing out of doors in the colder northern localities, but seldom killed by the severest frosts. Blue Hydrangeas are not normally of that colour, and all varieties do not "blue" well; those which are suitable for blueing are indicated with the letter B, and the best method to accomplish this is to use one of the recognised "blueing powders." *Pl.44.*

H. HORTENSIS BLUE PRINCE—is naturally dull-red, but "blues" to cornflower blue (B).

H. ,, COERULEA—is normally pink, but "blues" to Cambridge blue (B).

H. ,, DOMOTOI—has large, pale-rose flowers.

HYDRANGEA (continued)

H. HORTENSIS GEN. VICTOIRE DE VIBRAYE—has large, bright-rose flowers (B).
H. „ GERTRUDE GLAHN—has extra large heads of rich pink (B).
H. „ GOLIATH—is clear-pink.
H. „ F. MATHER—is salmon-rose.
H. „ HILGE—is deep-red.
H. „ LA MARNE—can be good blue or pink, with fimbriated edges (B).
H. „ LORELEI—is carmine.
H. „ MADAME E. MOULLIÈRE—has toothed white flowers with pink eyes.
H. „ MARÉCHAL FOCH—is a mixture of blue and red (B).
H. „ MARIESII—has very large, pale-pink flowers.
H. „ NIGRA—has black stems and bright-rose flowers.
H. „ PARSIVAL—is dwarf, has deep-red flowers with frilled edges.
H. „ SOUVENIR DE MADAME CHAUTARD—is another dwarf with brilliant pink flowers.
H. „ VEITCHII—is pure white.

2-*ft.*–4-*ft.*, *August-November*. *D*. 4-*ft.*–6-*ft.* *Sq*. *Cg*7. *ANC*.

H. INVOLUCRATA (Rolled together) Japan, is a very fascinating dwarf with the inner flowers of brilliant blue, and outer sterile flowers of blued-white. 1½-*ft.*, *August-November*. *D*. 3-*ft.* *Sq*. *Cg*7. *ANC*.

H. PANICULATA (Panicled) Japan, has large green leaves up to five inches in length, and bears large white clusters of flowers, the white, sterile florets ageing to pink.

5-*ft.*–7-*ft.*, *July-September*. *D*. 5-*ft.* *Sq*. *Cg*7. *ANC*.

H. PANICULATA VAR. GRANDIFLORA (Large-flowered) Japan, has very large clusters of clear white flowers, very freely produced if the shrub is pruned each spring, since the flower heads are borne upon the new wood. 5-*ft.*–7-*ft.*, *July-September*. *D*. 5-*ft.* *Sq*. *Cg*7. *ANC*.

H. QUERCIFOLIA (With leaves like the Oak) N. America, has large, deep-green leaves cut into seven lobes, and bears extremely large flower heads, the outer edges of which are heavily clustered with large, sterile, white florets. H. quercifolia is best grown in a shady site. 6-*ft.*, *July-September*. *D*. 6-*ft.* *Sq*. *Cg*7. *ANC*.

H. SARGENTIANA (Comm.) is a magnificent shrub with large, rough, green leaves, and terminal clusters of rose-violet, fertile flowers surrounded by large, white, sterile ones. In certain of the varieties the outer florets fade to deep-pink or even rose.

8-*ft.*–10-*ft.*, *July-September*. *D*. 8-*ft.*–10-*ft.* *Sq*. *Cg*7. *ANC*.

H. STRIGOSA (Covered with bristles) China, has bristly branches with large, hairy, green leaves, and bears wide flower clusters with small, central, white, fertile flowers with an annular zone of sterile, purple-blue florets.

6-*ft.*–8-*ft.*, *July-September*. *D*. 6-*ft.*–8-*ft.* *Sq*. *Cg*7. *ANC*.

Hydrangea aspera var.

Hypericum Kalmianum

H. villosa (Shaggy) China, has lance-shaped leaves, green above and hairy and grey below, and the central zone of small, pale-blue flowers is ringed and dotted with large, lavender-blue, sterile flowers.
6-ft.–8-ft., July-September. D. 6-ft.–8-ft. Sq. Cg7. ANC.

HYPERICUM (Hypericaceae) (possibly from Gr. hyper—over ; and ereike—a heath ; a reference to the native habitat of some of the species, or alternatively from hyper and eikon—an image ; the flowers having been used to decorate images).

The genus Hypericum is one of the most useful and beautiful of all garden shrubs, adding to its golden beauty the meed of easy culture. Wide variations exist in the size of the flowers, which are five-petalled, centred with a mass of thread-like stamens, and the species show a vast range in height and scope. Propagation is comparatively simple, either from seeds or from cuttings. The latter should be made about two inches in length and taken from the tips of the current year's growth, preferably as soon as possible—as early as June in most seasons.

H. aegypticum (Egyptian) Eastern Mediterranean, grows into an upright bush about a foot in height with very neat and small grey-green leaves, and bears at the tips of the shoots clusters of very small (quarter-inch) pale-yellow flowers with orange eyes. It seems to have acquired what must now be regarded as an undeserved reputation for tenderness, a trait which might be excused in view of its unconscionable flowering period.
1-ft., May-October. E. 1-ft. Sq. Cg6. ANC. 3/1.

H. anagalloides (Resembling a Pimpernel) N.W. America, is a flat-growing variety with round, green-grey leaves, almost stemless, small, pimpernel-like flowers of deep orange-yellow, and said to exist in nature with apricot, and even salmon-pink, flowers, desirable plants which fail to come into cultivation. This variety, at least in the south-west, needs less sun than any other.
1/6-ft., June-July. E. 2/3-ft. Sq. Cg6. Sd2. ANC.

H. aureum (Golden) U.S.A., is a flexibly branched shrub with blue-grey leaves, bearing the typical flowers in large clusters from the late summer onwards, and adds to its other merits the fragrance which its beauty so deserves.
4-ft., July-September. D. 4-ft. Sq. Sd2. Cg6. ANC.

H. balearicum (From the Balearic Isles) Mediterranean region, is an erect-growing shrub with dark-green, thick, crinkly foliage, edged with small warts both on the leaves and stems, which will only produce its flowers in a hot, dry site. It is said to be scented, but my own nose, though well to the fore, has failed lamentably to discern this in cultivation !
1½-ft., July-August. E. 1-ft. Sq. Cg6. ANC.

H. Buckleyi (Comm.) Eastern N. America, has the outstanding virtue of neatness so valuable both in man and plant, the rounded, pale-green leaves designed so well to fit the inch-wide flowers of bright-yellow. *1-ft., July-August. D. 1-ft. Sq. Cg6. ANC.*

H. CALYCINUM (An allusion to the cup-shaped flower) Orient, is the Rose of Sharon, a variety which will rampage, run, and respond in any shady site under the shelter of trees with complete abandon, and bear its beautiful, bright-yellow flowers with greater generosity if the knife is ruthlessly employed to trim it tightly in the spring.

1-ft., June-October. E. Indefinite. D3. Cg6. ANC.

H. CHINENSE (Chinese) Japan, China, is a very attractive shrub with a reputed tenderness, bearing sprays of very large, bright-yellow flowers of typical structure, sometimes exceeding two inches in diameter. *1½-ft., June-October. E. 1½-ft. Sq. Cg6. ANC.*

H. CORIS (Resembling Coris) Apennines, is a dwarf with fine, heathery, golden-green foliage, beautiful in itself, bearing sprays of starry flowers of clear gold which, if it is to attain its greatest glory, benefits by starvation, privation, and deprivation, in a poor soil.

⅔-ft., July-August. E. ⅔-ft. Sq. Cg5–6. Sd2. ANC. 602.

H. CUNEATUM (Having wedge-shaped leaves) Asia Minor, is a dwarf with attenuated red stems, likely to be blown away with a gust of wind, not heavily clothed with wedge-shaped, grey leaves, which bears, as its chief beauty, waxy buds of enamelled scarlet. That these buds open merely to display clear yellow petals should not prevent the grower from enjoying the pleasure of anticipation.

¼-ft., June-August. E. ⅔-ft. Sq. Cg3–6. ANC.

H. EMPETRIFOLIUM (Having leaves like the Crakeberry) Greece, is variable, a delightful prostrate form, and an equally beautiful erect form of the same plant being common in cultivation. Both have heathery-green foliage, and narrow-petalled flowers containing the precious golden stamens which convey the impression of starry-eyed, dewy freshness.

⅙-ft.–⅔-ft., July-August. E. ⅔-ft. Sq. Cg4–6. ANC.

H. FRAGILE (Brittle) Greece, is a cushion-like growth somewhat similar to H. Coris, the stems of which fall to make it more tangled and compact. *½-ft., June-July. D. 1-ft. Sq. Cg4. ANC.*

H. HOOKERIANUM (Comm.) Himalayas, is also known as H. oblongifolium and is an upright-growing variety with semi-evergreen leaves, which adorns itself with large, golden, cup-shaped flowers, often over two inches in diameter.

3-ft.–5-ft., August-October. DE. 3-ft.–5-ft. Sq. Cg6. ANC.

H. HYSSOPIFOLIUM (With leaves like Hyssop) N. Asia, is after the style of H. repens, but has longer strands of heathery, greeny-grey leaves, and larger sprays of starry, yellow flowers.

½-ft., June-July. E. 1-ft. Sq. Cg4. Sd2. ANC.

H. LESCHENAULTII (Comm.) Nepal, closely resembles H. Hookerianum but is more tender and requires the shelter of a wall in inclement districts, and under such circumstances produces the largest, golden, cup-shaped flowers of the species, sometimes quite three inches in diameter.

3-ft., August-October. D. 3-ft. Sq. Cg6. ANC.

H. MOSERIANUM (Comm.) Garden origin, adds more than a touch of burnished gold to the low cover afforded by its pleasant green leaves, and responds in due measure to the careful attention of the cultivator who will time his pruning to the breaking of the basal side shoots into growth.

1½-ft., July-October. E. 2-ft. Sq. Cg6. ANC.

H. MOSERIANUM VAR. TRICOLOR (Three-coloured) Garden origin, has all the beauties of its parent species, but makes up its leaves with a mixture of green-grey, cream and rose, so that its really beautiful flowers, when they appear, are but an anticlimax.

1½-ft., July-October. E. 2-ft. Sq. Cg6. ANC.

H. OLYMPICUM (From Mt. Olympus) Greece, is an upright-growing, small bush of grey-green leaves, borne upon wiry stems, which covers itself with terminal clusters of large, golden-yellow flowers about the size of a penny, but is completely outshone and outdone by its variety, M. olympicum var. citrinum or pallidum which, though slightly but not noticeably weaker in growth, borrows its paler tones from errant moonbeams to charm its observers with pale reflected sunlight. *1-ft., July-August. E. 1-ft. Sq. Cg4. ANC.*

H. PATULUM VAR. FORRESTII (Slightly spreading ; Comm.) China, has bushy, branching stems and its initial leaves turn from bright-red to green, and back again to gold and orange and crimson in the autumn. Add to this the presence from midsummer to late autumn of the large golden flowers and you have its unexaggerated charms modestly displayed.

2-ft.–3-ft., July-October. D. 2-ft.–3-ft. Sq. Cg6. ANC.

H. PATULUM VAR. GRANDIFLORUM (Large-flowered) China, adds to the beauties of H. patulum the merit of extra size in flowers, but loses a little in balance ; but then, if you like your favourites this way, it is an inevitable choice.

2-ft.–3-ft., July-October. D. 2-ft.–8-ft. Sq. Cg6. ANC.

H. PATULUM VAR. HENRYI (Comm.) China, is of the same type, a little larger in growth, but slightly smaller in flower than H. patulum var. grandiflorum. It responds very readily to pruning, as indicated for H. Moserianum, and will then dazzle rather than beguile the eye with its golden splendour.

3-ft.–4-ft., July-October. D. 3-ft.–4-ft. Sq. Cg6. ANC.

H. POLYPHYLLUM (Many-leaved) Cilicia, is not very different from H. olympicum but is more fully clothed with leaves, and adds tidiness of growth to the other virtues of H. olympicum, and much may thus be added to its balance.

½-ft., July-August. E. ⅔-ft. Sq. Cg4. ANC.

H. RODGERSII (Comm.) India, is the largest-growing of the species, attaining under favoured conditions up to ten feet in height, but more generally five feet, and at its best will dazzle the retina with its ready display of 2½-inch golden blooms.

5-ft.–10-ft., July-October. D. 5-ft.–10-ft. Sq. Cg6. ANC.

H. URALUM (From Ural) Himalayas, differs from H. patulum in its lax habit and pendent branches, and presents a picture of pathetic charm rather than that of dashing splendour.

1½-ft.–2-ft., July-October. D. 3-ft.–4-ft. Sq. Cg6. ANC.

HYSSOPUS (LABIATAE) (FROM A VERY OLD NAME USED BY THE GREEKS, POSSIBLY OF HEBREW ORIGIN).

The Hyssops are delightful shrubs, completely unexcelled by any others for hot, dry positions in poor or sandy soils. They prove the most attractive of all shrubs to bees and butterflies, and though they flower most readily and the display of colour they present is most generous upon a sunny day in late summer, they present a picture of as varied colours as those of Joseph's coat, for every fluttering butterfly will still its wings and compose itself to rest for a while, to sip what one must suppose must be the nectar of the gods. Of easy cultivation, it may be equally easily propagated from two- to three-inch cuttings of the current year's growth, taken and placed in sandy soil during August.

H. OFFICINALIS (Of the shop) S. Europe, is the Hyssop, a notable potherb with narrow, dark green leaves and long terminal sprays of small, violet-blue flowers, comparatively insignificant alone but impressive in the mass. H. officinalis albus differs only in having white flowers, and H. officinalis roseus in having pink flowers, but all are equally charming and each as attractive to insects.

2-ft., August-September. D. 2-ft.–3-ft. Sq. Cg8. ANC.

ILEX (AQUIFOLIACEAE) (FROM THE OLD LATIN NAME ILEX—THE HOLM OAK; TO WHICH HOLLY MAY HAVE BEEN SUPPOSED TO BEAR SOME RESEMBLANCE).

The varieties of I. Aquifolium provide among them the most beautiful of all the evergreen trees and shrubs, and combine with this beauty a degree of hardiness, together with ease of culture, which makes them outstanding among cultivated shrubs, especially for town use. In most varieties the sexes are borne in separate plants, which accounts for the fact that some of the shrubs never bear berries. It is not proposed to give an exhaustive selection of the varieties of I. aquifolium, but the varieties which follow may be regarded as among the best.

I. AQUIFOLIUM (With pointed leaves) Europe, Asia, is a remarkably good hedging plant with dark-green, prickly leaves which, cultivated in good soil, will often grow at least a foot each year.

6-ft.–60-ft., May-June. E. 25-ft.–35-ft. Sq. Ch8. ANC.

I. AQUIFOLIUM VAR. ARGENTEA MARGINATA (Silver-margined) is a silver variegated and free-berrying type.

I. AQUIFOLIUM VAR. FRUCTU LUTEO—has yellow berries.
I. " " GOLDEN KING—has deep golden variegations and produces red berries.

I. AQUIFOLIUM VAR. GOLDEN QUEEN—has golden leaves, but is sterile.

I. " " HODGINSII—has large, dark-green leaves, and berries freely.

I. " " POLYCARPA—has very distinct foliage, and berries readily.

I. " " PYRAMIDALIS—is of attractive shape and free berrying.

6-ft.–60-ft., May-June. *E.* *25-ft.–35-ft. Sq.* *Ch8.* *ANC.*

I. CRENATA (Crenellated) Japan, is a small-leaved, low-growing holly, making a very good low hedge.

5-ft.–7-ft., June. *E.* *3-ft.–5-ft. Sq.* *Ch8.* *ANC.*

I. CRENATA VAR. MARIESII (Comm.) is a smaller form, sometimes known as I. crenata var. nummularia, with very small, crenellated, rounded leaves. *3-ft., June.* *E.* *3-ft. Sq.* *Ch8.* *ANC.*

I. PERRYI (Comm.) China, is another very dwarf type with most attractive long, pointed, prickly leaves, and seldom exceeding five to six feet in height. *5-ft.–6-ft., June.* *E.* *4-ft. Sq.* *Ch8.* *ANC.*

ILLICIUM (MAGNOLIACEAE) (FROM THE LATIN ILLICIO—TO ATTRACT; A REFERENCE TO THE AROMA ATTRACTIVE TO ANIMALS).

This is the Aniseed Tree, best grown in a moist, peaty soil in partial shade, and propagated from layers which root readily.

I. ANISATUM (Anise-scented) Japan, bears oval, aromatic leaves and forms itself into a low-growing shrub with multi-petalled, greenish-yellow flowers about an inch in diameter.

3-ft.–6-ft., March-May. *E.* *3-ft.–6-ft. Sq.* *L4.* *AN.*

I. FLORIDANUM (From Florida) U.S.A., is another variety with larger, thicker leaves, with the same characteristic pleasant smell, with crimson to brown flowers freely borne, but with a reputation for tenderness which should confine its cultivation to the south-west of the British Isles.

6-ft.–8-ft., March-May. *E.* *6-ft.–8-ft. Sq.* *L4.* *AN.*

INDIGOFERA (LEGUMINOSAE) (FROM THE LATIN INDIGO—THE BLUE DYE; AND FERO—TO PRODUCE).

All the varieties are of easy cultivation in any good garden soil, and may be freely propagated from seed sown in February and potted on singly, or alternatively from cuttings taken with a slight heel in June or July and inserted in a warm sand frame and left until rooted. Suckers may also be detached from many of the varieties.

I. DECORA (Decorus) N. China, is a very beautiful shrub with red-brown stems and long, pinnate leaves divided into seven to nine green leaflets, grey-green upon the underside, which bears long sprays of many rose-pink pea flowers.

1-ft., Mav-September. *D.* *2-ft. Sq.* *Ch6.* *Sd2.* *ANC.*

INDIGOFERA (continued)

I. DECORA VAR. ALBA (White) China, is similar but has flowers of clear, pure white. *1-ft., May-September. D. 2-ft. Sq. Ch6. Sd2. ANC.*

I. GERARDIANA (Comm.) Himalayas, is a delightful shrub with pinnate leaves made up of thirteen to twenty-one leaflets, borne upon many-branched, low-growing bushes, which are decorated from June onwards with long sprays of numerous rose-pink pea flowers.
3-ft.–6-ft., June-September. D. 6-ft. Sq. Cg6. ANC. Pl.48.

I. HEBEPETALA (With petals resembling Hebe) Himalayas, is a shrub of low growth with long, pinnate leaves, often nine inches in length, and made up of nine to twenty-one leaflets, bearing long sprays of crimson and rose-coloured pea flowers.
3-ft., June-September. D. 4-ft. Sq. Cg6. ANC.

I. KIRILOWII (Comm.) China, Japan, is also I. macrostachya (long-spiked), is in fact a very dwarf-growing shrub, generally losing its top growth every winter, resembling in flower ROBINIA hispida. The leaves, divided into seven to eleven leaflets, are very attractive, but are inundated by the long sprays of rose-coloured flowers, drooping to more than half a foot in length.
2-ft.–3-ft., June-October. D. 4-ft. Sq. Cg6. ANC.

I. PENDULA (Pendulous) W. China, is a spreading shrub with arching, lacey branches clothed with long, pinnately divided leaves made up of eleven to twenty-seven leaflets, and which bears long, drooping sprays of Wistaria-like flowers of rose-purple, sometimes up to eighteen inches in length.
5-ft.–9-ft., July-October. D. 8-ft. Sq. Cg6. ANC.

I. POTANINII (Comm.) China, has light green leaves made up of five to nine leaflets, and bears sprays of clear rose-pink flowers up to ten inches in length.
6-ft., July-October. D. 6-ft.–8-ft. Sq. Cg6. ANC.

ITEA (SAXIFRAGACEAE) (DERIVED FROM ITEA, THE ANCIENT GREEK NAME FOR WILLOW, TO WHICH THE LEAVES OF I. VIRGINICA BEAR A CLOSE RESEMBLANCE).

Growing reasonably well in any good garden soil, I. ilicifolia is best propagated from cuttings of the current year's wood, about four inches in length, induced to root in a warm sand frame. I. virginica can be divided.

I. ILICIFOLIA (With leaves like Ilex, Holly) is a bushy shrub with elongated holly-like leaves of glossy green, and long, drooping, catkin-like sprays of small, white, scented flowers presenting a charming picture. Though it is said to be tender, established shrubs in Gloucestershire at more than one thousand feet defy the most rigorous winters, though planted in fully sunny sites.
6-ft.–8-ft., July-August. E. 6-ft. Sq. Cg7. ANC.

I. VIRGINICA (From Virginia) U.S.A., has oblong, willow-like, light-green leaves, is perfectly hardy and bears cylindrical, drooping sprays of small, creamy-white flowers which are sweetly scented and fitted with divine artistry into the general pattern.

5-ft., July-September. D. 5-ft. Sq. D3. ANC.

JAMESIA (SAXIFRAGACEAE) (NAMED IN HONOUR OF DR. JAMES, A MEMBER OF LONG'S EXPEDITION TO THE ROCKY MOUNTAINS).

This species is perfectly hardy in any good garden soil, and is propagated from seeds sown in February or from cuttings, about four inches in length, of the ripe wood taken in August.

J. AMERICANA (American) Western N. America, is a very compact shrub with oval, green, serrated leaves, greyish-white beneath, which bears terminal sprays of pure white flowers.

5-ft., June-July. D. 5-ft. Sq. Sd2. Ch8. ANC.

JASMINUM (OLEACEAE) (PROBABLY DERIVED FROM YSMYN, THE ARABIC NAME FOR JASMINE; KNOWN ALSO AS JESSAMINE, AND NUMBERING AMONG THE SPECIES SOME OF THE SWEETEST SCENTED OF ALL GARDEN SHRUBS).

All are easily grown in any good garden soil, and are propagated from cuttings of the half-ripened wood, taken during August.

J. BEESIANUM (Comm.) W. China, is a dwarf-growing shrub of lax habit, which bears small clusters of fragrant deep-rose flowers, often approaching red.

3-ft., July-August. D. 3-ft. Sq. Cg8. ANC.

J. FLORIDUM (Flowering freely) China, is a semi-evergreen shrub related to J. revolutum (humile) with many flowered sprays of bright-yellow, five-petalled flowers.

10-ft., July-August. DE. 6-ft. Sq. Cg8. ANC.

J. FRUTICANS (Bush-like) S.E. Europe, N. Africa, is a shrubby variety with weak stems, and two- to five-flowered clusters of bright-yellow flowers. *3-ft., July-August. D. 3-ft. Sq. Cg8. ANC.*

J. NUDIFLORUM (Naked flowers) China, is in all probability the best known of all the species, which decorates and ornaments many a cottage wall with its green stems and sweetly-scented sprays of yellow flowers during the winter months.

15-ft., November-February. D. Indefinite. Cg8. ANC.

J. OFFICINALE (Of the shop) Persia, is the climbing Jessamine with sprays of sweetly-scented white flowers, freely produced during the summer. *10-ft., June-October. D. Indefinite. Cg8. ANC.*

J. OFFICINALE VAR. AFFINE (Related) Garden origin, is also called J. grandiflorum, and is different solely upon the score of its still larger flowers. *10-ft., June-October. D. Indefinite. Cg8. ANC.*

J. PARKERI (Comm.) N.W. India, is a delightful dwarf with green twiggy growths, which eventually become covered with small sprays of starry yellow flowers in complete proportion to its dwarfed growth.

1-ft., June. E. 1-ft. Sq. Cg7. ANC. Shelter.

JASMINUM (continued)

J. PRIMULINUM (Resembling a primrose) Yunnan, is a remarkable evergreen species with double flowers of deep primrose-yellow, which is best situated upon a south or sheltered south-east wall.
8-ft., March-May. E. Indefinite. Cg8. ANC.

J. REVOLUTUM (With turned-back petals) Himalayas, is a delightful shrub with large, dark-green leaves and large, sweetly-scented, yellow flowers in attractive sprays.
10-ft., June-August. D. 8-ft. Sq. Cg8. ANC.

J. STEPHANENSE (Comm.) Garden origin, is a hybrid of J. Beesianum with J. officinale, and is a climber closely resembling J. officinale except in its terminal clusters of sweetly-scented pink flowers.
10-ft., June-October. D. Indefinite. Cg8. ANC.

J. WALLICHIANUM (Comm.) Nepal, is a climbing shrub with clusters of sweetly-scented yellow flowers, produced in clusters.
10-ft., June-August. D. Indefinite. Cg8. ANC.

KALMIA (ERICACEAE) (NAMED IN HONOUR OF PETER KALM, A PUPIL OF LINNAEUS).

Kalmias derive comfort in the southern and south-western parts of Great Britain from filtered sunlight provided by open shrubs placed upon the south side. They thrive on sandy, peaty soils, and are best propagated by cuttings of the current year's wood, taken from the tips and placed in sandy, peaty soil in a cold frame and left there until rooted in the spring.

K. ANGUSTIFOLIA (With narrow leaves) Eastern U.S.A., is a compact and very neat shrub with evergreen, dull-green leaves, producing, at the topmost parts of the previous year's growth, rosy-red flowers of the shape of inverted umbrellas, with projecting stamens.
2-ft.–3-ft., May-July. E. 2-ft. Sq. Cg8. AN.

K. ANGUSTIFOLIA VAR. OVATA (Elliptical, but rather broader at base) N. and S. Carolina, is slightly taller, with dark green, ovate leaves with a blue-grey surface beneath, and bears similar flowers of bright rose. *3-ft.–4-ft., May-July. E. 2-ft. Sq. Cg8. AN.*

K. ANGUSTIFOLIA VAR. RUBRA (Red) is similar to K. angustifolia but has flowers of deeper red shades.
2-ft.–3-ft., May-July. E. 2-ft. Sq. Cg8. AN.

K. CAROLINA (Carolinian) Western U.S.A., is a very compact variety with grey-green, narrow leaves, with many rose-red or pink flowers clustered around the stems.
1½-ft., May-June. E. 1½-ft. Sq. Cg8. AN.

K. CUNEATA (Wedge-shaped) N. America, is very erect, with wedge-shaped, grey-green leaves which colour well in autumn, and bears stem-clasping, clear white flowers of characteristic shape.
2-ft.–3-ft., June-July. D. 2-ft. Sq. Cg8. AN.

Laburnum Adami

Indigofera Gerardiana ACDH

Lonicera Periclymenum
BEFGJKLNP

Lonicera Periclymenum var. belgica
KMOQ

K. LATIFOLIA (With broad leaves) N. America, is an outstanding shrub with glossy green foliage, and innumerable saucer-shaped flowers of deep rose-pink borne upon the topmost growth of the previous year's wood. *3 ft., June-July. E. 3-ft. Sq. Cg8. AN.*

K. POLIFOLIA (With leaves like Germander) Eastern N. America, is also K. glauca, and is an exceptionally beautiful shrub of rather dwarf, spreading habit, with narrow grey-green leaves and saucer-shaped, pale-rose flowers which put in an appearance in April.

1-ft.–2-ft., April-May. E. 2-ft. Sq. Cg8. AN.

K. POLIFOLIA VAR. MICROPHYLLA (With small leaves) California, is a really beautiful miniature relative of the foregoing with very pretty saucer-shaped flowers of bright-pink.

$\frac{1}{3}$-ft., April-May. E. 1-ft. Sq. Cg8. AN.

KALMIA POLIFOLIA

KALMIOPSIS (ERICACEAE) (FROM KALMIA, AND OPSIS—A RESEMBLANCE).

A recently discovered variety with a resemblance to Kalmia.

K. LEACHIANA (Comm.) Western U.S.A., is a miniature with saucer-shaped, rose-pink flowers freely produced on long, thin stems.

1-ft., April-June. E. 1-ft. Sq. Cg8. AN.

KERRIA (ROSACEAE) (NAMED AFTER WILLIAM KERR, A KEW PLANT COLLECTOR).

These shrubs are easy to grow in any good garden soil, and may be readily propagated from divisions of the root in early spring.

K. JAPONICA (Japanese) Japan, has bright-green, lanceolate, serrated leaves which, for their topmost lengths, are wreathed with bright-yellow, five-petalled flowers.

3-ft.–6-ft., April-May. D. 3-ft.–6-ft. Sq. D3. ANC.

K. JAPONICA VAR. PLENIFLORA (Double-flowered) Garden origin, adds innumerable petals and an increased flowering period, and is one of the few double-flowered shrubs which is superior to its opposite single-flowered variety.

8-ft., April-September. D. 6-ft. Sq. D3. ANC.

KOELREUTERIA (SAPINDACEAE) (IS NAMED IN HONOUR OF J. G. KOELREUTER, A GERMAN BOTANIST).

K. PANICULATA (Having tufts of flowers) China, Japan, is a very handsome shrub or small tree with pinnate leaves of nine to fifteen leaflets, known as the Golden Rain Tree, which, in favoured positions, will reach thirty feet in height, but is more often about fifteen feet, and will propagate from cuttings taken in August. Seed is probably the best method of reproduction, but root cuttings will also provide another means of increase.

15-ft.–30-ft., July-August. D. 15-ft.–30-ft. Sq. Sd2. Cr4. Cg8. AN.

KOLKWITZIA (CAPRIFOLIACEAE) (NAMED IN HONOUR OF DR. KOLKWITZ, A GERMAN BOTANIST).

One species, easily grown in good garden soil, and propagated from cuttings of the current year's wood about two to three inches in length, placed in a warm sand frame in June or, at the latest, July.

K. AMABILIS (Lovely) C. China, is a pretty shrub with large, rough, hairy, oval, long, pointed leaves, with clusters of Weigela-like flowers of bright-pink with yellow throats, a little too small to balance its rather leafy growth.

3-ft.–6-ft., May-June. D. 5-ft.–6-ft. Sq. Cg6. AN.

LABURNUM (LEGUMINOSAE) (FROM THE OLD LATIN NAME FOR THE TREE, POSSIBLY DERIVED FROM ALBURNUM—SAPWOOD ; FROM ITS WHITENESS).

A group of trees and shrubs which has generally trefoil leaves and hanging sprays of yellow pea flowers, though in the case of one species, L. caramanicum, the flower sprays are erect. Laburnums thrive in limy soils, and grow well in all soils. The true species are best propagated from seeds, but the hybrids are grafted upon stocks of L. anagyroides. All are best grown in sunny sites.

L. ADAMI (Comm.) Garden origin, is sometimes known as Laburnocytisus Adami and is a graft hybrid of Cytisus purpureus with L. anagyroides, which closely resembles the Common Laburnum in its growth, but produces sprays of flowers similar to those of that species in long, deep-yellow, drooping sprays, and occasionally strands of foliage and flowers identical with those of Cytisus purpureus, but in addition, and often in majority, somewhat smaller sprays of less ample flowers of a shade of deep-apricot.

12-ft.–20-ft., May. D. 9-ft.–18-ft. Sq. G4. NC. Pl.47.

Magnolia Watsonii

Magnolia Lennei BCFGHLM

Rhododendron japonicum
Kersbergen strain JKNO

L. ALPINUM (Alpine) S.E. Europe, is known as the Scotch Laburnum; has the typical bright-green, trifoliate leaves of the group, and bears the largest sprays of flowers of any, producing them later than those of any other.

10-ft.–15-ft., June-July. D. 8-ft.–12-ft. Sq. Sd2. NC.

L. ANAGYROIDES (Like Anagyris) Europe, is also L. vulgare, and a delightful tree too well known to need description. L. anagyroides var. autumnale (autumn flowering) Europe, closely resembles L. anagyroides, but has the pleasant habit of flowering for a second time in the latter part of September, when its flowers deepen considerably in colour.

18-ft.–20-ft., May-June. D. 15-ft.–18-ft. Sq. Sd2. NC.

L. VOSSII (Comm.) Garden origin, is a hybrid of L. alpinum with L. anagyroides, makes a stiff, erect tree with a very rounded head, and bears the typical long sprays of bright-yellow flowers of the genus. *20-ft.–30-ft., May-June. D. 15-ft.–25-ft. Sq. G4. NC.*

L. WATERERI (Comm.) Garden origin, is another hybrid of the same parentage, and is a very beautiful tree with the long, slender, hanging sprays of flowers typical of L. alpinum.

15-ft.–20-ft., June. D. 12-ft.–18-ft. Sq. G4. NC.

LAURUSTINUS (*see* VIBURNUM TINUS).

LAVANDULA (LABIATAE) (FROM THE LATIN, LAVO—TO WASH ; THE ROMANS ARE SAID TO HAVE USED LAVENDER IN THE BATH).

The Lavenders are delightful shrubs which unite fragrance with silver-grey and purple in combination of consummate skill. All the species are easily grown in any good garden soil and propagate with ease from either seeds or cuttings. Varieties which are of general appeal are :—

L. DENTATA (Toothed) Mediterranean region, forms a stout shrub of from two to three feet in height with green leaves, symmetrically notched at the edges, and with only the lingering scent of lavender, bearing typical heads of "lavender" flowers of pale-mauve with the same meagre scent. It is unfortunately tender.

3-ft., July. E. 3-ft. Sq. Sd2. Cg5. ANC. Shelter.

L. LANATA (Woolly) Spain, makes a tufted growth of long, wide, white, woolly leaves, and bears its cylindrically clustered heads of sweetly-scented violet flowers upon long, grey, slender stems.

1½-ft., July-August. 1-ft. Sq. Sd2. ANC.

L. SPICA (Resembling an ear of corn) Mediterranean region, is also L. officinalis, and the Common Lavender of gardens, whose sweet-scented flowers make their presence most strongly felt as compensation for the declining summer, and modestly fit its grey-green, rolled back, narrow leaves. For hedges in certain districts it has few peers. Its varieties, L. Spica alba with white flowers, L. Spica compacta with more closely knit frame, and L. Spica nana, a midget, all have their parental characteristics as their main commendation, with the added strength of the revolutionary, rising to its best in L. Spica nana "Munstead Dwarf," about a foot in height and with extra dark flowers.

3-ft., July-August. *4-ft. Sq.* *Cg8.* *ANC.*

L. Stoechas (From Hyères, Stoechades) is very distinct and has grey-green, narrow leaves with rolled-back edges, and short, rather stout, four-angled spikes of deep, almost indigo-purple flowers.

1-ft., June-August. *E.* *1-ft. Sq.* *Sd2.* *N.* 633.

L. vera (True) Mediterranean region, is the so-called Dutch Lavender with leaves greener than those of L. Spica, and unbranching spikes, and is the source of the Old English Lavender Water.

3-ft., July-August. *E.* *4-ft. Sq.* *Cg8.* *ANC.*

LAVATERA (Malvaceae) (named in honour of a Zurich physician, Lavater).

The tree Mallows thrive in good garden soil in a sunny site, and benefit from being pruned back to within three feet of the ground each spring.

L. arborea (Tree-like) Europe, makes annual or biennial tree-like shoots, with round leaves made up of five to nine lobes, and bears hollyhock-like flowers of pale reddish-purple, veined at the centre with dark-purple.

5-ft.–10-ft., July-September. *D.* *6-ft. Sq.* *Sd2.* *ANC.*

LEDUM (Ericaceae) (the name is derived from the Greek for ladanum, a resinous substance obtained from the plant).

These ericaceous plants are best suited to moist spots in peaty soil, and may be propagated from cuttings about an inch in length, taken from the tips of the shoots and placed in very sandy peat, in August, under a bell glass in a cold frame, and allowed to remain until the following spring.

L. glandulosum (Glandular) N.W. America, has felted stems, elliptical green leaves of attractive aromatic odour, and bears, at the tips of the branches, wide clusters of clear-white, five-petalled, cup-shaped flowers. *2-ft.–3-ft., May-June.* *E.* *3-ft. Sq.* *Cg8.* *AN.*

L. groenlandicum (From Greenland) N. America, is also L. latifolium and the Labrador Tea Plant, and a very hardy shrub with narrow, scented leaves and terminal clusters of small white flowers. L. groenlandicum compactum is a proportionate dwarf.

2-ft.–3-ft., April-June. *E.* *3-ft. Sq.* *Cg8.* *AN.*

L. minus (Small) Japan, is another dwarf-growing variety with rugged, sweet-smelling, narrow, rolled-edged leaves, and many clusters of small white flowers at the ends of the stems.

1-ft.–1½-ft., April-June. *E.* *2-ft. Sq.* *Cg8.* *AN.*

L. NIPPONICUM (From Nippon) Japan, is still smaller and has wider leaves of bright-green, glaucous on the underside, and its stems overlaid with reddish-brown tomentum.

1-ft., May-June. E. 1-ft. Sq. Cg8. AN.

L. PALUSTRE (Of the swamp) Arctic regions, has smaller leaves than those of L. groenlandicum, with its young shoots covered with rusty down. In Sweden the leaves are used for brewing beer, but in other places it is said to scare away mice ! Indeed a pretty plant with possibilities. *1-ft.–3-ft., May-June. E. 3-ft. Sq. Cg8. AN.*

LEIOPHYLLUM (ERICACEAE) (FROM GR. LEIOS—SMOOTH ; AND PHYLLON—A LEAF).

This group of evergreen shrubs bear white flowers resembling those of Ledum, and require peaty soils in which to grow. They are propagated in a similar way a little earlier.

L. BUXIFOLIUM (With box leaves) New Jersey, is the Sand Myrtle, and a small shrub with dark, shiny, evergreen leaves and small, bright rose-red buds produced in terminal clusters opening to show clear-white, starry flowers. *1-ft., May-June. E. 1½-ft. Sq. Ch7. A.*

L. BUXIFOLIUM VAR. HUGERI (Comm.) Eastern U.S.A., is a little more dwarf, and has longer and more slender leaves, making as pretty a picture a little nearer the ground.

¾-ft., May-June. E. 1-ft. Sq. Ch7. A.

L. BUXIFOLIUM VAR. PROSTRATUM (Prostrate) Eastern U.S.A., is also L. Lyonii, has shorter leaves, less inches, and fits its flowers better than any other variety. *½-ft., May-June. E. 3-ft. Sq. Ch7. A.*

LEPTOSPERMUM (MYRTACEAE) (FROM THE GR. LEPTOS—SLENDER ; AND SPERMA—A SEED).

These are the New Zealand Manukas or Tea Trees, and though not generally hardy throughout the whole of the British Isles, they are undeniably so in the south and west and in the sea-coast districts, and in sheltered spots elsewhere. Contrary to general expectation they are not particular as to the texture of the soil in which they will grow, but prefer it without the added complication of lime. Propagation of the true species is best from seed thinly sown in sandy peat. Cuttings may be taken of the varieties, from two to three inches in length, from the tips of the shoots, and placed in sandy peat in a frame with gentle bottom heat.

L. BACCATUM (Shaped like a berry) Australia, forms a bush up to nine feet in height, neatly clothed with narrow, dark green leaves, silver below, and bears in the topmost leaf axils of the innumerable tiny branchlets small, well-opened, five-petalled flowers of white flushed at the centre with pink.

6-ft.–9-ft., June. E. 4-ft.–6-ft. Sq. Sd2. AN.

L. PUBESCENS (Slightly hairy) Australia, is also L. lanigerum, and a gracefully slender shrub of branching habit with sharply pointed,

green leaves covered with dense hairs which give it a frosted appearance. The small five-petalled flowers are clear-white.
6-ft.–9-ft., June. E. 6-ft.–9-ft. Sq. Sd2. AN.

L. SCOPARIUM (Brush-like) New Zealand, is an upright-growing shrub of almost columnar habit which decorates itself in June with innumerable white flowers produced in the leaf axils.
6-ft.–9-ft., June. E. 4-ft.–6-ft. Sq. Sd2. AN.

L. SCOPARIUM VAR. CHAPMANII (Comm.) Garden origin, has similar habit, but has flowers of bright-pink. L. scoparium var. Nichollsii has bronzy-red leaves and crimson flowers.
6-ft.–9-ft., June. E. 4-ft.–6-ft. Sq. Sd2. AN.

LESPEDEZA (LEGUMINOSAE) (NAMED IN HONOUR OF A SPANISH GOVERNOR).

A group of shrubs resembling DESMODIUM and INDIGOFERA, with hanging sprays of small pea-shaped flowers, they require similar cultivation in good, deep garden soil, in a dry position in a sunny site.

L. BICOLOR (Two-coloured) Japan, has three-parted leaves and bears clusters of hanging sprays of bright-purple pea flowers.
6-ft., July-September. D. 6-ft. Sq. Sd2. ANC.

L. FORMOSA (From Formosa) China, Japan, is an exceptionally attractive low-growing shrub, generally losing its top growth in winter, but bearing, during late summer and autumn, long, graceful sprays of rose-purple flowers sometimes exceeding two feet in length. *4-ft.–6-ft., August-September. D. 8-ft. Sq. Sd2. ANC.*

LEUCOPOGON (EPACRIDACEAE) (FROM GR. LEUKOS—WHITE ; AND POGON—A BEARD).

The one species is a very pretty little shrub which requires a peaty soil in a somewhat shaded site, and may be propagated from short cuttings taken at a junction with older wood, or may be divided and again firmly replanted in the early spring.

L. FRASERI (Comm.) New Zealand, is also CYATHODES Fraseri, and a very dwarf, heather-like plant with small, hairy, bronze-green leaves, and bears white tubular flowers, one in each leaf axil, every one with tufts of white hair in the throat, and followed by translucent orange berries. *½-ft., May-June. E. 1-ft. Sq. Ch7. D3. AN.*

LEUCOTHOE (ERICACEAE) (COMMEMORATES THE DAUGHTER OF KING ORCHAMUS, BURIED ALIVE BY HER FATHER BUT CHANGED BY HER LOVER APOLLO INTO A SHRUB WHICH GAVE INCENSE).

This group of shrubs is generally best suited by semi-shaded positions in soils free of lime, and may be successfully propagated from cuttings, from two to three inches long, of the branch tips or side shoots, taken with a slight heel, and placed in a cold frame in June, July, or August. Layering may also be practised with success.

Nierembergia frutescens

Rhododendron Augustinii

L. CATESBAEI (Comm.) Western N. America, has very beautiful, shining green leaves which turn crimson during the winter, held upon long, arching sprays which bear short spires of clear white, Lily-of-the-valley-shaped flowers from all the leaf axils, in May–June.

3-ft.–6-ft., May-June. E. 3-ft.–6-ft. Sq. Ch6–8. AN.

L. CATESBAEI VAR. ROLLINSONII (Comm.) Eastern N. America, is a variety with smaller, narrower leaves, generally bronze-green in colour and seldom exceeding two feet in height.

2-ft., May-June. E. 2-ft. Sq. Ch6–8. AN.

L. DAVISIAE (Comm.) Western U.S.A., is another neat shrub with oval leaves and erect terminal sprays of clear white, Lily-of-the-valley flowers. *3-ft., June-July. E. 3-ft. Sq. Ch6–8. AN.*

L. GRAYANA (Comm.) Japan, is yet another neat shrub with strong, red stems, carrying oval green leaves fringed with hairs, turning red and often falling in autumn, and terminal sprays of pale creamy-white flowers, flushed with pink.

3-ft., May-June. D. 3-ft. Sq. Ch6–8. AN.

L. KEISKEI (Comm.) Japan, is a pendulous shrub with pointed, shiny, green leaves, semi-prostrate red stems, and sweetly-scented, long, cylindrical, ivory-white flowers borne in short hanging sprays. The leaves colour attractively in autumn.

⅔-ft., June-July. E. 2-ft. Sq. Ch6–8. AN.

LEYCESTERIA (CAPRIFOLIACEAE) (NAMED IN HONOUR OF W. LEYCESTER, A BENGAL JUDGE).

One hardy species which will grow in any good soil, and is fully at home in positions which are partially shaded, and is propagated easily from the seed which it produces freely.

L. FORMOSA (From Formosa) Himalayas, is the Himalayan Honeysuckle, and is notable for its bottle-green, hollow stems, oppositely clad with simple leaves with tapering points. The flowers, which are funnel-shaped, are borne at the tips of the shoots and are white in colour, but are admirably set off by the claret-coloured bracts which enclose them.

6-ft.–8-ft., July-September. D. 5-ft.–6-ft. Sq. Sd2. ANC.

LIGUSTRUM (OLEACEAE) (FROM THE OLD LATIN NAME DERIVED FROM LIGO—TO BIND; PROBABLY BECAUSE THE TWIGS WERE USED FOR TYING).

The Privets are a generally well-known group of useful evergreen and deciduous shrubs with small, white, sometimes sweetly-scented flowers, easily suited by soil or position, and among the most patient of shrubs for growing in towns. The best varieties for various purposes may be stated thus: for hedging, L. ovalifolium and its varieties; for flower, L. sinense, L. Quihoui, and L. vulgare flore luteo; for foliage, L. japonicum, L. lucidum, and L. ovalifolium aureum. All varieties are propagated easily from cuttings, six to eight inches long, from the tips of the shoots taken in August.

L. HENRYI (Comm.) China, is a pleasant evergreen shrub with dark-green, shining leaves and five-inch sprays of small white flowers.
6-ft., July. E. 6-ft. Sq. Cg8. Sd2. ANC.

L. IONANDRUM (With violet anthers) W. China, is another evergreen species with a very erect, stiff habit, probably the smallest leaves of the genus, and small white flowers followed by generous helpings of purple-black berries. *8-ft., July. E. 6-ft. Sq. Cg8. Sd2. ANC.*

L. JAPONICUM (Japanese) Japan, is distinctive in its large leaves and very large sprays of white flowers, not unlike lilac, and strongly but sweetly scented. L. japonicum var. coriaceum differs by being slow growing, has rounded green-black leaves.
6-ft., July. E. 6-ft. Sq. Cg8. Sd2. ANC.

L. LUCIDUM (Shining) China, is one of the oldest inhabitants of British gardens, and is L. japonicum var. macrophyllum, with large green leaves like those of a Camellia, and long and wide sprays of clear-white flowers. *6-ft., August-September. E. 6-ft. Sq. Cg8. Sd2. ANC.*

L. OVALIFOLIUM (Oval-leaved) Japan, is the well-known Hedging Privet, with its variety aureo-variegatum, with golden leaves, and variegatum with variegated leaves.
3-ft.–15-ft., July. DE. 3-ft.–15-ft. Sq. Cg8. ANC.

L. QUIHOUI (Comm.) China, is a deciduous species which is probably the best example of the floral value of species, bearing its small flowers in large outstanding sprays.
8-ft., August-September. D. 8-ft. Sq. Cg8. Sd2. ANC.

L. SINENSE (Chinese) China, grows into a gracefully symmetrical bush with branches pendulous at the tips, and bears sprays of small white, pleasantly-scented flowers in July.
6-ft., July. DE. 6-ft. Sq. Cg8. Sd2. ANC.

L. VULGARE (Common) Great Britain, is the Common Privet of the hedgerow, delightfully scented when diluted by distance and stimulated by sunshine, but rising to its greatest height in its variety L. vulgare var. flore luteo, with buff-yellow or primrose-yellow flowers. *6-ft.–15-ft., July. DE. 6-ft.–15-ft. Sq. Cg8. Sd2. ANC.*

LINDERA (LAURACEAE) (NAMED IN HONOUR OF J. LINDER, A SWEDISH BOTANIST).

The " Spice Bush " requires a lime-free soil, generally in a sunny, sheltered site.

L. BENZOIN (Resembling Benzoin) U.S.A., is a neat shrub with yellow flowers produced before the leaves, which give out a strong but not particularly pleasant smell when crushed, and bears reddish-purple berries. *3-ft., April. D. 3-ft. Sq. Sd2. AN.*

LINNAEA (CAPRIFOLIACEAE) (NAMED IN HONOUR OF LINNAEUS).

L. BOREALIS VAR. AMERICANA (Northern ; American) N. America, is a tiny evergreen creeper with rounded green leaves carried in pairs

Rhododendron barbatum

Rhododendron Wardii

along the stems, which produces in the leaf axils twin flowers like tiny hanging trumpets of pink and white, upon stems of about two inches in length. It is best grown in leafy or peaty soil in some shade, and propagates by division.

⅙-ft., May-June. E. 2-ft. Sq. Ch5. D8. AN.

LINUM (LINACEAE) (DERIVED FROM THE GR. LINON—FLAX).

L. ARBOREUM (Tree-like) Crete, is a small shrub with oval, grey-green leaves and clusters of large golden-yellow flowers.

1-ft., June-September. E. 1-ft. Sq. Cg5. N. 2.

LIPPIA (VERBENACEAE) (NAMED AFTER A. LIPPI, A FRENCH BOTANIST AND EXPLORER).

L. CITRIODORA (Lemon-scented) S. America, is the lemon-scented Verbena so beloved of southern gardens, and also known as ALOYSIA citriodora. L. citriodora is best planted against a south wall and is much valued for its sweetly-scented leaves.

3-ft., June. D. 3-ft. Sq. Cg6. AN.

LITHOSPERMUM (BORAGINACEAE) (FROM THE GR. LITHOS—A STONE; AND SPERMA—A SEED; THE SEEDS OF THE SPECIES BEING STONE-LIKE).

A group of low-growing, evergreen shrubs growing best in soils which differ for each species.

L. DIFFUSUM (Loosely spread) Spain, is the L. prostratum of catalogues, and forms a mat of rough, green, narrowly oval leaves, bearing sprays of sky-blue flowers. It produces these in great quantity during the summer months and spasmodically at other times. The variety L. prostratum album has flowers of clear white, L. diffusum var. erectum has upright, shrubby growth, and L. diffusum var. Grace Ward has large flowers, but L. diffusum var. Heavenly Blue is the best-known variety with flowers of bright-blue.

½-ft., June-October. E. 2-ft. Sq. Cg8. A. 42.

L. OLEIFOLIUM (With leaves like the Olive Tree) Spain, is a very beautiful, low-growing shrub of running habit, grey-green, rounded leaves, and large, funnel-shaped flowers of opalescent blue, which is best suited by a light, leafy, gritty soil containing lime.

½-ft., May-August. E. ⅔-ft. Sq. Ch7. C. 43/1.

L. ROSMARINIFOLIUM (With leaves like Rosemary) S. Italy, is a rounded shrub with hard, woody stems, narrow green leaves, and very large flowers of intense blue. L. rosmarinifolium is best suited by a neutral soil, a sheltered spot, and a site where it can be kept dry in winter. *1⅓-ft., January-February. E. 1-ft. Sq. Cg3. N. 742/3.*

LOISELEURIA (ERICACEAE) (NAMED IN HONOUR OF LOISELEUR-DESLONGSCHAMPS, A FRENCH BOTANIST).

L. PROCUMBENS (Lying down) Northern Europe, is the Alpine Azalea, a small shrub with tiny, rounded, oval leaves forming a mat, and which bears small white or pale-pink flowers in some profusion when grown in sandy peat.

½-ft., June. E. 1-ft. Sq. Ch8. ANC.

LOMATIA (Proteaceae) (from the Gr. lòma—border ; the seeds of the species being winged).

A genus of plants drawn from Chile and Australia, with a reputation for being tender, but able to resist ten to fifteen degrees of frost when established if planted in a sheltered place unlit by morning sunlight. They are best suited by a lime-free soil, and can be increased in the same way as Grevillea, to which they are related, and bear similarly shaped flowers.

L. ferruginea (Rusty) Chile, is also known as L. pinnatifolia, with large, handsome, pinnate, bronze-green leaves with its leaflets pinnately lobed, bears Grevillea-like flowers of red and white in May, and is only suitable for south-western districts.

7-ft.–30-ft., May. E. 7-ft.–30-ft. Sq. Ch7. AN.

L. fraxinifolia (With ash-like leaves) Australia, has red-brown stems, large, grey, ash-like leaves, very irregularly cut, and bears ivory-white flowers closely resembling those of the Grevillea.

3-ft.–7-ft., May-July. E. 3-ft.–7-ft. Sq. Ch7. AN.

LONICERA (Caprifoliaceae) (named after A. Lonicer, a German botanist).

This genus Honeysuckle contains a number of evergreen and deciduous climbing shrubs, and for convenience the climbing types are marked with the letter C. Cultivation of both kinds is not difficult and may be said generally to consist of giving them reasonably good deep soil. Propagation is best from cuttings of the current year's wood, four to six inches in length, placed in sand in a closed frame with gentle bottom heat. The best months for this are July and August.

L. americana (American) (C) is a natural hybrid of L. caprifolium and L. etrusca, and a delightful climber with clusters of long, crescent-like, tubular flowers with flared-out lips, yellow and deep-pink externally and ivory-white within, and with a searching and fascinating scent.

12-ft.–18-ft., May-September. E. Indefinite. Cg7–8. ANC.

L. Brownii (Comm.) (C) is a hybrid of L. sempervirens and L. hirsuta, is commonly called the Scarlet Trumpet Honeysuckle, and is a magnificent climber for a semi-shaded site, which it will gaudily adorn with its elliptical leaves and its yellow, tubular flowers with orange-scarlet exterior decoration. L. Brownii var. fuchsioides is said to be more scarlet without, but is generally similar, and L. Brownii var. plantierensis is not so good in its habit of growth but has coral-red flowers which are orange within.

12-ft.–18-ft., June-September. D. Indefinite. Cg7–8. ANC.

L. Caprifolium (Resembling the genus) (C) Europe, is the early-flowering European Honeysuckle with two-inch long creamy-white flowers, sometimes tinged with pink, and sweetly scented.

12-ft.–18-ft., May-June. D. Indefinite. Cg7–8. ANC.

L. CHAETOCARPA (With bristly fruits) W. China, has stems, leaves and fruits covered with short hairs, and carries its one-inch-long primrose-yellow flowers in pairs in the leaf axils.

3-ft.–5-ft., June. D. 2-ft.–5-ft. Sq. Cg7–8. ANC.

L. CILIOSA (Fringed) (C) Western N. America, resembles L. sempervirens but has its leaves fringed with short hairs, and bears flowers varying in colour from yellow to deep orange. It is not particularly hardy and requires and deserves a shady, sheltered spot.

12-ft.–18-ft., June-September. D. Indefinite. Cg7–8. ANC.

L. DIOICA (With the sexes divided) (C) N. America, is also L. glauca, and has large, deep-green leaves at the base of the shoots, smaller leaves as it progresses, and carries clusters of small, yellow, trumpet-shaped flowers touched with carmine.

L. ETRUSCA (Etruscan) (C) Mediterranean region, is a quick-growing, partially evergreen climber with large clusters of very fragrant, creamy-yellow flowers which age to deep-yellow, flushed with purple. L. etrusca var. superba has leaves which are downy.

12-ft.–18-ft., June-July. DE. Indefinite. Cg7–8. ANC.

L. FRAGRANTISSIMA (Very fragrant) China, is a very pretty, partly evergreen shrub with small, stiff, oval, green leaves, and exceptionally sweetly scented, creamy-white flowers produced in pairs at the joints of the stems.

4-ft.–6-ft., December-February. DE. 4-ft.–6-ft. Sq. Cg7–8. ANC.

L. HECKROTTII (Comm.) (C) Garden origin, is a hybrid of the parentage L. sempervirens and L. americana, and is best suited to a shady site, which it will slowly fill with its oval green leaves and long, tubular, fragrant, two-lipped flowers, yellow within and pink without.

8-ft.–12-ft., July-September. D. Indefinite. Cg7–8. ANC.

L. HENRYI (Comm.) (C) China, has long, oval, dark-green leaves, rather thin and spare growth, clusters of yellow and purplish-red flowers, little worse than many much-publicised varieties, and with the added advantage of a strong constitution and blue-black berries in winter.

8-ft.–12-ft., July-September. E. Indefinite. Cg7–8. ANC.

L. HILDEBRANDIANA (Comm.) (C) China, Burma, is a very tender, rapid climber with large, oval, leathery, green leaves, hardy only in the extreme south-west, but is distinctive for the extremely long, slender, tubular, yellow flowers which age to orange.

20-ft., July-September. D. Indefinite. Cg6. ANC.

L. HISPIDA (Bristly) Central Asia, is an exceptionally hardy shrub with oval, dark-green, bristly-edged leaves, with wide, comparatively short-tubed flowers of pale-yellow, reminiscent of certain of the Diervillas.

3-ft.–5-ft., May-June. D. 3-ft.–5-ft. Sq. Cg7. ANC.

L. IBERICA (From Georgia) Transcaucasia, is a dense shrub with rounded, heart-shaped, dark-green leaves, clothed with down on both sides, bearing pale-yellow flowers in pairs at the tips and in the leaf axils, followed by bright-red berries.

6-ft., June. D. 8-ft.–10-ft. Sq. Cg7. ANC.

L. JAPONICA (Japanese) (C) China, Japan, is a very vigorous, semi-evergreen climber with oval leaves, and bears sweetly-scented white flowers, passing to yellow with age, generally in pairs in the leaf axils, but very crowded at the tips of the shoots.

L. JAPONICA VAR. AUREO-RETICULATA (C) has rounded leaves which are mottled with golden-yellow, and is extremely backward in flowering. L. japonica var. flexuosa (C) has sweetly-scented flowers which are white within and pale-red without, fading to buff. L. japonica var. Halliana (C) is similar but has white flowers fading to deep primrose-yellow.

20-ft.–30-ft., June-September. DE. Cg7. ANC.

L. MAACKII (Comm.) Manchuria, is a deciduous shrub with narrow, oval leaves and pure-white flowers produced in the leaf axils, and rising in vertical pairs upon almost horizontal branches, very crowded at the tips of the shoots and turning yellow with age. L. Maackii var. podocarpa is probably better, its yellow flowers being followed by attractive red fruits.

6-ft.–10-ft., May-June. D. 6-ft.–10-ft. Sq. Cg6–7. ANC.

L. MAXIMOWICZII (Comm.) America, is an attractive shrub with oval leaves and small, rose-purple flowers produced in pairs.

6-ft., June-July. D. 6-ft. Sq. Cg6–7. ANC.

L. MORROWII (Comm.) Japan, is neither particularly beautiful nor outstanding, bears creamy-white flowers fading to yellow, and is suited only to the wild garden.

6-ft., May-June. D. 6-ft. Sq. Cg6–7. ANC.

L. MYRTILLUS (Resembling Myrtle) Himalayas, has very small, oval leaves, and small, sweetly-scented, pinkish-white flowers, produced in pairs in the leaf axils.

3-ft., May-June. D. 3-ft. Sq. Cg6–7. ANC.

L. NITIDA (Shining) W. China, is the well-known hedging shrub with very small, glossy, dark, evergreen leaves, which produces small, sweetly-scented, white flowers in the leaf axils and translucent, purple-violet berries, which are gorgeously beautiful when light is transmitted through them. It clips remarkably well but seldom flowers or fruits under such treatment.

5-ft.–8-ft., May. E. 5-ft.–8-ft. Sq. Cg7. ANC.

L. PERICLYMENUM (Twining with tendrils) (C) Europe, is the Woodbine or Honeysuckle, which winds over hedges and ornaments with its oval green leaves, and bears its sweetly-scented, yellowish-white flowers, more or less flushed with red, with great generosity. L. Periclymenum var. belgica is the Early Dutch Honeysuckle, which bears clusters of long-tubed, yellow flowers freely tinged with red. L. Periclymenum var. serotina (Late in the year) is the Late

Dutch Honeysuckle, which flowers later and has similar yellow flowers flushed with red, paling with age.

12-ft.–20-ft., May-September. D. Indefinite. Cg6–7. ANC. Pl.48.

L. PILEATA (Headed like a mushroom) W. China, is a dwarf variety with rather larger, pale-green leaves than L. nitida, but bearing similar flowers and berries, and very useful for covering banks or hiding unsightly objects.

2-ft., May. E. 4-ft.–10-ft. Sq. Cg7. ANC.

L. PILEATA VAR. YUNNANENSIS (From Yunnan) W. China, is similar but is of erect habit, and as good a hedging shrub as L. nitida.

5-ft.–6-ft., May. E. 5-ft.–6-ft. Sq. Cg7. ANC.

L. PYRENAICA (Pyrenean) Pyrenees, is a very pretty dwarf shrub with grey-green, oval leaves, with rose and white, Diervilla-like flowers produced in groups of two in the leaf axils, and followed by many orange-red berries. *2-ft., June. D. 3-ft. Sq. Sd2. Cg7. ANC.*

L. SEMPERVIRENS (Evergreen) (C) South-Eastern U.S.A., is a rather tender climber, best flanked by a protecting wall, and bears six-flowered clusters of orange-scarlet flowers, white inside, which are delightfully set off by the grey-green leaves.

12-ft., June-September. ED. Indefinite. Cg7. ANC.

L. STANDISHII (Comm.) China, has pointed, oval, rather large, rough, green leaves, and exceptionally sweetly-scented cream flowers freely produced at the joints in the stems, from November to March.

5-ft., November-March. DE. 5-ft. Sq. Sd2. Cg7. ANC.

L. SYRINGANTHA (With flowers resembling Lilac) N.W. China, is an exceptionally pretty, arching shrub of comparatively dwarf habit, grey-green leaves and small, sweetly-scented flowers borne in pairs in groups at the leaf axils.

3-ft.–4-ft., May-June. D. 4-ft. Sq. Cg7. Sd2. ANC.

L. TATARICA (From Tartary) Turkestan, is a very vigorous shrub rising to quite eight feet, with pointed, oval, green leaves, paler upon the underside, with pink and white, two-lipped flowers about an inch in length, produced in pairs in the leaf axils towards the ends of the shoots, and replaced later in the year with bright-red fruits. L. tatarica var. lutea is about half as high and has bright-pink flowers similarly arranged, giving way to translucent amber-yellow berries at midsummer. L. tatarica var. sibirica is similar to the type, with large flowers.

4-ft.–8-ft., May-June. D. 4-ft.–8-ft. Sq. Cg7. Sd2. ANC.

L. TELLMANNIANA (Comm.) Garden origin, is a delightful hybrid of L. tragophylla and L. sempervirens, with oval, dark-green leaves and long, large-lipped flowers of deep-yellow tipped with bronze-red.

12-ft., June. D. Indefinite. Cg7. ANC.

L. TRAGOPHYLLA (Goat-leaved) (C) Central China, is a very attractive climber of vigorous habit, with oval, coppery-red leaves, whitish upon the undersides, with long, tubular, two-lipped flowers of orange-yellow, borne in heads of more than a dozen. Best grown

LONICERA (continued)

in a semi-shady site, L. tragophylla is one of the best of the climbing species. 10-*ft.*–12-*ft.*, *June-September.* *D.* *Indefinite.* *Cg7.* *ANC.*

LUPINUS (LEGUMINOSAE) (FROM LATIN LUPUS—A WOLF; POSSIBLY BECAUSE SOME OF THE SPECIES ARE VERY DEEPLY ROOTED AND WERE SAID TO IMPOVERISH THE SOIL).

The Tree Lupins are very quick-growing shrubs, are not long-lived, but freely propagated from the seed which they produce so generously, and are well suited by a good, deep loam in a sunny site.

L. ARBOREUS (Tree-like) California, is a vigorous, low-branching shrub with the typical leaves of the species, freely branching, woody stems, and sulphur-yellow flowers produced in cylindrical spires.

L. ARBOREUS VAR. SNOW QUEEN (Garden origin), is an attractive hybrid differing only in its snow-white spires of flowers.

4-*ft.*–6-*ft.*, *June-July.* *E.* 6-*ft.*–8-*ft.* *Sq.* *Sd2.* *ANC.*

LYCIUM (SOLANACEAE) (SAID TO BE DERIVED FROM THE GR. LYKION, THE NAME OF ANOTHER PLANT FROM LYCIA IN ASIA MINOR).

The common names given to the genus include Box Thorn and Matrimony Vine, and the species thrive in any normal soil, and may be increased by hardwood cuttings, from suckers, seeds or layers.

L. CHINENSE (Chinese) China, is a vigorous, somewhat rambling shrub, rather tender in reputation, with small, narrow, greyish-green leaves, and small, funnel-shaped, purple flowers with five spreading lobes, produced singly or in small groups in the leaf axils, and followed by oblong, orange-scarlet fruits, and much liked in and by south coast situations.

4-*ft.*–6-*ft.*, *May-July.* *D.* 6-*ft.*–8-*ft.* *Sq.* *Sd2.* *ANC.*

L. HALIMIFOLIUM (With leaves like Halimus) S.E. Europe, is very similar but has narrower leaves, and less diffuse habit.

4-*ft.*–6-*ft.*, *May-July.* *D.* 4-*ft.*–6-*ft.* *Sq.* *Sd2.* *ANC.*

MAGNOLIA (MAGNOLIACEAE) (NAMED BY LINNAEUS IN HONOUR OF PIERRE MAGNOL, A FRENCH BOTANIST OF MONTPELLIER IN THE SEVENTEENTH CENTURY).

There are few small trees or shrubs more beautiful or striking than the Magnolias, added to which many of the species diffuse upon the air the scent of many thousands of Freesias. The majority of the species are of slow growth and comparatively easy culture if they are given good, deep soil, a reasonably sheltered position, generally unlit by the morning sun, since they are liable to frost damage. Propagation of the species is undoubtedly best from seeds which should not be stored but be sown as soon as ripe. Layering is also practised and is preferable to grafting upon stocks of M. acuminata. Cuttings of the current year's growth, about four inches in length with a clean heel, in June, July or August, can be inserted in a warm sand frame, and should be potted on when rooted. Magnolias cannot as a rule be said to transplant well, and are generally best transplanted in the spring.

M. ACUMINATA (Long-pointed) U.S.A., is in reality a tree reaching one hundred feet in height, reminding one of Baron Munchausen in its common name, the Cucumber Tree, and outside our scope, but since it provides the stocks upon which many varieties are grafted it must perforce have mention. It has very large, bright-green, wavy-edged, oval leaves, and yellowish-green flowers up to three inches in length, seldom seen upon any but mature trees.

M. ACUMINATA VAR. CORDATA (Heart-shaped) rises not so high, at least in this country, and displays a commendably sweet, reasonable attitude by producing its upright, canary-yellow flowers upon even small bushes, dispensing sweet scents from both flowers and the aromatic leaves.

6-ft.–10-ft., May-June. D. 6-ft.–10-ft. Sq. Sd2. AN.

M. DENUDATA (Bare) Central China, is the Chinese Yulan, and is also M. conspicua, an outstanding large shrub or small tree which grows well in most gardens if given a sheltered position where it is unaffected by morning sun, when it will produce its snow-white, goblet-like flowers upon even small trees.

6-ft.–30-ft., March-June. D. 6-ft.–30-ft. Sq. Sd2. AN.

M. GRANDIFLORA (Large-flowered) Southern U.S.A., is a magnificent, evergreen tree with large, oval leaves, generally confined to south or west walls. In nature it reaches one hundred feet in height, but is more often seen varying from fifteen to forty feet in height, and spreading twenty-five to thirty-five feet wide, with dense growth and forking low down. The eight-inch, sweetly-scented flowers are creamy-white, and nestle in a circle of deep green leaves.

M. GRANDIFLORA VAR. FERRUGINEA (Rusty) differs only in having the undersides of its leaves covered with red-brown felt, and undoubtedly is better than any other variety for persisting in chalky soils. This variety only propagates from layers.

M. GRANDIFLORA VAR. LANCEOLATA is another variety sometimes known as Exmouth, propagated from layers, which has the advantage of flowering freely while the plants are still young. Its narrower leaves are rather rough, and the ivory-white flowers are quite as attractive.

15-ft.–40-ft., July-September. E. 10-ft.–35-ft. Sq. Sd2. L5. AN.

M. KOBUS (From Kobe) Japan, resembles a tree with long oval leaves and small, six-petalled, pure-white flowers, and is probably the least beautiful of all the species, but has charm. M. Kobus var. borealis has an outline more slender and graceful, wider leaves, and flowers which are larger. Both, however, fail to flower until they are reasonably mature.

30-ft., April. D. 25-ft.–30-ft. Sq. Sd2. L5. AN.

M. LENNEI (Comm.) Garden origin, is a hybrid of M. denudata and M. liliflora, and makes a large tree, forking low down and spreading wide, with large, dull-green leaves and goblet-shaped flowers, purple-rose on the outside and white inside. It is a splendid tree, however, in a sheltered place in the small garden, since it will flower while still young, certainly by the time it has reached a yard in height.

6-*ft.*–25-*ft.*, *April-May*. *D*. 8-*ft.*–35-*ft*. *Sq*. *L*5. *Cg*6. *AN*. *Pl*.50.

M. LILIFLORA (Lily-flowered) China, is probably the best variety of all for the small garden. It grows very slowly, ultimately reaching something less than ten feet, has oval, long, green leaves, paler below, and flowers before the leaves are produced, decorating its graceful frame with goblet-shaped, white flowers, wine-red upon the outside. M. liliflora var. nigra is the M. Soulangiana nigra of gardens, slow to grow and to flower. The flowers are dark purple upon the outside and paler within.

10-*ft.*, *March-May*. *D*. 10-*ft*. *Sq*. *Sd*2. *L*5. *Cg*6. *AN*.

M. MACROPHYLLA (Having long leaves) Southern U.S.A., may be either a large or small tree according to its locality, but requires a sheltered position for its greater glory. Its fragrant, creamy-white flowers, however, are not produced on any but established and mature trees. 15-*ft.*–50-*ft.*, *July*. *D*. 15-*ft.*–50-*ft*. *Sq*. *Sd*2. *AN*.

M. OBOVATA (With egg-shaped leaves) Japan, is a magnificent, straight tree, branching at about two-thirds of its height, and has large, dark green leaves, grey and felted beneath, over a foot in length, and bears exceptionally sweetly-scented, large, creamy-white flowers with a central ring of crimson stamens, overtopped by golden anthers. It is also known as M. hypoleuca.

10-*ft.*–50-*ft.*, *June-July*. *D*. 10-*ft.*–30-*ft*. *Sq*. *Sd*2. *AN*.

M. PARVIFLORA (With small flowers) China, is a pygmy among many giants, rarely exceeding three feet in height, with small, glossy, evergreen leaves, and born to be nursed in the shelter of a wall, preferably one facing west. This David produces very sweetly-scented, large, white flowers with pink sepals, and is well fitted to compete in beauty with its giant brethren.

3-*ft.*, *May-June*. *D*. 3-*ft*. *Sq*. *Sd*2. *L*5. *AN*.

M. SALICIFOLIA (Willow-leaved) Japan, makes a tree up to thirty feet in height, with elliptical leaves, pale green on top, glaucous beneath, and bears narrow-petalled, sweetly-scented flowers before the leaves are produced.

10-*ft.*–40-*ft.*, *April-May*. *D*. 10-*ft.*–35-*ft*. *Sq*. *Sd*2. *Cg*6. *AN*.

M. SARGENTIANA (Comm.) W. China, is a small, graceful tree, only producing its goblet-shaped, white flowers, tinted with violet, when mature, but is one of the most beautiful of the species.

25-*ft.*, *April*. *D*. 20-*ft*. *Sq*. *Sd*2. *AN*.

M. SIEBOLDII (Comm.) Japan, is a large shrub with many branches, and evergreen, oval leaves, heavily felted beneath. The attractive, white flowers are borne upon long stems, and form the perfect receptacle for the crimson stamens. It is exceptionally sweetly scented, and has the additional virtue of flowering while still young. M. Sieboldii is probably best suited by a shady site.

8-*ft.*–15-*ft.*, *May-August*. 8-*ft.*–15-*ft*. *Sq*. *Sd*2. *L*5. *Cg*6. *AN*.

Rhododendron dicroanthum ABCDEFHM
Rhododendron cinnabarinum JKNO
Rhododendron lepidotum KLMQ

Pieris Forrestii ABCDEFGH

Rhododendron russatum JKLNORS

Rhododendron didymum LMPQ

M. SINENSIS (Chinese) W. China, is the M. Nicholsoniana of gardens, and is a large shrub with rather large, oval leaves, rounded at the tips, bright-green on the topside, somewhat pubescent beneath. The cup-shaped, very fragrant, white flowers are centred with a cluster of rose-red stamens, over which appear the yellow styles.
10-*ft.*–20-*ft.*, *May-June*. *D*. 10-*ft.*–18-*ft. Sq*. *Sd*2. *L*5. *C*6. *AN*.

M. SOULANGIANA (Comm.) Garden origin, is a hybrid of M. denudata and M. liliflora, which quickly forms an outstanding tree. The long, rough, green, oval leaves are produced in April and May, with goblet-shaped, white flowers, flushed upon the outside with purple. M. Soulangiana is outstanding because it adds to its beauty hardiness beyond the ordinary.

M. SOULANGIANA VAR. ALBA has pure-white, scented flowers produced at first upon a leafless tree, but is succeeded by further flowers accompanied by the leaves.

M. SOULANGIANA VAR. ALEXANDRINA has similar flowers, stained at the base of the petals with reddish-purple.

M. SOULANGIANA VAR. BROZZONII has larger flowers than any of the type, freely produced upon even small plants.
10-*ft.*–30-*ft.*, *April-June*. *D*. 8-*ft.*–26-*ft. Sq*. *L*5. *Cg*6. *AN*.

M. STELLATA (Starry) Japan, is very slow-growing and covers itself before the leaves are in evidence with semi-double, white flowers made up of a number of narrow petals. It is one of the outstanding varieties, seldom exceeding ten feet in height and taking considerably more than half an average lifetime to reach this size. It is, however, a grand thought to plant one about a foot in height and to hope to retain one's sight long enough to see it at its best. Fortunately it flowers while still very young.
5-*ft.*–10-*ft.*, *March-April*. *D*. 5-*ft.*–10-*ft. Sq*. *Sd*2. *L*5. *Cg*6. *AN*.

M. THOMPSONIANA (Comm.) Garden origin, is a hybrid of M. virginiana with M. tripetala, which forms itself into a large open bush with impressive, long, oval, wavy-edged, light-green leaves, and large, very fragrant, creamy-white flowers borne upon small bushes, but most striking when ornamenting a wide, fully grown bush.
6-*ft.*–15-*ft.*, *May-September*. *D*. 8-*ft.*–20-*ft. Sq*. *Cg*6. *L*5. *AN*.

M. TRIPETALA (Three-petalled) Eastern U.S.A., is the Umbrella Tree, a name which it has derived from the arrangement of its very long, wide leaves at the tips of its branches, and is exceptionally handsome when it produces its large, creamy-white flowers centred with purple-red stamens, or when they are followed by the pleasant, large, rose-coloured, cone-shaped fruits, which it produces with regularity and in quantity. Most American authorities state that it is unpleasantly scented ; the perfume is certainly very strong, but I have known many people to like it, though I cannot say that I, personally, find it pleasant.
15-*ft.*–30-*ft.*, *May-June*. *D*. 15-*ft.*–30-*ft. Sq*. *Cg*6. *Sd*2. *AN*.

M. VIRGINIANA (From Virginia) U.S.A., is also M. glauca and the Sweet Bay, and in this country is generally represented by a slender, upright, small tree or large shrub with polished, olive-green, oval leaves which are green-grey upon the underside, and which vary in their persistence in winter in various plants. The sweetly-scented, narrow-petalled flowers are creamy-white and about three inches in diameter, and produced with great freedom.
6-ft.–15-ft., June-September. DE. 5-ft.–10-ft. Sq. Sd2. Cg6. L5. AN.

M. WATSONII (Comm.) Japan, is a very beautiful small tree with large, deep green, oval, round-topped leaves, and very large, cup-shaped flowers, centred with a circle of crimson stamens, and diffusing far and wide the sweetest fragrance of any of the species, and flowering while still a small tree.
8-ft.–25-ft., May-June. D. 8-ft.–25-ft. Sq. Sd2. Cg6. L5. AN. Shelter. Pl.49.

M. WILSONII (Comm.) W. China, is another species which grows into a large, branching shrub, and requires adequate protection to be able to fulfil its proper function. The flowers are smaller than those of M. Watsonii but similar in shape, and are borne when the narrow, deep-green leaves are fully formed.
6-ft.–15-ft., May-June. D. 6-ft.–15-ft. Sq. Sd2. Cg6. L5. AN. Shelter.

MAHONIA (*see* BERBERIS).

MARGYRICARPUS (ROSACEAE) (FROM THE GREEK MARGARITES—A PEARL; AND KARPOS—A BERRY; FROM THE PEARL-LIKE APPEARANCE OF THE BERRIES).

M. SETOSUS (Bristly) Chile, is a semi-prostrate evergreen with insignificant flowers, followed by large white berries strung out like pearl beads, and which is perfectly easy to grow in any position in good garden soil. *½-ft., August-January. E. 2-ft. Sq. Cg5. ANC.*

MENZIESIA (ERICACEAE) (NAMED AFTER A. MENZIES, A SCOTTISH BOTANIST).

This is a group of small shrubs closely resembling Erica, requiring the same methods of propagation, thriving in semi-shade or in woodland conditions, and preferably a peaty or leafy soil.

M. CILIICALYX (With fringed calyx) Japan, is a pretty shrub with stiff, erect growth, and rosettes of pointed, oval, green leaves fringed with hairs. The pink Lily-of-the-valley-like flowers are borne at the end of the previous season's growth and are a slightly deeper shade at the mouth. *2-ft., May-June. D. 2-ft. Sq. Cg6. A.*

M. MULTIFLORA (Many-flowered) Japan, is a larger shrub than the foregoing with smaller netted leaves, bristly at the edges, bright, copper-green above and blue-grey beneath. The very pretty clusters of flesh-pink flowers are slightly smaller than those of M. ciliicalyx. *3-ft.–4-ft., May-July. D. 3-ft.–4-ft. Sq. Cg6. A.*

M. PILOSA (Hairy) N. America, has oval, pale-green leaves, downy upon the underside, and bears sprays of attractive bell-flowers, varying in colour from white to yellow.

1½-ft.–2-ft., May-June. D. 2½-ft. Sq. Cg6. A.

M. PURPUREA (Purple) Japan, has oval, green leaves, blue-grey upon the underside, borne upon rather stiff, wiry shoots, with sprays of nodding bell-flowers of bright wine-red. It has the advantage also of colouring brightly in the autumn. A rare shrub but a very beautiful one. *3-ft.–5-ft. May-July. D. 3-ft.–5-ft. Sq. Cg6. ANC.*

MIMULUS (SCROPHULARIACEAE) (FROM THE LATIN MIMUS—A MIMIC; THE FLOWERS HAVING BEEN SUPPOSED TO BEAR SOME RESEMBLANCE TO A MASK OR A MONKEY'S FACE).

The species which follows is often known as Diplacus, and is only suited to growing against a south wall or in a cold house, though it is so easy to produce from cuttings of the soft wood, and grows so rapidly, that it may be increased each year from cuttings for planting out in the spring. Many winters it survives without trouble.

M. GLUTINOSUS (Sticky) California, has long, pointed, sticky, green leaves, and bears large, salmon-yellow flowers in the uppermost leaf axils and at the tops of the shoots. The flowers are reminiscent of the smaller-flowered Azaleas and are extremely beautiful, and best suited by a warm, sunny site. M. glutinosus var. puniceus has smaller leaves and deep-scarlet flowers which are not quite so large as those of the type. A host of hybrids now abound with flowers varying from white to purple.

4-ft., June-September. E. 3-ft. Sq. Cg7. ANC.

MITCHELLA (RUBIACEAE) (COMMEMORATIVE NAME).

The genus comprises only one species known to cultivators, a downy, creeping, evergreen shrub, commonly known as the Partridge-berry, and thriving in light, peaty soil in semi-shade.

M. REPENS (Creeping) N. America, has small, round, dark-green, shiny leaves borne upon wiry shoots which hug the ground, and produces pink, hanging bell-flowers in the leaf axils, in pairs, which are followed by irregularly shaped, orange-scarlet berries.

¼-ft., June-July. E. 2-ft. Sq. Sd2. ANC.

MITRARIA (GESNERACEAE) (DERIVED FROM THE GR. MITRA — A MITRE; FROM THE SHAPE OF THE CALYX).

One species from Chile is a plant more tender in reputation than in fact, withstanding up to twenty degrees of frost with fortitude and often equanimity. It does, however, flower more freely in a sheltered position, certainly in a soil free from lime.

M. COCCINEA (Scarlet) Chile, dots among its bright-green leaves the orange-scarlet, pendent flowers, shaped like those of the Foxglove.

2-ft., June-September. 2-ft. Sq. D. Cg7. AN.

MOLTKIA (Boraginaceae) (named in honour of count J. G. Moltke, a Danish naturalist).

The one species which follows is best grown in sandy peat in a fully sunny site.

M. petraea (Stony) S.E. Europe, makes a small, rounded bush clad with narrow, ash-grey leaves, and bears flowers like those of the Lithospermum, at first purple with touches of pink, but turning violet-blue with age.

1-ft., June-July. E. 1½-ft. Sq. Cg8. A.

MUEHLENBECKIA (Polygonaceae) (named in honour of H. Muehlenbeck, an Alsatian doctor).

Is also known as the Wire Plant, and is a pleasant shrub for covering that which were better hidden.

M. complexa (Interwoven) N. Zealand, is a trailing plant with round, polished, deep-green, fiddle-shaped leaves, greenish flowers borne in short spikes, and forms a tangled mat of very pleasant green. In addition to these other merits it will also climb.

1-ft.–6-ft., September. D. Indefinite. Cg7. ANC.

MUTISIA (Compositae) (named in honour of J. C. Mutis, a South-American botanist).

A group of climbing shrubs with very large, daisy-like flowers, comparatively rare in cultivation. The species are best grown with the root in a place which the sun cannot parch nor the frost wither. They are generally increased from the suckers, which they will send up with freedom when suited, but these require coddling for a while before they may be safely planted out.

M. decurrens (With the leaves hanging down) Chile, is an extremely beautiful climber, which is at its best planted to ramble through a shrub or hurdle fence, with its root protected from the sun's rays, when it will produce its astonishingly large, Gazania-like flowers with great freedom.

Indefinite, July-August. E. Suckers. 4. AN.

M. ilicifolia (Holly-leaved) S. America, has greyish-green leaves, much cut at the edges, furnished with tendrils at the tip, heavily felted beneath with white wool, and bears freely for almost the whole season. Its large daisy flowers vary in colour from white in a poor form to pink in a specimen with bluer blood.

Indefinite, May-October. E. Suckers. 4. AN.

M. retusa (Blunted) Chile, has all the advantages of M. ilicifolia with a botanical difference, but is probably a great deal more hardy.

Indefinite, May-October. E. Suckers. 4. AN.

MYRICA (MYRICACEAE) (DERIVED FROM THE GR. MYRIKE—TAMARISK).

A group of attractive shrubs grown for the benefit of their aromatic foliage, and suited to soils which are lime-free. They are propagated from divisions of the root in early spring, or from seeds.

M. CALIFORNICA (Californian) Western U.S.A., is an evergreen shrub with shining, bright-green, serrated-edged leaves covered with a deposit of white wax. M. californica is very hardy and is outstanding in its ability to succeed upon very poor, sandy soils.

10-ft.–12-ft., June. E. 10-ft.–12-ft. Sq. D3. L4. Sd2. AN.

M. CAROLINIENSIS (From Carolina) U.S.A., is the Bayberry, a rather more bushy and compact shrub, generally, but not always, deciduous, clothed with oval green leaves, quaintly lemon-scented, and assuming magnificent regal tones in autumn, and with similar catkins followed by greyish-white fruits overlaid with white wax. This also does well in poor soils.

6-ft.–8-ft., May-June. D. 6-ft.–8-ft. Sq. D3. L4. Sd2. AN.

M. CERIFERA (Producing wax) New Jersey, is the Wax Myrtle, was at one time the source of the wax from which early settlers made candles, and a comely shrub with dark-green leaves which are pleasantly scented, and with greyish-white, small berries covered with wax.

3-ft.–5-ft., May-June. D. 3-ft.–5-ft. Sq. D3. L4. Sd2. AN.

M. GALE (Probably an old name) Europe, is the Sweet Gale, a well-known native of our moors, with very pleasantly scented wood, glossy, dark-green leaves, and closely packed, stemless catkins, persisting in the case of the female ones as groups of nutlets of yellowish-brown enclosed in two brownish bracts.

2-ft.–4-ft., May-June. D. 2-ft.–4-ft. Sq. D3. Sd2. AN.

M. RUBRA (Reddish) China, has large, deep-green leaves, rather deeply notched, and shares the pleasant aroma of the species with the added beauty of red-purple nutlets.

5-ft.–8-ft., May-June. E. 5-ft.–8-ft. Sq. D3. Sd2. AN.

MYRSINE (MYRSINACEAE) (FROM MYRSINE, THE OLD GREEK NAME FOR MYRTLE).

A group of evergreen shrubs with small box-like leaves, often finely toothed like a miniature holly at the tips, with tiny flowers, about twenty-four to the inch, borne in three- to eight-flowered clusters, and followed, in the case of the female flowers, by small fruits.

M. AFRICANA (African) Azores, etc., has its long green flowers followed by orange-red berries.

2-ft.–4-ft., May-June. E. 2-ft.–4-ft. Sq. Sd2. AN.

MYRTUS (Myrtaceae) (from the old greek name myrtos, sacred to the goddess of love).

The Myrtles are as a rule suited only to the most sheltered positions against walls, but are otherwise of comparatively easy culture in good loam.

M. communis (Common) Mediterranean region, is the Myrtle of the classics, with its deep-green, scented, ovate leaves and creamy-white, four- to five-petalled flowers, centred with a cluster of stamens, followed by bluish-black fruits. M. communis var. tarentina varies only in its narrower, smaller leaves in four distinct rows, and its white fruits. *8-ft.–10-ft., July. E. 8-ft.–10-ft Sq. Cg7. N.*

M. nummularia (Like a coin) S. America, is a flat-growing shrub with shining, round leaves, and almost stemless white flowers, with a central tuft of stamens, followed by deep-pink, edible berries. It is best grown in a sheltered, sunny, but not sun-parched, spot.
¼-ft., June. E. 1-ft. Sq. Cg7. N.

M. obcordata (Of inverted heart-shape) N. Zealand, is an etherealised relative with thin, wiry branches, small grey leaves about half an inch in length, small flowers about four to an inch span, followed by dark-red berries of about the same size, turning with age to violet.
8-ft., July. E. 6-ft. Sq. Cg7. N.

NANDINA (Berberidaceae) (derived from the japanese name nandin).

N. domestica (Having domestic use) Japan, is a shrub with a particularly graceful appearance, erect in growth, and decorated with pinnately divided leaves with very narrow, long leaflets giving a grassy effect. The individual white flowers are small but are impressive in the mass, and in favoured places are followed by coral-red fruits, but the chief beauty of the plant is its attractive spring and autumn tones. *8-ft., June-July. E. 18-ft. Sq. Sd2. ANC.*

NEILLIA (Rosaceae) (named after dr. patrick neill, a nineteenth-century botanist of edinburgh).

The Neillias are a group of deciduous shrubs closely allied to and resembling Spiraea, which thrive in almost any soil and position. They can be freely propagated from cuttings of the tips of the shoots about four inches in length, placed in sand or sandy soil in July, or from suckers detached from the roots in early spring.

N. longiracemosa (Bearing long racemes) China, is probably the outstanding species, with alternate toothed and lobed green leaves and terminal clusters of drooping sprays of rose-pink flowers.
6-ft.–8-ft., May-June. D. 6-ft.–8-ft. Sq. Cg7. ANC.

N. opulifolia (With leaves like Viburnum opulus) has white flowers tinged with pink and is a splendid plant for the wild garden.
8-ft.–10-ft., June. D. 10-ft.–20-ft. Sq. D3. ANC.

N. RIBESIOIDES (Resembling the Flowering Currant) China, is a neater plant than N. longiracemosa, with wand-like, red-brown stems and shorter, closely packed sprays of bright-pink flowers.

4-ft.–6-ft., May-June. D. 6-ft.–8-ft. Sq. Cg7. D3. ANC.

N. THIBETICA (From Tibet) Tibet, differs little for garden purposes from N. longiracemosa.

6-ft.–8-ft., May-June. D. 8-ft.–10-ft. Sq. Cg7. ANC.

NIEREMBERGIA (SOLANACEAE) (THE NAME IS COMMEMORATIVE OF J. E. NIEREMBERG, A SPANISH SEVENTEENTH-CENTURY JESUIT AND NATURALIST).

N. FRUTESCENS (Shrubby) South America, is a very slender-leaved, wiry shrub with large, white, funnel-shaped flowers deepening in the centre to violet-blue.

1½-ft., May-Sept. E. 1½-ft. Sq. Ch6. N. Pl.51.

NOTOSPARTIUM (LEGUMINOSAE) (FROM GR. NOTOS—SOUTH; AND SPARTION—BROOM).

N. CARMICHAELIAE (Comm.) New Zealand, is a beautiful shrub of the habit of Spartium junceum, with whip-like branches, almost leafless, which becomes wreathed with small purplish-pink pea flowers produced along the bare branches in short sprays composed of upwards of a dozen flowers.

6-ft.–12-ft., June-July. D. 6-ft.–8-ft. Sq. Sd2. AN.

NUTTALLIA (ROSACEAE) (NAMED IN HONOUR OF THOMAS NUTTALL, A NORTH-AMERICAN BOTANIST. THE ONE SPECIES IS ALSO KNOWN AS OSMARONIA).

N. CERASIFORMIS (Shaped like a cherry) California, is an easily grown shrub, with oblong to lanceolate green leaves, bearing, while still leafless, short, drooping sprays of almond-scented, greenish-white flowers, succeeded by purple fruits with plum-like bloom.

6-ft.–10-ft., January-March. D. 6-ft.–10-ft. Sq. Ch7–8. D3. ANC.

OLEARIA (COMPOSITAE) (DERIVED FROM THE GR. ELAIA—THE OLIVE; THE LEAVES OF SOME OF THE SPECIES RESEMBLING THOSE OF THE OLIVE).

These are the so-called Daisy-bushes, only a few of which are completely hardy everywhere in the British Isles. Most varieties are endemic to the antipodes, and are very easily produced from cuttings of from four to six inches in length, placed in sandy soil in a frame with mild bottom heat during July to August, and grown on in pots before being planted out. All the varieties are best suited by sunny sites in sandy soil, but most will grow in any soil, however poor.

O. ALBIDA (White) New Zealand, is the O. oleifolia of gardens, and is a very hardy variety with dark-green, polished, oval leaves, which are very white beneath, and are relieved in July and August by small clusters of white composite flowers.

4-ft.–8-ft., July-August. E. 4-ft.–8-ft. Sq. Cg7–8. ANC.

O. CHATHAMICA (From the Chatham Isles) has long, rather narrow, lanceolate leaves, slightly serrated at the tips, dark green above and felted white beneath, and bears large, white, daisy flowers about the size of a penny, with a violet disc.

4-ft.–8-ft., July-August. E. 4-ft.–8-ft. Sq. Cg7–8. ANC. Shelter.

O. ERUBESCENS (Turning red) Australia, is a shrub of somewhat slender habit with red-brown stems, small oblong, unevenly toothed leaves, and small white flowers in large cylindrical sprays produced from the leaf axils.

3-ft.–4-ft., May-June. E. 3-ft.–4-ft. Sq. Cg7–8. ANC. Shelter.

O. GUNNIANA (Comm.) Tasmania, is one of the most popular species, and is of compact, rounded habit with narrow, grey, oval, slightly toothed leaves, and branching clusters of up to twenty white daisy flowers with a central yellow zone. Comber's varieties are similar but a little more lax in habit, slightly more tender and have flowers which include blue, violet, mauve and red, and are best suited to seaside districts.

3-ft.–5-ft., May. E. 3-ft.–5-ft. Sq. Cg7–8. ANC. Shelter.

O. HAASTII (Comm.) New Zealand, is the hardiest of the species, completely ubiquitous, and has small dark-green, oval leaves and masses of small, hawthorn-scented, white daisy flowers in rounded clusters. *3-ft.–8-ft., July-August. E. 3-ft.—8-ft. Sq. Cg7–8. ANC.*

O. ILICIFOLIA (With holly leaves) New Zealand, has shiny, dark-green, coarsely toothed, oblong leaves, and bears clusters of small, white, yellow-centred daisy flowers, which are sweetly scented in the way of Musk.

6-ft.–10-ft., June. E. 6-ft.–10-ft. Sq. Cg7–8. ANC. Shelter.

O. INSIGNIS (Remarkable) New Zealand, is also Pachystegia insignis, a low-growing, large, oval-leaved shrub, heavily felted with silver along the stems and upon the underside of the leaves, which are light green above, and very large, white daisy flowers upon thick, stiff stems. O. insignis is best suited by a sharply drained soil, but holds an undeserved reputation for tenderness.

4-ft., July. E. 6-ft. Sq. Cg7–8. ANC.

O. LINEATA (With narrow leaves) New Zealand, is a tall-growing shrub with thin, wand-like stems, pendent at the tips, and clothed with groups of five grass-like leaves, with many clusters of small white flowers in June.

6-ft.–12-ft., June. E. 2-ft.–4-ft. Sq. Cg7–8. ANC.

O. MACRODONTA (With long teeth) New Zealand, has grey-green, holly-like leaves, silvery underneath, and clusters of many small, white, sweetly-scented flowers, and is much more hardy than it is normally reputed to be, standing 20 degrees of frost when well established. *8-ft.–15-ft., June. E. 6-ft.–8-ft. Sq. Cg7–8. ANC.*

Rhododendron hybridum

Rhododendron hybrids

O. MOSCHATA (With a musky scent) New Zealand, is a compact shrub with small, silver-green-grey leaves, faintly musk-scented, and many few-flowered clusters of small white flowers.

1-ft.–3-ft., July-September. E. 1-ft.–3-ft. Sq. Cg7–8. ANC.

O. MYRSINOIDES (Resembling Myrsine) Tasmania, has small, oval, musk-scented, shiny, green, finely toothed leaves, grey beneath, is of loose growth and bears long sprays of small white flowers in July and August.

3-ft.–4-ft., July-August. E. 3-ft. Sq. Cg7–8. ANC. Shelter.

O. NUMMULARIFOLIA (With leaves rounded like a coin) New Zealand, has rounded green leaves with turned-back edges, felted grey upon the underside, is low and twiggy in its growth, and bears its solitary white flowers, made up of six to twelve creamy-white ray florets, above the leaves. *4-ft., June-July. E. 4-ft. Sq. Cg7–8. ANC.*

O. SEMIDENTATA (Toothed upon the upper half) Chatham Isles, is a magnificent shrub for clement districts, with long, bright-green, slightly toothed leaves, very white beneath, and large, solitary, aster-like flowers of lavender-pink with discs of violet. It is best suited by a sheltered site in sharply drained soil.

4-ft.–8-ft., July-August. E. 4-ft.–8-ft. Sq. Cg7–8. ANC.

O. SOLANDRI (Comm.) New Zealand, is an upright-growing shrub made up of many erect-growing branches, clothed with tiny, bright-green leaves which are yellow upon the undersides, and give the whole a golden-yellow appearance. It has small golden-yellow flowers, and is valuable only for its contrasting colour.

3-ft.–8-ft., August-October. E. 2-ft.–4-ft. Sq. Cg7–8. ANC. Shelter.

ONONIS (LEGUMINOSAE) (DERIVED FROM THE GR. ONOS—AN ASS; AND ONINEMI—TO DELIGHT; SOME OF THE SPECIES PROVIDING SUITABLE FODDER FOR ANIMALS).

All the species noted are more or less sub-shrubs, frequently losing the whole of their top growth in winter, and resemble the well-known Rest Harrow (O. arvensis) of the countryside. They are of easy cultivation—with the possible exception of O. cenisia—in any good, light garden soil in an open site, and can be most readily propagated from seeds.

O. CENISIA (From Mount Cenis) Europe, is a pretty, prostrate-growing shrub with trifoliate, light-green leaves and rather large, rose-pink pea flowers. It requires a well-drained site.

½-ft., June-July. D. 1½-ft. Sq. Sd2. ANC.

O. FRUTICOSA (Shrubby) S. Europe, is of open, spreading habit, with trifoliate, pale-green leaves, and freely produced, pinkish-white flowers in groups of three.

3-ft., June-July. D. 4-ft. Sq. Sd2. ANC.

O. NATRIX (Water-snake) S. Europe, is the Goat-root, with rather hairy, green, three-parted leaves, rather large, yellow pea flowers

ONONIS (continued)

which decline to a graceful old age by becoming flushed at the centre with reddish-brown, and present then an even more fascinating picture. *2-ft., May-June. D. 3-ft. Sq. Sd2. ANC.*

O. ROTUNDIFOLIA (With round leaves) S. Europe, is one of the most completely clothed of the species, its large, rounded leaves being again composed of three leaflets, and its rose-pink pea flowers are produced in groups of three from the axils of the uppermost leaves.
2-ft., May-June. D. 1½-ft. Sq. Sd2. ANC.

OSMANTHUS (OLEACEAE) (FROM THE GR. OSME—PERFUME OR SCENT; AND ANTHOS—A FLOWER; THE FLOWERS OF MOST OF THE SPECIES BEING VERY FRAGRANT).

Osmanthus comprises a group of evergreen shrubs with dark-green, polished, holly-like leaves, thriving in good loam and most easily increased by cuttings of the tips of the side shoots, three to four inches in length, placed in a sand frame with gentle bottom heat in July-August.

O. AQUIFOLIUM (Resembling Holly) Japan, is a shrub of exceptional beauty of leaf combined with small, white, very fragrant flowers and an ease of growth which make it a fine subject for hedges in mild districts.
4-ft.–8-ft., September-October. E. 3-ft.–6-ft. Sq. Cg7–8. ANC.

O. ARMATUS (Armed with thorns) China, has large, dull-green, leathery leaves, sharply spined when young, clusters of very sweetly-scented, small, creamy-white flowers produced in the leaf axils late in the year, and appreciates a shady site.
6-ft.–12-ft., September-October. E. 5-ft.–10-ft. Sq. Cg7–8. ANC.

O. DELAVAYI (Comm.) China, is another variety at its best in a shady spot, with very small, pointed, elliptical, shiny, green leaves, and clusters of clear white, tubular, sweetly-scented, lilac-like flowers, borne in small clusters in the leaf axils.
6-ft., April-May. E. 6-ft. Sq. Cg7–8. ANC.

O. FORRESTII (Comm.) China, has long, pointed, elliptical leaves edged with sharp teeth, with main ribs of cream, and creamv-white flowers produced in groups in the leaf axils.
8-ft., April-May. E. 6-ft. Sq. Cg7–8. ANC.

O. SERRULATUS (With minute teeth) China, is a smaller-growing variety with shiny, bright-green, narrow leaves with minute serrations, and axillary clusters of sweetly-odorous, clear-white flowers.
4-ft., February-March. E. 4-ft. Sq. Cg7–8. ANC.

O. SUAVIS (Sweetly-scented) Himalayas, has glandular stems with shiny, dark-green, spear-shaped leaves, finely toothed at the edges, and small clusters of small, very sweetly-scented, white flowers.
6-ft.–8-ft., December-March. E. 4-ft.–6-ft. Sq. Cg7–8. ANC.

OSMAREA (OLEACEAE) (THE NAME IS DERIVED FROM THE COMBINATION OF OSMANTHUS AND PHILLYREA).

A bigeneric cross between Osmanthus and Phillyrea, needing the same conditions for its growth as Osmanthus, and propagating in a similar manner.

O. BURKWOODII (Comm.) Garden origin, is a hybrid between Osmanthus Delavayi and Phillyrea decora. It has dark, glossy-green, elliptical, pointed leaves up to two inches in length, is of slow growth, and bears clusters of sweetly-scented, ivory-white flowers in the leaf axils and in terminal clusters.
4-ft., April. E. 4-ft. Sq. Cg7–8. ANC.

OSTEOMELES (ROSACEAE) (DERIVED FROM THE GR. OSTEON—A BONE; AND MELON—AN APPLE; A REFERENCE TO THE HARDNESS OF THE FRUIT).

A group of useful shrubs with pinnate leaves and small white flowers, followed by red haws, with a reputation for being tender—in the case of O. Schwerinae and its varieties—rather undeserved if grown in light and dry soil in a somewhat sheltered site.

O. SCHWERINAE (Comm.) W. China, is a tall evergreen shrub with slender, arching branches clothed with pinnate, grey leaves, made up of fifteen to thirty-one leaflets. The small white flowers are borne in clusters resembling those of the Hawthorn, and are followed by dark-red fruits.
6-ft.–8-ft., June. E. 6-ft.–8-ft. Sq. Sd10. Cg7. ANC.

O. SCHWERINAE VAR. SUBROTUNDA (Roundish) E. China, is a much dwarfer variety with smaller leaves made up of fifteen to nineteen tiny leaflets, but its flowers and fruits are not noticeably reduced in size. *3-ft., June. E. 3-ft. Sq. Sd10. Cg7. ANC.*

OXYCOCCUS (VACCINIACEAE) (DERIVED FROM THE GR. OXYS—SHARP; AND KOKKOS—A BERRY; A REFERENCE TO THE SHARPNESS OF TASTE OF THE FRUITS).

These are the Cranberries, which require very peaty or sandy soils in which to grow, but most certainly a complete absence of lime. The two species may be said to have little value from the point of view of garden beauty, but they do produce what we are told are the most attractively flavoured of all the wild berries.

O. MACROCARPUS (Large-fruited) Newfoundland, N. Carolina, is evergreen with creeping stems, and bears small pink flowers in terminal clusters, followed by largish red fruits up to three-quarters of an inch in diameter.
1-ft., June-August. E. 3-ft. Sq. Sd2. Cg7. AN.

O. PALUSTRIS (Swamp-loving) N.E. Europe, is the European or Small Cranberry, not quite so invasive in its growth, but with a much smaller but similar berry.
1-ft., May-July. E. 2-ft. Sq. Sd2. Cg7. AN.

OXYDENDRUM (Ericaceae) (from the Gr. oxys—sour ; and dendron—a tree ; from the taste of the sap).

O. arboreum (Tree-like) N. America, is also known as Andromeda arborea and the Sorrel Tree, and is generally in cultivation a small tree rarely exceeding twenty feet in height, and more often only ten feet, with branches right to the ground. Is best grown in a semi-shady site. The leaves are long and slender, pointed, generally assuming bright tints in autumn. While in flower the tree presents its most picturesque aspect, the long, drooping sprays of white, bell-shaped flowers exceeding six inches in length.

10-ft.–20-ft., July-September. D, 10-ft.–20-ft. Sq. Sd2. AN. Pl.34.

PACHYSANDRA (Buxaceae) (from the Gr. pachys—thick ; and andres—stamens).

P. terminalis (Terminal) Japan, is an interesting rather than a beautiful, low-growing evergreen with diamond-shaped leaves produced in curious whorls, separated each year by a length of bare stem. The flowers are green touched with purple and are produced in small spikes at the end of the previous year's growth. Its main advantage is that it can be grown in quite densely shaded sites under trees. *½-ft., April. E. 3-ft Sq. Cg6. AN.*

PAEONIA (Ranunculaceae) (derived from the old Gr. name given to the plant after Paion, physician to the gods, the plant being said to have medicinal qualities).

The Paeony is a genus composed mainly of herbaceous plants, but it numbers among it two species of shrubs, of which P. Moutan has been in cultivation in China and Japan for many centuries. The Tree Paeony is best grown as a solitary shrub in a site sheltered from the morning sun. It requires good, deep, rich soil and is benefited considerably by dressing occasionally with manure. Propagation is best done by layering, which should be done before growth for the season commences.

P. Moutan (King of the Flowers) China, Japan, is a rigid-branched shrub with rather hard outlines while still bare, but extremely pleasant when fully clothed. It rarely exceeds five feet in height, bears large, pinnate, alternate leaves, sometimes up to eighteen inches in length. The single varieties have from five to ten petals, and the double varieties produce fully double flowers, sometimes up to a foot in diameter. The original colour of the species was rose-purple, but now all shades of colour exist from white to crimson.

Arashiyama (Maple Mountain)—has double rose flowers flushed with copper.
Asahi (Rising Sun)—has double crimson-scarlet flowers.
Beni-Kirin (Crimson Giraffe)—has double orange-scarlet flowers.
Bijou de Chusan—is double and creamy-white in colour.
Choseiden (Temple of Long Life)—has variegated foliage and pale-mauve double flowers.

Daihasshu (Nippon)—is white at the edges, deepening to mauve at the centre, and is semi-double.

Elizabeth—has double flowers of bright salmon-pink.

Flora—has large, semi-double flowers with frilled petals.

fragans maxima plena (Large; scented; double)—has scented, double white flowers.

Fugi-no-Akebono (Dawn on Mount Fuji)—is double white, shaded with pink at the base.

Fuka-jishi (God of Lions)—has single flowers of bright carmine.

Gekkeikan (Laurel Crown)—is fully double with flowers of rose flushed with mauve.

Hana-Kagami (Standard of Flowers)—has fully double white flowers flushed at the base with pale pink.

Henryi—has fully double flowers of carmine edged with white.

Ima-Murasaki (New Purple)—is fully double with large purple flowers.

Jitsugetsu-Nishiki (Superlative Brocade)—has bright red, double flowers touched with white at the edges.

Kimpai (Golden Cup)—has semi-double flowers of clear cream.

Kokuho (Black Bird)—has double black-purple flowers.

Kumomana tsuki (Kumomana black)—has single flowers of purple-black.

Madame Louis Henry—has open, semi-double, carmine flowers flushed with orange-yellow.

Madame Stuart Low—has semi-double flowers of bright salmon-red.

Myoko (Clear Light)—has double yellow flowers flushed with rose at the base.

Nishi-no-Umi (Western Sea)—has large double flowers of peach-pink.

Nissho (Sunbeam)—has double scarlet flowers.

Otohime (Young Princess)—has double mauve flowers, purplish-red at the base.

Seiryuden (Refreshing Temple)—has large, white, fully double flowers, shaded at the base with pink.

Shirohata-Ryu (Irregular White)—has very double white flowers with irregular petals.

Souvenir de Duder—has fully double, violet-purple flowers.

Taiyo (Sun)—has double crimson flowers.

Yachiyo-Jishi (Immortal Lion)—has double, salmon-pink flowers with a deeper centre.

5-ft., May-June. D. 3-ft.–5-ft. Sq. L4. N.

PALIURUS (Rhamnaceae) (an old greek name of doubtful origin; containing as a genus only one cultivated species, which has biblical connections).

P. Spina-Christi (Christ's Thorn) S. Europe, is also P. australis and P. aculeatus, and a small tree or shrub seldom exceeding twenty feet, with small, ovate leaves and two spines at each joint, one pointing upwards and the other down, and innumerable small flowers of greenish-yellow, followed by fruits crowned with a curious ring which encircles them. The armed twigs are very pliable and are believed to have provided the material from which the Crown of Thorns was made.

20-ft., July-August. D. 15-ft.–20-ft. Sq. Cg7. ANC.

PASSIFLORA (PASSIFLORACEAE) (FROM THE LATIN PASSUS—SUFFERING; AND FLOS—FLOWER).

The one hardy member of the genus is endemic to South America, and was given the name Flos Passionis by the early Spanish Missionaries. The parts of the flower were regarded as emblematic of the Crucifixion. The three stigmas represented the three nails; the five wounds were represented by the five anthers; the corona was the Crown of Thorns; the ten sepals and petals, the ten apostles present; and the leaves and tendrils were symbolic of the hands and scourges of the persecutors.

P. COERULEA (Sky-blue) Brazil, is the so-called Blue Passion Flower, the flowers of which are three to eleven inches in diameter, and composed of five greenish-white sepals, five pale petals tinged with a purple flush, and a corona of purple and yellow. This climber is best suited to a sheltered, sunny wall where its greyish-green, palmate leaves will persist.

20-ft.–30-ft., July-September. E. Indefinite. Sd2. Cg7. ANC.

PENTSTEMON (or PENSTEMON) (SCROPHULARIACEAE) (FROM THE GR. PENTE—FIVE; AND STEMON—A STAMEN; THAT IS, HAVING FIVE STAMENS).

The Pentstemon is a magnificent shrub of comparatively easy culture in any good garden soil, and is propagated from cuttings of the stem three to four inches in length, placed in a cold frame in August.

P. CORYMBOSUS (With flowers in convex clusters) California, is a deciduous, woody shrub with rather small, serrated, deep-green leaves, and short sprays of small but intense-coral-red flowers.

1-ft., July-September. D. 1-ft. Sq. Cg8. ANC.

P. HETEROPHYLLUS (With variable leaves) California, is a woody shrub with oval to linear leaves of deep green, with long spires of large flowers of blue, prinked up with touches of purple and pink. The flower colours are variable, and seedling forms of merit should be propagated from cuttings. P. heterophyllus must be regarded as a tender shrub and be given a protected site in sharp and well-drained soil, with the added insurance of replacement cuttings confined to a cold frame during the winter.

1½-ft., June-August. E. 1¼-ft. Sq. Sd2. Cg8. ANC.

P. MENZIESII (Comm.) Oregon, is a small, woody shrub with shining, green, oval leaves, and violet-blue flowers with a bearded, sterile stamen. *½-ft., June-July. D. 1-ft. Sq. Cg4. ANC.*

P. NEWBERRYI (Comm.) California, is a small evergreen shrub with thick, rounded, greyish-green leaves, and making a humped bush decorated with bright-red, tubular flowers.

1-ft., June-July. E. 1¼-ft. Sq. Ch8. ANC.

P. ROEZLII (Comm.) California, is in reality a dwarf form of P. heterophyllus, with narrow foliage and pale-blue or violet flowers. The red-flowered P. Roezlii of catalogues is P. rupicola.

¾-ft., June-July. E. 1-ft. Sq. Cg4. ANC.

P. RUPICOLA (Growing in stony places) Washington, etc., is a low-growing shrub with grey-green, rounded leaves and larger flowers of intense crimson-rose.

⅓-ft., June-July. E. 1-ft. Sq. Sd2. Ch8. ANC.

P. SCOULERI (Comm.) British Columbia, has spear-shaped leaves of greyish-green, toothed at the edges, and bears large lilac flowers.

1-ft., June-August. E. 1¼-ft. Sq. Ch8. ANC.

P. × SIX HILLS HYBRID (Garden origin) is an exceptionally fine plant of low growth and with a fine constitution, which will smother itself with masses of sprays of flowers of lilac-rose.

1-ft., June-July. E. 1½-ft. Sq. Ch8. ANC.

PERAPHYLLUM (ROSACEAE) (FROM THE GR. PERA—BEYOND ; AND PHYLLON—A LEAF ; THE FLOWERS BEING PERSISTENT).

P. RAMOSISSIMUM (Much-branched) Western N. America, resembles Amelanchier and is definitely not so good a shrub, as it finds residence in these isles much more trying than its more tractable brethren.

3-ft., April-May. D. 3-ft. Sq. Cg7. ANC.

PERNETTYA (ERICACEAE) (NAMED IN HONOUR OF DOM PERNETTY, AUTHOR AND TRAVELLER).

The Pernettyas are undoubtedly best suited by a lime-free soil and revel in a moist peaty one. They may be propagated from layers or cuttings two to three inches in length, taken and inserted in sandy peat during August or September, and species may be freely raised from seed.

P. FURIANS (Wild) Chile, has oval, spear-shaped, green leaves, and bears numerous clusters of white lily-of-the-valley-like flowers, followed by purple-red fruits.

2-ft.—4-ft., May-June. E. 2-ft.–4-ft. Sq. Sd2. Cg8. AN.

P. LEUCOCARPA (With whitish fruits) Chile, is also P. GAYANA, has very small, pointed, green leaves, with small typical flowers followed by pinkish-white berries.

1-ft., May-June. E. 2-ft. Sq. Sd2. Cg8. AN.

P. MUCRONATA (With a stiff, sharp point) Magellan, makes a stiff, upright bush with pointedly oval leaves, small typical lily-of-the-valley flowers, followed by large crimson berries, which are retained throughout the winter. P. mucronata Bell's Seedling is an improved form with very large, crimson fruits which are retained throughout the winter and spring. P. mucronata Davis's Hybrids vary in the colour of their fruits, ranging from white to deep purple. P. mucronata rupicola has cream-coloured fruits.

2-*ft.*–2½-*ft.*, *May-June*. *E*. 2½-*ft. Sq*. *Cg*8. *AN*.

.PUMILA (Small) Patagonia, is also P. magellanica and P. empetrifolia, and a dwarf, running shrub with white flowers and deep pink berries. ⅓-*ft.*, *May-June*. *E*. 1-*ft. Sq*. *Cg*8. *AN*.

P. TASMANICA (Tasmanian) Tasmania, is a tiny, prostrate shrub with minute, pointed, green leaves upon almost microscopic stems, with white, nodding, bell-flowers, large for the size of the plant, followed by bright-red berries which sit tightly upon the tuft. P. tasmanica is best suited by shady conditions in soils which do not dry out quickly. ¼-*ft.*, *May-June*. *E*. 1-*ft. Sq*. *Cg*8. *AN*.

PEROWSKIA (LABIATAE) (THE NAME IS COMMEMORATIVE OF M. PEROWSKY, A RUSSIAN BOTANIST).

P. ATRIPLICIFOLIA (With leaves resembling Atriplex) Himalayas, is a tall growing sub-shrub with grey-green, pleasantly aromatic leaves, and substantial sprays of violet-blue flowers reminiscent of an enlarged Nepeta Mussini, which propagates freely from suckers, or from cuttings of the green wood taken during July, and is much at home in any well-drained garden soil.

3-*ft.*–5-*ft.*, *August-September*. *D*. 3-*ft.*–5-*ft. Sq*. *Cg*7. *ANC*. *Pl*.73.

PHILADELPHUS (SACIFRAGACEAE) (AN OLD GREEK NAME FOR A SWEETLY-SCENTED FLOWERING SHRUB, WHICH TOOK ITS NAME FROM THAT OF PTOLEMY PHILADELPHUS OF EGYPT).

These are the Syringas of gardens, a name which is unfortunately the botanic generic name for the shrubs generally known as Lilac. The Mock Orange is of exceptionally easy culture in any soil, thriving with alacrity upon either a well-limed or a lime-free soil, and is of easy propagation from cuttings three to four inches long of the side shoots, placed in a sandy soil in a cutting frame with gentle bottom heat in July. All the species are scented, but in certain cases the scent is so strong as to be repulsive to some people, and the attention of these folk should be centred upon the hybrids in which the odour of the flowers has been reduced.

P. BRACHYBOTRYS (With short branches) China, has slender, almost semi-pendent branches which become ornamented from end to end with sweetly-scented, single white flowers about the size of a halfpenny. 8-*ft.*, *June*. *D*. 8-*ft. Sq*. *Cg*7. *ANC*.

P. COULTERI (Comm.) N. Mexico, has cup-shaped flowers of approximately the same size, tinged at the base with purple, and is best suited to a south wall in any but the most clement districts. In open sites it rarely exceeds six feet in height.

6-*ft.*–12-*ft.*, *July*. *D*. 6-*ft.*–12-*ft. Sq*. *Cg*7. *ANC*.

Rhododendron obtusum
macrostemon BCEFGJKLMNOPQ

Rhododendron obtusum
Hatsu-Giri DHST

Rhododendron indicum hybridum

P. Delavayi (Comm.) China, closely resembles P. tomentosus, with large, green, rounded leaves, grey upon the underside, decorated with six-inch sprays of five to thirteen sweetly-scented flowers of a similar size. It is one of the prettiest of the species.

6-ft.–12-ft., May-June. D. 6-ft.–12-ft. Sq. Cg7. ANC.

P. hybridus (Hybrid) Garden origin, consists of a group of hybrids, all of considerable grace, with single or double flowers to taste.

P. hybridus var. Albâtre—has very large sprays of sweetly-scented, double white flowers.

P. ,, Argentine—has dense sprays of single, pure white flowers quite two inches in diameter.

P. ,, Avalanche—has semi-pendent branches weighed down with dense sprays of single, white, sweetly-scented flowers.

P. ,, Belle Etoile—has very large, single, white flowers each with a central purple zone.

P. ,, Boule d'Argent—has sprays of excellent double white flowers.

P. ,, Bouquet Blanche—has up to ten double white flowers in each spray.

P. ,, Dame Blanche—has very sweetly-scented, semi-double, frilled-edged flowers.

P. ,, Fantasie—has small, white, single flowers with fimbriated petals dyed at the centre with rose-purple.

P. ,, Favourite—is similar, with clear white, cupped flowers.

P. ,, Girandole—has double, creamy-white fimbriated flowers.

P. ,, Glacier—is of medium height with milky-white, frilled, double flowers.

P. ,, Lemoinei erectus—has small white flowers, but redeems them by its freedom.

P. ,, Manteau d'Hermione—is one of the neatest, rarely more than three feet in height, and in the flowering season ablaze with double, creamy-white flowers.

P. ,, Mont Blanc—is very upright, and has single flowers produced in impressive wreaths.

P. ,, Norma—has large, single, white flowers.

P. ,, purpureo - maculatus — has small, single, white flowers touched at the centre with purple.

P. ,, Pyramidal—is tall - growing, with extra large, double, white flowers.

P. ,, Rosace—has large, semi-double, white flowers.

P. ,, Virginale—is the outstanding double - flowered variety.

P. ,, Voie Lactée—has large, flat flowers of clearest white, and earns the praise of the best single-flowered variety.

3-ft.–8-ft., May-June. D. 3-ft.–8-ft. Sq. Cg7. ANC.

P. INCANUS (Hoary) China, has leaves very grey and hoary upon the underside, and short sprays consisting in the main of seven small, single, white flowers.

6-ft., May-June. D. 4-ft.–5-ft. Sq. Cg7. ANC.

P. INSIGNIS (Remarkable) Garden origin, is a hybrid of P. pubescens and P. californicus, and is outstanding in the beauty of its overlapping petals and large sprays of beautiful, cupped, single, white flowers. *6-ft., July. D. 5-ft.–6-ft. Sq. Cg7. ANC.*

P. MEXICANUS (Mexican) Mexico, is a tender species, fitted only for seaboard districts in the south and south-west, and is taller than most of the species, with large, single, white, sweetly-scented flowers.

10-ft., June-July. D. 8-ft. Sq. Cg7. ANC.

P. MICROPHYLLUS (With small leaves) Colorado, is a neat-growing species with very small, green leaves and innumerable sprays of small, white flowers, centrally stained with purple, which emit the odour of pineapples.

5-ft., May-June. D. 5-ft. Sq. Cg7. ANC.

P. SATSUMANUS (From Satsuma) Japan, is a strong-growing shrub with sprays of five to eleven large, single, white flowers.

8-ft., July. D. 6-ft.–7-ft. Sq. Cg7. ANC.

P. WILSONII (Comm.) China, is thin and slender in its growth, and bears sprays of white, bell-shaped flowers on slender stems.

4-ft.–6-ft., June. D. Cg7. ANC.

PHILESIA (LILIACEAE) (FROM THE GR. PHILESIS—LOVE OR LOVELINESS).

One species from Chile, P. buxifolia, is extremely hardy but is only at home in a peaty or sandy peaty soil. It can be propagated from cuttings of the stem, placed in sandy peaty soil in July and given gentle bottom heat, or from the suckers which it freely produces.

P. BUXIFOLIA (With leaves resembling Box) is most at home in a sheltered, shady spot in lime-free soil, when its virile, narrow, polished leaves are ornamented with long, tubular, rose-red flowers. Once made fully at home, this is one of the most remarkable of plants, which will devour space with an appetite never excelled, and is so beautiful that it will be the " cynosure of neighbouring eyes."

1-ft., June-October. E. Indefinite. Cg7. Suckers. 7. AN.

PHILLYREA (OLEACEAE) (IS MOST PROBABLY DERIVED FROM THE GR. PHILYRA—A LIME TREE ; AND SHOULD BE SO SPELT).

The outstanding feature of the genus is the axillary clusters of sweetly-scented flowers, produced in April. The flowers cannot be regarded as showy. The method of propagation is by cuttings of the stem, approximately four inches in length, made of the side shoots in July or August and placed in a sand frame with gentle bottom heat. When rooted the cuttings should be carefully potted on.

P. ANGUSTIFOLIA (With narrow leaves) Mediterranean region, is a neat shrub with many branches, and narrow leaves of dark-green, bearing in the leaf axils small, cream-coloured flowers of a fragrance seldom equalled and never excelled.

5-*ft.*–10-*ft.*, *May*. *E*. 5-*ft.*–10-*ft. Sq*. *Cg*7–8. *Suckers*. *AN*.

P. DECORA (Decorated) Black Sea region, is also P. Vilmoriniana, and an excellent shrub for a partially shaded site, with shining, dark-green leaves and very sweetly scented, small, white flowers freely produced from the leaf axils in April, followed by oval, purple fruits in autumn. 6-*ft.*, *April*. *E*. 6-*ft. Sq*. *Cg*7–8. *Suckers*. *AN*.

PHORMIUM (LILIACEAE) (DERIVED FROM THE GR. PHORMOS—A BASKET ; FOR WHICH THE FIBRE THE PLANT PRODUCES IS USED).

This is a plant which, though tender, does best near water or in swampy places.

P. COLENSOI (Comm.) New Zealand, is also P. Cookianum, and a dwarf, pretty plant with long spikes of bright yellow flowers.

3-*ft.*, *July*. *E*. 3-*ft. Sq*. *Sd*2. *ANC*.

P. TENAX (Tough) New Zealand, is the New Zealand Flax, with sword-like leaves of bright grey-green, and four- to five-foot spires of orange-red flowers. 5-*ft.*–6-*ft.*, *July*. *E*. 5-*ft. Sq*. *Sd*2. *ANC*.

PHOTINIA (ROSACEAE) (FROM THE GR. PHOTEINOS—SHINING ; A REFERENCE TO THE APPEARANCE OF THE LEAVES).

Photinias are easily adapted to any soil in a sunny position but transplant badly. Young plants should therefore be grown on in pots prior to being planted out. Propagation is from seeds, the seeds being sown in pots or pans and plunged in the open during the winter, then brought into a cool house in the spring. Cuttings may also be made of the half-ripened wood of the short side shoots, preferably with a heel, and these should be placed in a cold frame in sandy soil in July or August. When rooted they should be potted on before being planted out.

P. BEAUVERDIANA (Comm.) China, has oblong, pointed, shiny, green leaves which assume very beautiful shades of crimson and scarlet in the autumn, clustered, small white flowers produced at the tips of the shoots, followed by clusters of bright red, round fruits.

12-*ft.*–20-*ft.*, *May*. *D*. 12-*ft.*–20-*ft. Sq*. *Sd*10. *Ch*7–8. *ANC*.

P. DAVIDSONIAE (Comm.) China, is an evergreen species with oblong, neatly serrated leaves, shining, deep green above and pale green beneath, which bears large clusters of small white flowers, followed by the typical red berries.

20-*ft.*–25-*ft.*, *May*. *E*. 18-*ft.*–24-*ft. Sq*. *Sd*10. *Ch*7–8. *ANC*.

P. GLABRA (Smooth) China, is a smaller-growing species with smooth, obovate, evergreen leaves, which are attractively coloured in the spring, and wide clusters of sweetly-scented, white, " May " flowers, sometimes tinged with pink.

6-*ft.*, *May*. *E*. 6-*ft.*–8-*ft. Sq*. *Sd*10. *Ch*7–8. *ANC*. *Shelter*.

P. SERRULATA (Edged with small teeth) China, is another large shrub with long, dark-green, oblong leaves, yellowish-green upon the underside, which generally assume a bright red colour in the spring, when the large clusters of many small, white hawthorn-like flowers are borne.

15-*ft.*–30-*ft.*, *April.* *E.* 12-*ft.*–35-*ft.* *Sq.* *Sd*10. *Ch*7–8. *ANC.*

P. VILLOSA (Hairy) China, is a very hardy, small tree or shrub with obovate, green leaves, hairy upon the lower surfaces, and becoming tinted with every sunset shade in autumn, when it also carries the considerable clusters of bright red fruits which follow the hawthorn-like flowers.

6-*ft.*–15-*ft.*, *May.* *D.* 6-*ft.*–15-*ft.* *Sq.* *Sd*10. *Ch*7–8. *ANC.*

PHYGELIUS (SCROPHULARIACEAE) (FROM THE GR. PHUGE—FLIGHT ; AND HELIOS—THE SUN ; A REFERENCE TO THE FACT THAT IN ITS NATIVE HOME IT SEEMS TO PREFER SHADED SITES).

In cultivation the one species, P. capensis, the Cape Figwort, delights in a sunny site in a light, well-drained soil, and may be freely propagated from cuttings of the half-ripened wood, or from the seeds which it will produce readily in most seasons. Cut to the ground in the worst winters it takes refuge in running underground, but is rarely killed outright.

P. CAPENSIS (Of the Cape) S. Africa, has bright-green, wide, wedge-shaped leaves, and bears open, terminal clusters of fig-shaped buds of bright scarlet which open to display a yellow mouth. Grown against a south or west wall it will reach prodigious heights, but treated as a shrub in the open border rarely exceeds three feet in height.

3-*ft.*, *June-October.* *E.* 5-*ft.* *Sq.* *Sd*2. *Cg*7–8. *ANC.* *Pl.*74.

PHYLLODOCE (ERICACEAE) (THE NAME IS THAT OF A NYMPH ATTENDING CYRENE).

The genus comprises a group of dwarf, evergreen shrubs of very wide distribution throughout the northern hemisphere, which are most at home in moist, lime-free soils. Some of the species are known also under the names of BRYANTHUS and MENZIESIA. Propagation of the true species is best from seeds sown in sandy, peaty soil and plunged in the open in a north aspect. Cuttings may also be prepared similarly to those of Erica. The characteristics of the genus are the crowded, evergreen, narrow leaves and the small clusters of bell-shaped flowers on long stalks, which are bent forward.

P. ALEUTICA (From the Aleutian Islands) Alaska, is a very dwarf, spreading shrub with small, dark-green, serrated, linear leaves crowded round the twiggy stems, which become decorated in the uppermost leaf axils and the tips of the shoots with small bell-flowers of pale yellow.

¾-*ft.*, *May.* *E.* ¾-*ft.*–2-*ft.* *Sq.* *Ch*6. *AN.*

P. Breweri (Comm.) California, is also Bryanthus Breweri, and a neat, spreading shrub with salver-shaped flowers of rose-purple.

½-ft.–1-ft., May-June. E. 1-ft. Sq. Ch6. AN.

P. caerulea (Bluish) N. Europe, is a low-growing shrub composed of many tiny, branched stems clothed with short, dark-green, narrow leaves borne very close together, which bears hanging bell-flowers of pale violet in clusters of from three to six.

½-ft., March-April. E. 1-ft. Sq. Ch6. A.

P. empetriformis (Like the Crowberry) Western U.S.A., is another evergreen plant with low-growing habit, and linear leaves with blunt points of deep, glossy green, borne very closely together, which bears its small clusters of bell-shaped, bright-rose flowers in the leaf axils at the tips of the shoots.

½-ft., April. E. 1-ft. Sq. Ch6. A.

P. nipponica (From Nippon) Japan, is an upright-growing plant with glossy, green, narrow, oval leaves, very grey on the underside, and terminal clusters of snowy-white bell-flowers.

⅓-ft., April. E. ⅔-ft. Sq. Ch6. A.

PHYLLOTHAMNUS (Ericaceae) (the name is derived from phyllodoce and rhodothamnus).

The one representative of the genus, P. erectus, is a bigeneric cross between Phyllodoce empetriformis and Rhodothamnus Chamaecistus, and from the point of view of propagation should be treated as Erica.

P. erectus (Upright) Garden origin, is a very dwarf evergreen shrub of upright growth with bright-green, linear, alternate leaves, producing at the tips of the branches clusters of rose flowers of open bell shape, each borne upon a slender stalk. P. erectus needs a shaded site in a soil free of lime, and under such circumstances is very hardy.

8-ins.–18-ins., April-May. E. 2-ft. Sq. Cg7. AN.

PIERIS (Ericaceae) (derived from pieria, the birthplace of the muses).

The bulk of the species are evergreen and are best suited by shaded sites, and moist, lime-free soils, and may be propagated from cuttings of the side shoots, detached with a slight heel and placed in sand in a cold frame in August.

P. floribunda (Free-flowering) S.E. United States, is also known as Andromeda floribunda, and is an exceptionally attractive shrub with dark-green, oval, pointed leaves, and sprays of small, white, bell-shaped flowers, puckered in at the mouth, as if such sweetness has indeed found a sour world.

5-ft., March-April. E. 5-ft.–6-ft. Sq. Ch8. AN.

P. formosa (Beautiful) China, is a larger shrub in those parts where it remains uncut from winter's cold blasts, when its early growth is pink and crimson, and is followed by large sprays of white flowers similar to those of P. floribunda.

5-*ft.*-9-*ft.*, *May.* *E.* 5-*ft.*-9-*ft.* *Sq.* *Ch*8. *AN.* *Shelter.*

P. FORRESTII (Comm.) China, is a close relative of P. formosa, very like it, but even more brilliant in its early spring colour, the new leaves at a distance conveying the impression of large, exotic, crimson flowers, but alas, it also needs a sheltered spot where chill winds cannot sear it.

5-*ft.*-8-*ft.*, *April-May.* *E.* 5-*ft.*-9-*ft.* *Sq.* *Ch*8. *AN.* *Shelter.* *Pl.*56.

P. JAPONICA (Japanese) Japan, is an exceptionally beautiful, dwarf, evergreen shrub with pointed, elliptical, serrated, deep-green leaves, well branched close to the ground, and with its young growth brilliantly tinted with fascinating colours in spring, and gracefully decorated with clusters or sprays, built up into fan-shaped panicles, of small, inverted, pitcher-shaped, clear white flowers. P. japonica var. variegata differs not at all in habit but has its leaves composed of pale green, cream and pink in an artistic blend which just fails to be merely pretty.

5-*ft.*, *March-April.* *E.* 5-*ft.*-7-*ft.* *Sq.* *Ch*8. *AN.* *Pl.*24.

P. LUCIDA (Shining) S.E. United States, is a glittering star in a galaxy of beauty, with a veritable constellation of names, of which the Fetter Bush is probably the best known. P. lucida is also Andromeda coriacea, Pieris nitida, Xolisma lucida, Neopieris lucida, Desmothamnus lucidus and Lyonia lucida, and is just as tender a plant by whatever name it is known, suited only to the milder south and west, with slender, upright growth, deep-green, glossy, oval leaves, and terminal, axillary sprays of white flowers, heavily flushed with pink. 3-*ft.*-5-*ft.*, *June-July.* *E.* 3-*ft.*-5-*ft.* *Sq.* *Ch*8. *AN.* *Shelter.*

P. MARIANA (Named after the Virgin Mary) Eastern U.S.A., has almost as many names, differs from the other species in being deciduous, has an added hardiness, and appreciates a sunnier site than most of the species. Its beautiful sprays of larger white flowers are prettied with red tinges at the mouths, and the whole shrub subsides with Turneresque beauty into winter somnolence.

3-*ft.*-4-*ft.*, *June.* *D.* 3-*ft.*-4-*ft.* *Sq.* *Ch*8. *AN.*

P. TAIWANENSIS (From Taiwan) Formosa, is another very beautiful shrub with brilliantly coloured new leaves in spring, ageing to deep, shining green, and erect sprays of clear white flowers resembling more slender Lilies-of-the-valley, profusely produced in April.

3-*ft.*-8-*ft.*, *April-May.* *E.* 3-*ft.*-8-*ft.* *Sq.* *Ch*8. *AN.*

PILEOSTEGIA (SAXIFRAGACEAE) (FROM THE GR. PILOS—A CAP ; AND STEGE—A COVERING ; A REFERENCE TO THE CONSTRUCTION OF THE SEED CAPSULE).

P. VIBURNOIDES (Resembling Viburnum) Japan, is the so-called Climbing Hydrangea, also known as SCHIZOPHRAGMA, an attractive shrub with handsome, shiny, dark-green, oval leaves, which climbs by means of aerial roots and will cling to walls, with creamy-white inflorescences like those of a Hydrangea.

3-ft.–12-ft., August-September. E. Indefinite. Cg7. ANC.

PIPTANTHUS (LEGUMINOSAE) (DERIVED FROM THE GR. PIPTO—FALL ; AND ANTHOS—A FLOWER ; SO NAMED BECAUSE THE FLOWERS FALL QUICKLY).

A group of shrubs which may be deciduous or evergreen according to the severity of the winter, and which are generally best suited in more inclement districts by the shelter of a backing wall.

P. NEPALENSIS (From Nepal) Himalayas, is the so-called Evergreen Laburnum, with soft-green, three-parted leaves and clusters of bright-yellow pea flowers. Very vigorous in appearance, P. nepalensis is completely hardy in the south-west, where it readily reaches ten feet in height, but elsewhere it should receive the sheltered position it deserves.

10-ft., May-June. ED. 8-ft. Sq. Sd2. ANC. Pl.75.

PITTOSPORUM (PITTOSPORACEAE) (FROM THE GR. PITTA—PITCH ; AND SPOROS—A SEED ; A REFERENCE TO THE STICKY JUICE WHICH COVERS THE SEEDS).

They may be freely propagated from cuttings of the half-ripened wood, taken during August and placed in a cold frame, or from seeds when these are produced. The species are distinguished more by their fragrance than their beauty.

P. BICOLOR (Two-coloured) Tasmania, New South Wales, is a magnificent small tree or large shrub for providing shelter, growing quickly and being well clothed with narrowly oval leaves, greyish-green, rather like those of Laurel, felted beneath, with small, five-petalled flowers of purplish-brown and yellow.

10-ft.–15-ft., May. E. 8-ft.–12-ft. Sq. Sd2. Cg8. ANC.

P. BUCHANANII (Comm.) New Zealand, is upright in growth and has pale-green, alternate, oblong leaves up to five inches in length, with solitary, five-petalled flowers of purplish tone.

10-ft.–15-ft., May. E. 8-ft.–12-ft. Sq. Sd2. Cg8. ANC.

P. COLENSOI (Comm.) New Zealand, is another small tree or large shrub with somewhat smaller, acutely pointed leaves and deep purple flowers, usually borne singly.

10-ft.–15-ft., May. E. 8-ft.–12-ft. Sq. Sd2. Cg8. ANC. Shelter.

P. CORNIFOLIUM (With leaves like Dogwood) New Zealand, has brownish-green, oval, whorled leaves, and dull, reddish-purple flowers with a musk-like scent.

5-ft.–9-ft., March. E. 5-ft.–7-ft. Sq. Sd2. Cg8. ANC.

P. CRASSIFOLIUM (With thick leaves) New Zealand, is a large bush with shining, green leaves, felted upon the underside, and reddish-purple flowers borne in small terminal clusters, which generally fails to flower but makes up for this fact, when it can be prevailed upon to do so, by its ineffably sweet scent.

8-ft.–15-ft., May. E. 6-ft.–12-ft. Sq. Sd2. Cg8. ANC.

P. DALLII (Comm.) New Zealand, has pale-grey bark, dull-green, elliptical leaves, paler upon the under surface, and has larger white flowers than most of the species, with a very sweet scent.

10-ft.–15-ft., June. E. 8-ft.–12-ft. Sq. Sd2. Cg8. ANC.

P. DAPHNIPHYLLOIDES (With leaves like Daphne) W. China, has still larger, milky-white flowers, but is unfortunately one of the most tender of the species, which merits the most extreme care and forms eventually a small tree.

10-ft.–15-ft., April-June. E. 8-ft.–12-ft. Sq. Sd2. Cg8. ANC. Shelter.

P. HETEROPHYLLUM (With variable leaves) China, has open growth, leaves which are variable in shape, and bears small, pale-yellow, sweetly-scented flowers.

6-ft.–9-ft., June. E. 5-ft.–8-ft. Sq. Sd2. Cg8. ANC.

P. RALPHII (Comm.) New Zealand, differs but little from P. crassifolium except in the fact that its leaves are not turned back at the edges, but has a reputation for being hardier and just as shy to flower. *8-ft.–15-ft., May. E. 6-ft.–12-ft. Sq. Sd2. Cg8. ANC.*

P. TENUIFOLIUM (With fine leaves) New Zealand, is also P. Mayi and P. nigricans, and has black stems and smaller, green, oblong leaves, wavy at the edges, and sweetly-scented, dark-purple flowers produced, sometimes singly and elsewhere in small groups, in the leaf axils. *8-ft.–10-ft., May. E. 6-ft.–8-ft. Sq. Sd2. Cg8. ANC.*

P. TOBIRA (A Japanese name) Japan, is the best known of the species, and is most generally met as a shrub of some six feet or so in height, though in favoured districts it will reach up to twenty feet in height, and, with its dark-green, laurel-like leaves and very fragrant, creamy- or greeny-white flowers, makes a splendid hedge in seaside districts, but it is better for its safer custody to confine it to sheltered spots elsewhere.

6-ft.–20-ft., April-July. E. 6-ft.–12-ft. Sq. Sd2. ANC.

PLAGIANTHUS (MALVACEAE) (FROM THE GR. PLAGIOS—OBLIQUE; AND ANTHOS—A FLOWER; A REFERENCE TO THE SHAPE OF THE PETALS WHICH FORM THE FLOWERS).

P. DIVARICATUS (Spreading widely apart) New Zealand, is a pleasant, much-branched shrub with birch-like branches, with very small elliptical leaves and quite inconspicuous but scented yellow flowers.

4-ft.–6-ft., June. D. 4-ft.–6-ft. Sq. Sd2. Cg8. ANC.

P. LYALLII (*see* HOHERIA Lyallii).

POLYGALA (POLYGALACEAE) (FROM GR. POLUS—MUCH; AND GALA—MILK; ITS PRESENCE IN PASTURAGE BEING CREDITED WITH A FAVOURABLE EFFECT UPON THE MILK YIELD OF CATTLE).

The Polygalas are best suited in loam well laced with leafmould or peatmould in a not too sunny situation.

Rhododendron hybrids
Rhododendron (A) japonicum × sinense **GLM**
Rhododendron (A) japonicum × rusticum fl. pl. **ABCDEFGHJKPQRSTU**

Rhododendron japonicum
coccinea speciosa
ABEFJKN

Rhododendron japonicum
Emil Liebig GHLM

Rhododendron japonicum
Anthony Koster NOPRST

P. CHAMAEBUXUS (Dwarf Box) Europe, is a neat, dwarf, evergreen shrub with rounded, shining, green leaves, which creeps readily underground, and bears in the leaf axils pea-shaped flowers with cream wings and an elongated yellow central process which turns bronze as it ages. *½-ft., May. E. 1-ft. Sq. Cg6. C.* 64/3.

P. CHAMAEBUXUS VAR. GRANDIFLORA (Large-flowered) Europe, is also P. Chamaebuxus var. purpurea, and similar in all its characteristics except in the colour of its wings, which are of bright purple.
½-ft., May. E. 1-ft. Sq. Cg6. C. 035/1. 4/2.

P. VAYREDAE (Comm.) Spain, has more slender, pointed leaves than P. Chamaebuxus grandiflora, and slimmer flowers of yellow with more widely flung wings of crimson-magenta. P. Vayredae is more at home in a soil which is free of lime.
⅓-ft., May. E. 1-ft. Sq. Cg6. D3. A.

POLYGONUM (POLYGONACEAE) (FROM THE GR. POLUS—MANY; AND GONU—A JOINT; A REFERENCE TO THE MANY JOINTS IN THE STEMS OF THE SPECIES).

P. BALDSCHUANICUM (From Baljuan) Bokhara, is an extremely rampant climber with green, heart-shaped leaves, and very large, drooping sprays of creamy-white flowers produced with great freedom, and is probably the ideal climber for covering old tree stumps.
20-ft.–40-ft., August-October. D. Indefinite. Ch2 or 7. ANC.

POTENTILLA (ROSACEAE) (FROM THE LATIN POTENS—POWERFUL; FROM THE SUPPOSED MEDICINAL QUALITY OF SOME OF THE SPECIES).

All the Potentillas are of easy growth in any good garden soil, and are very hardy, thriving without let or hindrance in a sunny place. Seeds germinate readily if sown in February, but give rise to many quite attractive hybrids, though, where uniformity is desired, cuttings of the half-ripened wood three to four inches in length will root well if placed in sand in a cold frame in August.

P. DAHURICA (From Dauria) Siberia, is a dwarf shrub, oft-times known as P. davurica or P. glabra, with erect stems and drooping branches, and small, smooth, green, five-parted leaves and a steady flow of white strawberry flowers a little smaller than a halfpenny.
1-ft.–1½-ft., May-September. D. 2-ft.–3-ft. Sq. Cg8. ANC.

P. FRIEDRICHSENII (Comm.) Garden origin, is a hybrid of P. dahurica and P. fruticosa, with neat, bright-green, small, five-parted leaves, and a long succession of small, lemon-yellow flowers. The height is subject to considerable variation.
1-ft.–4-ft., May-September. D. 1-ft.–3-ft. Sq. Cg8. ANC.

P. FRUTICOSA (Shrubby) Great Britain, often reaches four feet in height, and is an upright shrub with three- to seven-parted leaves, often densely covered with short hair, and bears bright-yellow flowers, produced in many small sprays, for a long period.
*2-ft.–4-ft., May-September. D. 2-ft.–4-ft. Sq. Cg8. ANC. Pl.*75.

P. FRUTICOSA numbers among its varieties the following, all of which are beautiful, and provide some of the most generous of all flowering shrubs :—

P. FRUTICOSA VAR. ARBUSCULA—is dwarf, nearly prostrate in habit, is heavily felted with bronze hairs, and has many striking, golden-yellow flowers.

P. „ „ BEESII—is a hybrid of garden origin and dwarf habit, with large, deep-yellow flowers.

P. „ „ FARRERI—is notable for its dwarf and compact habit, very small, almost insignificant leaves, and flattish, butter-yellow flowers.

P. „ „ MANDSCHURICA—is exceptionally dwarf, has silvery-grey leaves which are densely felted, and spangles itself with round, white flowers throughout the summer months.

P. „ „ OCHROLEUCA—has the habit of growth of the species, and pale-yellow flowers.

P. „ „ PURDOMII—is of the best, with very slender growth and many golden-yellow flowers.

P. „ „ PYRENAICA—is a very flat-growing variety, with strands of buttercup-like flowers looping in all directions.

P. „ „ VEITCHII—is a very fascinating dwarf with flat, white flowers, which adequately fit the attractive grey-green foliage. *Pl.*75.

P. „ „ VILMORINIANA—is similar to the type, with silvery-grey leaves and creamy-white and pale-yellow flowers at the same time.

PRUNUS (ROSACEAE) (IS DERIVED FROM THE LATIN PRUNUS—A PLUM TREE).

The genus comprises the ALMONDS, known more often as AMYGDALUS, CHERRIES, sometimes known as CERASUS, the APRICOTS (ARMENIACA), the CHERRY LAURELS (LAUROCERASUS), the BIRD CHERRIES (PADUS), and the PEACHES (PERSICA). The so-called Japanese Flowering Cherries will be found under P. Lannesiana and P. serrulata. Cultivation of most of the species cannot be regarded as difficult as they appear to grow well upon almost any type of reasonably good garden soil, and to be quite indifferent to lime. Propagation of the species is best from seeds, but the process is a slow one. Cuttings of the firm wood, taken with a heel and given gentle bottom heat, will root with reasonable frequency, and, though the growing-on process cannot be said to be fast in most cases, the results are very satisfying. It is thought that, to retain alphabetical accuracy, it is better to indicate the section into which each variety falls individually. The flowering Almonds and Peaches are generally worked upon stocks of P. cerasifera (the Cherry Plum), and the Cherries upon P. Avium (the Gean). Nearly all the varieties are grown both as bushes and as standard trees. The heights given apply only to the bush varieties, but where standards are grown allowance should be made for the height of the stock, and the actual spread slightly discounted.

P. ACIDA (Sharp) Europe, is the Amarelle Cherry, and a bush of neatly spherical habit with upright stems, rather large, white flowers in tight, rounded clusters followed by dark-red, sour fruits.
8-ft., April-May. D. 8-ft. Sq. Sd2. Cg7. ANC.

P. AVIUM (Bird Cherry) Europe, is the Gean, a tree generally best suited to woodland planting, and available in many forms of different habits, with both double and larger flowers, but mentioned only as a species here since it provides the stocks upon which other varieties are grafted; is very beautiful both in spring and autumn.
20-ft.–60-ft., April-May. D. ——— Sd2. ANC.

P. BESSEYI (Comm.) Western N. America, is the Sand Cherry, a very hardy, diffuse or semi-prostrate bush with slender branches, green, elliptical, finely-toothed leaves, small white flowers very freely produced, and black, edible fruits so seldom produced as to prove the reverse of that.
2-ft.–4-ft., April-May. D. 3-ft.–5-ft. Sq. Sd2. ANC.

P. × BLIREIANA (Comm.) is a shrub of from six to ten feet in height with purple leaves and very attractive double flowers of bright rose-pink, and where it grows well is probably the best of the cerasifera hybrids.
6-ft.–10-ft., February-March. D. 6-ft.–10-ft. Sq. Cg7. ANC.

P. CANESCENS (Hoary) China, is a small Cherry of a little greater height than P. Besseyi, with small rosy-white flowers like those of P. subhirtella, but which are evanescent and liable to be carried away by the slightest puff of wind, and are followed by red, edible fruits. *4-ft.–5-ft., April. D. 4-ft.–5-ft. Sq. Sd2. ANC.*

P. CERASIFERA (Cherry-bearing) Caucasus, is the Cherry Plum or Myrobalan, varying in height up to thirty feet, and an extremely hardy and very beautiful tree, which varies its flowering period considerably in mild winters, often forming a cloud of snow-white flowers as early as January—and at other seasons in one of the following two months. The flowers are followed by cherry-shaped fruits which are both edible and suitable for jam-making, though in some seasons they fail to appear.
10-ft.–30-ft., January-March. D. 10-ft.–30-ft. Sq. Sd2. Cg7. ANC.

P. CERASIFERA VAR. PISSARDII (Comm.) is also P. cerasifera var. atropurpurea and follows the type, but has purple leaves of glowing splendour, and deep pink buds which open to display clouds of white flowers. P. Pissardii var. nigra has leaves of even deeper colour. *10-ft.–30-ft., March. D. 10-ft.–30-ft. Sq. Cg7. ANC.*

P. CERASUS (The Wild Cherry) S.E. Europe, is also known as the Dwarf or Morello Cherry, and is very similar in appearance to P. acida but appears to be more dwarf, and freely to produce suckers from the root.
10-ft.–20-ft., May. D. 10-ft.–15-ft. Sq. Cg7. Suckers. 2. ANC.

P. CERASUS VAR. RHEXII (Comm.) is a delightful variety with fully double flowers of longer duration.

10-ft.–15-ft., May-June. D. 10-ft.–12-ft. Sq. Cg7. ANC.

P. COMMUNIS (Common) is the Almond, known also as Amygdalus communis and Prunus Amygdalus, or more simply the Almond, one of the most popular of all small flowering trees, well known for the abundance of wreathed, single, pink flowers produced before the leaves.

12-ft.–25-ft., March. D. 8-ft.–18-ft. Sq. Sd10. Cg6. ANC.

P. COMMUNIS VAR. MACROCARPA (Bearing large fruits) is similar, with large flowers of paler pink which are followed by still larger fruits.

12-ft.–25-ft., April. D. 8-ft.–18-ft. Sq. Cg7. ANC.

P. COMMUNIS VAR. POLLARDII (Comm.) has large, deep-pink flowers, and is considered to be one of the most attractive of all the varieties, as its hybrid origin (P. communis × P. persica) would lead one to suppose.

12-ft.–20-ft., February-April. D. 8-ft.–18-ft. Sq. Cg7. ANC.

P. COMMUNIS VAR. ROSEA PLENA (Double rose) is a slower-growing and possibly more sedate variety, well suited to smaller spaces, and bears double, deep-pink flowers with the same freedom as the other varieties.

8-ft.–12-ft., March-April. D. 6-ft.–10-ft. Sq. Cg7. ANC.

P. CONCINNA (Elegant) China, is one of the most attractive of the Cherries, bearing its almost stalkless flowers in groups of three or four in a cluster, and of white—more or less flushed with pink at the centre—before the narrow, finely toothed leaves are produced, at which time it is amazingly beautiful.

6-ft.–10-ft., March-April. D. 5-ft.–8-ft. Sq. Sd10. Cg7. ANC.

P. CONRADINAE (Comm.) China, is another Cherry which can be an extremely attractive shrub or small tree in the way of P. concinna, and which produces its larger, almost stemless, white or pale-pink flowers in groups of approximately four before the leaves appear, at any time from the beginning of February until the middle of April, and thereafter continues to be ornamental with its peculiarly metallic green leaves. P. Conradinae fl. pl. is less strong in its growth, deeper in colour, and has extra petals.

8-ft.–20-ft., February-April. D. 6-ft.–16-ft. Sq. Sd2. ANC.

P. (PERSICA) DAVIDIANA (Comm.) China, is a Peach which makes a small tree, and bears its inch-wide pink-and-white flowers upon bare stems as early in the year as January, and is thus frequently damaged by frosts. It seems better when grown in the colder districts, where it consequently flowers later. P. Davidiana var. alba is similar with white flowers, and P. Davidiana var. rubra has rose-red flowers.

12-ft.–20-ft., February-March. D. 8-ft.–16-ft. Sq. Budding. ANC.

P. (Amygdalus) dehiscens (Opening freely when ripe) China, is a somewhat slow-growing, very densely branched Almond of medium height, with its small, narrow, finely crenated leaves, rosetted at the spurs and nodes, which bears single, wide-petalled flowers of peach-pink, and seems extremely hardy.

12-*ft.*, *April*. *D.* 15-*ft. Sq. Sd2. ANC.*

P. (Cerasus) demissa (Hanging down) Western U.S.A., is a Cherry sometimes known as P. virginiana var. demissa, and is generally a tall shrub, and more seldom a small tree, with small, white, slightly scented flowers borne in long clusters with the leaves, followed by small, red or yellow fruits.

12-*ft.*–20-*ft.*, *May*. *D.* 10-*ft.*–25-*ft. Sq. Sd2. ANC.*

P. (Amygdalus) glandulosa (Glandular) China, Japan, is also P. japonica and the so-called Flowering Almond of Japan, considered by some authorities to be more properly a cherry, and a dwarf, well-rounded bush, with roundly lance-shaped leaves, finely toothed at the edges, and small white or flushed flowers followed by tiny red fruits. While the species is very beautiful it is completely outshone by the double-flowered varieties, P. glandulosa var. albo-plena, with arched sprays of tiny, double, white flowers, and P. glandulosa var. sinensis, with a similar distribution of double flowers of bright pink. 4-*ft.*, *May*. *D.* 5-*ft. Sq. Ch7. L7. ANC.*

P. (Cerasus) incana (Hoary) Asia Minor, is the Willow Cherry, a dwarf bush with small, narrowly oval leaves, closely resembling P. nana in habit and in flower, the flowers of rosy-red appearing with the leaves. P. incana differs from P. nana in its fruits which are in fact cherries.

3-*ft.*–6-*ft.*, *April*. *D.* 3-*ft.*–6-*ft. Sq. Ch7. L7. ANC.*

P. (Cerasus) incisa (Deeply cut) Japan, is an extremely beautiful Cherry, which can be either a small tree or bush with ovate, double-serrated leaves, with the young leaves red, and nodding, flesh-pink, bell-shaped flowers produced with great freedom in March or April, followed by small, purplish-black fruits.

8-*ft.*–10-*ft.*, *March-April*. *D.* 8-*ft.*–10-*ft. Sq. Ch7. L7. Sd2. ANC.*

P. incisa serrata (Serrated) Japan, is another form said to be more dwarf, but in cultivation differing only in the serrations of the leaves. 8-*ft.*–10-*ft.*, *March-April*. *D.* 8-*ft.*–10-*ft. Sq. Ch7. L7. Sd2. ANC.*

P. (Cerasus) Jacquemontii (Comm.) Afghanistan, is an exceptionally handsome, shrubby Cherry with elliptical, acutely pointed leaves, serrated at the edges, producing its attractive, small, funnel-shaped, rose-pink flowers before the leaves, and adding much to its brightness with its small, red, round fruits in July.

6-*ft.*–10-*ft.*, *April-May*. *D.* 6-*ft.*–10-*ft. Sq. Ch7. L7. Sd2. ANC.*

P. (Cerasus) Lannesiana (Comm.) Japan, is the progenitor of many of the large-flowered Japanese Cherries, differing botanically from P. serrulata in its green rather than bronze spring leaves, and in the nature of its serrations and its scented flowers. It is impossible to be perfectly certain into which section the hybrids of garden origin fall, but the following distributions are probably of reasonable accuracy, and cross-references are given where any doubt exists. The type, which was definitely of garden origin, is a tree not unlike P. Avium in its habit, but with large, single, pink flowers bearing a slight sweet scent and fading to white with age. *Plate* 76. P. Lannesiana var. albida is more probably the true species and differs only in having white flowers. The hybrids, which fall into P. Lannesiana, are the following :—

P. LANNESIANA VAR. AFFINIS (Related to) is also P. serrulata affinis, and P. Jo-nioi (Superlative Fragrance), and bears single white flowers, bell-like in shape, offset by bronzy sepals, and is one of the prettiest of the hybrids.
15-ft., April-May. D. 12-ft. Sq. Cg7. Graftage. ANC.

P. LANNESIANA VAR. ALBIDA (White) is the most fragrant of all the Cherries and a sheer delight when fully adorned by the beauty of its single white flowers.
20-ft., April-May. D. 18-ft. Sq. Cg7. Graftage. ANC.

P. LANNESIANA VAR. AMANOGAWA (Galaxy) or P. Lannesiana var. erecta is a variety with very erect growth, like that of a Lombardy Poplar, which produces either single or semi-double flowers of apple-blossom-pink in very dense clusters. Its curious erect growth makes it an outstanding variety for the small garden.
10-ft.–20-ft., April-May. D. 6-ft.–8-ft. Sq. Cg7. Graftage. ANC.

P. LANNESIANA VAR. GIOKI (is also P. serrulata var. tricolor) is most likely only a variation of grandiflora ; its yellowish-green flowers are striped with green, and occasionally pink, and it is probably one of the most interesting of all the hybrids.
10-ft.–20-ft., April-May. D. 15-ft.–30-ft. Sq. Cg7. Graftage. ANC.

P. LANNESIANA VAR. GRANDIFLORA (Large-flowered) is the Ukon (yellowish), an exceptionally pretty variety with double flowers of greenish primrose-yellow which can be kept small in poor soils, and presents a most charming picture with its bronze-green foliage.
10-ft.–20-ft., April-May. D. 15-ft.–30-ft. Sq. Cg7. Graftage. ANC.

P. LANNESIANA VAR. HATAZAKURA (Tall Cherry) is the Flagstaff Cherry, and one of the most homely varieties with its captivating semi-double, flesh-pink flowers.
10-ft.–20-ft., April-May. D. 15-ft.–30-ft. Sq. Cg7. Graftage. ANC.

P. LANNESIANA VAR. JO-NIOI (*see* P. LANNESIANA VAR. AFFINIS).

P. LANNESIANA VAR. LONGIPES is also P. Lannesiana var. Oku-miyako, and is an outstandingly beautiful variety with large, double, pure white flowers with fimbriated petals, opening from pink buds and hanging upon long stalks.
10-ft.–20-ft., May. 15-ft.–30-ft. Sq. Cg7. Graftage. ANC.

P. Lannesiana var. Mikuruma Gaeshi (The Return of the State Carriage) has extremely large, single pink flowers, each hanging upon a long stem.

12-*ft.*–18-*ft.*, *April-May*. *D.* 10-*ft.*–16-*ft. Sq.* *Cg*7. *Graftage*. *ANC.*

P. Lannesiana var. Ojochin (Large Lantern) is extremely near to P. Ariake, and from pink buds produces single, very pale-pink or white flowers of the most enchanting elegance.

12-*ft.*–25-*ft.*, *April-May*. *D.* 10-*ft.*–35-*ft. Sq.* *Cg*7. *Graftage*. *ANC.*

P. Lannesiana var. Senriko (japonica alba) is a very vigorous variety with extremely large, single, white flowers, ageing to flesh-pink, but alas, it is very shy to flower.

10-*ft.*–20-*ft.*, *April-May*. *D.* 15-*ft.*–30-*ft. Sq.* *Cg*7. *Graftage*. *ANC.*

P. Lannesiana var. Shirotae (White Dress) has a multiplicity of names, among which may be recorded Kojima, Mount Fugi, Sirotae, and Snowflake, and is probably the most representative of the Lannesiana hybrids, and is a fine tree with stiff, flat branches, very vigorous habit, and semi-double, clear white flowers which fade with a suspicion of pink.

10-*ft.*–20-*ft.*, *April-May*. *D.* 12-*ft.*–25-*ft. Sq.* *Cg*7. *Graftage*. *ANC.*

P. Lannesiana var. Taizan-fukum (God of Taizan) is a sweetly genial double-flowered form of P. Lannesiana var. Amanogawa, and is a much more fully clothed variety, probably in the main a much better selection if solidity is required.

10-*ft.*–20-*ft.*, *April-May*. 6-*ft.*–8-*ft. Sq.* *Cg*7. *Graftage*. *ANC.*

P. Lannesiana var. Temari (Comm.) is a very strong grower in the early stages of its development and mixes without fear or favour single and double flowers, quite two inches in diameter, of apple-blossom pink which persist while fading until they fall.

10-*ft.*–20-*ft.*, *April-May*. *D.* 12-*ft.*–25-*ft. Sq.* *Cg*7. *Graftage*. *ANC.*

P. Lannesiana var. Ukon (*see* P. Lannesiana var. grandiflora).

P. Lannesiana var. Washino-o (The Eagle's Tail) is an open-headed tree or shrub with stiff branches, and has white single flowers ageing to pink at the centre, and is one of the strongest growing of all the varieties.

12-*ft.*–20-*ft.*, *April-May*. *D.* 15-*ft.*–30-*ft. Sq.* *Cg*7. *Graftage* *ANC.*

P. Laurocerasus (The Cherry Laurel) S.E. Europe, is the Common Laurel with small, dull-white, very fragrant flowers followed by purple-black fruits, and an extremely graceful evergreen when allowed untrammelled development in woodland surroundings, being completely undamaged by as much as twenty-five degrees of frost. It is available in a vast number of varieties, all of which vary in the size and width of the leaf, and in the main are all adapted for the same purposes.

4-*ft.*–20-*ft.*, *April*. *E.* 8-*ft.*–40-*ft. Sq.* *Cg*7. *Sd*10. *ANC.*

P. litigiosa (Replete with dispute) China, is also P. pilosiuscula media, and a tree of symmetrical pyramidal shape, of variable height, which obscures itself with clear white flowers, enclosing a cluster of yellow anthers just as the leaves appear, and is the best of the genus for small gardens.

8-ft.–20-ft., April-May. D. 4-ft.–10-ft. Sq. Cg7. Graftage. ANC.

P. LUSITANICA (Portuguese) Portugal, is the Portugal Laurel, very similar in most of its characteristics to P. Laurocerasus, but even more hardy, still taller, and one of the most outstanding of all evergreen shrubs. The flowers, which are dull-white, are borne in far from insignificant racemes, but the specimens usually seen in gardens suffer considerably from being overclipped.

10-ft.–20-ft. or more, June. E. 10-ft.–20-ft. Sq. Cg8. ANC.

P. MAACKII (Comm.) Manchuria, is a very handsome Bird Cherry, the outstanding feature of which is the peeling bark, which resembles that of the Birch, and is coppery-yellow, disclosing as it peels a fair and unblemished, polished surface like well-burnished metal. The flowers, borne in racemes on the wood of the previous year, are small and white.

10-ft.–20-ft., June. D. 10-ft.–20-ft. Sq. Cg8. ANC.

P. MIRA (Quaint) W. China, can be either a small tree or a large bush, with slender branches and narrow, toothed, spear-shaped, green leaves, bearing before their appearance wide, single, white, peach flowers, distributed with cunning skill upon the leafless branches.

10-ft.–20-ft., March-April. D. 10-ft.–20-ft. Sq. Sd2. ANC.

P. MUME (A Japanese name) Japan, is the Japanese Apricot, is a deciduous tree or, more generally, a shrub, with green and brown branches, pale-rose or white flowers with an exquisitely beautiful scent, produced upon the bare branches, when spared to do so by the kindness of Providence, in March. It rises to its most transcendent beauty in its varicties albo-plena and roseo-plena.

12-ft.–20-ft., March. D. 12-ft.–20-ft. Sq. Cg8. ANC.

P. (AMYGDALUS) NANA (Dwarf) S. Russia, is an exceptionally pretty, dwarf almond which runs underground when suited and forms a thicket, bearing upon its unclothed stems wreaths of rose-pink flowers of quite enchanting appearance.

3-ft., March-April. D. 3-ft.–8-ft. Sq. D2. ANC.

P. PADUS (Greek name for Bird Cherry) Europe, is the Bird Cherry, Padus racemosa and Cerasus Padus, a tree which will in time reach thirty feet or more, with elliptical, sharply serrated leaves and drooping racemes of white, fragrant flowers, each about half an inch in diameter. It is available in a number of forms :—

- P. PADUS ALBERTII (Comm.)—is a rather condensed tree of twiggy habit.
- P. „ PLENA—has flowers which are double white.
- P. „ WATERERI—is somewhat smaller in growth, but has sprays of larger flowers up to six inches in length.

10-ft.–30-ft., April-May. D. 10-ft.–30-ft. Sq. Sd2. ANC.

Rhododendron Thomsoni

Rhus typhina ABCDEFGH
Rhus typhina var. laciniata JKLMNOPQRSTU

P. PERSICA (Peach) China, is also Amygdalus persica and Persica vulgaris, and is a deciduous tree of up to twenty feet, with smooth branches and almost stemless flowers, borne before the leaves, of bright pink. The sub-varieties are :—

P. PERSICA VAR. DUPLEX—has double flowers of bright rose-pink.
P. „ „ CLARA MEYER—has deep salmon-pink, double flowers.
P. „ „ MAGNIFICA—has double, fiery-red flowers.
10-ft.–20-ft., April. D. 10-ft.–20-ft. Sq. Cg7. ANC. Pl.77.

P. SARGENTII (Comm.) Japan, is one of the most beautiful of all trees, its bronze-red foliage forming the most fitting foil for its single flowers of soft rose-pink, which are as large as a penny, and are produced in groups of from two to six upon stalks of about the same length, and are followed by small, black, cherry-like fruits. In the autumn its leaves are exquisitely tinted.
10-ft.–25-ft., March-April. D. 10-ft.–25-ft. Sq. Cg7. ANC.

PRUNUS SERRULA

P. SERRULA (Toothed) W. China, is one of the gems of the genus, which, strangely enough, is almost worthless as a flowering tree. Rising to its greatest height in its variety P. serrula var. tibetica, its greatest beauty is the coppery-red mahogany tones of its bark, which exhibit all the beauties of burnished bronze as the golden-brown outer skin peels away and discloses the underlying loveliness.
15-ft.–20-ft., April. D. 10-ft.–18-ft. Sq. Cg7. Sd2. ANC.

P. (CERASUS) SERRULATA (With minute teeth) China, is represented in the type by a tree up to twenty feet high in nature, with smooth, wide, spreading branches, bright-green leaves and double, white or rose-tinted flowers freely produced.
12-ft.–15-ft., April. D. 20-ft.–30-ft. Sq. Cg7. Budding. ANC.

PRUNUS (continued)

The following varieties are among the best :—

P. SERRULATA VAR. ALBO-ROSEA, which is also P. serrulata var. Shirofugen (White Goddess), and has double white flowers which fade to pink.

P. „ „ BENIFUGEN (Crimson Goddess)—has large, double, flesh-pink flowers.

P. „ „ FUGENZO (Brilliant Goddess)—is also P. serrulata Kofugen, and Veitchiana, and has double, rose-pink flowers.

P. „ „ HORINJI (Name of an ancient temple)—has deep-pink, double or semi-double flowers, and grows more slowly and climbs not so high.

P. „ „ KIRIN (Giraffe) — has double, rose-pink flowers.

P. „ „ KWANZAN (A Japanese mountain)—is also Sekiyama, purpurascens, Horingi, Ohnanden, Sekizan, New Red and rubra nova, and is the tallest of the varieties with very large, rosy-red flowers produced from deep-pink buds.

P. „ „ SHUJAKU (Southern Constellation)—has large, pale-rose flowers and exceptionally upright habit.

P. „ „ SPIRALIS (Coiled)—is also P. serrulata var. Udzuzakura, with large, double, pale-pink flowers which resemble P. Lannesiana var. Ojochin.

P. „ „ TORANO-O (Tiger's Tail)—has large, single, white flowers tinted at the base with pink.

P. „ „ UNIFOLIA (With one leaf only)—is also P. serrulata var. Ichiyo, with double, very pale-pink flowers of pendent habit, closely resembling P. serrulata var. Benifugen.

P. SIEBOLDII (Comm.) Central Japan, is a tree of exceptionally small growth with bronze-green young leaves and single or semi-double, rose-pink flowers in tight clusters, produced upon upright branches.

10-ft.–20-ft., April-May. D. 15-ft.–30-ft. Sq. Cg7. ANC.

P. SIEBOLDII VAR. WATERIANA (Comm.) is a variety with slower growth and more tightly massed flowers.

8-ft.–12-ft., April-May. D. 12-ft.–18-ft. Sq. Cg7. ANC.

P. SPINOSA (Spined) Europe, is the Sloe or Blackthorn, quite attractive in its varieties, P. spinosa var. purpurea with reddish-bronze leaves and neat habit, and P. spinosa var. flore pleno with its pleasant double white flowers.

8-ft.–12-ft., March. D. 8-ft.–10-ft. Sq. Suckers. ANC.

P. SUBHIRTELLA (Somewhat pubescent) Japan, is the Higan or Rosebud Cherry, a very remarkable tree with its branches crowded with rose-pink buds in April, opening to flesh-pink flowers.

10-*ft.*–20-*ft.*, *April.* *D.* 10-*ft.*–20-*ft.* *Sq.* *Cg*7. *ANC.*

P. SUBHIRTELLA VAR. ASCENDENS (Rising) is the Japanese Shiro-higan, has small, bell-shaped, pale-pink flowers and is of pyramidal habit, seldom exceeding twelve feet in height.

8-*ft.*–12-*ft.*, *April.* *D.* 6-*ft.*–10-*ft.* *Sq.* *Cg*7. *ANC.*

P. SUBHIRTELLA VAR. AUTUMNALIS (Autumn-flowering) is a tree which will reach thirty feet in height and which bears very lovely, semi-double, scented flowers of pale-pink during the winter months.

20-*ft.*–30-*ft.*, *November-April.* *D.* 20-*ft.*–30-*ft.* *Sq.* *Cg*7. *ANC.*

P. SUBHIRTELLA VAR. MAKINO is a weeping variety with tiny, rose-pink buds opening into double, carmine flowers.

10-*ft.*–20-*ft.*, *March-April.* *D.* 10-*ft.*–20-*ft.* *Sq.* *Cg*7. *ANC.*

P. SUBHIRTELLA VAR. PENDULA (Pendulous) is an exceptionally pretty weeping variety with its branches wreathed with a multitude of pale-pink flowers.

10-*ft.*–20-*ft.*, *March-April.* *D.* 10-*ft.*–20-*ft.* *Sq.* *Cg*7. *ANC.*

P. SUBHIRTELLA VAR. PENDULA RUBRA (Reddish) is similar, but has deep rose-red flowers.

10-*ft.*–20-*ft.*, *March-April.* *D.* 10-*ft.*–20-*ft.* *Sq.* *Cg*7. *ANC.*

P. TRILOBA (With three lobes) China, is also Amygdalopsis Lindleyi and one of the most attractive of the Almonds, making a bushy shrub which becomes spangled with bright-pink rosette-like flowers.

10-*ft.*–15-*ft.*, *March-April.* *D.* 10-*ft.*–15-*ft.* *Sq.* *Ch*8. *ANC.*

P. VILMORINII (Comm.) China, has coppery-green leaves preceded by white flowers tinged with rose.

10-*ft.*–20-*ft.*, *March-May.* *D.* 10-*ft.*–20-*ft.* *Sq.* *Cg*7. *ANC.*

P. YEDOENSIS (From Tokio) Japan, has large, white flowers, turning pale-pink with age.

20-*ft.*–30-*ft.*, *March-April.* *D.* 20-*ft.*–30-*ft.* *Sq.* *Sd*10. *Cg*7. *ANC.*

PTELEA (RUTACEAE) (DERIVED FROM THE GR. NAME FOR ELM, THE SEEDS OF BOTH GENERA BEING SIMILAR).

P. TRIFOLIATA (With three leaflets) Eastern U.S.A., is the Hop Tree, a tree of slow growth, seldom more than twenty feet in height, with aromatic wood, three-parted green leaves made up of leaflets about five inches in length, and sweetly-scented, greenish-white flowers in June and July.

10-*ft.*–20-*ft.*, *June-July.* *D.* 15-*ft.*–30-*ft.* *Sq.* *Sd*10. *ANC.*

PUNICA (LYTHRACEAE) (THE MEANING OF THE LATIN NAME IS "OF CARTHAGE," THE FRUIT HAVING BEEN KNOWN AS "THE APPLE OF CARTHAGE").

P. GRANATUM (Many-seeded) S.E. Europe, is the Pomegranate (Pomum granatum), a tender shrub with green, oval leaves and fiery-red flowers produced at the terminals of the shoots. Fruits are occasionally formed but seldom ripened, and this shrub and its varieties are best suited by a south wall. P. granatum var. flore pleno is outstandingly beautiful, and a magnificent specimen may be seen growing upon the wall of the Banqueting Hall in the Bishop's Palace at Wells.

12-ft.–20-ft., July-September. *D.* *Indefinite.* *Ch4.* *ANC.*

PYRACANTHA (Rosaceae) (the name is derived from the Gr. pyr—fire ; and akantha—a thorn ; from the colour of the berries, and the spiny nature of the plant).

The Pyracanthas present few difficulties in cultivation and are of extreme hardiness and particularly suitable for walls with a north or east aspect, where they are completely undaunted by the " brave north-easter." Propagation of the species is best from the seeds, which should be sown in the autumn. Cuttings of the current year's growth with a heel, selected up to six inches in length, may be made in July and August.

P. angustifolia (With narrow leaves) China, is also Crataegus angustifolia and Cotoneaster angustifolia, and is one of the tenderest of the species, a fact which renders it more dear to the heart, and which merits in the colder districts the shelter of a flanking wall, which it will embellish with its garish clusters of bright, orange-yellow fruits, which persist throughout the autumn and winter. The flowers of all the species closely resemble those of the Hawthorn and dispel a similar but less invasive scent.

10-ft.–12-ft., June. *E.* *10-ft.–12-ft. Sq.* *Sd10.* *Ch7–8.* *ANC.*

P. atalantioides (Resembling Atalantia) W. China, is also P. Gibbsii, is an outstanding variety with larger leaves and masses of bright orange-red berries, which impose a load upon the branches which they manfully bear. P. atalantioides forma aurea has just as many clusters of golden-yellow berries.

15-ft., June. *E.* *15-ft. Sq.* *Sd10.* *Ch7–8.* *ANC.*

P. coccinea (Scarlet) S. Europe, is another delightful evergreen of proved hardiness with small, oval leaves, white " May " flowers, and brilliant coral-red fruit, reaching the zenith of its perfection in P. coccinea var. Lalandii with even more vigorous growth and larger berries of bright orange-red.

15-ft., June. *E.* *15-ft. Sq.* *Sd10.* *Ch7–8.* *ANC.*

P. Rogersiana (Comm.) S.W. China, is also P. crenulata Rogersiana, which literally inundates itself with a snow cloud of white flowers, followed by orange berries in the same profusion, which nestle in complete comfort in rosettes of shining, green leaves. P. Rogersiana var. aurantiaca is similar, with berries of bright orange-red, and P. Rogersiana var. fructu luteo, which is also P. Rogersiana var. flava, has yellow fruits.

5-ft.–8-ft., June. *E.* *5-ft.–8-ft. Sq.* *Sd10.* *Ch7–8.* *ANC.*

P. YUNNANENSIS (From Yunnan) China, is another splendid evergreen, with fruits which are orange-red at first and become deeper in colour as time progresses, presenting a brilliant picture throughout the winter.

8-ft.–10-ft., June. E. 8-ft.–10-ft. Sq. Sd2. Ch7. ANC.

PYRUS (ROSACEAE) (FROM THE LATIN PYRUM—A PEAR).

A group of trees and shrubs which includes the Flowering Crabs or Apples, the Whitebeams, the Service and Mountain Ash trees. These are included, since they are pre-eminently fitted to the Shrub Garden to provide the features around which it stands. Most of the species are also suited to grow as specimens. The Genus includes MALUS (PYRUS MALUS), *Plate* 78, and species described will often be found catalogued as such.

P. (MALUS) ALDENHAMENSIS (Comm.) Garden origin, has exceptionally large, wine-red flowers, which are borne in rosettes of young, purple-red foliage, and rather flattened fruits of crimson touched with scarlet. It is also P. Malus aldenhamensis, P. floribunda var. aldenhamensis, and Malus purpurea aldenhamensis.

12-ft.–30-ft., April-May. D. 20-ft. Sq. Graftage. N.

P. AMYGDALIFORMIS (Almond-like) S.E. Europe, is the Almond Pear, a small tree sometimes reaching twenty feet, resembling a pear in growth, and bearing clusters of white flowers about an inch in diameter, followed by small, pear-shaped fruits.

20-ft., April-May. D. 20-ft. Sq. Graftage. N.

P. BACCATA (Berried) Siberia, is the Siberian Crab Apple and Malus baccata, is a small tree with masses of white flowers followed by small, round, bright-red, berry-like fruits. P. baccata var. mandschurica is similar and has slightly larger fruits.

10-ft.–20-ft., May. D. 10-ft.–20-ft. Sq. Cd2. N.

P. CORONARIA (Crown-bearing) Eastern U.S.A., is the Garland Crab Apple, Malus coronaria and Malus fragrans, and becomes wreathed with very sweetly-scented, rose-coloured flowers followed by yellow, long-stemmed fruits, which persist while the leaves assume the most gorgeous autumn tints. P. coronaria Charlottae has large, semi-double, rose flowers.

12-ft.–20-ft., May-June. D. 20-ft. Sq. Graftage. N.

P. EARLHAMENSIS (Comm.) Garden origin, has bronze-green foliage and pinkish-crimson flowers followed by large, apple-like, crimson fruits with attractive bloom.

12-ft.–30-ft., April-May. D. 20-ft. Sq. Graftage. N.

P. ELEYI (Comm.) Garden origin, is also Malus Eleyi and Pyrus Malus Eleyi, and blends red-bronze young leaves with the purple-red of its flowers, its succeeding fruits shading from bright-crimson to scarlet. *12-ft.–30-ft., April-May. D. 20-ft. Sq. Graftage. N.*

P. FLORENTINA (Florentine) Italy, is also P. crataegifolia. P. florentina has grey-green leaves like those of the Hawthorn, borne upon a tenuous, branched, slender-headed tree, clusters of small, clear white flowers, and smaller red fruits spangled with brown patches. In addition the foliage assumes the most amazing tints in autumn, rivalling those of a fine summer sunset.

8-ft.–12-ft., April-May. D. 12-ft. Sq. Sd2. Graftage. N.

P. FLORIBUNDA (Free flowering) Garden origin, is an exceptionally fascinating, large shrub or small tree, is very beautiful, literally submerging itself in an orgy of pale-pink flowers followed by small red fruits. P. floribunda var. atrosanguinea (*Plate* 76) is also Malus atrosanguinea. P. pulcherrima var. atrosanguinea belongs at least in its characteristics, differing only in the deeper tones of its wine-red flowers borne upon drooping branches. P. floribunda var. Scheideckeri (Comm.), with its attractive, semi-double, pale-pink flowers, probably belongs here.

12-ft.–20-ft., April-May. D. 12-ft.–20-ft. Sq. Graftage. N.

P. FUSCA (Brown) Western N. America, is the Oregon Crab Apple, growing in its native habitat to thirty feet, but seldom here exceeding fifteen feet, with slender, reddish-brown branches, dark-green, oval, three-lobed leaves, and brilliant, flesh-pink flowers fading to white, followed by reddish-yellow fruits.

8-ft.–15-ft., April-May. D. 8-ft.–15-ft. Sq. Sd2. N.

P. GLAUCESCENS (Somewhat glaucous) N. York to Alabama, has extremely pretty leaves, rather larger than those of P. coronaria, and distinctly three-lobed, and large, pale-pink flowers succeeded by rather large, greeny-yellow fruits, which are offset by the brilliant autumn foliage.

15-ft.–30-ft., May-June. D. 15-ft.–30-ft. Sq. Sd2. Graftage. N.

P. HARTWIGII (Comm.) Garden origin, is of parentage P. Halliana × P. baccata, and a magnificent small tree or large shrub with dark-green leaves and very large, white flowers, deep pink upon the reverse side.

15-ft.–20-ft., May-June. D. 15-ft.–20-ft. Sq. Graftage. N.

P. HUPEHENSIS (From Hupeh) W. China, is also known as P. theifera; is distinguished by its stiff branches, has quite broad, elliptical, serrated leaves and pink flowers, distinctly cup-shaped, succeeded by small, pear-shaped, purplish fruits.

12-ft.–18-ft., April-May. D. 12-ft.–18-ft. Sq. Graftage. Sd2. N.

P. IOENSIS (Violet-like) Central U.S.A., is the Prairie Crab, and has green-grey leaves similar to those of P. coronaria but a little larger, and large flowers of carmine which age to pale-pink, and are followed by red, oblong fruits. P. ioensis plena is similar but a trifle slower growing, with double pink flowers.

12-ft.–20-ft., May-June. D. 12-ft.–20-ft. Sq. Graftage. Sd2. N.

P. KANSUENSIS (From Kansu) N.W. China, is a small tree or large shrub which may reach twenty-five feet, with broadly ovate leaves, white "May" flowers, and long, narrow, dark-crimson fruits spotted with brown.

12-ft.–20-ft., May-June. D. 12-ft.–20-ft. Sq. Graftage. Sd2. N.

P. LEMOINEI (Comm.) Garden origin, has bronze-green leaves, deep crimson flowers, and small, bright-red fruits.

15-ft.–20-ft., April-May. D. 15-ft.–20-ft. Sq. Graftage. N.

P. × MAGDEBURGENSIS (From Magdeburg) Garden origin, is a hybrid of P. spectabilis and P. pumila, a straight tree with its branches wreathed with semi-double, pink flowers which, at their best, are near those of the double-flowered Peach or Almond, and are produced upon a tree which is more tractable.

15-ft.–30-ft., May. D. 15-ft.–30-ft. Sq. Graftage. N.

P. × MICROMALUS (With minute apples) Garden origin, is a hybrid of P. spectabilis and P. baccata, and is the P. Kaido or P. Riversii of gardens, and a delightful, large shrub or small tree, the chief attraction of which is the outstanding rosetted clusters of vinous-red flowers which pass with age to a more sedate rose-red.

8-ft.–12-ft., May. D. 8-ft.–12-ft. Sq. Graftage. N.

P. ORTHOCARPA (With straight fruits) Japan, is a large shrub or small tree, seldom exceeding ten feet in height, with clusters of flesh-pink flowers, the outstanding feature of which is the small, brilliant, orange or orange-scarlet fruits, which are produced in amazing prodigality.

6-ft.–10-ft., April-May. D. 6-ft.–10-ft. Sq. Sd2. Graftage. N.

P. PRATTII (Comm.) China, is an exceptionally strong-growing tree or shrub with wide, serrated leaves, small white flowers, somewhat insignificant red fruits, and magnificent autumn colouring which seems to be fitted with a delayed action fuse, so late in the year does it appear.

15-ft.–30-ft., April-May. D. 15-ft.–20-ft. Sq. Sd2. Graftage. N.

P. PRUNIFOLIA (With leaves like the Plum Tree) N.E. Asia, is a small tree with broadly oval leaves and white flowers, followed in even very young trees by persistent, small, yellowish to bright-red fruits. P. prunifolia var. rinki has flesh-pink flowers followed by yellow fruits. P. prunifolia var. xanthocarpa is outstanding for the quantity of its golden-yellow fruits.

15-ft.–30-ft., April-May. D. 15-ft.–30-ft. Sq. Graftage. N.

P. PUMILA (Small) Europe and W. Asia, is the Crab Apple, probably best represented by the following, all of which are known as MALUS pumila :—

P. PUMILA VAR. BEAUTY OF MONTREAL (Garden origin)—has the typical white flowers of the species, followed by conical fruits striped with brilliant red.

P. ,, ,, DARTMOUTH—has white flowers and plum-like fruits.

P. PUMILA VAR. JOHN DOWNIE—has fine, conical, yellow and bright-red fruits, which persist for a long time.

P. „ „ LADY NORTHCLIFFE—has pinky-white flowers and small, bright-yellow fruits.

P. „ „ VEITCH'S SCARLET—has white flowers and scarlet fruits.

P. „ „ WISLEY CRAB—has deep-rose flowers followed by large, deep-red fruits, borne upon trees with bronze-green leaves.

15-*ft.*–30-*ft.*, *April-May.* *D.* 15-*ft.*–30-*ft.* *Sq.* *Graftage.* *N.*

P. SALICIFOLIA (With willow-like leaves) S.E. Europe, is the Willow-leaved Pear, a small tree with a rough stem, small, white flowers, and silvery-grey, narrow, willow-like leaves.

10-*ft.*–30-*ft.*, *May.* *D.* 10-*ft.*–20-*ft.* *Sq.* *Sd2.* *Graftage.* *N.*

P. SARGENTII (Comm.) Japan, is a most exceptional small shrub with slow and short growth, seldom reaching anything greater in height than eight feet, and beautified by rosettes of small but exceptionally pretty white flowers, followed by clusters of small, shining, bright-red fruits.

5-*ft.*–8-*ft.*, *May.* *D.* 5-*ft.*–8-*ft.* *Sq.* *Graftage.* *Sd2.* *N.*

P. SIEBOLDII (Comm.) Japan, is also P. Torinyo, and a beautifully proportioned small tree or large shrub with rather small but exceptionally attractive apples held upon long stems which gives them the appearance of Cherries.

8-*ft.*–15-*ft.*, *May.* *D.* 8-*ft.*–15-*ft.* *Sq.* *Graftage.* *Sd2.* *N.*

P. SPECTABILIS (Showy) N. China, is another perfectly proportioned tree of spherical habit, which has the typical clusters of rose-red flowers paling with age to pink, followed by yellow fruits. P.× micromalus var. Riversii may really belong here.

8-*ft.*–15-*ft.*, *April-May.* *D.* 8-*ft.*–15-*ft.* *Sq.* *Graftage.* *Sd2.*

P.× SUBLOBATA (Slightly lobed) Garden origin, is a Japanese hybrid of very neat, conical habit of growth, with elliptic, moderately lobed leaves, felted upon the reverse side, clusters of pinky-white flowers followed by small, rounded, yellow fruits.

6-*ft.*–8-*ft.*, *April-May.* *D.* 6-*ft.*–8-*ft.* *Sq.* *Graftage.* *N.*

P. THEIFERA (*see* P. HUPEHENSIS).

P. TORINGOIDES (Resembling Toringo) W. China, has weeping or semi-weeping branches, white flowers resembling those of the Hawthorn, and pink and cream fruits borne upon long stems like cherries.

12-*ft.*–25-*ft.*, *April-May.* *D.* 10-*ft.*–20-*ft.* *Sq.* *Graftage.* *N.*

P. TRILOBATA (Three-lobed) S.E. Europe, has leaves which are markedly three-lobed and heavily toothed, and large, white flowers succeeded by pear-shaped, crimson fruits, enhanced in beauty and desirability by the fascinating autumn tones of the leaves.

10-*ft.*–15-*ft.*, *April-May.* *D.* 10-*ft.*–15-*ft.* *Sq.* *Sd2.* *Graftage.* *N.*

Rosmarinus corsicus EFJKLMNOP

Grevillea rosmarinifolia
BCDGH

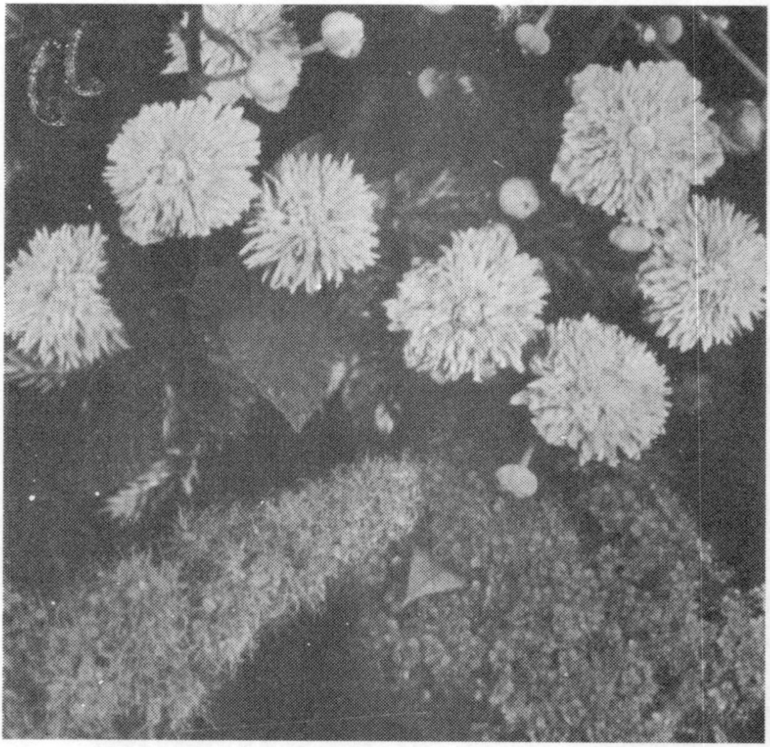

Rubus ulmifolius var. bellidiflorus
ABCDEFGH

Spiraea macrothyrsa
JKNO

Spiraea japonica var. Bumalda
Anthony Waterer LMPQ

P. Tschonoskii (Comm.) Japan, is a tree with felted leaves, young growth and almost insignificant white flowers which yield pride of place to greenish-yellow fruits, suitably ornamented with rouged cheeks, picked out with beauty patches of red-brown, and accompanied by brilliant orange-scarlet and blood-red leaves in autumn.

15-ft.–30-ft., April-May. D. 15-ft.–30-ft. Sq. Sd2. Graftage. N.

P. yunnanensis (From Yunnan) W. China, is a typical apple with large leaves, well felted upon the underside with a yellowish tomentum, and bearing small, white flowers, which are followed by equally small but undeniably attractive, round, bright-red fruits, smaller but brighter than cherries. P. yunnanensis var. Veitchii has somewhat larger leaves, more felt, but on the whole one comes to the conclusion that one of the species is sufficient for any small garden.

15-ft.–25-ft., April-May. D. 15-ft.–25-ft. Sq. Sd2. Graftage. N.

P. Zumi (Comm.) Japan, is a sedate shrub which can seldom be prevailed upon to rise above twelve feet, and modestly pales its flowers from pink to white, arrogantly replacing them with bright-red, small and select fruits. P. Zumi var. calocarpa is similar in almost all respects but the glory of its golden-yellow fruits, which are produced with prodigality and magnanimity.

8-ft.–12-ft., April-May. D. 8-ft.–12-ft. Sq. Sd2. Graftage. N.

RAPHIOLEPIS (Rosaceae) (derived from the Gr. raphis—a needle; and lepis—a scale; a reference to the shape of the bracts which subtend the flower).

These shrubs are excellent for seaside locations and are at home in any good garden soil. The best method of propagation of the species is from the seeds, which usually germinate freely, but if shy may be encouraged to do so by being subjected to the assistance of frost.

R. Delacourii (Comm.) Garden origin, is a hybrid of R. umbellata and R. indica, and is a somewhat tender shrub, meriting and needing some protection in winter, with dark-green, tough, obovate leaves, pyramidal sprays of farthing-sized flowers of beautiful rose-pink, borne in May and followed by blue-black berries.

3-ft.–5-ft., May. E. 3-ft.–5-ft. Sq. Sd2. Cg7. ANC.

R. indica (Indian) China, is also R. salicifolia, and another tender shrub only completely hardy in the extreme south-west, but quite a good wall shrub in more austere districts, which has lanceolate leaves, white flowers, washed with pink, in pyramidal panicles, and blue-black berries.

4-ft.–5-ft., April-May. E. 4-ft.–5-ft. Sq. Sd2. Cg7. ANC.

R. umbellata (Umbelled) Japan, is also R. japonica of gardens, and the Yeddo Hawthorn, a hardy shrub a little larger than its relatives, with sweetly-scented, Hawthorn-like flowers borne in intensely conglomerate sprays and followed by the typical blue-black berries of the genus.

4-ft.–6-ft., April-May. E. 4-ft.–6-ft. Sq. Sd2. Cg7. ANC.

RHAMNUS (Rhamnaceae) (derived from the Gr. rhamnos—an old Greek name for the ancient Buckthorn, or possibly from the Celtic rham—a tuft).

The Buckthorns are a group of shrubs, usually with black berries, but not essentially so. All are of easy cultivation in any soil and are eminently suitable to the wild garden. Propagation of the species is best from the seed, which is freely produced, or from cuttings of the stem, usually of the current year's growth, about four inches in length, taken during August.

R. cathartica (Of medicinal properties) Europe, is the "Native Buckthorn," a large shrub or small tree exceptionally at home upon chalky soils, with elliptical leaves up to three inches in length, and small, greenish flowers followed by black berries.

12-*ft.*, *May-June*. *D.* 8-*ft. Sq.* *Sd*2. *ANC.*

R. davurica (From Dauria) Siberia, is another very handsome shrub with oblong leaves up to four inches in length, greenish-white flowers and the typical blue-black berries of the group.

15-*ft.*–20-*ft.*, *May-June*. *D.* 20-*ft. Sq.* *Sd*2. *ANC.*

R. Frangula (The old name for the Buckthorn, meaning brittle) Europe, with greenish flowers and fruits at first green, changing to red and then to dark, purple-black, and used as an ingredient, via charcoal, of the finest gunpowders.

10-*ft.*, *May-June*. *D.* 15-*ft. Sq.* *Sd*2. *ANC.*

R. imeretina (From Transcaucasia) Caucasus, is an extremely handsome species with foliage resembling Rhododendron, assuming very beautiful autumn tints for outshining the greenish-white flowers and small, purple-black berries.

10-*ft.*, *May-June*. *D.* 12-*ft. Sq.* *Sd*2. *ANC.*

RHODODENDRON (Ericaceae) (the name is derived from the Gr. rhodon—a rose; and dendron—a tree).

The genus includes also Azalea and Rhodora. The botanical difference existing between Azalea and Rhododendron may briefly be described as follows. The Azalea bears, in the main, funnel-shaped flowers and is deciduous, and the Rhododendron is evergreen and bears bell-shaped flowers, though the differentiation is sweeping and cannot be regarded as complete. For further information the species sometimes known as Azalea are followed in the sequence by the letter "A" enclosed in parentheses. Taken as a whole, the genus Rhododendron thrives in a moist, leafy, sub-acid soil, which may be built up of a sandy peat or may consist of a lime-free loam. All of the genus are surface-rooted, and all that need concern the would-be cultivator is the surface soil, which should consist of nine inches of good lime-free loam, or sandy, sub-acid peat. Siting should be done with reasonable care; those flowering early in the season should be sheltered from the rays of the early spring sun, which can bring devastation in its path, and, as a general recommendation, one cites their requirements as being best suited by the north-west slope, or placed in the shelter of a woodland site. Propagation of the species is best from the seeds, which most of them produce with complete prodigality. The best method is to sow the seeds in the late autumn in pans, the surface layer of which is composed of completely sterilised sphagnum moss, passed through a 200-mesh sieve, and subjected to the complete rigours of the winter, placed upon germination in the shelter (that is, the shade) of a north wall. The hybrids are certainly most freely propagated from layers which root readily if the appropriate soil is prepared for their reception, but the would-be propagator should not disdain cuttings, which will acquire roots upon the whole length of their submerged stems if placed in a suitable mixture of subacid peat and sand in July.

It is not possible in a work of this length to deal exhaustively with the whole of the genus, and the following selection must be regarded only as an attempt to indicate the varieties at present in substantial commercial propagation.

The genus Rhododendron comprises in its scope practically all that the garden requires to furnish both attractive evergreen foliage and almost continuous flower of gorgeous coloration throughout the year.

R. ADENOGYNUM (With glandular pistil) China, is an extremely beautiful evergreen species with clusters of from six to twelve sweetly-scented flowers of white, tinted outside with pink and spotted with crimson.
6-ft., April-May. E. 6-ft.–8-ft. Sq. Sd2. L7–8. Cg7. A.

R. AERUGINOSUM (With leaves of verdigris colour) Sikkim, may be disregarded for its floral worth but is outstanding for the brilliance of its blue-green juvenile leaves.
6-ft., April-May. E. 6-ft.–8-ft. Sq. Sd2. L7–8. Cg7. A.

R. (A) ALBRECHTII (Comm.) Japan, is undoubtedly a magnificent species with large purple-rose flowers of open bell shape, with bronze-green to bronze-red foliage, changing to the loveliest of autumnal colours.
3-ft., May-June. D. 3-ft. Sq. Sd2. L7–8. Cg7. A.

R. AMBIGUUM (Doubtful : the colour) W. China, has pale-yellow flowers in groups up to six, with greenish-yellow spots on the face, but cannot be said to be either a distinctive or fascinating colour.
6-ft., April-May. E. 6-ft. Sq. Sd2. L7–8. Cg7. A.

R. ANTHOPOGON (With bearded flowers) Tibet, is an exceptionally interesting small shrub with aromatic, oval leaves of shining green and sulphur-yellow flowers in small terminal clusters.
1½-ft., April. E. 2-ft. Sq. Sd2. L7–8. Cg7. A.

R. APERANTUM (With naked flowers) Burma, is a dwarf evergreen species with somewhat hairy, oval leaves and terminal clusters of bell-shaped flowers, varying in number up to six, generally of orange-yellow, but exhibiting a considerable range of colour. When suited, R. aperantum is one of the most outstanding of all the dwarf Rhododendrons.
1-ft., June. E. 1-ft. Sq. Sd2. L7–8. Cg7. A.

R. (A) ARBORESCENS (Resembling a tree) N. America, is a deciduous species which has flesh-coloured, funnel-shaped flowers in July and later, and exhibits a fine range of colour in its leaves before they fall in autumn.

5-ft., July-August. D. 3-ft.–5-ft. Sq. Sd2. Cg7. L7–8. A.

R. ARBOREUM (Tree-like) Himalayas, is a tree-like species sometimes reaching forty feet, with deep-green leaves, very white or buff beneath, with clusters of white, pink or red flowers sometimes spotted within, and up to one-and-a-half-inches in diameter, not particularly outstanding in itself, but which provides the parent for many of the garden varieties now in existence. R. arboreum var. Blood Red is similar but has flowers of deepest red.

10-ft.–20-ft., March-May. E. 10-ft.–20-ft. Sq. Sd2. L7–8. Cg7. A.

R. AUGUSTINII (Comm.) China, is an exceptionally beautiful shrub of the Triflorum group, with evergreen, oval leaves and groups of up to ten lavender flowers borne terminally. The species rises to its greatest heights in R. Augustinii var. coerulea, which has flowers of lavender-lilac and gains still further approbation as one of the parents of R. × Blue Tit.

6-ft.–8-ft., May. E. 4-ft.–6-ft. Sq. Sd2. L7–8. Cg7. A. Pl.52.

R. AUGUSTINII VAR. COERULEA (Garden origin) is similar but has flowers which more closely approach blue.

6-ft.–8-ft., May. E. 4-ft.–6-ft. Sq. Sd2. L7–8. Cg7. A.

R. AUREUM (Golden) China, is a dwarf with its dark-green, young leaves scaly upon the reverse side, with clusters of from three to five funnel-shaped flowers, which may be of a good, deep yellow, but are sometimes of a greenish tinge.

3-ft.–4-ft., May. E. 3-ft.–4-ft. Sq. Sd2. Cg7. L5. A.

R. AURICULATUM (Shaped like an ear) Central China, has large, dull, dark-green leaves, rusty upon the underside, and is one of the latest varieties to start into growth, with large, funnel-shaped, white flowers borne in groups of from four to eight.

8-ft.–20-ft., August. E. 8-ft.–20-ft. Sq. Sd2. Cg7. L5. A.

R. BAILEYI (Comm.) Tibet, is a neatly habited dwarf shrub with somewhat small, deep, glossy, green, oval leaves with a distinct point, and buff upon the reverse side, with funnel-shaped flowers with an open face of reddish-purple, freely spotted with darker tones upon the uppermost three lobes.

3-ft.–5-ft., May. E. 3-ft.–5-ft. Sq. Sd2. C7. L5. A.

R. BALFOURIANUM (Comm.) China, is an exceptionally beautiful evergreen shrub with sharply pointed, long, narrow, deep-green leaves and bell-shaped flowers of very pale rose, much flushed and spotted with crimson, borne in clusters of from six to nine.

8-ft., April-May. E. 5-ft. Sq. Sd2. C7. L5. A.

R. **barbatum** (Bearded) Nepal, is a tree-like shrub of open growth with dark-green leaves and small, rounded clusters of bright-crimson flowers, produced in March. A magnificent specimen, over twenty-five feet in height, was an amazing sight when it held over 1,000 clusters of its startling flowers. R. barbatum carneum is similar but has flowers of flesh-pink.

6-ft.–25-ft., March. E. 4-ft.–20-ft. Sq. Sd2. C7. L5. A. Pl.53.

R. × **Blue Tit**, Garden origin, is a hybrid of R. impeditum and R. Augustinii, is one of the finest of the dwarf Rhododendrons of hybrid origin, its neatly elliptical, pale-green leaves being set upon bushes of symmetrical habit, which are eclipsed in May by masses of funnel-shaped flowers of deep-mauve.

3-ft., May. E. 2-ft. Sq. Cg7. A.

R. **brachyanthum** (With short flowers) W. China, is a dwarf evergreen with small, dark-green leaves, much lighter upon the underside, with flowers of bell to funnel shape of yellow—bright in a good form, greenish-yellow in a poor one.

3-ft., June. E. 3-ft. Sq. Cg7. Sd2. A.

R. **brachycarpum** (With short fruits) W. China, has narrowly oval leaves of deep green, felted grey upon the reverse side, with rounded heads of wide, creamy-white flowers, shaded freely with pink, and adds to its other merits that of great hardiness.

5-ft.–7-ft., June. E. 5-ft.–7-ft. Sq. Cg7. Sd2. L5. AN.

R. **bracteatum** (With bracts) China, has small, rather narrow leaves of dark green, and small, white flowers freely spotted with purple.

3-ft.–6-ft., June. E. 3-ft.–5-ft. Sq. Cg7. Sd2. L5. AN.

R. **brevistylum** (With a short style) W. China, is a very hardy, tall shrub with rather long, narrow, dark-green leaves, paler upon the underside, and clusters of funnel-shaped flowers of rose, painted with crimson spots upon the uppermost lobes.

5-ft.–9-ft., June. E. 3-ft.–8-ft. Sq. Cg7. Sd2. L5. A.

R. (A) **calendulaceum** (Resembling Marigold) N. America, is the Flame Flower of Northern America, a medium to tall-growing, deciduous shrub with somewhat narrow, long green leaves, widely funnel-shaped flowers of brilliant buff-yellow, ageing to orange-yellow. The best form is probably R. calendulaceum var. aurantiacum, the flowers of which are deep orange and become, as time passes, a brilliant crimson. The species bears a distinct resemblance to R. nudiflorum but is, notwithstanding, a clearly separate species.

5-ft.–10-ft., May. D. 4-ft.–7-ft. Sq. Cg7. Sd2. A.

R. **calciphila** (Lime-loving) Burma, a shrub reputed to love lime, with very small, grey-green leaves and clusters of small, rose-pink, funnel-shaped flowers.

1-ft., May-June. E. 2-ft. Sq. Cg7. Sd2. ANC.

R. **callimorphum** (Of beautiful form) China, is a symmetrical, well-clothed shrub with roundish, netted, green leaves with a distinct point, and rings of bell-shaped flowers of pale rose, painted with deep crimson upon the base.

6-ft., April-May. E. 6-ft. Sq. Cg7. Sd2. L5. A.

R. CALOSTROTUM (With beautiful covering) Burma, has an easy temperament, is one of the most dwarf species, and has small, aromatic leaves heavily covered with grey scales upon the upper side and buff beneath, and salver-shaped flowers of deep-rose deepening almost to crimson. *1-ft., April-May. E. 2-ft. Sq. Cg7. Sd2. L5. A.*

R. CAMPANULATUM (Bell-shaped) Himalayas, is outstanding because of its very hardy, beautiful foliage, smooth, dark green above and reddish-brown upon the underside, and loose clusters of white or lavender, bell-shaped flowers spotted with purple upon the upper lobes. *6-ft.–10-ft., April. E. 6-ft.–8-ft. Sq. Cg7. Sd2. L5. A.*

R. CAMPYLOCARPUM (With bent fruits) Sikkim, is an extremely beautiful, symmetrical shrub with oval, pointed leaves with a glossy, dark-green surface, and glaucous undersurface, and clusters of half a dozen or so pale-yellow, fragrant, bell-shaped flowers.

4-ft.–8-ft., May. E. 4-ft.–8-ft. Sq. Cg7. Sd2. L5. A.

R. CAMPYLOGYNUM (With bent style) Yunnan, is a dwarf with small, stiff, oval, bronze-green leaves, closely resembling the better-known R. myrtilloides, and with similar drooping, bell-shaped flowers with wider lobes of bright brownish-red, each borne upon a rather long and slender stem.

1-ft.–2-ft., May-July. E. 2-ft. Sq. Cg7. Sd2. L5. A.

R. CAMTSCHATICUM (From Kamchatka) Alaska, is also known as Therorhodion camtschaticum, and is a very dwarf, dense shrub with densely hairy leaves and wide, rose-crimson flowers, which are produced with great freedom if it is placed in a moist, shady spot.

1-ft., May-June. D. 2-ft. Sq. Sd2. Ch7. A.

R. (A) CANADENSE (Canadian) North-East and N. America, is also known as Rhodora canadensis and Azalea Rhodora, and is a much-branched, deciduous shrub with green leaves of approximately two inches in length, grey felted on the underside, with rose-purple, funnel-shaped flowers produced in April and May.

3-ft., April-May. D. 3-ft. Sq. Sd2. Cg7. A.

R. CANTABILE (*see* R. RUSSATUM. *Pl.*56).

R. CATAWBIENSE (From Catawba) South-eastern U.S.A., is an evergreen species of wide-spreading habit with oval, shining, green leaves, pale and smooth on the underside. The lilac-purple flowers are produced in large clusters and are spotted with crimson. This Rhododendron is one of the easiest to grow, and one of the hardiest of the species.

6-ft.–9-ft., May-June. E. 8-ft.–12-ft. Sq. Sd2. Cg7. L5. ANC.

R. CAUCASICUM (From the Caucasus) S.W. Asia, is another extremely hardy, low-growing shrub, seldom more than two feet in height, with narrow, oval leaves of deep, dark-green with rusty hair upon the undersides, and with narrow, bell-shaped flowers of creamy-white flushed with pink, opening to two inches across. E. caucasicum var. album has white flowers and R. caucasicum var. pictum has flowers of soft rose, and grows a little taller.

2-ft., April-May. E. 3-ft. Sq. Sd2. Cg7. L5. A.

R. CEPHALANTHUM (Bearing heads of flowers) W. China, has small, dark-green, narrow leaves, and low-growing, stiff habit and bears clusters of Daphne-like flowers of creamy-white or pale-yellow.

1-ft.–1½-ft., April. E. 2-ft. Sq. Sd2. Cg7. ANC.

R. CHAETOMALLUM (With bristly down) W. China, is a dwarf, evergreen shrub with pale-green, oval leaves, roundly blunt at the tips, with clusters of bell-shaped, vivid crimson flowers in groups of from four to ten.

2-ft.–3-ft., April-May. E. 3-ft.–4-ft. Sq. Sd2. Cg7. A.

R. CHAMAETORTUM (Twisted dwarf) Yunnan, is another very dwarf species seldom exceeding one foot in height, which bears a close resemblance to R. cephalanthum, but has similar groups of flowers of rose-pink a little later.

1-ft., May-June. E. 2-ft. Sq. Sd2. Cg7. A.

R. CHARIDOTES (Gracefully endowed) Upper Burma, is a splendid, dwarf-growing species of semi-prostrate appearance, with flattish flowers of brilliant magenta. *½-ft., April-June. E. 2-ft. Sq. Sd2. A.*

R. CHARITOPES (Gracefully cut) Upper Burma, has small, grey-green leaves, paler on the underside, and dotted with yellow scales, bears clusters of few apple-blossom-pink, bell-shaped flowers spotted with crimson. A feature of the species is the large calyx, which is cut into five distinct lobes.

1-ft.–2-ft., May. E. 2-ft.–3-ft. Sq. Sd2. Cg7. L5. A.

R. CHARTOPHYLLUM (With papery leaves) China, is an evergreen with long, narrow, green leaves, scaly beneath, and narrow, bell-shaped flowers of pale-pink, spotted with crimson.

3-ft., May. E. 3-ft. Sq. Sd2. Cg7. A

R. CHRYSEUM (Golden-yellow) Yunnan, is a multiple-branched, evergreen shrub with grey-green leaves heavily scaled beneath with brown, bearing broad, open, yellow flowers singly or in pairs.

⅔-ft., June. E. 1½-ft. Sq. Sd2. Cg6. A.

R. CILIATUM (Fringed) Sikkim, has elliptical, bristly leaves, and its young branches covered with the same type of bristles, bears wide, bell-shaped flowers, red in the bud, but fading continuously until they become either very pale-pink or white.

2-ft.–4-ft., March. E. 3-ft.–5-ft. Sq. Sd2. Cg7. AN.

R. CINNABARINUM (Vermilion-red) Himalayas, is a taller-growing shrub with long, slender branches moderately clothed with oval, metallic-green leaves, and hanging, slender, bell-shaped flowers orange-red on the outside and paler within; borne in groups of from five to eight. R. cinnabarinum var. Roylei is similar but has flowers of bright red a little smaller in size.

6-ft.–10-ft., May. E. 4-ft.–8-ft. Sq. Sd2. Cg7. A. Pl.55.

R. CONCINNUM (Elegant) W. China, has slender, oval, evergreen leaves pale upon the underside, eventually becoming brown, and bears trusses of purple, bell-shaped flowers in groups of four or more. The flowers are spotted with deeper purple.
6-ft.–10-ft., May. E. 6-ft.–10-ft. Sq. Sd2. Cg7. A.

R. CROCEUM (Orange-yellow) Yunnan, is a very beautiful, hardy, small tree with oval leaves of polished green, bearing clusters of soft-yellow flowers, widely bell-shaped and hanging in groups upon individual stems nearly as long as the flower is wide.
10-ft.–15-ft., May. E. 8-ft.–12-ft. Sq. Sd2. Cg7. L5. A.

R. CYCLIUM (With bluish fruits) Yunnan, has smooth, oval leaves gracefully clothing somewhat stiff stems, and bears white, sweetly-scented, polished flowers in clusters of from seven to eight.
4-ft.–9-ft., March-April. E. 3-ft.–8-ft. Sq. Sd2. Cg7. L5. A.

R. DAURICUM (From Dauria) Siberia, is a deciduous species with small, oval leaves of glossy green and rosy-purple flowers freely produced in February. *3-ft.–5-ft., February. D. 3-ft. Sq. Sd2. Cg7. A.*

R. (A) DAVIESII (Comm.) Garden origin, is also Azalea Daviesii and a hybrid between Rhododendron molle and Rhododendron viscosum, with large white flowers heavily spotted with deep-yellow.
4-ft.–6-ft., May. D. 4-ft.–6-ft. Sq. Cg7. L5. A.

R. DELEIENSE (From Deleyi Valley) Assam, is a somewhat tender shrub best suited to a site which will provide a harbour against the storms and stresses of the early spring, where it will make a compact and rounded bush with orbicular green leaves and deep, rose-coloured, funnel-shaped flowers produced with considerable freedom.
1½-ft.–2-ft., May-June. E. 1½-ft.–2-ft. Sq. Sd2. Cg7. A.

R. DICROANTHUM (With bi-coloured flowers) China, is a dwarf evergreen of rather stiff, tight growth, with blunt-ended, dark-green leaves culminating in a sharp point, and with long, rather narrow, bell-shaped flowers of orange often touched and beautified with pink.
2-ft.–5-ft., May. E. 2-ft.–4-ft. Sq. Sd2. Cg7. A. Pl.55.

R. DIDYMUM (Formed in pairs) Tibet, is a most attractive small shrub varying somewhat in its height, but generally approximating to two feet, with small, dark-green leaves and groups of half a dozen or so crimson-black, wide, bell-shaped flowers.
2-ft., June-July. E. 2-ft.–3-ft. Sq. Sd2. Cg7. L5. A.

R. DISCOLOR (Different colours) W. China, is a strong-growing, tall shrub with deep-green leaves of elliptical shape, with very large, white, open, bell-shaped flowers flushed with pink.
10-ft.–15-ft., June. E. 10-ft.–15-ft. Sq. Sd2. Cg7. L5. A. Pl.32.

R. EDGARIANUM (Comm.) W. China, is a dwarf, bushy species with small, oval, grey-green leaves and bluish-purple, salver-shaped flowers which deepen in colour, produced generally twice in the

Sorbus Meinchii
ABGHLMNORS

Viburnum Opulus
CDGHQU

Hippophae rhamnoides FJKNOPTU

Spiraea Aitchisonii ABCDEFGH
Spiraea difformis GHKLMN
Buddleia Davidii (variabilis) MPQST

same season. It is also known as R. oresbium and bears a close botanical resemblance to R. fastigiatum.

1½-ft.–2½-ft., April-June. E. 1½-ft.–2-ft. Sq. Sd2. A.

R. FASTIGIATUM (With erect, clustered branches) Yunnan, can be clearly distinguished by its erect habit of growth and its small, violet-purple to lilac-rose flowers, produced in small clusters. Many of the species obtained under this name are more correctly R. impeditum, which is similar in colour but has a horizontal rather than a vertical habit of growth.

1½-ft., June. E. 1½-ft. Sq. Cg6. A.

R. FERRUGINEUM (Rusty-leaved) Central Europe, is the Alpine Rose, and a shrub of compact growth with shiny, green leaves covered with rusty scales upon the undersides, and clusters of funnel-shaped, carmine-pink flowers borne at the tips of the shoots.

2½-ft., June-August. E. 2½-ft. Sq. Cg6. N.

R. FORRESTII (Comm.) W. China, is also known as R. repens, and is a very dwarf, flat-growing, shiny, green-leaved shrub with thick, woody stems, which bears large, bell-shaped, deep-crimson flowers during April and May and is reputedly difficult to establish, but can be made at home if a cool, well-drained, shady position can be found with a northern aspect. R. Forrestii var. chamaethauma (Wonderful dwarf) has much larger leaves which decorate its stiff, horizontal growths, and bears its bell-shaped, crimson flowers in groups of three or four.

½-ft., April-May. E. 1¼-ft.–2½-ft. Sq. Sd8. Cg7. L5. A.

R. FORTUNEI (Comm.) China, is a very hardy species which in time will reach ten or twelve feet, with as much width, but which is more generally represented by a shrub of half these dimensions, with oblong, pointed, pale-green leaves, and loose clusters of large, sweetly-scented, pale-pink flowers, fading in colour as they age.

6-ft.–12-ft., May. E. 6-ft.–12-ft. Sq. Sd2. Cg7. ANC.

R. FULGENS (Shining) Sikkim, has glossy, green leaves borne upon rigid branches, with brown, peeling bark, which are flat in shape, shining green above and reddish-brown beneath. The beautiful, brilliant crimson flowers are borne in spherical clusters, each well packed with large flowers, and its outstanding colour is unequalled by any of the species other than R. barbatum.

6-ft.–12-ft., February-March. E. 4-ft.–10-ft. Sq. Sd2. Cg7. L5. A.

R. FULVUM (Reddish-brown) W. Yunnan, is a large shrub, the young shoots of which are covered with yellowish-brown tomentum, with oval, thick, dark-green leaves with a sharp point, red-brown underneath, and a distinctly paler midrib. The rounded trusses of flowers are of clear, pale rose, painted with an outstanding crimson patch. *8-ft.–18-ft., April. E. 8-ft.–18-ft. Sq. Sd2. Cg7. L5. A.*

R. GLAUCUM (Grey-blue) Sikkim, is one of the few of the species which does not dislike a reasonably sunny site where its small, rather narrow, aromatic, oval leaves with their glaucous under-surface provide a splendid setting for the rose-coloured flowers, which are borne in clusters of six or more, and are of narrow bell-shape with outflung lobes.

2-ft.–4-ft., April-June. E. 4-ft.–6-ft. Sq. Sd2. Cg7. L5. A.

R. GLOMERULATUM (Club-shaped) Himalayas, is of dwarf, erect habit and bears neatly disposed, small, grey-green, oval leaves, and produces in the spring and autumn small, rounded clusters of purple-mauve flowers. *1-ft.–2-ft., April-May. E. 2-ft. Sq. Sd2. Cg7. A.*

R. HEMITRICHOTUM (Half-felted) S.W. Szechuan, has slender, almost wiry growth, small, rather narrow, dull-green leaves, silvery-white on the underside, and clear, pale-rose, open-faced flowers deeper at the edges. *3-ft., April. E. 2-ft.–3-ft. Sq. Sd2. Cg7. L5. A.*

R. HIPPOPHAEOIDES (Resembling the Sea Buckthorn) Yunnan, has small, grey-green, aromatic leaves carried upon upright bushes of dense, twiggy growth, and bears small clusters of bluish-mauve or bluish-pink flowers.

2-ft., June. E. 1½-ft. Sq. Cg6. Sd2. A. 636/1.

R. HIRSUTUM (Hairy) Switzerland, has narrow, dark-green, shiny leaves, hairy beneath and at the edges, and bears clusters of funnel-shaped flowers of bright carmine-pink, and is best suited by a moist site. *2-ft., June. E. 1½-ft. Sq. Cg6. Sd2. A.*

R. HYBRIDUM comprises Rhododendrons of hybrid origin, the parentage of which, if known, is stated. Many of the varieties have R. ponticum as one parent, and are fully at home in conditions which suit also the bulk of the species, namely, shade from the fiercest of the sun's rays, and cool root run in surface soil which is free of lime and composed of sub-acid peat, leafmould or loam. *Pl.*57.

A. C. Kenrick—has lilac-pink flowers with deeper markings, borne in large, spherical clusters.

album elegans—is a very fine, robust, clear white flowering variety, and is only outstripped by

album grandiflorum, which has still larger flowers.

Alice—is a variety which, flourishing in sunnier positions than most, has large, glowing, pink trusses of flowers, produced with certainty in May.

Ascot Brilliant, which unites R. Thompsonii with a variety of garden origin, has flowers of deep, blood-red in April.

atrosanguineum—has flowers of deepest scarlet.

Bagshot Ruby is still deeper in colour, and

Baron Schroeder has flowers the colour of a ripe plum, starred in the centres with yellow.

B. de Bruin—has bright-red flowers a little later than most.

Bernard Crisp—has well-rounded groups of bright-pink flowers.

Blandyanum—has pink flowers which deepen to crimson, produced early in the year.

Bodartianum—is a remarkably fine, white derivative from R. arboreum.

Christmas Cheer suggests an early-flowering variety with pale-rose flowers, and

Cornubia is a pink variative of R. arboreum.

Corona—has flowers which exhibit varied shades of coral-pink.

Corry Koster—has frilled flowers of pale pink, generously enlivened with crimson.

Dawn's Delight—is a tender but well-loved hybrid of R. Aucklandii with flowers of almost ruby-red which pale to carmine.

Doncaster, than which few can be better known, is one of the finest of the late reds.

Dr. Stocker—is a grandchild of R. Aucklandii and R. caucasicum, with flowers of creamy or yellowish-white.

Essex Scarlet is another late-flowering, brilliant-red variety, and everestianum has frilled flowers of pale lilac.

fastuosum or fastuosum fl.pl.—has semi-double flowers of pale-purple.

Gomer Waterer freely produces large trusses of white flowers, well flushed with pink.

Hugh Koster has the colour of Doncaster, but produces it in still larger trusses, and

Ivorianum has flowers of brilliant scarlet.

Jacksonii—is a variety of medium height with flowers of brilliant scarlet produced as early in the year as any of those of the hybrids.

John Waterer—has nicely rounded groups of flowers of bright-carmine.

kewense—has sweetly-scented, white flowers shaded with pink.

Lady Clementine Mitford—has flowers of pale, orange-red, deepening at the margins.

Lady Eleanor Cathcart—has rose-pink flowers patched with chocolate-brown.

Langley Park—is a fine variety with large trusses of deep-crimson flowers, and

Loderi, which is a lovely child of R. Fortunei and R. Aucklandii, has fascinatingly beautiful, large, mottled leaves, and flowers of white flushed with pale-pink.

Luscombei is another grand variety with parentage R. Fortunei and R. Thompsonii, with large and ample flowers of rose-pink.

Manglesii—has white flowers marked with red, and is an Aucklandii hybrid which requires the same protection.

Michael Waterer—is another vivid, scarlet-flowered variety.

Minnie—has flowers of pale mauve, exquisitely marked with orange.

Mrs. E. C. Stirling—has flowers of pale pink, touched with lilac.

Mrs. Edwin Hillier—is an extremely fine variety with flowers of bright, almost crimson, cerise.

Mrs. R. S. Holford—has flowers of soft salmon-pink.

Mrs. John Clutton—is of clear, unsullied white.

Nobleanum—is very early flowering, with bright scarlet flowers.

Pelopidas—has very fine groups of bright-crimson flowers.

Pink Beauty has flowers of pure, pale pink, and

Pink Pearl is a grand variety with nicely formed groups of flesh-pink flowers, which is perhaps outshone by

Professor Hugo de Vries, which is similar but has flowers of slightly deeper pink.

Queen Wilhelmina—has large groups of flowers, each of exceptional size, of bright scarlet fading to deep pink.

Raoul Millais—is of salmon-pink, picked out with yellow-brown patches.

Rosamund Millais—has similar markings on flowers of cherry-red.

The Bride—is white in colour with patches of green.

Unknown Warrior—has crimson-scarlet flowers, and

White Pearl, known also as R. Gauntlettii, has flowers of very pale pink which fade with age to white.

R. HYPOLEPIDOTUM (Somewhat scaly) China, is a small, round, tight bush with shiny-surfaced, small, green leaves, close and scaly on the underside, with groups of lemon-yellow, flattish flowers of up to six, produced at the tips in June.

*1½-ft.–3-ft., June. E. 1½-ft.–3-ft. Sq. Sd*10. *Cg*7. *A.*

R. IMPEDITUM (Impeded) Yunnan, closely resembles R. fastigiatum but is more horizontal in its habit, is less hairy and has leaves of duller green. *1-ft.–1½-ft., June. E. 1½-ft. Sq. Cg*6. *Sd*10. *A.*

R. IMPERATOR (General) Yunnan, makes a flat mat with very small, shiny, green leaves, with large, bright-red buds opening to salver-shaped flowers of reddish-purple.

*½-ft., May-June. E. 2-ft. Sq. Ch*7. *Sd*2. *A.* 631/2.

R. (A) INDICUM (Indian) China or Japan, has bright-green leaves which may or may not be persistent, are paler upon the underside, and bears wide-faced, funnel-shaped flowers, often as much as two inches in diameter, generally singly borne and of red or pink. R. indicum var. balsaminiflorum is sometimes known as Azalea rosaeflora and is a rather smaller shrub of somewhat more composite habit which bears many double flowers of clear salmon-pink.

*1-ft.–1½-ft., May. E. 1½-ft. Sq. Cg*6. *A. Pls.*59, 60.

R. INTRICATUM (Much entangled) W. Szechuan, differs but little from R. fastigiatum, bearing similar flowers of lavender-blue.

*1½-ft., April. E. 1½-ft. Sq. Sd*2. *Cg*7. *A.*

R. (A) JAPONICUM (Japanese) Japan, is also Azalea mollis, originally known as R. molle, and a deciduous shrub, generally round in outline, made up of erect, tough branches with oval leaves of dark green, slightly hairy above, bearing clusters of six to ten rose, salmon-red, or orange flowers at the tips of the leafless shoots, and ranging in size from two to three inches. Between R. japonicum and R. molle—that is, the old R. sinense—exist a large number of hybrids which have been of great use in the garden and for forcing for early bloom, among which one can enumerate such varieties as the Kersbergen strain (*Plate* 50), Anthony Koster (*Plate* 62), Koster's Brilliant Red,

Hugo Koster,a nd the double-flowered hybrids known as rusticum fl.pl. (*Plate* 61). Ghent Azaleas will be found dealt with in R. luteum.

4-ft.–8-ft., April-May. D. 4-ft.–8-ft. Sq. Ch7. AN.

R. KELETICUM (Swift) Tibet, has narrow, green leaves borne upon an almost prostrate shrub of woody growth, and bears flat, open-mouthed flowers of bright purple, either singly or in pairs.

⅔-ft., June. E. 1½-ft. Sq. Cg7. Sd2. A. 31/1.

R. LEDOIDES (With leaves resembling Ledum) Yunnan, is an extremely neat shrub with long, linear leaves of pale green, bearing small flowers in rounded groups, reminiscent of those of the Daphne, of white flushed with rose.

1½-ft.–2-ft., April-May. E. 2-ft. Sq. Sd2. Cg7. A.

R. LEPIDOSTYLUM (With a scaly style) China, is a compact growing bush with small, rounded, blue-grey leaves, more or less covered with hair, which are even more beautiful when decorated with the salver-shaped, primrose-yellow flowers which accompany them at mid-summer.

1½-ft.–2-ft., June-July. E. 1½-ft.–2-ft. Sq. Sd10. Cg7. A.

R. LEPIDOTUM (Scaly) Himalayas, has small, rather hairy, young leaves becoming glabrous with age, and flat, rosy-crimson flowers with five distinct lobes, in May and June.

*1-ft.–2-ft., May-June. E. 2-ft. Sq. Sd10. Cg7. A. Pl.*55.

R. LEUCASPIS (White-shielded) Tibet, is an upright, evergreen shrub with rounded, elliptical leaves, yellowish-blue upon the underside, bearing flat, pure-white flowers either singly or in groups of two or three, in April. *2-ft., April. E. 2-ft. Sq. Sd2. Cg7. A.*

R. LUTESCENS (Yellowish) China, is an interesting evergreen shrub of loose, upright habit, with long, slender, green leaves, shiny above and paler and scaly below, and bears lemon-yellow flowers in groups of one or two at the tips of the shoots. Planted in a group it is one of the most attractive of the yellow-flowered Rhododendrons, and, pruned with care, can be made to form a very pleasant specimen.

3-ft.–7-ft., March. E. 2-ft.–4-ft. Sq. Sd10. Cg7. A.

R. (A) LUTEUM (Yellow) Caucasus, is also R. flavum and Azalea pontica, a deciduous species which rises to eight feet or more, with rather stiff, upright growth, and bears large, sweetly-scented, bright-yellow flowers in small clusters at the ends of the shoots. It is very hardy and is used as the stock for grafting the choicer hybrids, propagating well from seed. The propagation of young plants presents no difficulty.

6-ft.–10-ft., May. D. 6-ft.–8-ft. Sq. Sd2. A.

R. flavum is one of the parents, together with R. calendulaceum and R. nudiflorum, of the so-called Ghent Azaleas, of which may be mentioned :—

Gloria Mundi—crimson.
Nancy Waterer—yellow.
William III—orange.
Bouquet de Flore—salmon.

It seems better to leave these as hybrids of R. luteum.

R. (A) MOLLE (Soft) China, is the first name given to R. sinense or Azalea sinensis. It differs from R. japonicum only slightly, and it appears better to allow this for garden purposes to remain. In the main the true plant is extremely rare, the whole blood of R. japonicum and R. molle having become inextricably knit. It therefore seems better to leave the hybrids under R. japonicum or R. luteum.

R. MOUPINENSE (From Moupine) China, is a dwarf, evergreen shrub with oval, dark, smooth, green leaves, scaly upon the underside, bearing scented, white flowers spotted with purple or red dots.
2-ft., March. E. 2-ft. Sq. Sd2. Cg7. A.

RHODODENDRON LUTESCENS

R. MUCRONULATUM (With a small, sharp point) Manchuria, produces its rose-purple flowers singly, from a cluster of buds at the ends of the naked shoots, in the middle of winter, but sometimes in the severest of winters flowering is delayed until later. Evergreen or deciduous according to circumstances, it is a charming shrub which may reach six feet in height.
4-ft.–6-ft., December-February. ED. 4-ft.–6-ft. Sq. Sd2. Cg7. A.

R. MULIENSE (Of Muli) China, is an extremely hardy, evergreen shrub with small, oval, dull-green leaves, grey upon the underside, producing terminal clusters with a small number of bright-yellow flowers on a neat and tidy bush.
1½-ft.–2-ft., May-June. E. 2-ft. Sq. Sd2. Cg7. A.

R. MYRTIFOLIUM (With leaves like Myrtle) Garden origin, is also the R. ovatum of catalogues, has Myrtle-like, bronzy-green leaves, and bears its rose-pink, open-mouthed flowers in great profusion in June. It is said to be a hybrid between R. hirsutum and R. minus.

2½-ft., June. E. 2-ft. Sq. Cg7. A.

R. MYRTILLOIDES (Resembling Myrtle) Burma, is a dwarf, evergreen shrub with tiny, Box-like leaves, making a multiplicity of well-clothed, short, upright stems. The leaves often become purple in a severe winter. The flowers, which are vivid-claret, covered with a plum-like bloom, are each borne upon a long, slender stem arising from the uppermost leaf axils.

½-ft., May. E. 1-ft. Sq. Sd2. Cg6. A.

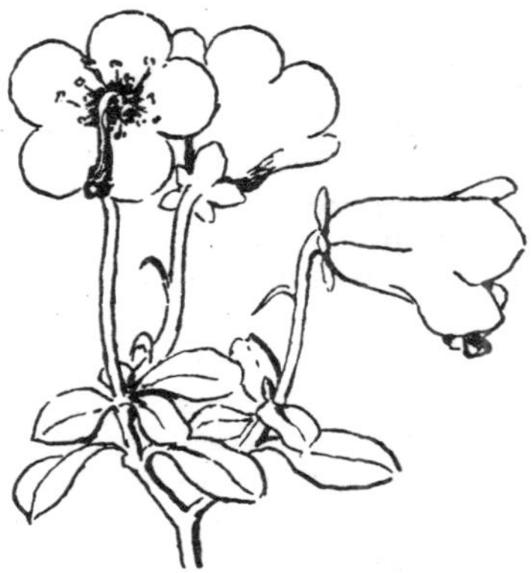

RHODODENDRON MYRTILLOIDES

R. NERIIFLORUM (With flowers resembling Oleander) Yunnan, has pointed, oblong, dark-green leaves, whitish upon the underside, and groups of rich crimson, narrow, bell-shaped flowers in clusters of up to twelve. It is one of the most beautiful of the red-flowered species. R. neriiflorum euchaites is a taller plant and has even brighter and larger flowers.

6-ft.–8-ft., April-May. E. 6-ft.–8-ft. Sq. Sd2. Cg7. A.

R. (A) NUDIFLORUM (With bare flowers) Eastern U.S.A., is the Pinxter Flower or Azalea nudiflora, a deciduous shrub which reaches six feet in height, and bears flowers of varying shades of pink to white, funnel-shaped in form and one inch or more in diameter. It is one of the parents of the so-called Ghent Azaleas.

6-ft., April-May. D. 5-ft.–6-ft. Sq. Sd2. Cg7. A.

R. (A) OBTUSUM (With blunt leaves) Japan, is a much-branched, evergreen shrub, once known as Azalea indica var. obtusa, with blunt, shiny leaves and terminal clusters of from two to four red flowers of funnel-shape. *1¼-ft., April-May. E. 1½-ft. Sq. Cg6. A.*

R. **OBTUSUM AMOENUM** is a rather taller variety with smaller hose-in-hose flowers of bright-magenta.

2-ft., April-May. E. 2-ft. Sq. Cg6. 29. *A.*

R. **OBTUSUM MACROSTEMON** (With long stamens) Japan, is another dwarf with very large, solitary flowers of clear pink.

*1½-ft., April-May. E. 1½-ft. Sq. Cg6. A. Pl.*59.

The following Obtusum varieties are worth special mention :—

Apple Blossom—pink flushed with white.
Beni-giri—semi-double crimson flowers.
Christmas Cheer—double crimson flowers.
Hatsu-giri—crimson-purple flowers. *Pl.*59.
Hino-manyo—salmon-pink flowers.
Hinode-giri—bright-red flowers.
Kirishima—lilac-mauve flowers.
Kokin-shita, brilliant salmon-red flowers.

R. **OREODOXA** (Mountain beauty) China, is one of the most attractive of the open shrubs, with oblong leaves, blunt at the tip, of deep green, and eight to ten rose-pink, bell-shaped flowers held in loose clusters.

6-ft.–10-ft., March-April. E. 6-ft.–10-ft. Sq. Sd2. L5. A.

R. **ORTHOCLADUM** (With straight stems) Yunnan, is a very compact shrub with small, straight, brownish-green leaves, and groups of small, mauve flowers produced with great freedom.

1½-ft., April. E. 1-ft. Sq. Sd2. Cg7. A.

R. **PATULUM** (Slightly spreading) Assam, is a tiny variety with small, evergreen leaves and large, funnel-shaped flowers of rose-red, passing to pink as they age.

½-ft., March-May. E. 1½-ft. Sq. Sd2. Cg7. A.

R. **PEMAKOENSE** (From Pemakoe) Tibet, is a tightly-growing, semi-prostrate shrub with shining, elliptical, green leaves and large, funnel-shaped flowers of pale lavender.

1-ft., April. E. 2-ft. Sq. Sd2. Cg7. A.

R. **PONTICUM** (From Pontus) Asia Minor, is the well-known magenta-flowered Rhododendron, naturalised in many parts of Great Britain, which makes a very large bush up to fifteen feet in height by thirty feet in diameter, and provides a stock upon which a number of the other varieties may be grafted.

15-ft., June. E. 30-ft. Sq. Sd2. L5. A.

R. **PRAECOX** (Early) Garden origin, is a hybrid of R. ciliatum and R. dauricum, interesting because of its early flowering and its easy culture, and bearing bright, rose-purple flowers from February to late March. *2-ft.–4-ft., February-March. E. 4-ft. Sq. Cg7. A.*

R. **PROSTIGIATUM** (Combined name) Garden origin, is a hybrid of R. prostratum and R. fastigiatum, of small growth, small, greyish-blue leaves and tidy clusters of violet-blue flowers.

1½-ft., June. E. 1½-ft. Sq. Cg6. A.

Spiraea japonica var. Bumalda Anthony Waterer **ACDEG**
Spiraea Margaritae **BEFJKLO**
Berberis Moseri **NPQRSTU**

Syringa vulgaris Madame Francisque Morel

R. PROSTRATUM (Prostrate) China, is a very small, flat-growing shrub with rigid branches, small, green leaves turned back at the edges, and decorative, salver-shaped flowers of deep rose-purple, about the size of a penny.

½-ft., April-May. E. 1½-ft. Sq. Sd2. Cg7. A.

R. RACEMOSUM (Flowering in clusters) W. China, is a strong-growing shrub of upright growth with small, oval leaves of polished green, bearing clusters of rather small flowers at the tips of the shoots during April and May. There is a considerable amount of variation, both in height and flower, in some of the varieties, R. racemosum var. compactum seldom exceeding fifteen inches in height.

1¼-ft.–3-ft., April-May. E. 1½-ft.–3-ft. Sq. Cg7. A. 627/3.

RHODODENDRON RACEMOSUM

R. RADICANS (Rooting) Tibet, makes a flat mat of small, evergreen, shining leaves, grey upon the underside, and carries large, solitary, flat flowers of rose-purple or violet-purple.

¼-ft., April-May. E. 1-ft. Sq. Sd8. A.

R. RAVUM (Grey) Yunnan, is a very hardy, and moderately dwarf species with oval, shining, dark-green leaves, buff and scaly below, bearing terminal clusters of four or more funnel-shaped flowers of deep rose.

2-ft.–3-ft., May-June. E. 2-ft.–3-ft. Sq. Sd2. Cg7. A.

R. RIPARIUM (Of the river bank) is a species of bushy habit with sticky, grey-green, elliptical leaves, tawny below, bearing reddish-pink flowers in small clusters at the tips of the shoots.

1½-ft.–2-ft., April-June. E. 1½-ft.–2-ft. Sq. Sd10. A.

R. ROXIEANUM (Comm.) S.W. China, is an attractive, slow-growing shrub of tight habit, with long, narrow, pointed, glossy, green leaves, rolled at the edges and rusty beneath, and tightly packed trusses of white flowers flushed with rose.

4-ft.–6-ft., May. E. 6-ft. Sq. Sd2. L5. A.

R. RUPICOLA (Growing in stony places) China, is a pleasant shrub of moderate height with thin, branching growth, small, green, oval leaves, somewhat resembling R. fastigiatum, and small, reddish-purple flowers as deep in colour as those of any of the small-flowered varieties. *2-ft., April-May. E. 2-ft. Sq. Sd2. Cg7. N.*

R. RUSSATUM (Somewhat brownish-black) N.W. Yunnan, is also R. cantabile and a very beautiful small shrub of rounded habit, dark-green, elliptical leaves, scaly below, bearing terminal clusters of upwards of five deep, purple-blue flowers, sometimes twice during the year. In a good form is one of the most beautiful of all the smaller Rhododendrons.
3-ft.–4-ft., March-April. E. 3-ft.–4-ft. Sq. Sd2. Cg7. A. Pl.56.

R. SALUENENSE (From Salween) China, has small, grey-green leaves, ochred below, borne upon stems of upright growth, with large, deep, purple-red flowers produced in groups of two or three at the ends of the shoots.
2-ft., May-August. E. 1½-ft.–2-ft.Sq. Sd2. Cg7. A.

R. SANGUINEUM (Blood-red) China, has narrowly oval, dark-green leaves, felted with greyish-white, and brilliant crimson, bell-shaped flowers borne in loose clusters of up to six.
3-ft., May-July. E. 3-ft. Sq. Sd2. Cg7. L5. A.

R. SARGENTIANUM (Comm.) W. China, is a splendid miniature, seldom more than two feet in height, with small, dark, glossy, green, oval leaves, bearing at the tips of the shoots pale-yellow, Daphne-like flowers, making it an extremely dainty and desirable plant.
1-ft.–2-ft., May-June. E. 1½-ft.–3-ft. Sq. Sd2. Cg7. A.

R. (A) SCHLIPPENBACHII (Comm.) Japan, is also Azalea Schlippenbachii, is a shrub of stiff habit with smooth, green, almost rhombic leaves and very large Azalea flowers of pale rose-pink spotted with reddish markings.
3-ft.–5-ft., April-May. D. 3-ft.–5-ft. Sq. Sd2. A.

R. SCINTILLANS (Scintillating) Yunnan, is a compact bush of erect habit, comfortably covered with small, oblong but sharply pointed, dark-green leaves with lavender-blue to dark, purplish-blue flowers, borne in clusters of from three to six at the tips of the shoots with great freedom.
1½-ft.–2½-ft., March-April. E. 1½-ft.–2½-ft. Sq. Sd2. Cg7. A.

R. SMIRNOWII (Comm.) Caucasus, is an extremely hardy shrub, seldom more than six feet in height, with long, dark-green leaves felted at first with white and becoming buff with age. The rosy-lilac flowers are borne in large trusses, and its hardiness makes it of great use in the colder districts.
5-ft.–6-ft., May. 6-ft.–8-ft. Sq. Sd10. Cg7. A.

R. TEPHROPEPLUM (Ashy-robed) Tibet, is a splendid variety with bushy, spreading growth, moderately long, narrow, glandular leaves, very grey and scaly on the underside. Pretty pink, funnel-shaped flowers are borne in trusses of from three to four.

3-ft.–4-ft., May. *E.* *3-ft.–4-ft. Sq.* *Sd2.* *Cg7.* *N.*

R. Thomsonii (Comm.) Nepal, is probably one of the most beautiful of all the Rhododendron species, with rounded, dark-green, oval leaves, grey-white below, and translucent, blood-red, bell-shaped flowers borne in loose, annular clusters. Varying in height and scope according to climate, R. Thomsonii is best grown in a sheltered place. It has provided the parent of many garden hybrids with red colouring.

6-ft.–12-ft., March-April. *E.* *6-ft.–12-ft. Sq.* *Sd2.* *L5.* *Cg7.* *A.* *Pl.63.*

R. trichocladum (With hairy twigs) China, has stiff, loose, upright growth with hairy, dark-green leaves and clusters of salver-shaped flowers of yellowish green or sulphur-yellow, and needs the occasional attention of the knife to keep it in character. It has the advantage of being particularly hardy.

2-ft.–3-ft., May. *DE.* *3-ft.–3½-ft. Sq.* *Sd2.* *Cg7.* *A.*

R. Wardii (Comm.) China, is an extremely beautiful species with roundly-oval, shiny, deep-green leaves and large, open, bell-shaped flowers of pale yellow produced from pink-tipped buds in loose clusters. Of splendid, symmetrical growth, R. Wardii does not grow quickly but probably exceeds eight feet in height, and more in scope when fully grown.

8-ft., May. *E.* *10-ft. Sq.* *Sd2.* *Cg7.* *L5.* *A.* *Pl.54.*

R. Williamsianum (Comm.) W. China, a shrub generally wider than it is high, with rounded, shiny, green leaves and large, hanging, pale-rose bell-flowers in terminal clusters, generally in twos. R. Williamsianum is best placed in a spot where it is shaded from the morning sun.

1-ft.–1½-ft., April-May. *E.* *1½-ft.–2½-ft. Sq.* *Cg7.* *A.* 422/2.

RHODOTHAMNUS (Ericaceae) (the name is derived from the Gr. rhodon—a rose; and thamnos—a bush).

R. Chamaecistus (Dwarf Box) Alps, is a dwarf shrub with small, bright-green, narrowly-oval leaves up to half an inch in length, fringed with short hair and bearing terminal, rose-coloured, flattish flowers, generally single, at the tips of the shoots. It seems to require a more moist, peaty soil, and though in nature it is found in limestone districts, these conditions do not appear to suit it in cultivation, where an acid soil seems to be a more appropriate medium.

¾-ft., April. *E.* *1-ft. Sq.* *Sd9.* *A.*

RHODOTYPOS (Rosaceae) (from the Gr. rhodon—a rose; and typos—shape; the flower suggesting a small rose).

R. kerrioides (Resembling Kerria) Japan, is an upright, branching shrub with opposite, ovate leaves and solitary, white, four-petalled flowers up to two inches in diameter, produced at the end of the short twigs during May and June.

4-ft.–6-ft., May-June. *D.* *4-ft.–6-ft. Sq.* *Sd10.* *Cg7.* *ANC.*

RHUS (ANACARDIACEAE) (THE NAME IS DERIVED FROM THE GR. RHOUS, THE OLD NAME FOR SUMACH).

Sumachs are of easy culture, growing well in any ordinary soil, and are noted for the excellence of their autumn colour. The pinnately-leaved kinds can be increased from cuttings placed in sandy soil in the spring. The simple-leaved kinds, of which R. Cotinus is an example, can be increased either by layering in the spring or by cuttings up to three inches in length, taken of the current year's wood in July or August.

R. CANADENSIS (Canadian) N. America, is also known as Rhus aromatica, and is a much-branching, lax shrub with three-parted, green leaves giving a pleasant aroma and becoming tinted with orange-gold and crimson in autumn. The flowers, which are yellowish and are borne in tight, round clusters, are insignificant in themselves but impressive in the group. The fruits which follow are red.
4-ft., April. D. 5-ft.–6-ft. Sq. Sd2. Ch3. Cr3. ANC.

R. COPALLINA (Giving copal) Eastern U.S.A., is a comparatively slow-growing species with pinnately-divided leaves made up of nine to twenty-one leaflets, with greenish flowers in dense clusters followed by red, hairy fruits.
8-ft.–10-ft., July-August. D. 8-ft.–10-ft. Sq. Ch3. Sd2. ANC.

R. COTINOIDES (Like Cotinus) Southern U.S.A., is a rare species with large, blue-grey leaves borne upon orange-red stems, forming one of the most beautiful of all the shrubs which provide autumn colour. *12-ft., June. D. 10-ft. Sq. Cg7. ANC.*

R. COTINUS (Wild olive) Europe, is commonly known as the Smoke Tree, with oval leaves up to three inches in length, panicles of flowers of purplish flesh colour, turning to smoky-grey and accompanied by the yellowing of the leaves, which make it a magnificent plant for autumn colour. R. Cotinus var. atropurpurea has its leaves and inflorescences of bright purple.
12-ft.–15-ft., July. D. 10-ft.–12-ft. Sq. Cg7. Suckers. 3. ANC.

R. GLABRA (Smooth) U.S.A., has pinnate leaves divided into eleven to thirty-one leaflets of bluish-green colour, green flowers in dense panicles produced in June or July, followed by red, hairy fruits. R. glabra var. laciniata has foliage more cut, but colours just as brightly as the year closes.
9-ft.–10-ft., July-August. D. 9-ft.–10-ft. Sq. Ch3. Cr3. ANC.

R. TYPHINA (Like a stag's horn) N. America, is a small tree or large shrub with pinnate leaves divided into eleven to thirty-one leaflets, and greenish flowers turning red as the fruits form. Its variety, laciniata, has leaves which are more cut.
10-ft.–30-ft., July-August. Cg3. Cr3. ANC. Pl.64.

RIBES (SAXIFRAGACEAE) (THE NAME IS THE ARABIC ONE FOR THAT OF A SOUR FRUIT, MIS-APPLIED TO THIS GENUS).

The Flowering Currants are of easy culture and are outstanding for their ability to produce their attractive, hanging sprays of bright flowers under town conditions, where they speedily become indispensable plants. They are easily produced from cuttings of one foot or so in length of the current year's wood, taken in late September or October and trodden firmly in on the open border, or from cuttings of one-third of this length, taken in July or August and placed in sandy soil in a warm, sheltered frame.

R. AMERICANUM (American) N. America, with large, black-currant-like leaves, clusters of yellowish-white flowers, and smooth, black fruits. The foliage assumes the most brilliant colours in the autumn, and the garden usage of the plant is confined mainly to obtaining the benefit of these colours.

5-*ft.*, *April*. *D*. 5-*ft*. *Sq*. *Cg*7–10. *ANC*.

RIBES GORDONIANUM

R. AUREUM (Golden) Western N. America, is the Golden or Buffalo Currant with yellow flowers, borne in five- to fifteen-flowered sprays upon slender, arching branches. This, too, assumes the most beautiful colours, compensating in the autumn for the loss of its spring sweetness.

4-*ft.*–5-*ft.*, *April*. *D*. 4-*ft.*–5-*ft*. *Sq*. *Cg*7–10. *ANC*.

R. FASCICULATUM (In tight clusters) Japan, is another currant with leaves divided into five lobes, hanging sprays of sweetly-scented, yellow flowers, five to nine in number, followed by smooth, red currants in the autumn.

3-*ft.*–6-*ft.*, *April*. *D*. 3-*ft.*–6-*ft*. *Sq*. *Cg*7–10. *ANC*.

R. GORDONIANUM (Comm.) Garden origin, is a hybrid of R. sanguineum with R. aureum, resembling R. aureum in growth, but has the greater freedom of the hybrid. It has exceptionally attractive, bronzy-red flowers, yellow within, and the leaves follow the pattern set for it by its parents.

4-ft.–5-ft. April. D. 4-ft.–5-ft. Sq. Cg7–10. ANC.

R. LACUSTRE (Lake-dwelling) N. America, is a dwarf shrub seldom exceeding three feet in height, clustered with bristles and bearing many drooping clusters of greenish-white flowers with brown sepals followed by small, purplish, gooseberry-like fruits.

3-ft., April. D. 3-ft. Sq. Cg7–10. ANC.

R. LAURIFOLIUM (Laurel-leaved) China, has large, evergreen, coarsely toothed, leathery, pointed leaves, and attractive, drooping sprays of greenish-white flowers during February and March.

3-ft., February-March. E. 3-ft.–4-ft. Sq. Cg7–10. ANC.

R. LOBBII (Comm.) California, is a Gooseberry with long spines and drooping, small, Fuchsia-like flowers with red sepals and white petals, followed by purplish fruits.

3-ft.–4-ft., April-May. D. 3-ft.–4-ft. Sq. Cg7–10. ANC.

R. LURIDUM (Dingy) W. China, is a Gooseberry without spines, the chief glory of which is a bright-red bark.

4-ft.–6-ft., April. D. 4-ft.–6-ft. Sq. Cg7–10. ANC.

R. MENZIESII (Comm.) N. America, is a densely branched shrub with bell-shaped flowers made up of white petals tinged with pink and red sepals, and foliage which colours beautifully in the autumn.

8-ft.–10-ft., April. D. 8-ft.–10-ft. Sq. Cg7–10. ANC.

R. SANGUINEUM (Blood-red) California, is the well-known "Flowering Currant," noted for its hanging sprays of reddish-pink flowers in April.

R. SANGUINEUM VAR. ALBIDUM—is similar and has white flowers tinged with pink.
R. " " ATRORUBENS—is earlier flowering and has crimson-red flowers.
R. " " KING EDWARD VII—is more compact in habit and later to flower, but has some excellent colour.
R. " " SPLENDENS—has blood-red flowers tinged with crimson.

4-ft.–10-ft., March-April. D. 4-ft.–8-ft. Sq. Cg7–10. ANC.

R. SPECIOSUM (Showy) California, is a Gooseberry which decorates itself in the spring with sprays of slender, crimson-red, hanging flowers, reminiscent of those of the Fuchsia. A rampant grower when suited it will reach ten feet in height and more in width, but is best pleased by a semi-shady spot in the warmer districts.

10-ft., April-May. 10-ft.–15-ft. Sq. Cg7–10. ANC.

ROBINIA (Leguminosae) (the name is derived from that of jean robin, a celebrated french botanist).

The members of this genus are of easy growth and well suited to either chalk or sandy soils. The two varieties described have one drawback, their branches are brittle and are apt to be swept away by high winds. They should therefore be planted in sheltered places. Cultivation of the true species is best from seed, but suckers of both varieties are produced which can be tipped and grown on. In some cases they are worked on to stocks of R. pseudo-acacia which is, in the main, best excluded from the garden, and one thoroughly recommends that both the species mentioned should be grown on their own roots.

R. hispida (Bristly) Southern U.S.A., has pinnately-divided leaves made up of seven to thirteen leaflets, and hanging, Wistaria-like sprays of deep-pink flowers freely produced during May and June.
4-ft.–6-ft., May-June. D. 4-ft.–6-ft. Sq. Sd10. ANC.

R. Kelseyi (Comm.) N. Carolina, is somewhat larger in height with leaves divided into nine to eleven leaflets, and rose-pink flowers followed by bristly pods.
10-ft.–12-ft., May-June. D. 10-ft.–12-ft. Sq. Sd2. ANC.

ROMNEYA (Papaveraceae) (the name is derived from that of t. romney robinson, an irish astronomer).

These are the Californian Tree Poppies, generally cut to the ground each year, but spreading with rapidity underground once they are suited, and are propagated with ease from the root cuttings made in the early spring. They resent disturbance, and plants are better grown on in pots until ready to be planted out.

R. Coulteri (Comm.) California, has grey, much-cut, poppy-like foliage, and bears majestic, white, sweet-smelling, poppy-like flowers with golden anthers from July to September.
4-ft., July-September. D. 4-ft.–6-ft. Sq. Cr3. ANC.

R. trichocalyx (With hairy calyx) California, is probably a more easily grown plant, differing only botanically and in its lack of a few inches. *3-ft., July-September. D. 4-ft.–6-ft. Sq. Cr3. AN.*

ROSA (*see* " Roses in Colour and Cultivation ").

ROSMARINUS (Labiatae) (from the latin ros—dew; and marinus—of the sea).

R. corsicus (Corsican) Corsica, is more congested in its growth, with spiny, grey leaves, and flowers approaching Cambridge blue in colour. *3-ft., April-May. E. 3-ft. Sq. Cg6. N.* 441/1. *Pl.*65.

R. officinalis (Of the shop) Mediterranean region, is the Rosemary, with bright-green, aromatic, linear foliage clustered along the stems and grouped heads of lavender-blue flowers.
4-ft.–6-ft., April-May. E. 4-ft.–6-ft. Sq. Cg6. N. 441/1.

RUBUS (Rosaceae) (derived from the old latin name, rubus, in its turn from ruber—red ; the colour of the fruit).

These are the Brambles, grown as a rule for the benefit of their flowers or the value of their coloured stems for winter decoration. Propagation of the white-stemmed varieties is best from seed, the others may be effectively increased by division in the spring. The genus is a large one, of which the following may be regarded as representative :—

R. biflorus (Two-flowered) Himalayas, has white stems when cut back regularly each year, and small, white flowers and yellow fruits when they are allowed to remain.

R. biflorus var. quinqueflorus is a magnificent variety, hailing from China, which is no better and no worse.
8-*ft.*, *May-June*. *D*. 8-*ft*. *Sq*. *Sd*2. *ANC*.

R. deliciosus (Delicious) Rocky Mountains, has attractive, vine-like leaves on long, arching branches wreathed in early summer with very large, pure white flowers.
5-*ft.*–8-*ft.*, *May-June*. *D*. 6-*ft.*–10-*ft*. *Sq*. *D*3. *ANC*.

R. Giraldianus (Comm.) China, is outstanding for the beauty of its arching, white stems and its grey-green, pinnately-divided leaves.
6-*ft.*–8-*ft.*, *June*. *D*. 10-*ft*. *Sq*. *Sd*2. *ANC*.

R. lasiostylus (With a hairy style) China, is another white-stemmed shrub, this time densely armed with spines.
6-*ft.*–8-*ft.*, *June*. *D*. 10-*ft*. *Sq*. *Sd*2. *ANC*.

R. thyrsoideus var. plenus (Flowering in thyrses) Europe, is the double-flowered White Bramble, which decorates itself with clusters of double, white, button-like flowers all the time that the Blackberry is so busily producing its flowers in the hedgerows.
8-*ft.*, *June-September*. *D*. *Indefinite*. *Cg*8. *ANC*.

R. ulmifolius var. bellidiflorus (With leaves like the Elm Tree ; daisy-flowered) Europe, has foot-long sprays of pink, double, daisy flowers, and forms an outstanding flowering shrub when flowers are scarce in the shrub garden.
8-*ft.*, *June-September*. *D*. *Indefinite*. *Cg*8. *ANC*. *Pl*.66.

RUSCUS (Liliaceae) (the name is said to be a corruption of an old herbalists' name for the butcher's broom).

The Butcher's Broom will grow almost anywhere, and may be freely propagated by division of the roots. As a rule the sexes are contained in separate plants, and seed will give rise to plants of both sexes.

R. aculeatus (Prickly) Europe. This dwarf-growing shrub, with its bright-green, sharply pointed, spear-like leaves, provides a great deal of pleasant colour when ornamented with its large, round, bright-red berries. 2-*ft.*–3-*ft.*, ——— *E*. 2-*ft*. *Sq*. *D*3. *ANC*.

Syringa vulgaris Lemoinei flore pleno

Syringa persica

SALIX (Salicaceae) (is derived from the celtic sal—near ; and lis—water).

The Willows can be of great use in the garden, both from the point of view of their ornamental catkins and the colour of their bark. They are most suited by moist positions, and propagate with great ease from cuttings of the bare wood placed firmly in the ground in March. Among the varieties which can be recommended are the following :—

S. Arbuscula (Little tree) Europe, is an exceptionally dwarf shrub with broad, glossy leaves, felted down the middle, which makes a tiny tree of only a few inches in height, and particularly attractive when ornamented with its large, yellowish catkins.

$\frac{1}{3}$-*ft.*–$\frac{1}{2}$-*ft.*, *April.* *D.* $\frac{1}{2}$-*ft. Sq.* *Ch*6. *N.*

S. Bockii (Comm.) W. China, is a neat shrub with its young shoots covered with dense, grey down, with oblong leaves of deep green, felted below with bluish-white. The attractive catkins are produced in the autumn while the leaves are still present, and it provides one of the most beautiful of the dwarf-growing types.

6-*ft.*, *October.* *D.* 6-*ft. Sq.* *Cg*3. *ANC.*

S. Caprea×lanata, Garden origin, is a most attractive hybrid of low growth with grey, heart-shaped leaves and large, woolly, yellowish catkins produced with prodigality in March and April.

4-*ft.*–6-*ft.*, *March-April.* *D.* 4-*ft.*–6-*ft. Sq.* *Ch*6. *ANC.*

S. cinerea (Ash-grey) England, is best in its variegated form called S. cinerea tricolor, has leaves tipped with white and yellow and forms an attractive shrub, seldom exceeding six feet in height.

6-*ft.*, *March-April.* *D.* 6-*ft. Sq.* *Ch*6. *ANC.*

S. Fargesii (Comm.) W. China, is a wide-spreading bush with long, narrow, channelled, dark-green leaves veined with crimson, and silvery upon the underside, enhanced in appearance by the shiny, deep-red, young shoots and pinkish buds.

5-*ft.*–8-*ft.*, *March-April.* *D.* 6-*ft.*–9-*ft. Sq.* *Ch*6. *ANC.*

S.×Grahamii (Comm.) Scotland, is a natural hybrid of S. herbacea and S. myrsinites, which has round, grey leaves and forms a most attractive tree, rarely more than a foot in height.

1-*ft.*, *May.* *D.* 1-*ft. Sq.* *Ch*6. *ANC.*

S. herbacea (Herbaceous) N. Europe, makes a prostrate-growing, gnarled and contorted tree with shining, green leaves, and livened with yellow catkins. $\frac{1}{4}$-*ft.*, *April.* *D.* 1$\frac{1}{2}$-*ft. Sq.* *Ch*6. *ANC.*

S. lanata (Woolly) Europe, is a dwarf, woolly Willow forming stout, dwarf twigs decorated with round, silvery-grey, furry leaves, and bearing large, rounded catkins. Seldom exceeding three feet in height, it is one of the most attractive of all the species.

2-*ft.*–3-*ft.*, *April-May.* *D.* 3-*ft.*–4-*ft. Sq.* *Ch*4–6. *ANC.* *Pls.*36, 37.

S. Lapponum (From Lapland) Europe, N. Asia, shows but a slight botanical difference, the leaves being longer and a little narrower than those of S. lanata.

2-*ft.*–3-*ft.*, *April-May.* *D.* 3-*ft.*–4-*ft. Sq.* *Ch*7. *ANC.*

S. MAGNIFICA (Magnificent) W. China, is one of the most beautiful of the Willows, with upright habit, young growths with purplish bark, large, wide, oval leaves of bluish-grey, and exceptionally large catkins.

7-ft.–15-ft., March-April. D. 6-ft.–12-ft. Sq. Ch6. ANC.

S. × MOOREI (Comm.) Ireland, is a hybrid of S. herbacea with S. phylicifolia, and a semi-prostrate shrub with leaves like those of the Myrtle, and catkins which at times are red.

1-ft., April. D. 1-ft. Sq. Ch6. ANC.

S. MYRTILLOIDES (Resembling Myrtle) Europe, is a large-branched, erect-growing Willow with green leaves, shiny both above and below, which decorates itself with its attractive yellow catkins before the leaves appear. *1-ft., March-April. D. 1-ft. Sq. Ch6. ANC.*

S. REPENS (Creeping) Europe, runs along the surface of the ground, which it decorates with its shining, elliptical leaves, which are silky while young, and bears small catkins of great fascination when they bronze in colour after having been fertilised.

¼-ft., April. D. 2-ft. Sq. Ch6. N.

SALVIA (LABIATAE) (THE NAME IS DERIVED FROM THE LATIN SALVEO—TO BE WELL ; FROM THE MEDICINAL PROPERTIES OF CERTAIN OF THE PLANTS).

All the species of the shrubby Sages must be regarded as being tender, but many of them are very beautiful and can be relied upon to give a charming display of bright colour throughout the whole of the summer season. Propagation is of the easiest, from cuttings of the half-ripened wood taken during July or the succeeding months. Such cuttings when rooted should be potted on and protected during the ensuing winter in a cold frame suitably placed.

S. CHAMAEDRIFOLIA (With leaves like the Germander) Mexico, is a woody shrub with stems at first prostrate, but rising, clothed with green, netted leaves, over which, at the tips of the shoots, are borne the brilliant blue, broad-lipped flowers. It is one of the finest of all blue-flowered shrubs, and, though its hardiness is subject to considerable doubt, it is well worth the early propagation which will most certainly be the lot of those who wish to keep it permanently.

1-ft., June-September. E. 1-ft. Sq. Cg6–7. ANC.

S. GRAHAMII (Comm.) Mexico, makes a shrub of some two feet in height in the open, but much more when sheltered against a warm wall. Though its leaves have some merit as a herb its chief glory is in the brilliance of the scarlet flowers it produces with great freedom. Said to be the hardiest of all the Salvias, it is worth the same attention as its blue-blooded brother.

2-ft. or more, June-September. E. 3-ft. Sq. Cg7. ANC.

SANTOLINA (Compositae) (from the Latin sanctus—holy ; and linum—flax ; a reference to its reputed medicinal qualities).

These aromatic shrubs are of easy growth and admirably suited to form low hedges, or for growth as specimens where the variation afforded by their attractive foliage colour is needed. Progagation is by cuttings of the half-ripened wood taken in June.

S. Chamaecyparissus (Ground Cypress) Mediterranean region, is also known as S. incana or the Lavender Cotton, and makes a low bush of feathery, silvery-grey leaves, pinnately divided into small lobes. The yellow buttons it produces are not individually attractive but are pleasant in the mass.
1½-ft., June-August. E. 2-ft. Sq. Ch6. ANC.

S. Chamaecyparissus var. nana (Small) Garden origin, is a reduced and refined counterpart with foliage even more intensely silver, and with all the charm of the tiny.
¾-ft., June-August. E. 1-ft. Sq. Ch6. N.

S. pinnata (Feathered) Italy, has bright-green, feathered leaves and flowers of creamy-white. *1-ft., July. E. 1-ft. Sq. Ch6. N.*

S. viridis (Dark green) S. Europe, has even deeper green foliage, similarly feathered, and with like button-heads of flowers of pale-yellow. *1-ft., July. E. 1-ft. Sq. Ch6. N.*

SARCOCOCCA (Buxaceae) (the name is derived from the Gr. sarx—flesh ; and kokkos—a berry ; from the nature of the berry).

Propagation is best from the seed, which should be sown in the late autumn.

S. Hookeriana (Comm.) Himalayas, is an upright shrub of loose growth, ultimately reaching a yard or so in height, with its uppermost growths decorated in the first few months of the year with sweetly-scented, creamy-white flowers, which are followed by elliptical, blue-black berries.
3-ft., January-March. E. 4-ft. Sq. Sd10. A.

S. Hookeriana var. digyna (With two styles) W. China, is more slender in growth, has flowers of pale flesh-pink, and larger berries to succeed them. *3-ft., January-March. E. 4-ft. Sq. Sd10. A.*

S. humilis (Of low growth) W. China, is another tiny with upright and dense growth, fully furnished with small, oval leaves, enlivened with many small, white, fragrant flowers followed by black fruits.
1-ft., February-March. E. 1½-ft. Sq. Sd10. A.

S. ruscifolia (With leaves resembling Butcher's Broom) C. China, has neat, erect growth and leaves reminiscent of Butcher's Broom, very sweetly-scented, five-petalled male and female flowers borne in the uppermost leaf axils, and followed by bright-red fruits.
3-ft., February-March. E. 3-ft. Sq. Sd10. A.

S. saligna var. angustifolia (Willow-like ; narrow-leaved) Himalayas, in common with the other varieties of the species, thrives best in a semi-shady site. Its long, willow-like leaves and purple-blue berries make it one of the most attractive of all.

2-ft.–3-ft., February-March. E. 3-ft. Sq. Sd10. A.

SATUREIA (LABIATAE) (IS DERIVED FROM THE OLD LATIN NAME FOR SAVORY).

A group of dwarf and attractive shrubs related to the Hyssop, and propagating from cuttings of the stem in June. It is at home in any soil.

S. MONTANA (Of the mountains) Europe, is the Winter Savory, a leaf-losing shrub with white or pale-lilac, broad-lipped flowers produced in the uppermost leaf axils in dense heads. The whole plant is pleasantly aromatic and well worth a place at the front of any shrub garden. *1¼-ft., July-August. D. 1½-ft. Sq. Cg6. ANC.*

SCHIZANDRA (MAGNOLIACEAE) (FROM THE GR. SCHIZO—TO CUT; AND ANDRES—ANTHERS; I.E., WITH SPLIT STAMENS).

A group of climbing shrubs of vigorous growth, related to the Magnolia and well suited to growing upon well-sheltered, shady walls. They are propagated from cuttings of the half-ripened wood taken in July.

S. CHINENSIS (Chinese) China, is a fine climber with red branches, long, elliptical leaves, and clusters of sweetly-scented, pale-rose flowers followed, in the case of the females, by scarlet fruits, which add considerably to its charm.

Indefinite, April-May. D. Indefinite. Cg7. ANC.

S. GLAUCESCENS (Somewhat glaucous) C. China, has leaves somewhat grey-green, and orange-red flowers followed by similar fruits.

Indefinite, April-May. D. Indefinite. Cg7. ANC.

S. PROPINQUA (Related) W. China, is the hardiest of the species, is evergreen and has dark-green, spear-shaped leaves and orange-yellow flowers followed by scarlet fruits.

6-ft.–8-ft., July. E. 6-ft.–8-ft. Sq. Cg7. A.

SENECIO (COMPOSITAE) (FROM THE LATIN SENEX—AN OLD MAN; THE APPEARANCE OF THE SEED RECEPTACLE SUGGESTING A BALD HEAD).

The genus Senecio is a vast one containing a host of personable herbaceous plants, a number of attractive shrubs and a mass of undesirable weeds. The following, which can be accepted with some pleasure, may be propagated from cuttings of the half-ripened wood, taken in July or August. All can be grown with ease in any good garden soil and are indubitably hardy only in seaside districts, though elsewhere they may be kept going from the cuttings, which root with celerity.

S. COMPACTUS (Compact) N. Zealand, makes a wide bush of about two feet or so in height, with neat, silvery, serrated leaves and heads of yellow marguerite-like flowers produced well on into the autumn.

2-ft., August-September. E. 3-ft.–4-ft. Sq. Cg7. ANC.

S. Monroi (Comm.) N. Zealand, has smaller, crinkly-edged, oval leaves, greyish-green towards the sky, silvery below, and in their way as sound and as beautiful a plant as the other members of this genus. *2½-ft., June-September. E. 4½-ft. Sq. Cg7. ANC.*

SKIMMIA (Rutaceae) (from a Japanese name skimmi—the name for an indigenous species).

The members of the genus are of easy culture in good garden soil, thriving in shady positions and bearing male and female flowers upon separate plants, so that it is necessary to plant members of both sexes if one is to be rewarded by the berries which comprise the chief beauty of the plant, and which appear to be completely distasteful to British birds. Cuttings root readily in June and July, and seed will produce plants of both sexes.

S. Foremanii (Comm.) Garden origin, is a hybrid of S. Fortunei with S. japonica, and is noted for its larger, smoother, evergreen leaves and its bright, scarlet berries. *2-ft., April. E. 2-ft. Sq. Cg7. ANC.*

S. Fortunei (Comm.) China, has dark-green leaves, small, sweetly-scented, white flowers, and is a hermaphrodite species freely producing its large, deep-crimson berries.
2-ft., April. E. 2-ft. Sq. Cg7. ANC.

S. japonica (Japanese) Japan, is still larger, with aromatic foliage and similar, small, white, fragrant flowers followed by clusters of bright-red fruits. The variety Veitchii is a hybrid combining both sexes, with dark-green, oval, glossy leaves and coral-red fruits following its small, white flowers.
3-ft.–4-ft., April. E. 4-ft.–8-ft. Sq. Cg7. ANC.

SOLANUM (Solanaceae) (derived from the old Latin name for the nightshade ; possibly connected with L. solor—to soothe ; a reference to the narcotic properties of some of the species).

S. aviculare (Liked by birds) New Zealand, is a particularly handsome climber with digitate, green leaves, and flowers of bluish purple borne in loose sprays reminiscent of the flowers of the Potato. *Climber, June-July. E. Indefinite. Sd2. Cg7. ANC.*

S. crispum (Curled) Chile, is another fine, partially climbing shrub, sometimes evergreen, with large, open clusters of bluish-purple flowers with yellow eyes. Best grown in the protection of a wall, it provides a most attractive picture during the summer and early autumn. S. crispum var. autumnale is slightly more graceful in growth and has deeper flowers with a prolonged season of flowering.
10-ft.–15-ft., June-August. DE. Indefinite. Sd2. Cg7. ANC.

S. jasminoides (Jasmine-flowered) Brazil, grows fast and closely resembles S. crispum, with flowers of blue-grey. It is also available in the form which is more properly S. jasminoides var. album, with flowers of white, and both varieties are admirably suited to growing in the shelter of a south or south-westerly wall.
Climber, June-November. DE. Indefinite. Sd2. Cg7. ANC.

SOLLYA (PITTOSPORACEAE) (IS NAMED AFTER R. H. SOLLY, AN ENGLISH NATURALIST).

S. HETEROPHYLLA (With leaves of variable shape) Australia, is a very tender, slender, twining shrub with pale-blue flowers borne in small, nodding clusters, sometimes known as the Australian Bluebell. It can be propagated from cuttings of the half-ripened wood, taken during July or August and kept during the winter in the shelter of a warm house. *Climber, June-August. D. Cg7–8. ANC.*

SOPHORA (LEGUMINOSAE) (DERIVED FROM AN ARABIC NAME).

A group of large shrubs or small trees with pinnate leaves and pea-shaped or tubular flowers, and may be regarded as being hardy in the south and west when grown in a sunny position in good, rich soil.

S. TETRAPTERA (Four-winged) New Zealand, is also known as Edwardsia grandiflora, and in the open is a small tree of ten feet or so, with pinnately-divided, green leaves and sprays of tubular, golden-yellow flowers hanging in some profusion. S. tetraptera var. microphylla differs only in its somewhat smaller leaflets and smaller flowers.
10-ft.–12-ft., May-June. E. 10-ft.–12-ft. Sq. Cg7. ANC.

S. VICIIFOLIA (With leaves like Vetch) is a deciduous shrub of much-branched growth, bearing small pinnate leaves and hanging clusters of violet-blue and white pea flowers at the tips of the shoots. To be seen at its best it should be grown in a reasonably sheltered site. *4-ft.–8-ft., June. D. 4-ft.–8-ft. Sq. Cg7. ANC.*

SORBUS (ROSACEAE) (IS DERIVED FROM THE LATIN SORBUS—NAME FOR THE SERVICE TREE).

Comprises a group of small trees, generally distinguished by their white flowers and red or yellow berry-like fruits, and propagated from the seed which they produce with some freedom. *Pl.67.*

S. AMERICANA (American) Eastern N. America, is the American Mountain Ash, which will reach thirty feet in height, has a neat head, and bears ash-grey leaves made up of eleven to seventeen leaflets. Attractive when it bears its large groups of bright-red fruits and equally so when the red, gummy buds make their appearance in the spring. *30-ft., May. D. 30-ft. Sq. Sd2. ANC.*

S. AUCUPARIA (Bird-catching) Siberia, Europe, is the well-known Mountain Ash, rising sometimes to as much as fifty feet, but more generally a much smaller tree. Its variety Fifeana is similar, with habit a little more erect, and glorified in late summer and autumn by its clusters of bright-yellow fruits.
15-ft.–50-ft., May. D. 15-ft.–50-ft. Sq. Sd2. ANC.

S. COMMIXTA (Mixed) Japan, is a smaller tree with attractive, upright habit, dark-green leaves and brilliant-red fruits in large clusters late in the year. *15-ft.–25-ft., May. D. 10-ft.–18-ft. Sq. ANC.*

S. GRACILIS (Graceful) Japan, is a very slow-growing variety with small, pinnate leaves forming a dense coating, and proving a most fascinating setting to the clusters of pear-shaped, bright-orange fruits. *8-ft.–12-ft., May. D. 8-ft.–12-ft. Sq. Sd2. ANC.*

S. MUNDA VAR. SUBARACHNOIDEA (Lightly covered with spiders' webs) W. China, is also known as S. Prattii, and a beautifully shaped, small tree or large shrub with ferny leaves made up of a great number of tiny leaflets, bearing masses of pearly-white, large fruits. *10-ft.–15-ft., May. D. 10-ft.–15-ft. Sq. Sd2. ANC.*

SPARTIUM (LEGUMINOSAE) (FROM THE GR. SPARTION, MEANING SMALL CORD).

S. JUNCEUM (Rush-like) Spain, is the Spanish Broom, a magnificent shrub of erect habit, almost inconspicuous, tiny leaves, and clusters of large, fragrant, butter-yellow pea flowers in long, slender groups. It provides one of the most floriferous of all garden shrubs during the months of June, July, and August, and still further proves its imperturbability by flourishing in almost any soil. *5-ft.–10-ft., June-September. D. 5-ft.–10-ft. Sq. Sd2. ANC.*

SPIRAEA (ROSACEAE) (IS DERIVED FROM THE GR. SPEIRA—WREATH).

A group of deciduous shrubs, the Spiraea is outstanding for producing in the garden colour late in the year, and is generally indifferent as to the soil in which it grows. Propagation of the species is best from cuttings of the half-ripened wood, made in July, and seed will germinate readily when sown but will give rise to half a hundred hybrids.

S. AITCHISONII (Comm.) Afghanistan, is also known as Sorbaria Aitchisonii, and forms a nicely balanced, symmetrical shrub with pinnately-divided, green leaves, bearing at the tips of the shoots long sprays of fluffy, white flowers. *8-ft.–12-ft., July-August. D. 10-ft.–14-ft. Sq. Cg7. ANC. Pl.68.*

S. ARBOREA (Tree-like) W. China, is somewhat similar in appearance, with large leaves and long sprays of creamish, plumey flowers. S. arborea var. subtomentosa differs only botanically. *8-ft.–15-ft., July-August. D. 10-ft.–14-ft. Sq. Cg7. ANC.*

S. ARGUTA (Sharply serrated) Garden origin, is a hybrid of S. Thunbergii and S. multiflora, and is a neat, gracefully branching shrub bearing small heads of closely set, white flowers in wreath-like masses at the tops of the shoots of the previous year. *3-ft.–5-ft., April-May. D. 3-ft.–5-ft. Sq. Cg7. ANC.*

S. BELLA (Beautiful) Himalayas, bears small, compound clusters of bright-pink flowers neatly distributed upon rounded bushes which seldom exceed three feet in height. *3-ft., May. D. 3-ft.–4-ft. Sq. Cg7. ANC.*

S. BRACTEATA (Bearing bracts) Japan, is also S. nipponica, and is an outstanding variety of strong, bushy growth, completely wreathed with clusters of clear-white flowers borne in large composite groups. *6-ft.–8-ft., June. D. 6-ft.–8-ft. Sq. Cg7. ANC.*

SPIRAEA (continued)

S. BULLATA (Studded) Japan, is a small species of compact growth, often less than eighteen inches in height, and with flat heads of bright, rosy-crimson flowers.

1¼-*ft.*, *July*. *D*. 1½-*ft. Sq*. *Cg7*. *ANC*.

S. CANESCENS (Greyish-white) Himalayas, is a tall, elegant shrub with gracefully arching branches and large, flat clusters of creamy-white flowers. Its variety glaucophylla is distinguished by the outstanding greyness of the underside of the leaves.

8-*ft.*–10-*ft.*, *June*. *D*. 6-*ft.*–8-*ft. Sq*. *Cg7*. *ANC*.

S. DISCOLOR (Of two colours) N.W. America, which is also known as S. ariaefolia, is another variety of extra graceful habit, tall in growth and with far-flung plumes of creamy-white flowers. It has the advantage of colouring exquisitely in the late autumn.

6-*ft.*–12-*ft.*, *June-July*. *D*. 5-*ft.*–10-*ft. Sq*. *Cg7*. *ANC*.

S. DOUGLASII (Comm.) N.W. America, is an attractive variety reaching eight feet or so, with greenish leaves felted white upon the underside, and long, narrow sprays of deep-rose flowers produced in July and August.

8-*ft.*, *July-August*. *D*. 8-*ft. Sq*. *Cg7*. *ANC*.

S. JAPONICA (Japanese) Japan, is also S. callosa, and a tightly growing, bushy shrub, generally well rounded and covered with compound corymbs of pink flowers.

S. JAPONICA VAR. ALBA—is small, but has white flowers.
S. „ „ BUMALDA "ANTHONY WATERER" — is much dwarfer and continues to produce its flat, crimson flower heads for a long time. *Plates* 66 *and* 69.
S. „ „ ATROSANGUINEA—has deep-red flowers.
S. „ „ RUBERRIMA—has rosy-red flowers.

2-*ft.*–4-*ft.*, *June-September*. *D*. 2-*ft.*–4-*ft. Sq*. *Cg7*. *ANC*.

S. LINDLEYANA (Comm.) Himalayas, is a wide-spreading variety with ash-like leaves, very large sprays of white flowers, and is suited by a moist spot near the water, where it will make one of the best waterside plants.

12-*ft.*–15-*ft.*, *July-August*. *D*. 15-*ft.*–20-*ft Sq*. *Cg7*. *ANC*.

S. MACROTHYRSA (With long thyrses) Garden origin, is an attractive hybrid with fluffy, rose-pink flowers.

6-*ft.*, *June-July*. *D*. 6-*ft. Sq*. *Cg7*. *ANC*. *Pl*.66.

S. MARGARITAE (Comm.) Garden origin, is a hybrid of S. japonica, very largely resembling it with flowers of bright rose.

6-*ft.*, *July-September*. *D*. 6-*ft. Sq*. *Cg7*. *ANC*. *Pl*.69.

S. MENZIESII (Comm.) Western N. America, is best in the form known as var. triumphans, with long, broad sprays of bright and deep rose. 5-*ft.*–8-*ft.*, *June-September*. *D*. 5-*ft.*–8-*ft. Sq* *Cg7*. *ANC*.

Perowskia atriplicifolia

Phygelius capensis

S. PRUNIFOLIA VAR. PLENA (With plum-like leaves) China, makes a dense bush composed of slender, curved branches clothed with small oval leaves and groups of button-like flowers of clear white, made up of a large number of tiny petals.

5-ft.–8-ft., April-May. D. 5-ft.–8-ft. Sq. Cg7. ANC.

S. SORBIFOLIA (With leaves like Sorbus) Asia, has ash-like leaves borne upon strong, dwarf, freely running bushes, and differs from S. Aitchisonii mainly in its sharper, stiffer habit of growth.

3-ft.–6-ft., July-August. D. 6-ft.–8-ft. Sq. Suckers. ANC.

S. TRICHOCARPA (Bearing hairy fruits) Korea, is another graceful variety with arching branches which become wreathed with clusters of pure-white flowers.

5-ft.–7-ft., June-July. D. 5-ft.–7-ft. Sq. Cg7. ANC.

S. TRILOBATA (With three-lobed leaves) N. China, has leaves which have the appearance of those of the Gooseberry, and which are redeemed by the attractive clusters of small, clear-white flowers produced along the whole length of the shoots.

3-ft.–4-ft., June. D. 3-ft.–4-ft. Sq. Cg7. ANC.

S. VEITCHII (Comm.) China, combines grace of habit and distribution, wreathing its long, slender growths with symmetrically placed clusters of clear-white flowers.

6-ft.–10-ft., June-July. D. 6-ft.–10-ft. Sq. Cg7. ANC.

STACHYURUS (TERNSTROEMIACEAE) (FROM THE GR. STACHYS—AN EAR OF CORN ; AND OURA—A TAIL).

Both species, which flower before the leaves are produced, are easily grown and may be propagated from cuttings of the half-ripened wood placed in a warm sand frame in July.

S. CHINENSIS (Of Chinese origin) W. China, bears its yellow flowers in stiff, hanging sprays on the leafless branches in winter, and then presents a most picturesque sight.

6-ft.–8-ft., February-March. D. 6-ft.–7-ft. Sq. Cg7. ANC.

S. PRAECOX (Early) Japan, provides its flowers a trifle earlier than those of the foregoing and needs therefore a little extra protection.

6-ft.–8-ft., February-March. D. 6-ft.–7-ft. Sq. Cg7. ANC.

STAPHYLEA (STAPHYLEACEAE) (FROM THE GR. STAPHYLE—A BUNCH OF GRAPES).

A group of shrubs which, in the main, prefer sheltered conditions in rich, leafy soil. The flowers are, as a rule, small, but grouped in large clusters, and are followed by bladder-like fruits. Propagation is comparatively easy from cuttings of the half-ripened wood taken in July or August.

S. COLCHICA (From Colchis) Asia Minor, is a shrub of erect growth, leaves made up of five—occasionally three—leaflets, with clusters of upright, white flowers, and is probably the best of the white-flowered species.

5-ft.–8-ft., May. D. 5-ft.–8-ft. Sq. Cg7–8. N.

STAPHYLEA (continued)

S. HOLOCARPA (With entire fruits) China, is probably just as beautiful and more rare, but is completely outshone by its variety S. holocarpa rosea with flowers of pleasing pink.

5-ft.–8-ft., May. D. 5-ft.–8-ft. Sq. Cg7–8. N.

STEPHANANDRA (ROSACEAE) (FROM THE GR. STEPHANOS—A CROWN ; AND ANDRES—STAMENS).

Two shrubs of medium size, related to the Spiraeas, with small, greenish-white flowers in loose terminal sprays, but which are grown mainly for their very pleasing leaf colour in the autumn. Both are freely propagated from cuttings of the half-ripened wood taken in August or September.

S. INCISA (Deeply cut) Japan, has deeply lobed leaves, gracefully held upon weeping branches, and colours pleasantly during the autumn.

8-ft., June. D. 8-ft.–10-ft. Sq. Cg8–9. ANC.

S. TANAKAE (Comm.) Japan, has three-lobed, triangular, large, bronzy-green leaves which ultimately colour brilliantly before they fall. *8-ft., June. 8-ft.–10-ft. Sq. Cg8–9. ANC.*

STEWARTIA (TERNSTROEMIACEAE) (NAMED IN HONOUR OF JOHN STEWART, EARL OF BUTE).

They can be freely grown in lime-free soils, preferably where, during establishment, their roots are shaded from the worst effects of the sun. They resemble in growth the Camellia, and are useful because they flower at a time when flowers are rare. Probably the conditions most suitable are those which suit the Rhododendron. Propagation can be made from layers or from cuttings taken in July or August, and placed in sandy peat in a warm cutting frame.

S. KOREANA (From Korea) Korea, is a deciduous, small tree, probably not less than fifteen feet in height, with white Camellia-like flowers centred by golden-tipped stamens, and adding to this beauty in the autumn by colouring its leaves before they fall.

15-ft., June-July. D. 15-ft. Sq. Cg7. ANC.

S. PENTAGYNA (With five styles) South-Eastern U.S.A., is a delightful, large shrub with big, creamy-white flowers centred by clusters of yellow stamens. S. pentagyna var. grandiflora has flowers which are delicately fringed and centred by purple stamens.

6-ft.–12-ft., July-August. D. 6-ft.–12-ft. Sq. Cg7. L5.

S. PSEUDO-CAMELLIA (False Camellia) Japan, is a shrub of conical shape with large, five-petalled, cup-shaped flowers enclosing innumerable golden-yellow stamens, and colours brilliantly in the autumn.

8-ft.–15-ft., July-August. D. 8-ft.–15-ft. Sq. Ch8. AN.

S. SINENSIS (Of Chinese origin) China, is an exceptional species with flattened boughs, many branches clad with serrated, tomentose, elliptical leaves, and smaller, saucer-shaped flowers of clear white, enlivened by its golden stamens. Add to these merits those of the dying splendour of its foliage as it passes, and S. sinensis provides one of the finest of the smaller trees.

15-*ft.*, *June-July*. *D*. 15-*ft*. *Sq*. *Ch*8. *AN*.

STRANVAESIA (ROSACEAE) (THE NAME COMMEMORATES W. F. STRANGWAYS, AN ENGLISH BOTANIST).

The genus comprises a group of small trees related to and bearing some resemblance to the Hawthorn. S. Davidiana is the best known of the species, which quickly attains small tree size, as does S. lucida and S. Nussia. Propagation may be freely effected from seeds.

S. SALICIFOLIA (With willow-like leaves) W. China, has dark-green leaves like those of the Willow, lightly grey-green on the reverse side, and bears flat heads of white, hawthorn-like flowers, which are replaced by clusters of bright-red fruits whose riot of colour is amplified by the brightening of some of the persistent leaves to tones of orange, crimson, and scarlet.

8-*ft*.–12-*ft*., *May-June*. *E*. 8-*ft*.–12-*ft*. *Sq*. *Sd*2. *ANC*.

S. UNDULATA (Waved) W. and C. China, is a fine dwarf, the outstanding characteristics of which are its bright stems, its flat heads of white flowers and its vivid, orange-red berries.

3-*ft*.–4-*ft*., *May-June*. *E*. 3-*ft*.–4-*ft*. *Sq*. *Sd*2. *ANC*.

STYRAX (STYRACACEAE) (THE NAME IS DERIVED FROM AN OLD ARABIC ONE).

A genus of deciduous shrubs related to Halesia, and commonly called the Snowdrop Trees. All the species grow best in lime-free soils composed of sandy loam with some leafmould or peatmould. They may be propagated from the seeds which they produce or from cuttings of the stem of half-ripened wood with a slight heel, taken in July and August and carefully potted on.

S. AMERICANUS (American) Virginia, is the American Storax, suited only to the milder parts of the country, and resembles the so-called Japanese Snowdrop Tree, but has oval leaves slightly felted, and up to three inches in length, and small, hanging clusters of drooping, white flowers giving the impression of narrow-petalled snowdrops.

6-*ft*.–10-*ft*., *June-July*. *D*. 6-*ft*.–10-*ft*. *Sq*. *Cg*7. *AN*.

S. DASYANTHUS (Having woolly flowers) China, has shining, widely oval leaves and small clusters of pendulous, white flowers borne at the tips of the shoots.

6-*ft*.–12-*ft*., *July*. *D*. 6-*ft*.–12-*ft*. *Sq*. *Cg*7. *AN*. *Shelter*.

S. JAPONICUS (Japanese) Japan, is the Snowdrop Tree, a splendid small tree which will reach ten feet or more, with pointed, oval leaves of dark, shining green, and hanging five-petalled flowers borne at the ends of the small side shoots. A particularly graceful and beautiful tree, it flourishes in those places where it is not struck by the rays of the sun too early in the day.

10-*ft*.–15-*ft*., *June-July*. *D*. 10-*ft*.–15-*ft*. *Sq*. *Sd*2. *Cg*8. *AN*.

SYCOPSIS (Hamamelidaceae) (from the Gr. sykon—a fig; and opsis—like; a reference to the shape of the fruit).

A shrub allied to Hamamelis, suited by the same conditions and propagating readily from cuttings of the half-ripened wood with a heel, taken in July. It is best grown in a shaded site.

S. sinensis (Of Chinese origin) China, is a wide-based shrub with dark-green leaves and red-brown and yellow flowers, the bracts being red-brown and the stamens yellow.
5-ft.–8-ft., February-March. E. 5-ft.–8-ft. Sq. Cg7. AN.

SYMPHORICARPUS (Caprifoliaceae) (from the Gr. symphoreo—to gather; and karpos—fruit; a reference to the clustered fruits of some of the species).

A group of shrubs of hardy characteristics, grown for the benefit of their white, or occasionally coloured, berries, and growing well in any soil. They can be propagated from the seeds they freely produce or from cuttings of the half-ripened wood made in July. Certain varieties may also be divided.

S. albus (White) N. America, is also S. racemosus, a name by which it is probably better known, with oval leaves resembling those of the Honeysuckle and pinkish-white bell-flowers followed by snow-white berries. The variety laevigatus is similar but has berries which are even larger.
7-ft.–10-ft., June-July. D. 7-ft.–10-ft. Sq. Sd2. Cg7. D3. ANC.

S. orbiculatus (Circular) N. America, is the Indian Currant or Coral-berry, with dull-white flowers, oval, dark-green leaves and pinkish-purple fruits borne throughout the winter.
5-ft.–6-ft., August-September. D. 5-ft.–6-ft. Sq. Sd2. Cg7. ANC.

SYRINGA (Oleaceae) (is derived from the Gr. syringx—a tube; from the hollow stems of some of the species).

Syringa is the botanical name for Lilac, a group of shrubs of outstanding beauty and a very large measure of popularity which is undoubtedly deserved. Most of the species grow well in any good garden soil, but appreciate a rich soil when it is available. The hybrids are best if they can be obtained upon their own roots, and layers and hardwood cuttings present few difficulties. The species may be propagated from seed or in the same way.

S. amurensis (From Amur) China, is also known as S. siberica, and resembles S. pekinensis, with ovate, smooth leaves and loose sprays of small, yellowish-white flowers freely borne during May and June.
8-ft.–10-ft., May-June. D. 8-ft.–10-ft. Sq. Sd2. Ch6. L5. ANC.

S. chinensis (Chinese) Garden origin, is better known as the Rouen Lilac and is a hybrid of S. vulgaris with S. persica, is a moderately dwarf variety of compact, branching growth with graceful sprays of carelessly disposed, drooping flowers of lilac. The varieties are alba with white flowers, metensis with lilac-pink flowers, and rubra with flowers of reddish-lilac.

6-*ft.*–8-*ft.*, *May-June*. *D*. 6-*ft.*–8-*ft. Sq*. *Ch*7. *L*5. *ANC.*

S. Emodi (Comm.) Himalayas, is a strong-growing variety with large, oval, smooth, green leaves, greyish-white upon the undersides, and dense heads of pale-mauve flowers eventually fading to white.

8-*ft.*–12-*ft.*, *June*. *D*. 8-*ft. Sq*. *Cg*7. *L*5. *ANC.*

S. japonica (Japanese) Japan, can become a small tree when suited in a warm, sheltered spot, which it will embellish with the beauty of conical heads of white flowers.

12-*ft.*–20-*ft.*, *June-July*. *D*. 12-*ft.*–20-*ft. Sq*. *Sd*2. *Ch*7. *L*5. *ANC.*

S. Josikaea (Comm.) Transylvania, is the Hungarian Lilac, with large, oval, shining, green leaves, grey beneath, and large sprays of deep-lilac flowers produced at the terminals.

8-*ft.*–12-*ft.*, *May*. *D*. 8-*ft.*–12-*ft. Sq*. *Sd*2. *Ch*7. *L*5. *ANC.*

S. Julianae (Comm.) W. China, is a symmetrical shrub with privet-like leaves, felted upon both sides, and sweetly-scented, lilac-grey flowers produced in small, upright sprays.

6-*ft.*, *May-June*. *D*. 6-*ft. Sq*. *Sd*2. *Ch*7. *L*5. *ANC.*

S. Komarowii (Comm.) W. China, is also known as S. Sargentiana, has ovate to oval, deep-green, corrugated leaves, and large, nodding, terminal sprays of lilac-pink flowers.

8-*ft.*–10-*ft.*, *May-June*. *D*. 8-*ft.*–10-*ft. Sq*. *Cg*7. *L*5. *ANC.*

S. persica (Persian) is probably a native of China and is a neat, much-branched shrub with slender stems, small, narrow leaves, gay with small sprays of lilac-coloured flowers in May.

4-*ft.*–6-*ft.*, *May*. *D*. 4-*ft.*–6-*ft. Sq*. *Sd*2. *Ch*7. *ANC*. *Pl*.72.

S. reflexa (Bent back) Central China, has enormous, oblong, green leaves, strong growth, and large, wind-swept, drooping sprays of deep-pink flowers making a picture of considerable grace in the month of June.

6-*ft.*–15-*ft.*, *June*. *D*. 6-*ft.*–12-*ft. Sq*. *Sd*2. *Ch*7. *L*5. *ANC.*

S. Sweginzowii (Comm.) W. China, is a shrub of slender growth with ovate, wavy, green leaves and very sweetly-scented, loose sprays of flesh-pink flowers.

6-*ft.*–10-*ft.*, *May-June*. *D*. 6-*ft.*–10-*ft. Sq*. *Sd*2. *Ch*7. *L*5. *ANC.*

S. tomentella (Finely felted) W. China, is also known as S. Wilsonii, and is a vigorous species with oval, pointed leaves, felted on the underside, and sweetly-scented, pink flowers in large, compact sprays.

6-*ft.*–8-*ft.*, *May-June*. *D*. 6-*ft.*–8-*ft. Sq*. *Sd*2. *Ch*7. *L*5. *ANC.*

S. vulgaris (Common) E. Europe, is the sweetly-scented Common Lilac of gardens.

S. vulgaris var. alba—has single, white flowers. (Single.)

S. „ „ Charles Joly—is a variety with double, dark-red flowers. (Double.)

SYRINGA (continued)

S. VULGARIS VAR. CHARLES X—a charming variety which has flowers of deep, purplish-lilac. (Single.)

S. „ „ CONDORCET—has enormous flowers of lavender. (Semi-double.)

S. „ „ CONGO—has compact sprays of reddish-purple flowers. (Single.)

S. „ „ HUGO KOSTER—is a variety with flowers of purplish-crimson. (Single.)

S. „ „ J. C. VAN TOL—has loose sprays of pure-white flowers. (Single.)

S. „ „ LAVANENSIS—has flowers of pale-pink. (Single.)

S. „ „ LEMOINEI FLORE PLENO—produces light, mauve-pink flowers. (Double.) *Pl.71.*

S. „ „ L'ONCLE TOM—has sprays of dark-crimson flowers. (Single.)

S. „ „ MADAME FRANCISQUE MOREL—has very long sprays of lovely, violet-pink flowers. (Single.) *Pl.70.*

S. „ „ MADAME LEMOINE—a very popular, double, white-flowered variety. (Double.)

S. „ „ MICHAEL BUCHNER—has flowers of pale, rosy-lilac. (Double.)

S. „ „ MISS ELLEN WILLMOTT—produces large panicles of pure-white flowers. (Double.)

S. „ „ MONT BLANC—the white flowers are produced in very long trusses. (Single.)

S. „ „ SOUVENIR DE L. SPATH—a beautiful variety with flowers of dark-crimson. (Single.)

S. „ „ VIRGINITÉ—has flowers of pale pink. (Double.)

S. WOLFII (Comm.) N. China, makes a symmetrical bush of erect contour with large, crinkled, green leaves, and outstandingly beautiful sprays of mauve flowers, prinked up by protruding yellow anthers.

8-ft.–10-ft., May-June. D. 6-ft.–8-ft. Sq. Sd2. Ch7. ANC.

S. YUNNANENSIS (From Yunnan) China, is of upright, symmetrical growth, bears large, deep-green, netted, pointed, oval leaves, and wide sprays of pale-pink flowers which pass to white as they age.

8-ft.–10-ft., June. D. 6-ft.–8-ft. Sq. Sd2. Ch7. ANC.

TAMARIX (TAMARICACEAE) (FROM TAMARIS, A RIVER IN SPAIN ASSOCIATED WITH THE DISCOVERY OF ONE OF THE PLANTS).

The genus is generally found in districts near the coast, sometimes swept by salt spray, and inland requires to be planted in really moist places. It can be freely propagated from cuttings of the hard wood, at least of full season's age, buried to a half or one-third of its length in suitably moist loam. The general features of the genus are the graceful, slender branches clad with small, heather-like leaves, and the large sprays of small, pink or white flowers with four or five petals.

T. ANGLICA (English) W. Europe, has bright-green, tiny leaves and minute, white flowers tinted with pink, borne in small but very graceful sprays.

3-ft.–8-ft., August-October. E. 3-ft.–8-ft. Sq. Ch10. AN.

T. GALLICA (Of French origin) Mediterranean region, differs but very little from T. anglica, and may be regarded for garden purposes as being synonymous.

3-ft.–8-ft., August-October. E. 3-ft.–8-ft. Sq. Ch10. AN.

T. HISPIDA (With stiff hairs) E. Europe, is a dwarf species with grey-green, feathery leaves and sprays of pink flowers, and should be cosseted in a sheltered place.

3-ft.–4-ft., August-September. D. 3-ft.–4-ft. Sq. Ch7. AN.

T. PENTANDRA (With five stamens) S.E. Europe, is a very strong, tall-growing variety which becomes a frothy mass of soft, pink flowers late in the year, making one of the finest of all the late-flowering shrubs. *12-ft., August-September. D. 8-ft. Sq. Ch10. AN.*

T. TETRANDRA (With four anthers) S. Europe, is a May-flowering variety with very small, bright-pink flowers borne in long, slender, much-branched sprays.

12-ft., May. D. 8-ft.–10-ft. Sq. Ch10. AN.

TECOMA (BIGNONIACEAE) (THE NAME IS SAID TO BE A CONTRACTION OF THE MEXICAN NAME TECOMAXOCHILI).

A group of climbing shrubs suited best by sheltered, southern walls, with clusters of gloxinia-like flowers borne late in the year. Members of the species are eminently suited to growth upon a south or west wall, and may be freely propagated from cuttings of the green wood, taken in the early autumn and given gentle bottom heat. The genus is sometimes known as Campsis, and of all the species only T. radicans can be regarded as in common cultivation.

T. RADICANS (Rooting) N. America, is a climber which will readily grip a wall, which it will decorate with its bright-green, pinnate leaves resembling those of the Ash, and in late summer will bear its clusters of five-lipped, fiery flowers of bright, orange-red, pale-yellow on the outside. It will exceed twenty-five feet in height when well suited.

10-ft.–25-ft., August-September. D. Indefinite. Cg7. ANC.

TEUCRIUM (LABIATAE) (NAMED AFTER TEUCER, A TROJAN PRINCE WHO USED MEMBERS OF THE GENUS MEDICINALLY).

T. FRUTICANS (Bush-like) S. Europe, has woolly stamens, grey-green leaves, and produces its lavender flowers with their enlarged lower lips for a long period, but is not sufficiently hardy to be grown except in a sheltered spot.

3-ft., June-October. E. 3-ft. Sq. Cg7. ANC.

TRACHELOSPERMUM (APOCYNACEAE) (FROM THE GR. TRACHELOS—NECK; AND SPERMA—A SEED; A REFERENCE TO THE NARROW SEED PODS).

This is a group of tender climbers, suited only to the sheltered wall, with leaves like those of the Periwinkle and flowers of the same shape. They are easily grown in light, peaty loam and can be relied upon to root readily from cuttings of the half-ripened wood placed in sandy peat.

T. ASIATICUM (Asiatic) Japan, is also T. crocostomum and T. divaricatum, and bears deep-cream, sweetly-scented flowers with yellow eyes in loose sprays at the ends of the shoots.
10-*ft.*–15-*ft.*, *July-August.* *E.* *Indefinite.* *Cg*7. *AN.*

T. JASMINOIDES (Resembling Jasmine) China, has similar, shining, green vine leaves and sprays of delightfully-scented, white flowers, a little larger and with petals turned back at the edges.
10-*ft.*, *July-August.* *E.* *Indefinite.* *Cg*7. *AN.*

TRICUSPIDARIA (TILIACEAE) (DERIVED FROM THE LATIN TRI—THREE; AND CUSPIS—A POINT; FROM THE THREE-POINTED PETALS).

Often known as Crinodendron, these large shrubs are best suited by lime-free soils in sheltered positions, and may be propagated from cuttings of the half-ripened wood, three to four inches in length, taken and placed in a warm sand frame in July.

T. DEPENDENS (Hanging down) Chile, is a strong-growing shrub or small tree with deep-green, elliptical leaves and white, bell-shaped flowers upon long stems, produced singly in the leaf axils.
6-*ft.*–12-*ft.*, *August-October.* *E.* 6-*ft.*–12-*ft. Sq.* *Cg*7. *AN.*

T. LANCEOLATA (Like a lancet) Chile, is hardy in the extreme south and west, and has deep-green, elliptical, pointed leaves and bears its quaint hanging flowers of sealing-wax red upon long red stems each from a leaf axil.
6-*ft.*–12-*ft.*, *May-August.* *E.* 6-*ft.*–12-*ft. Sq.* *Cg*7. *AN.* *Pl.*79.

ULEX (LEGUMINOSAE) (FROM THE OLD LATIN NAME FOR THE GORSE—ULEX).

For covering bare banks of poor, sandy soil nothing could be more appropriate than the native Furze, which will bespangle any open and dry situation with much fine gold for many a month. Propagation should be from cuttings of the current year's growth, potted singly in small pots and kept close throughout the winter. They will be found to be rooted in the following spring.

U. EUROPAEUS (European) is the Common (but beautiful) Gorse. U. europaeus var. plenus doubles its flowers and proves just as hardy and as charming.
2-*ft.*–5-*ft.*, *March-June.* *E.* 2-*ft.*–8-*ft. Sq.* *Cg*7–8. *NC.*

Piptanthus nepalensis BCGHKL

Potentilla fruticosa
var. Veitchii AEJNORS

Potentilla fruticosa
DMPQTU

Prunus (Cerasus) Lannesiana ABCDEGH
Cydonia Maulei EFJ
Pyrus floribunda var. atrosanguinea KLMNOPQ

U. NANUS (Small) W. Europe, is a little fellow which in nature is prostrate but waxes bigger and stronger under the benefits of cultivation, but seldom then gets beyond a modest eighteen inches, and literally gilds itself with golden-yellow flowers in the late summer.

1-ft.–1½-ft., July-September. E. 3-ft. Sq. Cg7–8. ANC.

VACCINIUM (VACCINIACEAE) (THE NAME IS OF DOUBTFUL ORIGIN, BUT WAS APPLIED BY VIRGIL TO A PLANT WITH BLACK BERRIES, AND IT IS SUGGESTED IT MAY HAVE BEEN DERIVED FROM THE LATIN BACCINEUM, A LITTLE BERRY—REFERRING TO THE FRUIT OF THE SPECIES).

Vaccinium is a group of evergreen or deciduous shrubs which thrive upon moist, peaty soils, and are notable among other reasons for their attractive autumn foliage.

V. BRACTEATUM (Bracted) China, is an evergreen shrub with shining, narrow, oval, deep-green leaves, red while young, with short sprays of egg-shaped, white flowers, heavily set with bracts and emitting a sweet scent. It is best suited by a somewhat shaded site.

5-ft., July-October. E. 3-ft.–5-ft. Sq. Cg7. AN.

V. CAESPITOSUM (Tufted) N. America, is the dwarf Bilberry, has narrow, rounded, wedge-shaped leaves and small, solitary, pink, bell-flowers, drawn in tightly at the mouths, and followed by edible, blue-black berries. *½-ft., May. D. 1½-ft. Sq. Sd2. AN.*

V. CILIATUM (Fringed) Japan, has oval, green leaves with bristly margins and sprays of greenish-yellow, Lily-of-the-valley flowers tinged with red and set heavily with leaves which usually contrive to conceal the flowers. V. ciliatum var. glaucum differs only in the grey underside to it leaves.

3-ft.–5-ft., June. D. 3-ft.–5-ft. Sq. Sd2. AN.

V. CORYMBOSUM (Corymbose) N. America, is the Highbush Blueberry with bright-green, elliptical leaves up to one-third of an inch in length, fully clothing a dense, twiggy bush, and sprays of bell-shaped, pale-pink flowers, puckered at the mouth, and maturing to small, blue-black berries.

4-ft.–6-ft., May. D. 4-ft. Sq. Sd2. AN.

V. CRASSIFOLIUM (With thick leaves) U.S.A., is an admirable, dwarf shrub with small, oval, reddish-green leaves borne upon red stems, and bell-shaped flowers of reddish-pink.

½-ft., May. E. 1½-ft. Sq. Cg7. AN.

V. ERYTHROCARPUM (Red-fruited) N. America, is a deciduous species forming a bush of some five feet in height, with oval, pointed leaves up to three inches in length, and four-parted, pale-rose flowers borne singly in the leaf axils, and followed by red fruits which age to black-purple.

3-ft.–5-ft., June. E. 3-ft.–4-ft. Sq. Sd2. Cg7. AN.

V. HIRSUTUM (Hairy) N. Carolina, is the Hairy Huckleberry, with oval, felted, green leaves and short, dense clusters of bell-like flowers of white tinged with pink, replaced by purplish-black fruits.
2-ft.–3-ft., May-June. D. 3-ft. Sq. Sd2. C7. AN.

V. MORTINIA (Mortinia) Andes, is a dwarf evergreen shrub of up to three feet in height with shining, dark-green leaves up to one inch in length, which turn bronzy-red in winter, and pale-pink, bell-shaped flowers freely produced in dense clusters in the leaf axils.
2-ft.–3-ft., May. E. 3-ft. Sq. Cg7. A.

V. OVALIFOLIUM (With oval leaves) N. America, is an erect shrub with sharply-pointed, oval, grey-green leaves and small, solitary, translucent, pinkish-white flowers borne in the leaf axils, and purplish fruits. *2-ft.–3-ft., June. D. 2-ft.–3-ft. Sq. Sd2. AN.*

V. OVATUM (Egg-shaped) Western N. America, is a pretty, evergreen species with dark-green leaves, slightly exceeding an inch in length, and pale-pink, egg-shaped flowers in short sprays, followed in favoured places by bright-red fruits and beautiful autumn tints.
7-ft.–8-ft., June-July. E. 7-ft.–8-ft. Sq. Cg7. AN.

V. PARVIFOLIUM (With small leaves) Western N. America, is a neat shrub of erect habit with small, oval leaves, small, pink, globular flowers and minute red fruits, and is notable mainly for its bright-red colour in autumn.
5-ft.–7-ft., May-June. D. 3-ft.–5-ft. Sq. Cg7. AN.

V. PENNSYLVANICUM (Pennsylvanian) Eastern U.S.A., is the Lowbush Blueberry, a dwarf variety with elliptical, serrated leaves and pale-pink flowers, with blue-black fruits, and generally provides excellent autumn colour.
1-ft.–2-ft., April-September. D. 3-ft. Sq. Cg7. Sd2. AN.

V. STAMINEUM (Long-stamened) Eastern N. America, is also Polycodium stamineum and the Deerberry ; is outstanding in the open, bell-shaped form of its unusual, five-petalled, white flowers with protruding yellow stamens, borne in short, leafy sprays. The oval, green leaves, which are blue-grey beneath, assume the most glorious tones before they fall.
3-ft., May-June. D. 3-ft. Sq. Cg7. Sd2. AN.

V. VACILLANS (Swaying) Eastern N. America, is the Dryland Blueberry, and a neat shrub with oval, green leaves, grey-blue below, heavy, dense clusters of pale-pink, cylindrical flowers touched with red, replaced by small, blue-black berries.
2-ft.–3-ft., May. D. 3-ft. Sq. Cg7. Sd2. AN.

V. VIRGATUM (With willowy twigs) Eastern U.S.A., is the Rabbit-eye Blueberry, with glossy, narrow, green leaves, bluntly elliptical, and pale-pink flowers, about a third of an inch in length, in rather short, rounded sprays.
3-ft.–5-ft., April-May. D. 3-ft.–5-ft. Sq. Cg7. Sd2. AN.

V. VITIS-IDAEA (Vine from Mount Ida) N. America, is the Cowberry, and a low, diffuse species with shining, evergreen leaves, and terminal sprays of pinky-white, Lily-of-the-valley flowers, at home in a peaty soil in some shade.

1-ft., May. E. 3-ft. Sq. Sd2. Cg7. AN.

VERBASCUM (SCROPHULARIACEAE) (FROM THE LATIN BARBASCUM—BEARDED ; THE STAMENS OF THE FLOWERS BEING BEARDED).

V. SPINOSUM (Thorny) Crete, is an irregular, spiny bush with silver-grey-green leaves and sprays of small, yellow flowers typical of those of the herbaceous species, but with a grace seldom equalled in them.

1-ft., August-September. E. 1-ft. Sq. Ch5. N. 601.

VERONICA (SCROPHULARIACEAE) (THE DERIVATION IS OPEN TO CONSIDERABLE DOUBT, IT BEING SUGGESTED THAT IT MAY BE FROM HIERA EIKON, AN ALLUSION TO ST. VERONICA'S SACRED HANDKERCHIEF, HER NAME BEING IN ITS TURN DERIVED FROM PHERO-NIKE—BEARING VICTORY. SITTSTEIN SUGGESTS VERO-UNICA — TRULY UNIQUE. LINNAEUS GIVES VETONICA, AN ANCIENT ROMAN NAME FOR A PROVINCE OF SPAIN).

The genus HEBE, given to the shrubby and tree-like species from New Zealand, remains here but is distinguished by the letter (H) after the initial V.

The Veronicas are of easy cultivation in sunny positions in any good garden loam, and may be freely propagated from short lengths of the young, green wood placed in sandy soil in a close frame. The hybrids of V. speciosa are tender and are only fitted for coastal districts and very sheltered positions inland.

V. (H) ANGUSTIFOLIA (With narrow leaves) is a variety with narrow leaves up to three inches in length, and sprays of pale, lilac-white flowers in somewhat longer sprays than those of V. (H) parviflora.

3-ft.–6-ft., July-September. E. 3-ft.–6-ft. Sq. Cg5. ANC.

V. (H) ANOMALA (Irregular) New Zealand, is akin to V. buxifolia, with narrow, dark-green leaves and sprays of small, starry-white flowers with blue stamens.

3-ft.–5-ft., July-August. E. 3-ft.–5-ft. Sq. Cg5. ANC.

V. (H) ARMSTRONGII (Comm.) New Zealand, is a small, golden shrub with thin, whipcord-like stems, tightly clasped by the small, golden leaves, except at the tips, where the clusters of small, white flowers are borne. *1½-ft.–3-ft., July-August. E. 1-ft.–3-ft. Sq. Cg5. N.*

V. (H) BUXIFOLIA (With leaves like Box) New Zealand, has a close and compact habit, with dark-green, myrtle-like leaves and sprays of flowers resembling those of V. (H) anomala.

4-ft., July-August. E. 4-ft. Sq. Cg5. ANC.

V. (H) COLENSOI (Comm.) New Zealand, has oblong, sharply-pointed leaves, blue-grey when young, deepening with age to green, and small clusters of starry-white flowers.

1½-ft.–2-ft., July-August. E. 2-ft.–3-ft. Sq. Cg5. ANC.

V.(H) CUPRESSOIDES (Resembling Cypress) New Zealand, has tiny, scale-like leaves of bright-green arranged in rows of four about the stems, and bears clusters of small, white, or very pale-purple, flowers at the tips of the shoots. The whole plant is pleasantly aromatic of cedarwood.

1-ft.–3-ft., July-August. E. 1-ft.–3-ft. Sq. Cg5. ANC.

V. (H) ELLIPTICA (Elliptical) New Zealand, is one of the hardiest of the broad-leaved types, with upright, twiggy growth and pale-green leaves up to half an inch in width. It has the largest flowers of the species in groups of up to twelve in a cluster. V. Autumn Glory with small heads of violet-blue flowers probably belongs here.

2-ft.–3-ft., July-September. E. 2-ft.–3-ft. Sq. Cg5. ANC.

V. (H) HECTORI (Comm.) New Zealand, is an exceptionally curious shrub with stems thicker than those of V. (H) Armstrongii, more flattened, greener in colour and less dense in their production, with white, or sometimes pale-lilac, flowers.

1½-ft.–2-ft., August-September. E. 1½-ft.–2-ft. Sq. Cg7. ANC.

V. (H) HULKEANA (Comm.) New Zealand, must hold the palm as the loveliest of all shrubs, with spoon-shaped, serrated leaves and long, diffuse and slender sprays of lavender-blue flowers like a glamorised and refined Lilac. Thus it can be recommended that it may be planted in the company of such stalwarts as will protect it from the slings and arrows of outrageous fortune in whatever guise of wind and weather these may come.

2-ft.–6-ft., June-July. E. 2-ft.–4-ft. Sq. Cg5. AN. 437/1. *Pl.*3.

V. (H) KIRKII (Comm.) New Zealand, is also known as V. (H) salicifolia var. Kirkii, and is an exceptionally hardy, large-flowered species with willow-like leaves and lilac flowers in long sprays.

4-ft.–10-ft., July-August. E. 4-ft.–10-ft. Sq. Cg5. ANC.

V. (H) MACRANTHA (Large-flowered) New Zealand, is a dwarf evergreen with short, thick, bright-green leaves and rather bare legs, bearing clusters of very large, pure-white flowers at the tips of the shoots. It bears the largest flowers of any of the Veronicas, and, kept going from cuttings which root readily, provides one of the most attractive of the whole genus.

1-ft.–2-ft., June-July. E. 1-ft.–2-ft. Sq. Cg7. ANC.

V. (H) MACROCARPA (With large fruits) New Zealand, is another variety resembling V. (H) salicifolia, with longer and larger leaves and long spires of white flowers.

4-ft.–8-ft., July-August. E. 4-ft.–8-ft. Sq. Cg7. ANC.

V. (H) PARVIFLORA (With small flowers) New Zealand, is a particularly graceful, small shrub with thin, willowy leaves and short, gracefully-disposed sprays of pale-lilac flowers. It bears a close resemblance to V. (H) angustifolia, and, though it attains tree-like size at home, it can be either a very good small shrub or a good large one, according to the way it is treated and the location in which it is grown.

1-ft.–6-ft., July-September. E. -ft.–5-ft. Sq. Cg7. ANC.

Prunus Persica

Pyrus Malus

V. (H) PIMELEOIDES (Resembling Pimelea) New Zealand, is a semi-prostrate, small shrub with small, elliptical leaves of greyish-blue tone, with pale-lavender flowers.

1-ft., July-August. E. 2-ft. Sq. Cg7. ANC.

V. (H) PINGUIFOLIA (Greasy-leaved) New Zealand, is a small bush with a stilted appearance, pointed, spoon-shaped leaves of a delightful blue-grey tone, reddened at the edges, and which flowers so freely that the distribution of its white inflorescences gives it the appearance of snow. *1½-ft., July-August. E. 1½-ft. Sq. Cg8. ANC.*

V. (H) SALICIFOLIA (With leaves like Salix) New Zealand, is an erect-growing shrub with narrow, willow-like leaves of pale green, and slender spires of small, white flowers tinged with lilac, reaching five feet in height or more.

5-ft. and upwards, July-August. E. 5-ft.–8-ft. Sq. Cg7. ANC.

V. (H) SPECIOSA (Showy) New Zealand, has deep, shining, green leaves borne symmetrically on the stems, stout, erect branches and long, cylindrical sprays of flowers, generally in the type of reddish-purple. Its hybrids, however, have a vast range of blues, reds and purples, and are eminently suited to seaside districts or sheltered spots inland in the south and west.

V. (H) SPECIOSA VAR. "ALICIA AMHERST"—has flowers of deep, rich purple.
V. (H) ,, ,, COOKIANA—has white flowers.
V. (H) ,, ,, "DIAMENT"—has bright-crimson flowers.
V. (H) ,, ,, "GLORIOSA"—is bright-pink.
V. (H) ,, ,, "PURPLE QUEEN"—has bright-purple flowers.
V. (H) ,, ,, "SIMON DELEAUX"—has large flowers of rich crimson.

5-ft., July-September. E. 5-ft. Sq. Cg7. ANC.

V. (H) TETRASTICHA (Arranged in four vertical rows) New Zealand, is a very tiny species with heather-like leaves which clasp the stem in four distinct vertical rows, and bears flowers which, when they can be persuaded to appear, are small and white. This is an exceptionally attractive plant whose appearance alone is exciting.

½-ft., July-August. E. 1-ft. Sq. Cg7. ANC.

V. (H) TRAVERSII (Comm.) New Zealand, is a small shrub reaching five feet in height, with narrow, dull-green leaves neatly ranged in four distinct rows, and small, white flowers produced in small clusters from the axils of the uppermost leaves.

3-ft.–5-ft., July-August. E. 3-ft.–5-ft. Sq. Cg7. ANC.

VIBURNUM (CAPRIFOLIACEAE) (IS POSSIBLY DERIVED FROM THE LATIN VIERE—TO BEND; FROM THE PLIANT NATURE OF THE BRANCHES OF CERTAIN OF THE SPECIES).

Among the Viburnums may be numbered some of the most beautiful of the hardy, ornamental shrubs. All have attractive leaves and berries, and some have large, white flower heads. In addition they colour in the most amazing fashion in the declining months of the year, and present few difficulties in the matter of cultivation. They may be readily propagated from cuttings of the half-ripened wood, taken in July or August and placed in sandy soil in the shelter of a cold frame or north wall. Among the varieties selected for special mention are the following :—

V. ACERIFOLIUM (With leaves like Maple) Northern U.S.A., is a shrub reaching six feet in height with wide, maple-like leaves with coarse teeth, and almost negligible flowers followed by handsome, bright-red fruits turning black in autumn.

6-*ft.*, *May-June*. *D*. 6-*ft. Sq*. *Cg*7. *ANC*.

V. AFFINE VAR. HYPOMALACUM (Related; rather soft) U.S.A., is a leggy bush with a dense head of ovate, coarsely toothed leaves, smallish guelder roses of clear-white followed by bluish-black berries, and colouring brilliantly scarlet in the autumn.

6-*ft.*–8-*ft.*, *May-June*. *D*. 6-*ft.*–8-*ft. Sq*. *Cg*7. *ANC*.

V. ALNIFOLIUM (With leaves like Alder) Eastern N. America, is the Hobble-bush, reaching something in excess of five feet, clothed with round, irregularly toothed leaves about six inches in diameter, and bearing sessile heads of white flowers five inches across, margined with sterile flowers about the size of a halfpenny. It should be grown in shaded, sheltered conditions in a lime-free soil.

5-*ft.*–8-*ft.*, *May-June*. *D*. 5-*ft.*–8-*ft. Sq*. *Cg*7. *AN*.

V. BETULIFOLIUM (With leaves like Birch) China, is an upright growing type with ovate, toothed, birch-like leaves, and white flowers in short-stemmed clusters followed by bright-red fruits which weigh down the branches.

8-*ft.*–12-*ft.*, *June-July*. *D*. 6-*ft.*–8-*ft. Sq*. *Cg*7. *ANC*.

V. BITCHIUENSE (From Bitchiu) Japan, is also known as V. Carlesii var. syringiflorum, and resembles that variety with smaller, similar leaves and rather looser growth, bearing loose heads of pinky-white, sweetly-scented flowers.

5-*ft.*, *April-May*. *D*. 5-*ft. Sq*. *Cg*7. *ANC*.

V. BUDDLEIFOLIUM (With leaves like the Buddleia) China, has long, pale-green, oblong leaves, grey upon the underside, and clusters of white flowers, three inches in diameter, followed by groups of berries, at first red but ageing to black.

6-*ft.*–8-*ft.*, *May*. *DE*. 6-*ft.*–8-*ft. Sq*. *Cg*7. *ANC*.

V. BURKWOODII (Comm.) Garden origin, is a hybrid between V. Carlesii and V. utile, which grows into a well-rounded, much-branched bush, best pleased by a somewhat shady site, and carrying at the tips of the branches many clusters of sweetly-scented, tubular flowers. 4-*ft.*–6-*ft.*, *April-May*. *DE*. 4-*ft.*–6-*ft. Sq*. *Cg*7. *ANC*.

V. CARLESII (Comm.) Korea, has oval, toothed, felted leaves, dull-green above and grey beneath, turning bright-red in autumn, and forms a shrub of rounded outline, three to four feet in height. The flowers resemble those of V. fragrans, but are held in trusses of about three inches in diameter, of white tinged with a characteristic pink, and pervade the surrounding atmosphere with the scent of the carnation. Best suited to lime-free soils, V. Carlesii deserves a place in which it is sheltered from the worst excesses of wind and sun.

3-ft.–4-ft., April-May. D. 3-ft.–4-ft. Sq. Cg7. Gr. L5. AN.

V. CASSINOIDES (Resembling Cassinia) Newfoundland to N. America, is the Withe-rod, with oval, dark-green leaves, brightly coloured both in spring and autumn, and white flowers in large clusters, followed by wide groups of bright-red fruits eventually turning blue-black. *5-ft.–8-ft., June. D. 5-ft.–8-ft. Sq. Cg7. ANC.*

V. CINNAMOMIFOLIUM (With leaves like Cinnamon) N. China, has long, narrow, elliptical leaves, white flowers borne in tight clusters, and open sprays of small, dark-blue berries.

5-ft., June. E. 5-ft. Sq. Cg7. AN.

V. COTINIFOLIUM (With leaves like Sumach) Himalayas, is a splendid plant for a sheltered position near a wall, with green, rounded leaves, grey upon the underside, white flowers tinged with pink, egg-shaped fruits at first red, changing to black, and brilliantly coloured autumn foliage.

6-ft.–10-ft., May. D. 6-ft.–10-ft. Sq. Cg7. ANC.

V. CYLINDRICUM (Cylindrical) W. China, is a large shrub of rounded outline with large, elliptical, grey-green leaves covered with a waxy deposit, and white flowers with lilac anthers, followed by black fruits.

8-ft.–10-ft., July. E. 8-ft.–10-ft. Sq. Cg7. ANC.

V. DAVIDII (Comm.) W. China, is a low, compact, well-rounded bush with elliptical leaves, slightly toothed at the edges, whose outstanding beauty is the bright-blue fruits which follow the small, white flowers. Existing in two forms, it is necessary to plant both, in order that the fruits may be obtained.

2-ft.–3-ft., June. E. 3-ft.–5-ft. Sq. Cg7. Sd2. ANC.

V. DILATATUM (Extended) Japan, is a tall-growing species with rounded or oval, coarsely toothed leaves up to five inches in length, hairy upon both sides, many clusters of white flowers followed by its bright-red fruits.

5-ft.–8-ft., May-June. D. 5-ft.–8-ft. Sq. Cg7. Sd2. ANC.

V. FRAGRANS (Fragrant) N. China, is a grand shrub, generally at least five feet in height and sometimes double this, with oval, netted, toothed leaves, and small groups of pink buds opening to sweetly-scented, white, tubular flowers borne through the late winter.

5-ft.–10-ft., January-March. 3-ft.–6-ft. Sq. Cg7. ANC.

V. FURCATUM (Forked) China, is a variety related to the rarer V. alnifolium, of more upright growth, with large, rounded, rugged, crenate leaves, changing their colour before they fall.

5-ft., June. D. 5-ft. Sq. Cg7. AN.

V. HARRYANUM (Comm.) W. China, is a rounded, compact shrub with small, circular, leathery leaves and small, white flowers followed by bluish-black berries.

2-ft.–4-ft., June. E. 2-ft.–4-ft. Sq. Sd2. Cg7. ANC.

V. HENRYI (Comm.) Central China, is one of the finest of the berrying varieties with oblong, toothed, evergreen leaves, wide panicles of white flowers developing into bright-red, and finally black, berries, which weigh down the branches.

10-ft., June. E. 10-ft. Sq. Cg7. Sd2. ANC.

V. HUPEHENSE (From Hupeh) China, is an erect, branched shrub with green, coarsely toothed, ovate leaves, heavily covered with a thick down giving the appearance of greyness, and with small clusters of white flowers followed by shining, red fruits.

6-ft., June. D. 4-ft.–6-ft. Sq. Sd2. Cg7. ANC.

VIBURNUM FRAGRANS

V. JAPONICUM (Japanese) Japan, is an evergreen shrub with large, shining, ovate leaves and white, sweetly-scented flowers in flat clusters succeeded by red fruits.

6-ft.–8-ft., June. E. 6-ft.–8-ft. Sq. Cg7. ANC.

V. LANTANA (Old name) Europe, is the native Wayfaring Tree, notable among shrubs in the hedgerow for its clusters of bright-red fruits and deep-red leaves.

6-ft.–15-ft., May-June. D. 6-ft.–15-ft. Sq. Sd2. ANC.

V. LENTAGO (Tough) U.S.A., is the Sheep-berry, thirty feet high in nature but one-third of this height in cultivation, with oval, finely toothed, green leaves, and white flowers in wide heads followed in nature by blue-black berries.

6-ft.–10-ft., May-June. D. 6-ft.–10-ft. Sq. Sd2. Cg7. ANC.

V. LOBOPHYLLUM (With lobed leaves) W. China, has long, pointed, elliptical, green leaves, widely toothed, and wide heads of white flowers followed by shining, red fruits.
6-ft.–10-ft., May-June. D. 6-ft.–10-ft. Sq. Sd2. Cg7. ANC.

V. MACROCEPHALUM (Large-headed) China, is a rather tender, slow-growing shrub, suited only to sheltered positions, with wide, hanging heads of sterile flowers.
5-ft.–6-ft., May. DE. 5-ft.–6-ft. Sq. Cg7. ANC.

V. OPULUS (Old name) Northern hemisphere, is the native Guelder Rose with maple-like, green leaves, grey beneath, and white flowers in large clusters. The marginal ones are sterile and larger than the others, and succeeded by masses of bright-red fruits accompanying the brilliant autumn foliage. V. Opulus var. sterile is the Snowball Tree whose sterile flowers look like round snowballs dotted all over the bush. V. Opulus var. xanthocarpum is similar to V. Opulus but has yellow fruits.
5-ft.–10-ft., May-June. D. 5-ft.–10-ft. Sq. Cg7. Sd2 (except sterile). Pl.67.

V. PHLEBOTRICHUM (With hairy veins) Japan, has long, pointed, bronze-green, narrow, reticulated leaves, and white flowers followed by hanging clusters of crimson fruits.
6-ft.–10-ft., June. D. 6-ft.–10-ft. Sq. Cg7. Sd2. ANC.

V. PROPINQUUM (Related) China, is a compact, twiggy bush with dark, glossy, green, long, pointed leaves, paler on the underside, and greenish-white flowers followed by blue-black fruits.
3-ft.–5-ft., June. E. 3-ft.–5-ft. Sq. Sd2. Cg7. ANC.

V. PRUNIFOLIUM (With plum-like leaves) N. America, is a large shrub or small tree, sometimes reaching fifteen feet in height, known as the Black Haw, with white flowers, broad, oval, finely toothed leaves and dark-blue, plum-like fruits.
6-ft.–15-ft., June. D. 6-ft.–12-ft. Sq. Sd2. Cg7. ANC.

V. PUBESCENS (Slightly hairy) N. America, has rounded leaves, coarsely toothed and rather hairy, with long-stalked groups of white flowers occasionally followed by blue-black fruits.
4-ft.–6-ft., June. D. 4-ft.–6-ft. Sq. Cg7. Sd2. ANC.

V. RHYTIDOPHYLLUM (With leaves like the Poppy) Central China, is an exceptionally hardy, brilliant, evergreen shrub with long, deeply wrinkled, green leaves, shining above and grey below, and yellowish-white or pinkish-white flowers in wide heads, followed by red fruits turning with age to black. It is best grown in a sheltered site.
8-ft.–15-ft., May-June. E. 8-ft.–15-ft. Sq. Sd2. Cg7. ANC.

V. RIGIDUM (Stiff) Canary Isles, is a shrub for milder districts, with bright-green, heavily veined, hairy leaves, small, white flowers and bluish-black fruits, forming a large, symmetrical bush.
5-ft.–8-ft., March-May. E. 5-ft.–8-ft. Sq. Cg7. ANC.

VIBURNUM (continued)

V. RUFIDULUM (Pale-red) Southern U.S.A., has its young growth heavily powdered with rusty felt, has oval leaves, finely toothed and rusty felted on the underside, and wide corymbs of large, white flowers followed by blue berries.

5-*ft.*–10-*ft.*, *May-June.* *D.* 5-*ft.*–10-*ft.* *Sq.* *Sd2.* *Cg7.* *ANC.*

V. SARGENTII (Comm.) N. China, is a Guelder Rose with large, three-lobed leaves and wide clusters of creamy-white flowers surrounded by sterile flowers of a larger size, and brilliant, crimson fruits larger than any of the type. The foliage colours well in autumn and it is of comparatively easy growth.

6-*ft.*–10-*ft.*, *May-June.* *D.* 6-*ft.*–10-*ft.* *Sq.* *Cg7.* *Sd2.* *ANC.*

V. SIEBOLDII (Comm.) Japan, is also V. reticulatum, and a well-balanced shrub with glossy, dark-green leaves, unpleasant to the smell, and creamy-white flowers followed by pink fruits ultimately becoming blue-black.

6-*ft.*–8-*ft.*, *June.* *D.* 6-*ft.*–8-*ft.* *Sq.* *Sd2.* *Cg7.* *ANC.*

V. SUSPENSUM (Hanging down) Japan, has oval leaves, toothed towards the points and paler on the underside, and with small groups of tubular, sweetly-scented, pale-pink flowers produced in June and July.

4-*ft.*, *June-July.* *E.* 4-*ft.* *Sq.* *Cg7.* *ANC.*

V. TINUS (Old name) Mediterranean origin, is the Laurustinus, an evergreen shrub with dark-green, ovate, oblong leaves, producing with great regularity its flat clusters of pinkish buds, opening to sweetly-scented, white flowers during the winter months and early spring.

5-*ft.*–10-*ft.*, *November-April.* *E.* 5-*ft.*–10-*ft.* *Sq.* *Cg7.* *ANC.*

V. TOMENTOSUM (Felted) Japan, is a compact bush with ovate leaves and flattish flower heads up to four inches in diameter, with large, sterile flowers on the margins.

V. TOMENTOSUM VAR. MARIESII—has still more sterile flowers.
V. ,, ,, PLICATUM—has all its flowers of the sterile type, punctuating its branches with large, round flower heads of snowy white.
V. ,, ,, PLICATUM GRANDIFLORUM—has still larger sterile heads, but lacks a little in height.

5-*ft.*–8-*ft.*, *May-June.* *D.* 5-*ft.*–8-*ft.* *Sq.* *Cg7.* *ANC.*

V. UTILE (Useful) China, is a thin, open shrub of artistic disposition with dark, glossy, green leaves and small, fertile flowers followed by blue-black fruits.

6-*ft.*–8-*ft.*, *May.* *E.* 5-*ft.*–8-*ft.* *Sq.* *Cg7.* *ANC.*

V. WILSONII (Comm.) China, is a slender, graceful shrub with oval, dark-green leaves and small, pinkish-white, tubular flowers followed by dark-red fruits.

5-*ft.*–8-*ft.*, *June.* *D.* 4-*ft.*–7-*ft.* *Sq.* *Sd2.* *Cg7.* *ANC.*

VITIS (Vitaceae) (from the old Latin name for the vine).

A group of climbing plants, including Ampelopsis, invaluable for covering walls, rambling through old trees, and over outhouses and buildings. All are of easy cultivation and can be propagated from cuttings of the ripe, dormant wood, about one inch in length, taken with an eye and placed on the surface of the soil so that the eye alone protrudes, and brought into growth with slight bottom heat.

V. amurensis (From Amur) China, is grown for the beauty of its large, vine-like leaves which turn rose and scarlet in the autumn.

Indefinite. ——— D. Indefinite. Eyes. ANC.

V. Coignetiae (Comm.) Japan, is probably the finest of all ornamental vines, with large, heart-shaped leaves which in the autumn assume every shade of yellow, crimson and orange.

Indefinite. ——— D. Indefinite. Eyes. ANC.

V. Davidii (Comm.) Central China, has large, shiny, dark-green leaves and is heavily armed with prickles. Again it is grown for the brilliance in the range of its autumn colours.

Indefinite. ——— D. Indefinite. Eyes. ANC.

V. Henryana (Comm.) China, is a very beautiful, self-clinging climber, growing easily to twenty feet or more, with composite leaves of three or five leaflets of bright-green, veined with silver and pink, and turning bright-red in autumn.

Indefinite. ——— D. Indefinite. Sd2. ANC.

V. heterophylla (With variable leaves) is a climber with very variable leaves, dark green above and paler below, and insignificant flowers followed by porcelain-blue berries.

Indefinite. ——— D. Indefinite. Sd2. ANC.

V. inconstans (With variable leaves) China and Japan, is a taller-growing, large-leaved, self-clinging species, with leaves either trifoliate or entire. V. inconstans var. Veitchii is the popular Ampelopsis Veitchii with small leaves and startling autumn colours, not excelled by any other variety.

Indefinite. ——— D. Indefinite. Sd2. ANC.

V. pulchra (Beautiful) Japan, is a very robust variety with large, green, lobed leaves, purplish upon the underside, and as brilliantly coloured in autumn as any of the Vines.

Indefinite. ——— D. Indefinite. Eyes. ANC.

V. vinifera (Yielding vine) Asia Minor, is the Wild Grape Vine used for decorative purposes in the following varieties :—

V. vinifera var. apiifolia (Parsley Vine)—is an extremely attractive variety with much-cut leaves and considerable beauty.

V. „ „ purpurea—has claret-coloured leaves, deepening in colour just before they fall.

Indefinite. ——— D. Indefinite. Eyes. ANC.

WISTARIA (Leguminosae) (named in honour of professor Wistar, of Philadelphia).

The Wistarias are among the élite of the climbing shrubs, with pinnate leaves of bright green and long, slender sprays of blue, purple or white flowers. They should be grown in sunny positions in good soil, but are not particular as to soil once they are established. The main problem is that of adequate support ; a south wall in most cases provides the right answer, but the Wistaria can be grown, at least in the southern half of the country, anywhere, provided that sufficient support is given to it.

W. floribunda (Free-flowering) Japan, has long, drooping sprays of violet-blue flowers of variable length, and varies considerably both in colour and size of flower spray.

W. floribunda var. alba—has white flowers produced in sprays often eighteen inches in length.

W. „ „ macrobotrys—has exceedingly long sprays of flowers, often a yard in length, of pale lilac.

W. „ „ rosea—has pale-pink and purple flowers.

Indefinite. May-June. D. Indefinite. L5. Cg8. ANC.

W. macrostachya (Having long spikes) U.S.A., has pinnate leaves divided into nine leaflets, and long, light-blue or lilac-purple flowers in hanging, crowded sprays of one foot in length.

Indefinite. May-June. D. Indefinite. L5. Cg8. ANC.

W. sinensis (Chinese) China, is the outstanding variety of all, the one most seen and noted for its foot-long sprays of large, mauve, scented flowers. *Indefinite. May-June. D. Indefinite. L5. Cg8. ANC. Pl.7.*

W. venusta (Lovely) China, has short sprays of hanging, sweetly-scented, white flowers.

Indefinite. May-June. D. Indefinite. L5. Cg8. ANC.

XANTHOCERAS (Sapindaceae) (derived from the Gr. xanthos—yellow ; and keras—a horn ; a reference to the glands produced between the petals).

A small tree or large shrub suited to moist positions generally in a shady or woodland site.

X. sorbifolia (With leaves like Sorbus) is an extremely pretty small tree with pinnate leaves made up of nine to seventeen sharply-toothed, dark-green leaflets, and spikes of flowers resembling those of the Horse Chestnut.

8-ft.–15-ft., May. D. 8-ft.–15-ft. Sq. Sd10. Cr3. ANC.

YUCCA (Liliaceae) (derived from the native Peruvian name).

The Yuccas are a small group of evergreen shrubs with stiff, sword-like leaves and erect spikes of flowers resembling lilies, all suited to hot, dry sites and of easy cultivation, expecially in towns. They may be propagated from seeds, rarely from offsets, and occasionally from cuttings of the root.

Tricuspidaria lanceolata

80

Zauschneria microphylla

Y. FILAMENTOSA (Thread-like) U.S.A., makes a rosette of numerous sword-like, grey-green leaves edged with long, curling, thread-like hairs, and sending up sprays, up to five feet in length, of hanging, deep-cream flowers.

2-ft.–5-ft., July-August. E. 2-ft.–5-ft. Sq. Sd10. Cr3. ANC.

Y. FLACCIDA (Limp) U.S.A., has shorter, stiffer leaves, but is otherwise similar to Y. filamentosa.

2-ft.–4-ft., July-August. E. 2-ft.–5-ft. Sq. Sd10. Cr3. ANC.

Y. GLAUCA (Sea-green) U.S.A., has narrow, grey-green leaves edged with white, and three-foot sprays of greeny-yellow flowers produced in July and August.

3-ft.–4-ft., July-August. E. 3-ft.–4-ft. Sq. Sd10. Cr3. ANC.

Y. GLORIOSA (Noble) U.S.A., is commonly known as Adam's Needle, and a small tree reaching eight feet in height, with stout, oval, short leaves and creamy-white flowers in large, upright sprays, four feet long and a foot wide.

8-ft., July-September. E. 4-ft. Sq. Sd10. ANC.

Y. RECURVIFOLIA (With curved-back leaves) U.S.A., is similar to Y. gloriosa, with a naked trunk, sometimes reaching six feet in height, long, wide, recurving leaves at the top, and sprays of similar, creamy-white flowers produced with much more freedom.

8-ft., July-September. E. 4-ft. Sq. Sd10. ANC.

Y. WHIPPLEI (Comm.) Western U.S.A., has very rigid, sword-like leaves in striking rosettes, and white flowers tinged with green in a huge inflorescence.

1-ft.–12-ft., June-July. E. 3-ft. Sq. Sd2. ANC.

ZANTHORHIZA (RANUNCULACEAE) (DERIVED FROM THE GR. XANTHOS—YELLOW; AND RHIZA—A ROOT; FROM THE COLOUR OF THE ROOT).

Z. APIIFOLIA (With leaves like Celery) U.S.A., is a deciduous shrub of some two feet in height, suited to a damp position, with pinnate leaves made up of five-lobed leaflets, and small, brownish-purple flowers in hanging sprays. The flowers are of little importance, but the leaves assume attractive colours in the autumn.

2-ft., May-June. D. 2-ft. Sq. D3. ANC.

ZAUSCHNERIA (ONAGRACEAE) (NAMED AFTER J. B. ZAUSCHNER, A GERMAN BOTANIST).

Z. MICROPHYLLA (Small-leaved) California, is a low-growing shrub running freely underground, with small, linear, ash-grey leaves on long, woody, arching stems, and sprays of brilliant-scarlet, tubular flowers. It will survive very low temperatures when once established.

1½-ft., September-October. D. 1½-ft. Sq. D3. N. 17/1. Pl.80.

ZENOBIA (ERICACEAE) (NAMED AFTER AN EMPRESS OF PALMYRA).

Z. PULVERULENTA (Powdered over) Eastern N. America, has oval to oblong leaves powdered with glaucous bloom, and white, bell-shaped flowers, half an inch across, in terminal clusters, and is suited by a semi-shaded site in lime-free soil. Z. pulverulenta var. nuda (Bare) is a little taller in height, has green leaves, and flowers a little smaller.

3-ft., May-June. D. 3-ft. Sq. Sd10. L5. Cg7. AN.

AN INDEX OF COMMON NAMES
WITH THEIR BOTANICAL EQUIVALENTS

Box Sand-Myrtle. *Leiophyllum buxifolium*
— Thorn. *Lycium*
Bramble. *Rubus*
Bridal Wreath. *Spiraea prunifolia*
Broom. *Cytisus ; Genista ; Spartium*
—, Arrow-. *Genista sagittalis*
—, Butcher's. *Ruscus*
—, Spanish. *Spartium junceum*
Buckberry. *Gaylussacia ursina*
Buckthorn. *Rhamnus*
—, Common. *Rhamnus cathartica*
—, Sea. *Hippophaë*
Bush Clover. *Lespedeza*
— Honeysuckle. *Diervilla*
Butcher's Broom. *Ruscus*
Butterfly Bush. *Buddleia*

Calico Bush. *Kalmia latifolia*
— Flower. *Aristolochia elegans*
Californian Bayberry. *Myrica californica*
— Fuchsia. *Zauschneria*
— Lilac. *Ceanothus*
— Tree-Poppy. *Romneya Coulteri*
Cape Figwort. *Phygelius*
— Honeysuckle. *Phygelius capensis*
Carpenter's Leaf. *Galax aphylla*
Checkerberry. *Gaultheria procumbens*
Cherry. *Prunus* (*Cerasus*)
—, Bird. *Prunus Padus*
—, Cornelian. *Cornus Mas*
—, Dwarf. *Prunus Cerasus*
—, Higan. *Prunus subhirtella*
—, Japanese. *Prunus Lannesiana; Prunus serrulata*
— Laurel. *Prunus Laurocerasus*
—, Morello. *Prunus Cerasus*
— Plum. *Prunus cerasifera*
—, Sand. *Prunus Besseyi*
—, Willow. *Prunus incana*
Chinese Witch Hazel. *Hamamelis mollis*
— Yulan. *Magnolia denudata*
Christ's Thorn. *Paliurus Spina-Christi*
Cinquefoil. *Potentilla*
Climbing Hydrangea. *Pileostegia*
Clover, Bush. *Lespedeza*
Common Buckthorn. *Rhamnus cathartica*
Confederate Jasmine. *Trachelospermum jasminoides*
Coral-berry. *Symphoricarpus orbiculatus ; Berberidopsis corralina*
Cornel. *Cornus*
Cornelian Cherry. *Cornus Mas*
Cowberry. *Vaccinium Vitis-idaea*
Crab Apple. *Pyrus* (*Malus*)
— —, Garland. *Pyrus coronaria*
— —, Oregon. *Pyrus fusca*
— —, Prairie. *Pyrus ioensis*
— —, Siberian. *Pyrus baccata*
Cranberry. *Oxycoccus*
— Bush. *Viburnum Opulus*
Crinkle Blush. *Lomatia*
Cross-Vine. *Bignonia capreolata*
Crown-Vetch. *Coronilla*
Crystal Tea. *Ledum palustre*
Cucumber Tree. *Magnolia acuminata ; Magnolia macrophylla*
Cup-flower. *Nierembergia*
—, Tall. *Nierembergia frutescens*
Currant, Flowering. *Ribes*
—, Indian. *Symphoricarpus orbiculatus*

Dagger, Spanish. *Yucca gloriosa*
Daisy-Bush, — -Tree. *Olearia*
Dangleberry. *Gaylussacia frondosa*
Deerberry. *Vaccinium stamineum*
Devil-wood. *Osmanthus*
Dogwood. *Cornus*
Dryland Blueberry. *Vaccinium vacillans*
Dutchman's Pipe. *Aristolochia Sipho*
Dwarf Bilberry. *Vaccinium caespitosum*
— Cherry. *Prunus Cerasus*
Dyer's Greenwood. *Genista tinctoria*

Evergreen Laburnum. *Piptanthus nepalensis*

False Acacia. *Robinia pseudo-acacia*
— Bittersweet. *Celastrum scandens*
Fetter Bush. *Pieris lucida*
Figwort, Cape. *Phygelius*
Fire-thorn. *Pyracantha*
Flame Flower. *Rhododendron calendulaceum*
Flannel Bush. *Fremontia californica*
Flax, New Zealand. *Phormium tenax*
Fleece Flower. *Polygonum*
Flowering Cherry. *Prunus* (*Cerasus*)
— Currant. *Ribes*
— Gooseberry. *Ribes*
— Quince. *Cydonia*
French Mulberry. *Callicarpa*
Fringe Tree. *Chionanthus*
Fuchsia, Californian. *Zauschneria*
Furze. *Ulex*

Sea Buckthorn. *Hippophaë*
— Heath. *Frankenia*
Senna. *Cassia*
—, Bladder. *Colutea*
—, Scorpion. *Coronilla Emerus*
Service Tree. *Sorbus*
Service-berry. *Amelanchier*
Shad-bush. *Amelanchier*
Sheep Laurel. *Kalmia angustifolia*
Sheep-berry. *Viburnum Lentago*
Shrub Althaea. *Hibiscus syriacus*
Siberian Crab Apple. *Pyrus baccata*
Silk-Tassel Bush. *Garrya*
Silver Bell. *Halesia*
Silver-berry. *Elaeagnus argentea*
Slipper-wort. *Calceolaria*
Sloe. *Prunus spinosa*
Smoke Tree. *Rhus Cotinus*
Snowball Tree. *Viburnum Opulus sterile*
Snowberry Tree. *Symphoricarpus*
Snowdrop Tree. *Halesia; Styrax japonicus*
Sorrel Tree. *Oxydendrum arboreum*
Sourwood. *Oxydendrum arboreum*
Southernwood. *Artemisia Abrotanum*
Spanish Broom. *Spartium junceum*
— Dagger. *Yucca gloriosa*
— Gorse. *Genista hispanica*
Spice Bush. *Lindera*
Spike Heath. *Bruckenthalia*
Spindle Tree. *Euonymus*
Spiraea, Blue. *Caryopteris*
Spurge Laurel. *Daphne Laureola*
Squaw-berry. *Mitchella repens*
Star Jasmine. *Trachelospermum jasminoides*
— Magnolia. *Magnolia stellata*
Storax. *Styrax*
Strawberry Tree. *Arbutus Unedo*
Sumach. *Rhus*
—, Myrtle-leaved. *Coriaria*
Summer Lilac. *Buddleia Davidii*
Summer-Sweet. *Clethra alnifolia*
Sun Rose. *Helianthemum*
Sweet Bay. *Magnolia virginiana*
— Gale. *Myrica Gale*
— Pepper Bush. *Clethra alnifolia*
Syringa (of gardens). *Philadelphus*

Tall Cup-flower. *Nierembergia frutescens*
Tamarisk. *Tamarix*
Tawhiwhi. *Pittosporum tenuifolium*
Tea, Crystal. *Ledum palustre*
—, Labrador. *Ledum groenlandicum*
Tea Tree. *Leptospermum*
Tea-berry. *Gaultheria procumbens*
Thorn, Box. *Lycium*
—, Christ's. *Paliurus Spina-Christi*
—, Fire-. *Pyracantha*
—, Goat's. *Astragalus Tragacantha*
—, Jerusalem. *Paliurus Spina-Christi*
Trailing Arbutus. *Epigaea repens*
Traveller's Joy. *Clematis Vitalba*
Tree Hollyhock. *Hibiscus syriacus*
— Lupin. *Lupinus*
— Mallow. *Lavatera*
— Paeony. *Paeonia Moutan*
— -Poppy, Californian. *Romneya Coulteri*
— Purslane. *Atriplex Halimus*
Trumpet Flower. *Tecoma*
Twinberry. *Mitchella repens*

Ukon. *Prunus Lannesiana var. grandiflora*
Umbrella Tree. *Magnolia tripetala*

Vetch, Crown. *Coronilla*
Vine. *Vitis*
—, Cross-. *Bignonia capreolata*
—, Matrimony. *Lycium*
Virgin's Bower. *Clematis*

Wax Myrtle. *Myrica cerifera*
Wax-berry. *Symphoricarpus albus*
Waxwork. *Celastrus scandens*
Wayfaring Tree. *Viburnum Lantana; Viburnum alnifolium*
White Alder. *Clethra*
Whortleberry. *Vaccinium*
Wild Rosemary. *Ledum palustre*
Willow. *Salix*
— Cherry. *Prunus incana*
Willow-leaved Pear. *Pyrus salicifolia*
Winter Hazel. *Corylopsis*
— Savory. *Satureia*
Wintergreen. *Gaultheria procumbens*
Winter-sweet. *Chimonanthus fragrans*
Wire Plant. *Muehlenbeckia*
Witch Hazel. *Hamamelis*
— —, Chinese. *Hamamelis mollis*
Withe-rod. *Viburnum cassinoides*
Woad-waxen. *Genista tinctoria*
Woodbine. *Lonicera Periclymenum*
Wormwood. *Artemisia*

Yeddo Hawthorn. *Raphiolepis umbellata*
Yulan, Chinese. *Magnolia denudata*

A	B	C	D
E	F	G	H
J	K	L	M
N	O	P	Q
R	S	T	U

IDENTIFICATION

For the positive identification of the species illustrated in the pictures, the transparent template enclosed in the book will be found of exceptional usefulness. Place the template over the picture, and the species named below will be found to lie within the squares indicated by the letter following the name. Thus in Plate 76 for example :

Prunus (Cerasus) Lannesiana falls in the squares A, B, C, D, E, G and H,
Cydonia Maulei in the squares Q and U, and
Pyrus floribunda atrosanguinea in the squares K, L, M, N, O, P and Q.